11kg

Cl. o.p. pap. i.p.

D0210689

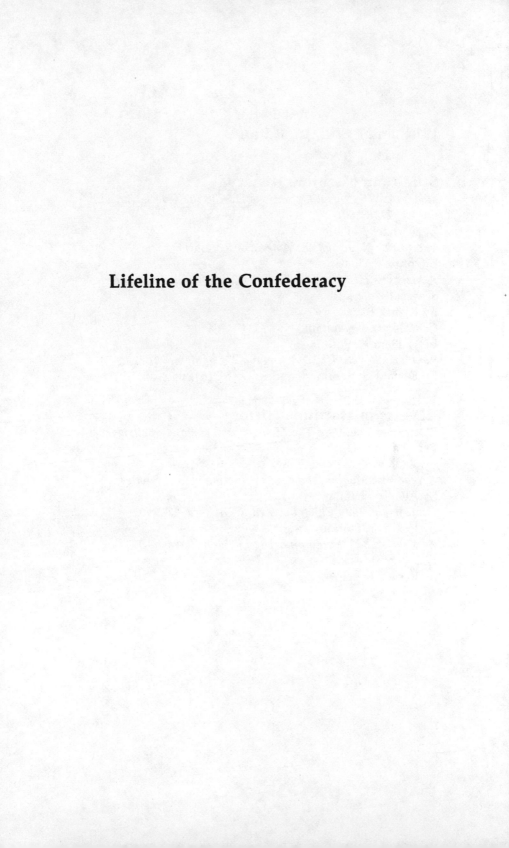

# Lifeline of the Confederacy

William N. Still, Jr., Editor

## Studies in Maritime History
*Stoddert's War: Naval Operations During the Quasi-War with France, 1798-1801*
by Michael A. Palmer
*The British Navy and the American Revolution*
by John A. Tilley
*A Maritime History of the United States: The Role of America's Seas and Waterways*
by K. Jack Bauer
*Confederate Shipbuilding*
by William N. Still, Jr.
*Raid on America: The Dutch Naval Campaign of 1672–1674*
by Donald G. Shomette and Robert D. Haslach

## Classics in Maritime History
*What Finer Tradition: The Memoirs of Thomas O. Selfridge, Jr., Rear Admiral, U.S.N.*
by Thomas O. Selfridge, Jr.
*A Year on a Monitor and the Destruction of Fort Sumter*
by Alvah F. Hunter
*Confederate Navy Chief: Stephen R. Mallory*
by Joseph T. Durkin
*Admiral of the New Empire: The Life and Career of George Dewey*
by Ronald Spector

# Lifeline of the Confederacy

---

## *Blockade Running During the Civil War*

by Stephen R. Wise

University of South Carolina Press

Copyright © University of South Carolina 1988

Published in Columbia, South Carolina, by the
University of South Carolina Press

Manufactured in the United States of America


LIBRARY OF CONGRESS
Library of Congress Cataloging-in-Publication Data

Wise, Stephen R., 1952–
    Lifeline of the Confederacy : blockade running during the Civil
War / by Stephen R. Wise.
        p.   cm. — (Studies in maritime history)
    Bibliography: p.
    Includes index.
    ISBN 0-87249-554-X
    1. United States—History—Civil War, 1861–1865—Blockades.
    2. United States—History—Civil War, 1861–1865—Naval operations.
    I. Title.   II. Series.
    E600.W57  1988
    973.7′5—dc 19                                                  88-20524
                                                                          CIP

# Contents

# Maps

# Illustrations

# Acknowledgments

While preparing this work I have received a great deal of assistance and encouragement from institutions, teachers, colleagues, and friends. The staffs of a number of institutions greatly facilitated my research. Allen Stokes of the South Caroliniana Library consistently assisted me in locating material. The staffs of the National Archives; Library of Congress; Southern Historical Collection, University of North Carolina; the manuscript division of Duke University Library; Thomas Cooper Library, the University of South Carolina; and the South Carolina Historical Society were very helpful in locating valuable source materials.

I have also benefited from the suggestions and criticisms of friends and colleagues while working on the various aspects of blockade running. I would like to give special thanks to William N. Still Jr. for his help and backing. I would also like to thank Dave Ruth, Chris Fonvielle, Lacy Ford, Alex Moore, George Terry, Peter Coclanis, Sharon Bennett, Kenneth Mackenzie, Ian Grant, Mike Higgins, Barbara Graham, David Carlton, Barbara Bellows, David Sadowski, Larry Connin, Frank and Virginia Lenz, Jack Meyers, Steve and Julia Corkett, George Devlin, Ethel Nepveux, Mike Miller, John Hildreth, Martha Bergmann, Jack Von Ewegen, Zulma Von Ewegen, Carter Wolff, John Roberson, Kelly McGowan, Don Moore, George and Cecily McMillan, Gerald Mahle, Bill Lockwood, Marsha Curles, Ellen Tillet, and Bill Earle for their aid and moral support.

Also very beneficial were the comments of Professors Walter Edgar, Edward Cox, Richard Wright, and Charles Kovacik.

Special thanks go to a number of people who gave invaluable support whenever needed. Melissa Cox Douglas, Sarah Alden Heron, and Louise Kruszewski Paradis were extremely helpful in facilitating my research. Also thanks to William Piston for his help and patience throughout the initial phases of this work. Gary Bailey and Peggy Perry Copulsky, made a number of comments on the work while Curt Bay did yeoman work in proofreading the manuscript. Other indispensable people that assisted in the project were Dave and Mona Grunden, who helped in doing the pedantic preparation of the tables and appendix; Rod Lee and Katie Mason, who drew the maps; Jackie Terry and Becki Wass, who typed various drafts; Kevin Foster, who provided technical data on blockade runners and their builders; Bob Holcombe, who drew the finely detailed silhouettes of the blockade runners and Bud Wass for his excellent art work. A number of the illustrations were made available through the detective work and generosity of Charles Peery, who is the world's greatest blockade running enthusiast and student.

This work began as a dissertation under the direction of Thomas L. Connelly, who originally suggested the idea to me. I will always be grateful for his guidance, patience, and friendship in helping me to complete the study that has led to this publication.

Last, but not least, I would like to especially thank my parents, without whose understanding and love, this work could never have been completed.

# Lifeline of the Confederacy

# Introduction

Even before President Lincoln issued his blockade proclamation on April 16, 1861, leaders of the Confederacy realized that they would have to obtain great quantities of their military supplies from abroad. Their new nation did not contain the needed industrial base to support a country at war; nor did the South have a large enough merchant fleet to bring in the required goods. For both vessels and supplies, the South looked to Great Britain and, once the British realized the immense profits that could be made by running cargoes through the blockade, a large and enthusiastic trade soon opened between Bermuda, Nassau, Havana and the Confederacy.

Blockade running not only brought to the South the supplies needed to sustain the nation, but also caused a revolution in ship building. By the second year of the war, the goods coming into the Confederacy were carried on fast, light-drafted, steel- and iron-hulled steamers. These vessels, designed to carry an immense amount of cargo, slipped past the Union warships at night, delivering valuable supplies to the South.

The trade also grew into a sophisticated business, carried on by both the Confederacy and private companies. Its importance to the South was tremendous. Without blockade running, the Confederacy could not have properly armed, clothed, or fed its soldiers. As long as there were ports that the steamers could utilize, the Confederacy survived; but, once the seaports were captured, the nation was destined to die.

For such a vital wartime operation, the writings on blockade running have always been incomplete. During the war, Southern newspapers glorified the exploits of blockade runners, in a sense, making them the cavaliers of the sea. However, reporters were not very careful in their accounts and, in order to keep up morale, stories were repeated and accuracy often forgotten. Union sources were also misleading as they often relied on Southern and foreign accounts, tales of Southern deserters, reports of misinformed captains, and statements from nervous consuls in unfriendly ports. When the official records of the war were

3

compiled, a number of these stories were reprinted with little or no attempt to prove their accuracy.

After 1865, the saga of blockade running became highly romanticized. Exploits grew with the growing age of the men who served on the vessels. During this period books by Thomas Taylor, Augustus Hobart-Hampden, John Wilkinson, and James Sprunt dominated the writing on blockade running. These works, plus articles in the *Southern Historical Society Papers, Confederate Veteran*, and other period journals, became the primary sources for those who would later write on blockade running.

Unfortunately these works, like many wartime reports, contained a number of inaccuracies. Time had taken its toll on the old seamen, and their reminiscences and memoirs were filled with inconsistencies and wrong information, which have been perpetuated by authors to the present time.

During the latter part of the nineteenth and early portion of the twentieth centuries, three scholarly works were produced that attempted to understand blockade running's impact on the war. The first of these was Robert Soley's *The Blockade and the Cruisers,* published in 1883. The book was one of a series written by naval authorities on the Civil War. Soley examined blockade running from the perspective of the Union blockade and drew heavily on naval sources for his data.

Francis B. C. Bradlee's *Blockade Running during the Civil War and the Effect of Land and Water Transportation on the Confederacy* (1925) drew on popular accounts to retell the blockade-running story. Bradlee was one of the first authors to attempt to look at individual blockade-running companies, but his sources were inadequate for any concise study.

The third important work done on blockade running before World War II was Frank L. Owsley's *King Cotton Diplomacy.* In his book Owsley used some sources, such as the Pickett Papers, that had never before been examined by authors working on blockade running. Owsley also placed blockade running in its rightful position as one of the most important, if not *the* most important, factor in supplying the Confederate armies. However, Owsley, like Bradlee and Soley before him, used inaccurate and romanticized accounts that had been written during or just after the war.

After World War II, there appeared a series of articles in the journal *American Neptune*, written by Marcus Price, that quickly became a highly quoted source on blockade running. Price's works were based on the holdings of the National Archives, and, for the most part, were lists giving the number of violations of individual blockade runners and their masters. He also wrote an article on blockade-running companies operating out of Charleston, South Carolina. This was the first attempt to compile an accurate list of blockade runners and their runs through the blockade. Price's accomplishment was a monumental achievement, but it contained flaws. Price defined a blockade runner as any vessel that cleared or entered a Southern port after Lincoln ordered the blockade of the Southern Coast. This meant that ships using the ports before the actual establishment of the blockade were defined as blockade runners, and any port of call made along the coast was considered a violation, even if the ship never left Southern waters. In this way, a vessel operating between Charleston and Savannah, before Union warships appeared off the coast, was considered a blockade runner, and a violation was counted for every whistle stop. Because of such record keeping, Price's statistics were heavily inflated.

Another important work that, with Price's, established a corpus of statistical information on blockade running was Frank E. Vandiver's book *Confederate Blockade Running through Bermuda, 1861–1865*. In his study, Vandiver uses letter books of individuals involved in blockade running and reproduced Bermuda cargo manifests. Because of these new sources, valuable insight on the trade originating from Bermuda was documented, but it was not an overall account of blockade running.

During the Civil War Centennial and the following years, a number of books appeared on blockade running, but none produced a comprehensive view of the trade. For the most part they relied on previous sources and usually retold the sometimes faulty but exciting chase scenes originally detailed by those who had run the blockade. At the same time, a number of articles were produced that covered a range of topics from the profitability of the trade to histories on individual vessels.

Because none of the previous works on blockade running gave a totally accurate or concise view of the trade, a study was needed to pull together the entire story. Blockade running was more than a romantic piece of Civil War history. On board the frail steamships were carried the munitions and supplies that sustained the South in its four-year struggle. It is the purpose of this work to give a detailed study of blockade running. By using past accounts and heretofore unused manuscript and newspaper accounts, this analysis gives the first detailed view of the trade. Among the sources consulted were records from admiralty courts, consul despatches, port records, the Wilmington Ordnance Account Book, Quartermaster Records, the Vessel Papers of the National Archives, and numerous manuscript sources. With these materials, a more precise picture of blockade running can be obtained.

This study offers an examination of blockade running and its effects on the war effort. It explains how cargoes were obtained; how they were brought in; where they were landed and how they aided the Confederate war effort. This work also describes the important companies and individuals that developed blockade running into the lifeline of the Confederacy.

# Chapter One

# We Have No Commercial Marine

The time was December 1864. Winter had not yet released her grip on the struggling Confederacy, nor had the Union armies. The seaports of Charleston and Wilmington were still receiving supplies from Europe. In the past six months the towns received over 500,000 pairs of shoes, 300,000 blankets, 3.5 million pounds of meat, 1.5 million pounds of lead, 2 million pounds of saltpeter, 50,000 rifles, 43 cannon plus huge amounts of uniform cloth, medicine, and other essential supplies. From these imported goods came supplies that were forwarded to Confederate field armies. In the heartland of the South, the remaining 25,000 soldiers of the shattered Army of the Tennessee were each sent a blanket, jacket, two shirts, and four pairs of pants, shoes, and drawers. The Army of Northern Virginia, huddled in the trenches around Richmond and Petersburg, received 100,000 jackets, 140,000 pairs of pants, 167,000 pairs of shoes, 170,000 pairs of drawers, and 150,000 shirts, all for an army of 72,000 men. These supplies, plus an unbroken flow of munitions, provided the Southern troops with the equipment needed to resist the Federals.

The Confederacy was able to supply their troops because of a reliance on a system based on steam vessels carrying essential goods through the Federal Navy's blockade. It was these vessels that allowed the new nation to survive as long as it did. On blockade runners came 60 percent of the South's arms; one-third of its lead for bullets, ingredients for three-fourths of its powder, nearly all of its paper for cartridges, and the majority of its cloth and leather for uniforms and accoutrements.[1]

7

As long as the South's ports were open, blockade runners maintained a lifeline of supplies. But it did not come easily. The government employees involved in the trade had to work against unscrupulous, private operators and a government that constantly refused to interfere with private shipping. At best it was a very tenuous supply line, which was kept open by calculating businessmen, hard-working patriots, valiant seamen, and revolutionary steamships. As long as blockade runners reached the South, the system worked. For at no time in the war did the Confederacy lack the proper tools of combat. The individuals involved in the business began their work early in the war, but in 1861 few realized the volume of trade that would eventually exist between the Confederacy and the outside world.

Early afternoon of a stormy blustery day—April 9, 1861—the U.S. Mail Steamer *James Adger* headed out through rough seas from Charleston harbor. To the starboard the American flag snapped taut over Fort Sumter while on the portside the banner of the rebelling South flew over Fort Moultrie. For five days the *James Adger* had been ready to clear the South Carolina port, but heavy weather had kept the large steamer tied to moorings in the Cooper River. Finally, the captain of the *James Adger*, believing that the storms were less of a threat than the political situation in Charleston, decided to defy the weather and take his vessel out to sea. The covenant of 1789 had come apart, and war between the separated states seemed inevitable; when it came, Charleston would be no place for a Northern merchantman.

The *James Adger* had arrived in Charleston on her usual run from New York City in late March, and even though South Carolina and six other Southern states had seceded from the Union, the Charlestonians still accepted the Federal mail and "foreign imports" brought in on Northern merchantmen. After docking at Charleston, the *James Adger* transferred part of her cargo and mail to the small sidewheel packet *Carolina* for distribution along the Southern coast. Under the command of Thomas J. Lockwood, the *Carolina* carried passengers, supplies, and mail from Charleston to Jacksonville, Florida. Lockwood made a good living as captain of the *Carolina* and, by 1861, had gained a solid reputation as a skilled and trustworthy seaman.

On the same day that the *James Adger* arrived in Charleston, the *Carolina* finished a round trip from Florida. On board she carried 150 bales of cotton. Part of this cargo would eventually find its way into the cargo holds of the *James Adger* for shipment to Northern textile mills. Before he was able to clear for another trip, Lockwood and his vessel were hired by local authorities for a harbor cruise. This was not to be an ordinary excursion; passengers aboard the steamer included a number of civilian and military personalities, including the commander of Charleston, Brigadier General Pierre G.T. Beauregard, and his aide States Rights Gist.

The *Carolina* was followed by the smaller steamer *General Clinch* carrying the Palmetto Brass Band, which serenaded the passengers on the *Carolina*. The two ships sailed around the harbor, visiting the newly constructed fortifications and inspecting the numerous cannons trained on Fort Sumter. When the passengers had completed their tour, Lockwood turned the *Carolina* back toward the city, guiding the vessel close to the walls of Fort Sumter, and, as if on cue, the band on the *General Clinch* struck up "Dixie Land."

While this excursion was taking place, Charleston businessmen were meeting to take advantage of the breakup of the Union. Until now, the overseas steamship trade of Charleston, as well as the rest of the South, had been controlled by Northern interests. Vessels like the *James Adger* brought Northern and European imports to the South and carried away Southern produce. With the forming of the Confederacy, numerous Charlestonians saw tremendous opportunities to exploit the national split to their own advantage.

By early April the Charleston businessmen had appointed a committee of four to supervise the formation of a Liverpool to Charleston steamship line. Among its members were Charles Gourdin, one of the city's most influential bankers and Charles K. Prioleau, a prominent member of the city's largest shipping firm, John Fraser and Company. At the first meeting, the committee decided to hire John Fraser and Company as their agents. This decision placed the venture on firm ground. The company was well known overseas, and its president, George Alfred Trenholm, was one of the wealthiest and most influential men in the South. His firm, with offices in Charleston, New York, and Liverpool, commanded such high regard that Trenholm could secure unlimited credit abroad.

While business moves were underway, other events were dominating public attention. On April 12, the Charleston papers proudly announced that the onetime commander of the Charleston arsenal,

Captain Josiah Gorgas, had resigned from the United States Army and offered his services to the Confederacy. Also reported was a speech given in the city by the firebrand Texas senator, Louis T. Wigfall, now back in his native state of South Carolina serving as an aide to General Beauregard. In a stirring oration, Wigfall predicted an easy Southern victory under the proven leadership of Jefferson Davis. At the same time, Charlestonians were told of the coming of William Howard Russell, the prominent reporter from the *London Times*. The citizens of Charleston were eager to greet Russell and let him know of their great friendship and admiration for Great Britain.

The events in Charleston were known to the captain and the crew of the *James Adger*. Bad weather had kept the steamer in port, and time was running out. While the ship remained moored at her dock, the final guns were mounted against Fort Sumter, and Southern-owned steamers were impressed into military service. Some officials were calling for the seizure of private Northern holdings in the city. As yet, no action had been taken against the *James Adger* but, once Sumter was attacked, Charleston would be no place for the Northern merchantman.

It was for these reasons that the *James Adger* left Charleston before the weather cleared. There were other Northern-owned vessels in the harbor, and they too would escape before the firing began. However, another steamer, owned by the same firm that operated the *James Adger*, was due in Charleston sometime after April 14. If hostilities had begun, the powerful sidewheeler *Nashville* would prove a great prize.

The sailing of the *James Adger* and the other Northern ships did keep them from being seized; however the *Nashville* arrived after the capture of Fort Sumter, and was being fitted out as a privateer when Russell made his appearance.[2]

Charleston was among the first stops that Russell made during his tour of the South. Yet, even this early in his trip, the British correspondent found Southerners holding unrealistic views concerning the war and England's role in the conflict. Russell discovered Southerners were completely confident in defeating the North. Russell found these convictions "remarkable," since before secession, the South was nearly dependent on imports for both its daily goods and its industrial supplies. Now the Confederates would need not only these basic necessities, but also immense amounts of arms and munitions. Russell, noting the South's lack of industries, questioned where these items would come from. To his astonishment, the Southerners candidly told him that they expected England to serve the new nation. One of his informants, Colonel Louis T. Wigfall, stated:

> We are an agrarian people; we are a primitive people. We have no cities—we don't want them. We have no literature—we don't need any yet. We have no press—we are glad of it. . . . We have no commercial marine—no navy—we don't want them. We are better without them. Your ships carry our produce, and you can protect your own vessels. . . . As long as we have our rice, our sugar, our tobacco and our cotton, we can command wealth to purchase all we want from those nations with which we are in amity, and to lay up money besides.

Views such as Wigfall's were common throughout the South. From the eastern seaboard to the Mississippi River, Russell found Southerners shared a "lively all-powerful faith" in the doctrine of "King Cotton," which they felt would sustain and protect their new nation.[3]

"King Cotton" was a belief, based on the economic power of Southern cotton, which held that the economy of England was dependent upon the supply of the staple to British textile mills (See Appendix 1). After all, in 1859 England had imported 78 percent of the South's cotton crop. The cotton textile industry of Great Britain provided four to five million Englishmen with jobs and, in 1860, produced a profit of over fifty-nine million pounds. Without their cotton, Southerners argued, the English textile industry would collapse and send the island nation into economic ruin.[4]

Russell considered the theory of King Cotton to be a "grievous delusion," one that mistakenly pictured England as an "appanage of their cotton kingdom," with the textile cities of Liverpool and Manchester obscuring "all Great Britain to the Southern eye." Yet it could not be denied that cotton was a great asset to the South, and gave the Confederacy a powerful economic and political weapon.

However, Southerners forgot that the supply of their commodity was not the only determining factor in the trade. They tended to ignore the South's reliance upon imports. Because of the success of its agricultural system, the region had found little need to develop industries that could effectively serve the new nation. Such a situation had not hindered the area before 1860, but now as an independent state facing war with the industrialized North, the Confederacy had to develop an efficient trade with Europe to secure, not only their daily manufactured needs, but also military goods.[5]

Before secession, the majority of these needed goods had arrived by way of internal trade routes from the Northern states. Direct imports from Europe were negligible. For the most part, supplies from overseas that did reach the South were landed in New York City and carried south by internal routes. Most foreign vessels coming to the region came exclusively for cotton, and usually arrived in ballast. The majority of the goods that did arrive came from the North on railroads, river steamboats, and ocean-going steamers working out of New York City. These vessels operated on set schedules and served the ports of Richmond, Norfolk, Wilmington, Charleston, and New Orleans. From these cities the products were distributed inland by railroads, canals, coasting packets, and river steamboats.[6]

Secession and the prospect of war ended this trade from the North. To make up for this loss, the South, led by the state legislatures of South Carolina, Alabama, Georgia, and Louisiana, began efforts to develop direct trade routes with England; however, the passage of bills could not create this trade from thin air; established ports, commercial connections, and an ocean-going merchant marine were needed by the Confederacy.

Such marine traffic would require numerous vessels capable of transporting large quantities of goods. In 1860 this type of trade was carried on large sailing ships supplemented by a few transatlantic steamship lines. The domain of the sailing ship as the principal carrier of cargo had yet to be challenged by the steamship. The world's commerce was still transported on brigs, ships, barks, and brigatines, which were unburdened by space-consuming engines and coal bunkers. It was to such vessels that the Confederacy would have to turn for its new lifeline, but the nation was not given the opportunity to develop a normal marine trade.[7]

All hope for conventional trade with Europe ceased four days after the firing on Fort Sumter when President Lincoln declared that soon a "competent force" would be posted off the coasts of South Carolina, Georgia, Alabama, Florida, Mississippi, Louisiana, and Texas "to set on foot a blockade." Eight days later Lincoln added to the blockaded area the shorelines of North Carolina and Virgina. Once established, the blockade could stop and search vessels attempting to reach the Confederacy. If a ship was found to be carrying contraband of war, it would be seized.[8]

The prospects of a Union blockade did not worry many Southerners. In addition to their strong faith in King Cotton and British intervention, they believed that the North could never effectively cover a
coastline of 3,549 miles, a length greater than the distance from New
York to Liverpool. However, the Union officials in charge of developing
the blockade did not concern themselves with the size of the Confederate shoreline.[9]

In June 1861 a joint "Blockade Strategy Board" was organized under
the Union Navy Department to devise a plan to properly blockade the
Southern coast. The board consisted of Professor Alexander D. Bache,
head of the Coast Survey, Major John G. Bernard of the Corps of
Engineers, Commander Charles H. Davis, and Commander Samuel
Francis Du Pont, who chaired the committee. The board, knowing that
the Confederacy would be dependent on a constant flow of materials
and munitions from Europe, concluded that the main effort of the
blockade should be placed against the region's major ports, where such
a trade could originate.[10]

By 1860, the shipping industry had grown so large that only a few
harbors could qualify as profitable ports of entry. If a coastal city was to
be a successful port, it had to have a bar of at least twelve to twenty feet; a
navigable channel; and an anchorage of good depth. It also had to be a
commercial and banking center and have transportation to inland markets via railroads, steamboats, or canals. Only at such coastal cities could
the supplies and materials needed by the Confederacy be effectively and
efficiently received. Ports of this type were not common along the
southern coast, so, the Blockade Board was able to easily identify the
Confederacy's most important ports.[11]

Beginning at the mouth of the Chesapeake Bay, the Southern coast
was described as becoming low to the water and, for the greater part,
sandy. A ridge of sand, occasionally broken by the mouths of rivers,
extended its entire length. In some places this ridge reached out from the
mainland, forming sounds of varying width and depth. Where the ridge
was broken, low marshy land bordered the outlets of the region's rivers.

The nature of the country through which the rivers flowed was such
that their banks were constantly eroding and the waters deposited
alluvium to form extensive submarine banks, shoals, and bars. Because
of this alluvium, the South had no harbors that were unobstructed by
sifting bars, and few large ports.[12]

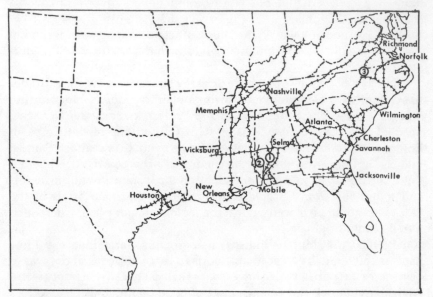

**CONFEDERATE RAILWAYS, 1861–1865**
COMPLETION DATES
1. November 1861
2. December 1862
3. May 1864

not to scale

Even though the South contained one-third of the national railroad mileage in 1860, the network was inefficient as a transportation system. It was composed of short lines that varied in gauge and relied on supplementary water transportation. During the war the South managed to complete new track lines that greatly facilitated the shipping of supplies. These ran between Mobile and the line running to Montgomery, 1: Meridian, Mississippi, and Selma, Alabama, 2; and Greensboro, North Carolina, and Danville, Virginia, 3.

One of the first marine sites studied by the Blockade Board and the Confederacy's best port area was that of the Hampton Roads, James River, and Norfolk region. Located just west of the mouth of Chesapeake Bay, the deep anchorage of Hampton Roads was formed by the convergence of the James, Nansemond, and Elizabeth rivers, and was connected to the Chesapeake by a channel running between Old Point Comfort on the north and Willoughby Point to the south.

Access to the two ports of Richmond and Norfolk led through the roadstead. Richmond, on the James River, could not be reached by the largest merchantmen, but the city's excellent railroad connections to the west and south, made Richmond an important commercial center. On the other hand, Norfolk was by far the better port, and though primarily serving the navy, it did have canals and railroads that allowed the city to control the trade of most of eastern Virginia and North Carolina.

Norfolk and Richmond together were considered the South's best ports on the Southeast coast, but their outlet to the Atlantic Ocean led through Hampton Roads, the anchorage site of the United States Navy's Home Squadron and past the Federal-occupied Fort Monroe at Old Point Comfort and Fort Calhoun on Rip Rap Shoals. Norfolk and Richmond were of little use as commercial ports until these forces were cleared from the roads.[13]

South from Hampton Roads, past Cape Henry, stretched 200 miles of low-lying sand bars known as the Outer Banks of North Carolina. These barrier islands enclosed a vast inland sea divided into large, broad sounds. Though impressive in size, the region was too shallow for contemporary merchantmen, and only vessels drawing ten feet or less could enter the sounds. Because of this, the prewar exports of the area, mostly tobacco, naval stores, and grains, had been sent to Norfolk for shipment overseas.[14]

Located on Topsail Inlet, Beaufort Harbor was the first deep-water port south of Norfolk. The harbor could be approached by vessels drawing up to fifteen feet at low tide and eighteen at higher water. By 1860, the old picturesque town of Beaufort, situated on the northeast side of the bay, was being superseded by Morehead City as the inlet's main port. Positioned on the southern side of the harbor, the newer town owed its rise to the Atlantic and North Carolina Railroad, which connected Morehead City to New Bern and the interior of the state. Only three years old, Morehead City was not yet an established major seaport, but, with its railroad, the town held great promise for the Confederacy.[15]

North Carolina's other deep-water port was at Wilmington, some ninety miles south of Beaufort on the Cape Fear River. Similar to Morehead City, Wilmington was still a developing port. Located twenty-eight miles from the mouth of the Cape Fear River, Wilmington lacked the established commercial houses and banking facilities to attract international trade, but it did have excellent internal communications through three railroad lines: the Wilmington and Manchester, which connected the port to Charleston and Columbia; the Wilmington and Weldon, which ran north to Virginia; and the unfinished Wilmington, Charlotte and Rutherford, which extended into the interior of North Carolina. The town was also served by daily steamboat service up the Cape Fear River to Fayetteville.

By 1860 the wharves of the port were filled with schooners and brigs loading Wilmington's main exports of turpentine, resin, tar, and grains. Steamers were also regular visitors to the city's docks as Wilmington was served by steamboat lines to Charleston and more recently to New York City.[16]

The port of Wilmington could be entered through two channels connecting Cape Fear River to the Atlantic. The main channel, which led out to the southwest, was called Old Inlet. It had a treacherous shifting bar that varied in depth from ten to fifteen feet. The second entrance, appropriately named New Inlet, had been formed in 1761 when a hurricane made a northeast cut through Federal Point Peninsula. The new pass was shallower than the main channel, but was quite navigable by small and medium-sized vessels.[17]

Both Morehead City and Wilmington were extremely valuable ports for the new Confederacy. Their harbors were adequate for deep-water trade, and their growing internal connections gave them command over a vast producing area that could supply large quantities of exports. Though not yet centers of world shipping, their potential as ports of entry was obvious, and given time the two towns could provide considerable service to the new nation.

The next port along the Atlantic seaboard was the old colonial village of Georgetown, South Carolina. Since the town had no direct railroad connections, it had long ceased to be used as a site for any overseas shipping. Georgetown was located ten miles from where Winyah Bay met the Atlantic Ocean and was approached by a winding channel that had a low-water depth of eight feet. The only commercial shipping that took place at the port was carried on shallow-drafted schooners and steamers that transported the goods to Charleston, the Confederacy's main Atlantic seaport.[18]

As a Southern port, Charleston ranked second only to New Orleans. Even though Charleston could not in any way compare to the Louisiana port in terms of wealth, volume of trade, or entrances and clearances of vessels, it was the Confederacy's dominant shipping point on the Atlantic coast. Formed by the convergence of the Ashley and Cooper rivers, Charleston Harbor offered a safe, deep-water anchorage to merchantmen of all sizes, however, entrance to the harbor was not easy. Four channels led into Charleston, but only two, Maffitt's or Sullivan's Island Channel of eleven feet and the Main Ship Channel, which had a varying depth of seventeen to twenty-two feet, allowed ships of any size to enter the harbor. Both were difficult to navigate, but once across the bars, vessels found easy passage to the city's wharves.

Railroad and steamboat connections supplied Charleston with its major exports of cotton, rice, tar, and pitch. These products were often controlled by one of a number of commercial houses headquartered in Charleston. The largest firms operated sailing ships to Liverpool, and plans were being made to open up steamship service to England. Such foreign connections were very important to the Confederacy as they could be used for direct trade to Europe with Charleston as the focal point of such intercourse.[19]

Running southward out of Charleston Harbor toward Savannah, vessels could move along a series of inland water routes that allowed ships drawing less than ten feet the advantage of not having to venture into the ocean. When using this passage, ships would usually make a port of call at Beaufort, South Carolina. Beaufort, situated on the Beaufort River, was one of the most accessible ports on the southeast coast. The river had a depth of fifteen to eighteen feet at low water, and the entrance from the Atlantic was through the easily navigable Port Royal Sound. The Beaufort–Port Royal area offered everything in terms of natural features that a port of entry would need, but the site was virtually useless to the Confederacy as it had only limited dock facilities and no railroad connections.[20]

Just south of Beaufort was Savannah, Georgia, the Confederacy's second major commercial port on the Atlantic. The city, situated eighteen miles from the mouth of the Savannah River, was built on a sandy bluff, fifty feet above sea level. Savannah was renowned for its tree-lined streets, large town squares, the variety of "many-colored little houses," and large population of merchants whose wealth was reflected in their huge homes of "New York Fifth Avenue character."[21]

The main export of Savannah was rice, but the city owed its prosperity to cotton. Savannah was the nation's third largest shipper of cotton, exporting close to 500,000 bales in 1861. The "white gold" poured into the city on steamboats coming down the Savannah River from the great cotton depot of Augusta, and on the Central Georgia Railroad, which linked Savannah to Macon and Columbus, tapping the state's cotton-growing interior.[22]

The main ocean entrance to Savannah was by the narrow, winding channel of the Savannah River. The river had a bar that accommodated vessels with an eighteen-foot draft, but only ships drawing fifteen feet could reach the city. The deeper-drafted vessels had to anchor two miles down river and be served by lighters. A second entrance to Savannah lay to the south at Wassaw Sound. Vessels coming through this channel could reach the city by an intricate passage from the sound through ten-foot-deep St. Augustine Creek, a small stream that emptied into the Savannah River just below the city. The passage was too shallow for the larger merchantmen and was mainly used by steam packets that ran from Charleston to Florida.[23]

South of Savannah were a number of deep-water sites that had not yet been developed into major commercial centers. They included Brunswick, Georgia, and Fernandina and Jacksonville, Florida, which had great potential for use as overseas ports. All of these cities had recently been connected to the Southern interior by railroads, but none had attracted any foreign trade. Given time, all could become valuable ports.[24]

Farther down the Florida peninsula, there were few harbors that could materially support the Confederacy. Such sites as St. Augustine, Mosquito Inlet, and Indian River Inlet could be used by schooners and very light-drafted steamers, but none had efficient transportation facilities to distribute incoming supplies. Only in extreme emergencies would these shallow ports be put to use by the Confederates.[25]

At the southern extremity of Florida, located at the end of a chain of islands curling out to the west from the tip of the peninsula was the tiny port of Key West, which was firmly in the hands of the Union troops stationed at Fort Taylor. From this point the Union planners divided the blockade between those squadrons that patrolled the Atlantic coast and those that watched the shores of the Gulf of Mexico.[26]

The western coastline of the Florida peninsula, from its tip at Cape Sable to Cedar Key, contained a few shallow and unimportant inlets leading to small fishing towns surrounded by wilderness. The harbors, including Charlotte Harbor and Tampa Bay, were valuable only as safe anchorage in storms or as hiding spots for blockade runners heading for St. Marks or Mobile, Alabama.[27]

The only port of any commercial value on the western side of the Florida peninsula was Cedar Key, a small town located ten miles south of the mouth of the Suwannee River. It was the western terminus of the Florida Railroad, which connected Cedar Key to Fernandina. The port, along with Fernandina, was being developed as part of Florida Senator David Yulee's grand plan of circumventing the New York-to-New Orleans trade by having ship cargoes unloaded at Fernandina and hauled by rail to Cedar Key, where coasting vessels would carry the shipments on to New Orleans.[28]

The scheme had merit, but entrance to the harbor was narrow and had a channel depth of only eleven feet. This would keep all but medium-sized vessels out of Cedar Key. The town was also without any established commercial houses and was in a very precarious position to defend. Even with rail connections, Cedar Key was of limited value.[29]

One hundred miles up the coast, at the point where the Florida peninsula met the mainland, was the town of St. Marks. Located on the St. Marks River, only vessels drawing ten feet could reach the small port city. However, those that did found railroad connections to the interior via the Tallahassee Railroad.

West of St. Marks, past the tiny town of Apalachicola, was the military port of Pensacola, described by army engineers as the "finest harbor on the Gulf coast." Pensacola had the "raw properties to become a port of inappreciable value." The water on the bar measured twenty-two feet, and the anchorage inside the bay was deeper, making the port capable of handling any vessel in the world.[30]

Pensacola had originally been developed as a military port to give the United States Navy a base on the Gulf of Mexico, but the city had tremendous commercial potential. Railroads connected it to the interior of Alabama and placed it in a position to secure vast amount of produce. This, coupled with the fine harbor and dock area, made the city a very valuable port; however it was not destined to serve the South. When Florida seceded, state troops managed to seize Fort Barrancas, McRee, and the navy yard, but failed to take Fort Pickens, located at the mouth of the harbor on the western tip of Santa Rosa Island. From this position Fort Pickens alone could maintain an effective blockade of Pensacola Bay, thus denying its use as a Confederate port of entry.[31]

Forty miles west of Pensacola was the Alabama port of Mobile, the Gulf's "second place of entry," after New Orleans. Founded in 1711, Mobile had grown with the rise of the Cotton Kingdom to become the nation's number two cotton port. In 1860, nearly 850,000 bales were shipped from the city. Mobile owed its prosperity to its location at the mouth of the Alabama and Tombigbee River system, whose branches stretched over the upper part of Alabama. These rivers were navigable by steamboats almost to their source in the Cumberland Mountains and, consequently, were utilized to transport huge amounts of cotton from the state's plantations.

Mobile was also well served by two important railroads. The Mobile and Ohio Railroad ran northwest through the interior of Mississippi and western Tennessee before terminating on the Mississippi River at Columbus, Kentucky, while the Alabama and Florida Railroad linked the city to the Chattahoochee River valley and Central Georgia. Such communications brought to Mobile even more cotton and other produce.[32]

Southward from the city stretched Mobile Bay, a large sheltered body of water that was thirty miles long and six to fifteen miles wide. The principal entrance from the Gulf was the main channel, which ran directly into the bay between Mobile Point on the east and Dauphin Island to the west. The bar had a good depth of twenty feet, and the channel was some two thousand yards wide. Once across the bar, vessels found excellent anchorage in an area known as Lower Fleet.

Shallow secondary entrances to Mobile were Swash Channel, which ran along Mobile Point before joining the main channel just outside the harbor, and Grant's Pass, located south of Dauphin Island between that island and the mainland. Grant's Pass had been excavated for seven miles through oyster reefs with a depth of about five feet at low water and nearly seven at high. The pass was used by coastal steamers that operated between New Orleans and Mobile by way of the Mississippi Sound.[33]

Mobile's major disadvantage as a port was that the bay was lined with banks of shoals that allowed only vessels drawing eight feet or less to reach the city's wharves. All other ships had to anchor in the lower reaches of the bay and be serviced by lighters. Because of this, Mobile was an active international port only during the shipping of cotton, when hundreds of vessels were seen riding at anchor just inside the mouth of the bay. When the cotton season was over, Mobile reverted to being a secondary port with its commerce being carried by light-drafted steamers and sailing ships.[34]

West of Mobile Bay a line of low-lying sand islands lay parallel to the shore forming the Mississippi Sound. This protected body of water was too shallow for heavy shipping, but it did provide a convenient and safe route for small coastal ships drawing six feet or less. As reported by Union engineers, "considerable trade" was "carried on between Mobile via Grant's Pass and New Orleans by way of Bayou St. Jean and Lake Pontchartrain."[35]

Located on the mainland side of the sheltered waterway were the small towns of Pascagoula, Biloxi and Mississippi City. These tiny fishing ports were too shallow and devoid of internal communications to be of any value to the Confederacy. Mississippi Sound, however, was of great strategic value as it provided the most direct route between New Orleans and Mobile. By employing small steamers, the South could quickly and easily transfer supplies, arms, and men between the two cities, thus developing an extremely valuable line of communication.[36]

The largest city in the South and the only Confederate port of entry that could be rightfully called a major site of world commerce was New Orleans. The strategically located city, founded as a French outpost in 1718, controlled the commerce of the great Mississippi River system, and dominated the trade of the Gulf and Southwestern states. By 1860 New Orleans had grown to become the South's largest and most industrialized city. It was second to New York in volume of trade and stood fourth in the nation in the amount of revenue collected.[37] (See Appendix 1.)

In 1860 New Orleans was the focal point of the world's cotton trade. Cotton arrived at the city on Western-styled steamboats, coastal vessels, small sailing ships, and on the most recent addition to the city's transportation system, the New Orleans, Jackson and Great Northern Railroad. The railroad ran north through the interior of the Mississippi to Grenada, where it was joined by lines running to Memphis and northward to the Ohio River. This system, plus the marine transportation, carried most of the Texas, Louisiana, Arkansas, Tennessee, Mississippi, and western Florida cotton crops into the city for shipment overseas. In the year prior to the outbreak of the war nearly two million bales of cotton were shipped from New Orleans. This total was more than the combined cotton exports of all other United States ports (Appendix 3).[38]

The importance of such a seaport to the Confederacy was immeasurable. New Orleans had the wealth, commercial connections, internal communications, and shipping needed to develop direct trade with Europe. Once this occurred, the city could become the new nation's exporting capital, and, by reversing the extensive transportation systems that brought cotton to the city, become the Confederacy's main import center. Yet New Orleans did have some natural features that limited its use and could keep it from reaching its full potential as the South's main seaport.[39]

New Orleans had numerous entrances to the Gulf, but only a few could be utilized by the larger ships that frequented the port. Connections east through Lake Pontchartrain were limited to vessels drawing seven feet or less. To the west the city could be approached via Barataria Bay, Berwick Bay, and Bayou la Fourche. However, only low-draft, square-rigged sailing ships and small steamboats could navigate the shallow canals and bayous that often measured only four feet of water.[40]

The main route to the city was via the Mississippi River, which entered the Gulf about 100 miles from the city. Three major passes existed at the river's mouth: Pass a l'Outre, South Pass, and South West Pass. Pass a l'Outre was actually three separate passes, the largest allowing vessels drawing seventeen feet to enter the river. Vessels were guided by a lighthouse, and three miles up the river was a small settlement that housed a revenue station, pilot station, boat depot, telegraph station, and an office of the New Orleans and Mississippi Towboat Company.[41]

Towboats served as an extremely important function to the port of New Orleans. Because of silt deposited in the river, the bar was constantly moving and shifting. The silt was not firmly packed, thus permitting the powerful towboats to move vessels with drafts up to twenty feet through the bar.[42]

South Pass had only six feet of water on its bar and was rarely used. South West Pass had for many years been the deepest entrance to the Mississippi River, but by 1860 the pass was filled with silt, leaving a depth of only thirteen feet. A lighthouse stood near South Pass, and a small settlement of pilots was located near South West Pass, but both passes had been eclipsed by Pass a l'Outre in use and importance.[43]

Besides the river and lake approaches, New Orleans was also connected to the Gulf by a port of entry some eighty miles to the west at Brashear City. This small town was the western terminus of New Orleans, Opelousas and Great Western Railroad, which had been started in 1853 to provide New Orleans with rail connections to Texas and, eventually, California. Unfortunately the funds of the company were badly sapped by construction costs, and in 1857 the project bogged down in the swamps of Louisiana. The owners of the railroad, in order to avoid bankruptcy, struck a deal with steamship companies to connect Brashear City to the ports of Texas.

West of Brashear City stretched the long Texas seaboard, an area that made up one-fourth of the Confederacy's coastline. The terrain of the coast was one of long sand islands and peninsulas that formed a protective bank for the inner shoreline. Numerous broad inlets and bays studded the shore, giving the impression that the Texas coast abounded with sites for bustling ports, but this was not the case. The Texas waters, though very picturesque, were deceptively shallow, thus restricting marine trade to only a few sounds that could be used as ports of entry.[44]

The depth of water along its coastline and the lack of railroad connections to the Mississippi River left the growing trade of Texas in the hands of New Orleans-based steamship companies that served three Texas harbors. The two smaller ports were those of Sabine City and Indianola. Both had incomplete railroad connections to the interior, and shallow bars limited their trade to light-drafted steamers and schooners. Only Galveston could accommodate vessels of any size.[45]

Galveston was the only port along the four-hundred-mile Texas coast that could put forth any claim to being a deep-water port, but even this was somewhat dubious. Located on Galveston Island, a long, narrow, sandy barrier island, the town looked inward onto a spacious but very shallow bay. Entrance to the harbor was by four channels, but only the main channel with a bar of twelve feet would allow large vessels to reach the town. A two-mile-long railroad bridge carrying the tracks of the Galveston and Houston Railroad connected Galveston to Houston and the rich cotton area of central Texas. Besides the railway, numerous small steamboats operated between the coastal city and Houston by way of Buffalo Bayou.[46]

Galveston's internal communications and useable entrance to the Gulf resulted in the town's becoming the commercial center of the state.

Its rows of warehouses and the elaborately constructed homes of its merchants reflected the prosperity of the city built in the sands. However, because of the depth of the bar and channel, Galveston was not a highly accessible port and, like the rest of the Texas marine trade, the town's commerce was in reality an appendage of the New Orleans trade. In 1860 the major portion of the 252,000 bales of cotton that passed through Galveston were sent to New Orleans before being shipped overseas.[47]

So, in their study of the Southern coastline, the Blockade Board did show that, at least potentially, the Confederacy did have ports of entry with which to build an overseas trade. The best ports were New Orleans, Mobile, Savannah, and Charleston, which combined good physical features with strong internal connections and active commercial houses. From these cities, European trade could be undertaken almost immediately. The remaining deep-water ports of Beaufort and Wilmington, North Carolina, Brunswick, Georgia, and Fernandina, Florida, had everything save the merchant interest, but given time the lure of profit would bring growth to these seaports. However, time was something that the Union blockade would try to deny the Confederate ports.

In 1861 most of Western Europe based blockades on the Declaration of Paris, and though the United States was not a signatory of the pact, Lincoln and Seward planned their blockade on the provisions of the treaty. The catch phrase of the document stated that: "Blockades, to be binding must be effective, that is to say, maintained by a force sufficient really to prevent access to the coast of the enemy." Most observers thought the United States would adopt a "cabinet blockade," in which squadrons of warships would operate off the Southern coast searching for violators on the high seas. Such an arrangement would provide enough of an "imminent danger" to vessels trying to reach the Confederacy that European powers would, at least for a while, accept the North's blockade.[48]

However, the Union leaders had no intention of using a cabinet blockade. Such a measure would not provide a stranglehold over Southern trade. Instead, the Union Navy planned to post warships off all major shipping centers to check commerce at the points of entry and departure. This was to be the first modern blockade. Its focal points were the Southern ports, and its power would come from steam engines.[49]

Steam was coming of age in 1861. Even the swiftest sailing vessel would eventually be overtaken in the open sea by a steamer. The organizers of the blockade knew that the majority of the Southern trade was carried by sailing ships, and soon they were despatching converted steam merchantmen to cruise off the Southern ports. Many of these new warships were the same powerful steamboats that had run between the two sections of the country before the war. As fighting vessels they were rather weak, but their appearance off the Southern coast would stop merchant sailing ships.[50]

Both the Confederates and the European powers doubted the Union's ability to effectively blockade the Confederacy, but the nations of France and England were willing to await the results of the blockade and in May 1861 declared their neutrality, thus giving the North's actions their tacit approval. The Southerners were disappointed by Europe's recognition of the blockade, but still held their belief in the power of cotton. The 1860 crop, for the most part, had been shipped by the time of the firing on Fort Sumter. Not until the following fall would the next crop be ready for export and, at that time, Southerners expected the lack of cotton in the world market would force England and France to break the blockade. Until then, Southerners seemed content to ignore the growing blockade.[51]

It took time for the United States Navy to put a blockade into effect. Slowly warships and converted merchantmen began to take their positions off Southern ports. As was the custom, the commander of the vessels would serve notice to the Confederate authorities of the establishment of the blockade, and a grace period of fifteen days would be given for neutral vessels to leave port. Any ship approaching the city would be warned off, and, if caught again, seized. On April 30, 1861, Norfolk became the first blockaded port. Slightly less than a month later, on May 28, Charleston, Savannah, and Mobile received notification, followed by New Orleans on the thirty-first. On July 2, Galveston was blockaded and, almost as an afterthought, on July 21 the small converted merchantman *Daylight* placed Wilmington under blockade.[52]

Even before the blockaders appeared off the Southern ports, the great exodus of shipping had begun. During May and June the majority of foreign vessels left, often before the blockade was established. At New Orleans a special arrangement had to be made to allow the tugboats to pull foreign vessels out of the Mississippi River.

The powerful steamers did their work quickly, but in pulling the sailing ships into the Gulf, they were removing the last of the prewar style of shipping that the Confederacy would see. In the Southern ports there remained a strange mixture of ocean steamers, coasting vessels, river steamboats, and sailing ships that made up the merchant marine of the Confederacy (see Appendix 4).[53]

The Confederacy had ten steamships capable of some sort of overseas trade, but none was put to immediate use. At the start of the war the large paddlewheelers *Jamestown* and *Yorktown* were seized at Richmond and converted to warships; the new screw steamer *North Carolina*, docked at Wilmington, was put up for sale; and the Charleston vessels *Isabel*, and the older *Governor Dudley* were sold to private interests while the *Nashville* became a warship. Tied up at New Orleans were the steamers *Tennessee*, the recently seized *Star of the West* of Fort Sumter fame, and the smaller *Habana* and *Marquis de la Habana*. All of these would eventually be taken over by the Confederate Navy, though the *Tennessee* was later released into private hands. None of the ocean vessels ventured out as commercial steamers during the first summer of the war, leaving what little steam-borne trade that did go on in the hands of smaller vessels.[54]

The ships that did keep up a limited service early in the war were a class of steamers commonly referred to as coasters or coasting packets. These ships were built with low free boards and light drafts, allowing them to work in the shallow Southern coastal waters. Along the East coast there were only a few vessels which could be considered as coasting packets (see Appendix 4). The majority of the Southern coasters operated in the calm waters of the Gulf of Mexico, which served as the perfect setting for these light-drafted steamers.[55]

There were two major steamship companies operating coastal packets in the Gulf. The smaller one ran four sidewheelers between Mobile and Lake Pontchartrain. The largest company in the Gulf, and in the South, was Charles Morgan's Southern Steamship Company of New Orleans. Operated by Israel C. Harris, Morgan's son-in-law, the firm ran fifteen vesels from New Orleans to Key West, Havana, and along the coast of Texas, carrying passengers, cargo, and mail.

The Gulf and Atlantic coasters were efficient vessels within their scope of operations, but they were incapable of providing the newly founded Confederacy with the ships needed to develop a trade with England. However, their owners, unlike those of the ocean steamers, provided limited service for the first few months of the war, but their impact was negligible. They did not venture beyond coastal waters, and only Confederate diplomats, wishing to impress British and French authorities, considered them blockade runners. They did little to support the war effort and nothing to relieve the growing shortages in the Confederacy.[56]

As early as May 1861, the reduction of goods in the South was beginning to have an effect on the Southern economy. The mere announcement of the blockade had a profound effect on businesses. In May a Wilmington merchant reported that "the only way to get money is to sell goods for cash. All of our merchants have therefore adopted the cash principle for the present." Prices in the larger cities were going up, and in the isolated towns costs were even higher. Towns that depended on supplies from coasting vessels found merchants charging outrageous prices for cargoes. Even in the great city of New Orleans, goods were becoming scarce and prices going up.[57]

The reason for this sudden upsurge in costs was obvious. The South, so long dependent on imports for its daily existence, was no longer being served by the world's trading vessels. From June through August not one steamer entered or cleared a Confederate port for a foreign destination. The record of the sailing ships was not much better. Arriving at the ports of Wilmington, Charleston, Savannah, Mobile, and New Orleans were some eighty-six sailing ships, but only seven brought in foreign goods and of these only two were larger than schooners. In departures, some ninety-two cleared the ports but only eleven for foreign destinations, and all were schooners. Such a trade could not sustain the Confederacy, much less relieve the economic pressures that were beginning to bear on the nation. The larger sailing ships were easy prey for steam blockaders, and schooners, which could slip by the Union warships, could not carry enough cargo. To defeat the blockade, steamers had to be employed, but in 1861 Southerners were reluctant to put their vessels to use.[58]

Simple logistics partially explains the absence of Southern steamboats. Ocean vessels were either taken over by the military or put up for sale by their Southern stockholders, who were cut off from their Northern partners. At New Orleans the Morgan vessels were frequently seized and inspected for use as gunboats by either the state of Louisiana, the Confederate States Navy, or the Confederate Army. Other coastal vessels were taken for gunboats and transports. Those owners who did retain their ships often lacked the connections necessary for overseas trade.

The packet vessels and their parent companies were not geared for foreign trade. The coasting vessels had limited fuel space, which restricted their range in open sea. The only feasible foreign ports that the vessels could reach were St. George, Bermuda, Nassau, Bahamas, and Havana, Cuba, and even then, the packets had no commercial connections to facilitate such a trade. They had no consigners to sell or transship their goods or to have a return cargo ready.[59]

But even more important than these conditions was the fact that Southern shippers and boat owners suffered from the same illusion that infected all areas of the South—that cotton would prove to be the Confederacy's salvation. Many of the commercial and shipping interests in the South could have worked out the mechanical difficulties in organizing an overseas trade by the fall of 1861, but they saw little need to risk their vessels, cargoes, and capital against the blockade when they, like the political leaders of the Confederacy, believed that European intervention over cotton would be soon coming.

Not even foreign recognition of the blockade could sway the Southerners from their faith in cotton. Instead, during the summer of 1861, local politicians, merchants, newspapermen, and planters banded together to force an embargo to prohibit the shipping of cotton from any Confederate port. It was reasoned that such a policy would soon coerce the British to intervene for Southern cotton. The embargo never had official sanction from the Confederate government, but Jefferson Davis and his advisors gave it their tacit approval, believing in its ultimate success.[60]

Unfortunately for the Confederacy the cotton embargo proved to be an ineffective political weapon. England, much to the astonishment of many Southerners, proved itself not to be an "appanage of their cotton kingdom." However, this realization on the part of Confederate leaders did not occur until sometime after the embargo was imposed. In the meantime the South lost an opportunity to develop an early steamboat trade to ports outside the Confederacy while the blockade was still weak. But, no one as yet was willing to abandon the concept of King Cotton. Southerners still clung to their belief that England would have to break the blockade for the cotton, and so the Confederacy waited for phantom fleets to arrive off their shores.[61]

While the embargo kept Southern commercial vessels at anchor, it did not stop armed private and government vessels from challenging the blockade. Early in the war, the Confederate Navy readied three steamers for use as commerce raiders. At New Orleans the *Habana*, renamed *Sumter*, and the *Marquis de la Habana*, now called the *McRae*, were fitted out and on June 30, 1861, the *Sumter* slipped out of Pass a l'Outre and out ran the blockader *Brooklyn* into the open sea. The *McRae* was also stationed at the Head of the Passes to await a chance to dash out of the river, but the opportunity never came, and she eventually became the flagship for the Confederate Naval Squadron based at New Orleans.[62]

The third vessel the Confederates planned to convert into a warship was the fast ocean steamer *Nashville*. In many ways she was an excellent choice. When built in 1853 for the New York-Southhampton-Havre run, the *Nashville* was considered "the fastest and finest steamer along the Atlantic coast." Her speed and size made her a logical choice for a commerce raider, but in fitting her out at Charleston it was discovered that her deck was too weak to hold the weight of heavy ordnance. Given two small twelve-pounders, the *Nashville* ran out of Charleston on October 21, 1861, for England, where the Confederates hoped to properly outfit her as a privateer.[63]

Besides the regularly commissioned warships, privately owned vessels took to the high seas in search of prizes. Taking advantage of the government's offer to issue letters of marque, and lured by profit and adventure, companies readied privateers. Before long, a number of sailing ships and steamers were cruising the coastline looking for victims. However, only two steamers, the tug *Mariner* out of Wilmington and the Charleston-based *Gordon* ever ran the blockade to undertake their raids. By the end of August 1861, both vessels had returned to port, their privateering days ended by increased Union vigilance. Though technically blockade runners, these steamers had done nothing to ease the growing shortages of goods and munitions in the Confederacy. Precious time was being wasted, and the problem of supply was growing.[64]

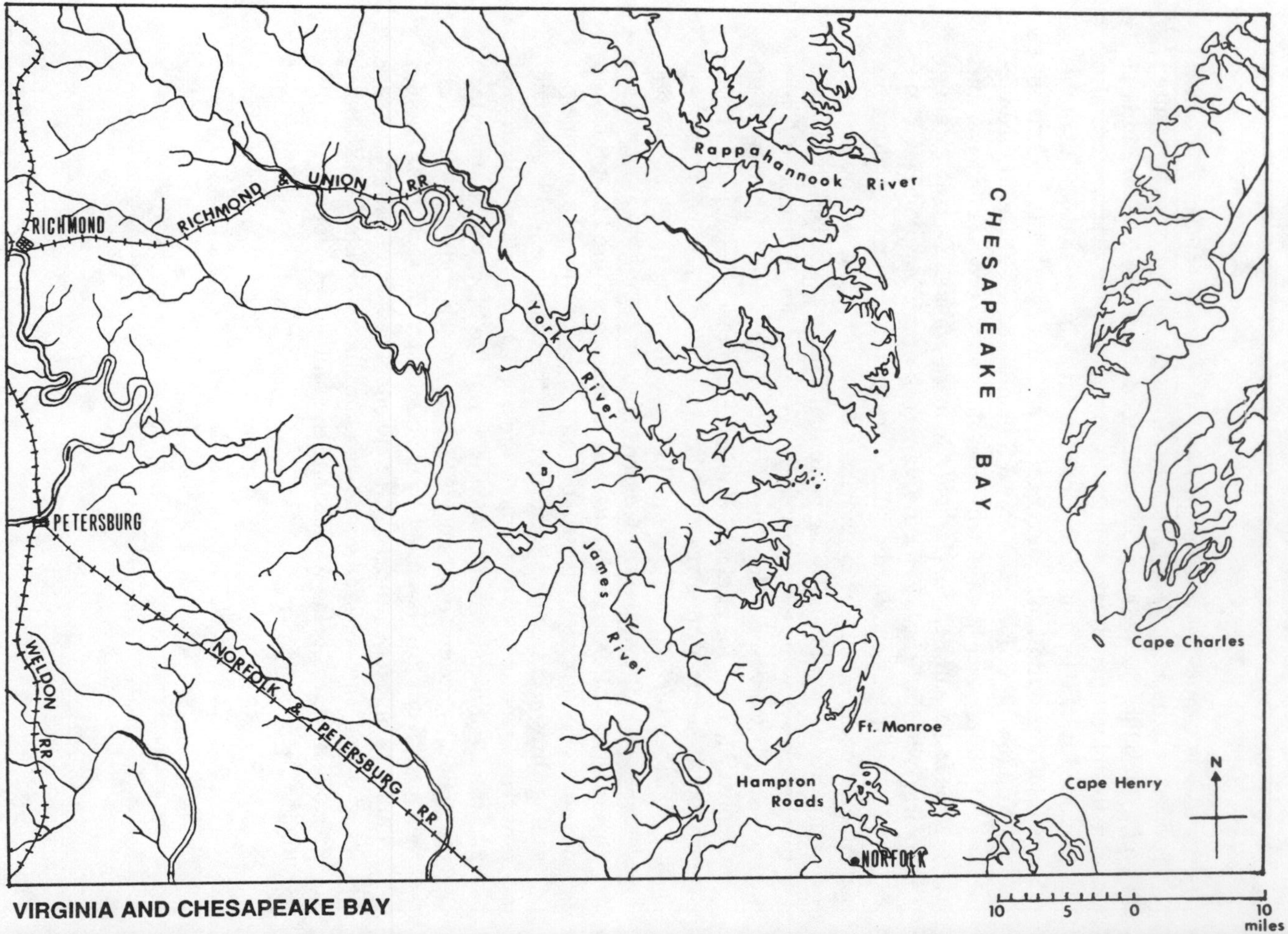

CHESAPEAKE BAY

Cape Charles

Cape Henry

NORFOLK

Ft. Monroe

Hampton Roads

Rappahannock River

York River

James River

RICHMOND & UNION RR

NORFOLK & PETERSBURG RR

PETERSBURG

WELDON RR

10 miles

N

**VIRGINIA AND CHESAPEAKE BAY**

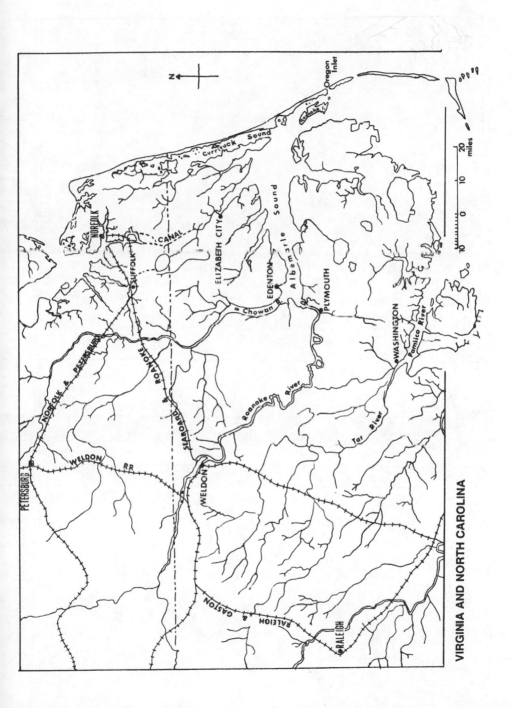

**VIRGINIA AND NORTH CAROLINA**

**WILMINGTON AND THE CAROLINAS**

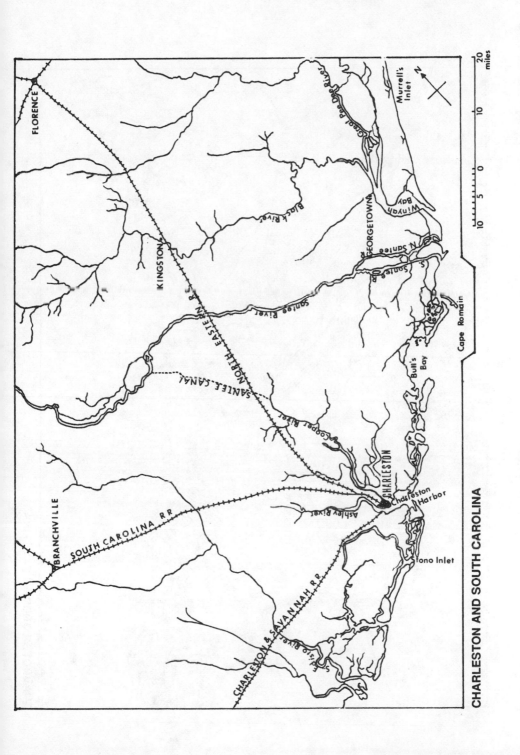

CHARLESTON AND SOUTH CAROLINA

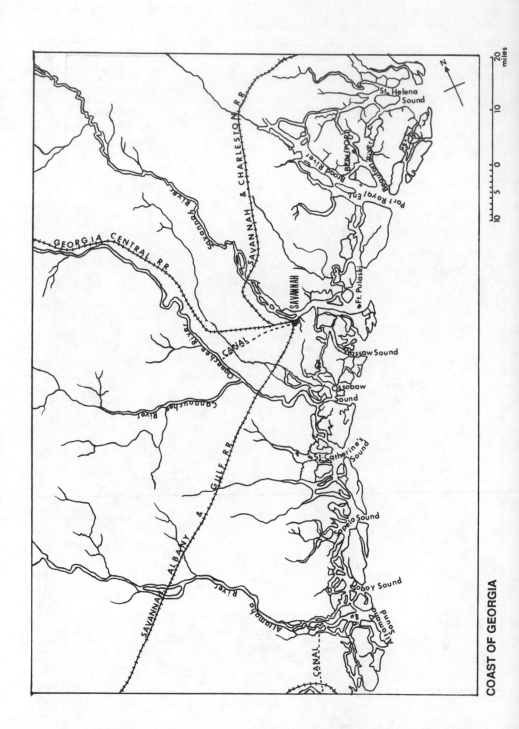

COAST OF GEORGIA

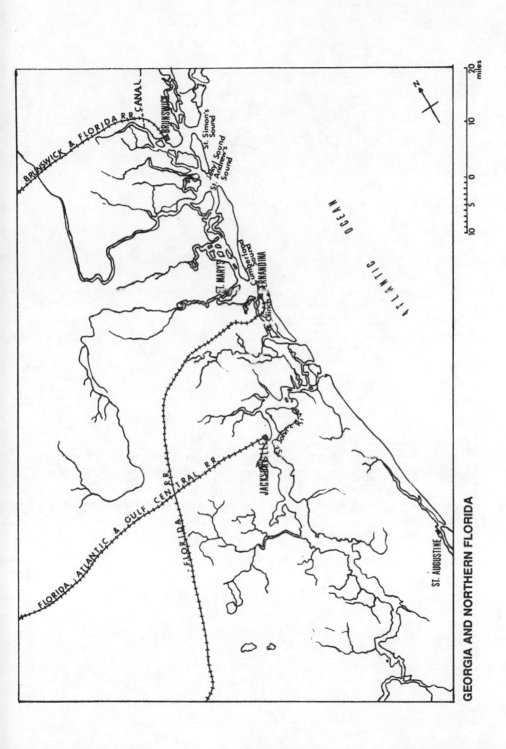

**GEORGIA AND NORTHERN FLORIDA**

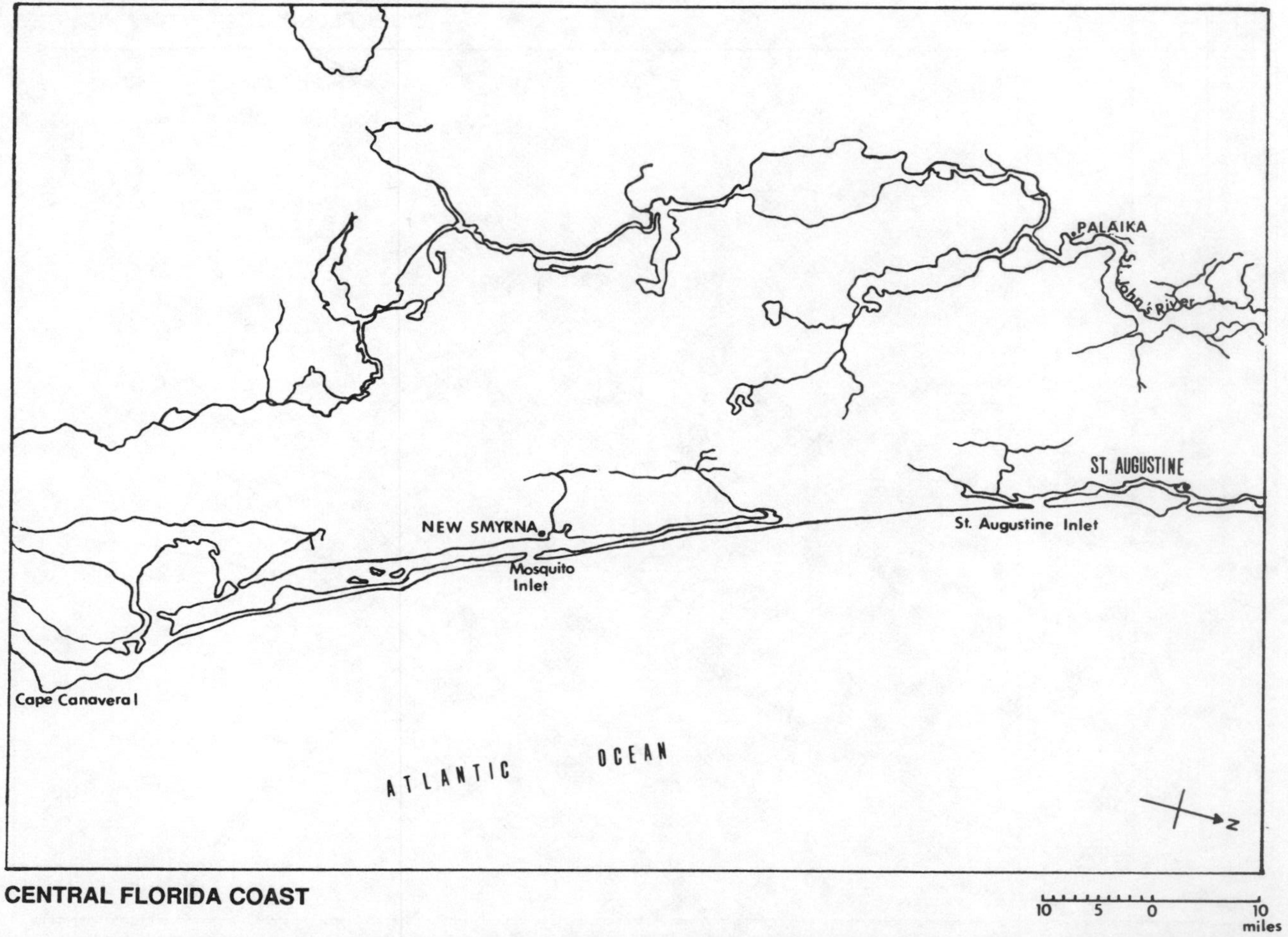

PALAIKA

St. John's River

ST. AUGUSTINE

St. Augustine Inlet

NEW SMYRNA

Mosquito Inlet

ATLANTIC OCEAN

Cape Canaveral

N

10    5    0                    10
                              miles

**CENTRAL FLORIDA COAST**

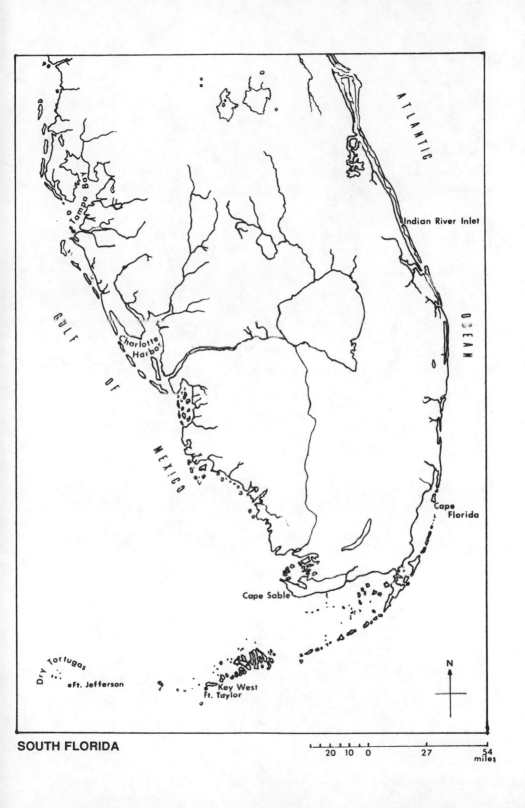

ATLANTIC

OCEAN

Indian River Inlet

GULF

OF

MEXICO

Tampa Bay

Dry

Charlotte
Harbor

Cape
Florida

Cape Sable

Dry Tortugas

•Ft. Jefferson

Key West
Ft. Taylor

N

**SOUTH FLORIDA**

20 10 0        27       54
miles

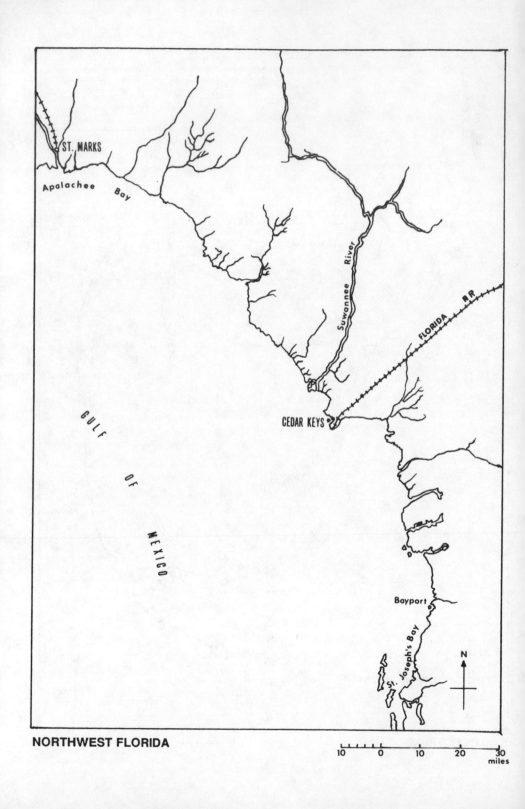

ST. MARKS

Apalachee Bay

Suwannee River

FLORIDA RR

CEDAR KEYS

GULF

OF

MEXICO

Bayport

St. Joseph's Bay

N

**NORTHWEST FLORIDA**

10    0    10    20    30
                        miles

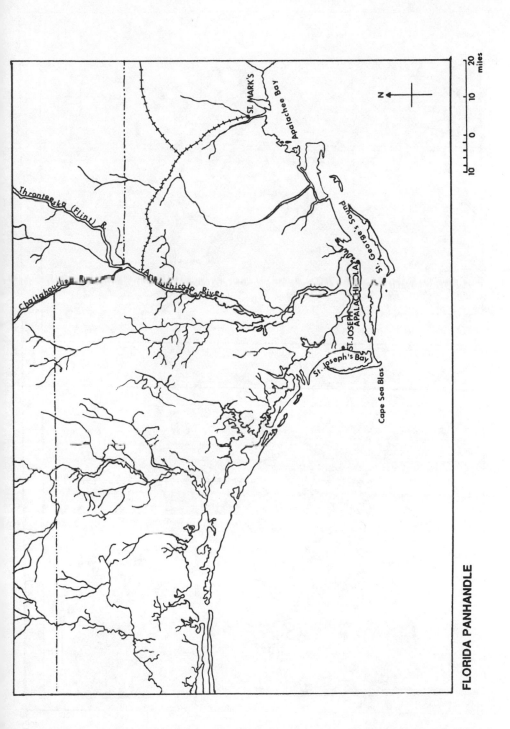

**FLORIDA PANHANDLE**

ALABAMA AND MISSISSIPPI COAST

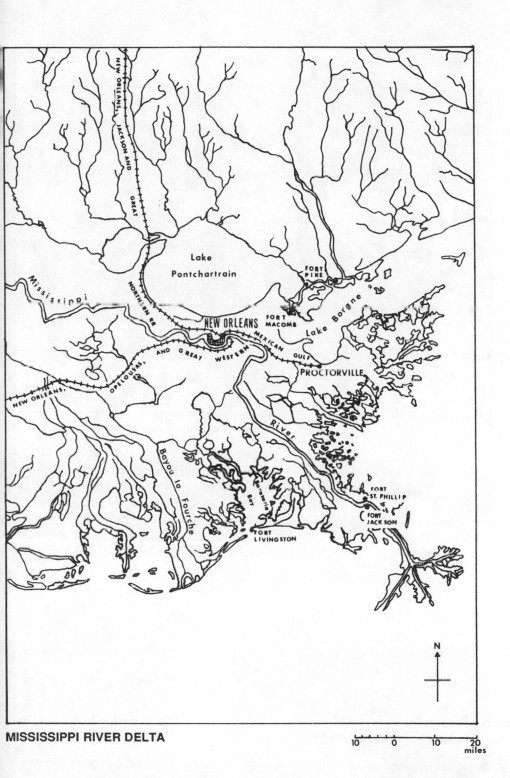

**MISSISSIPPI RIVER DELTA**

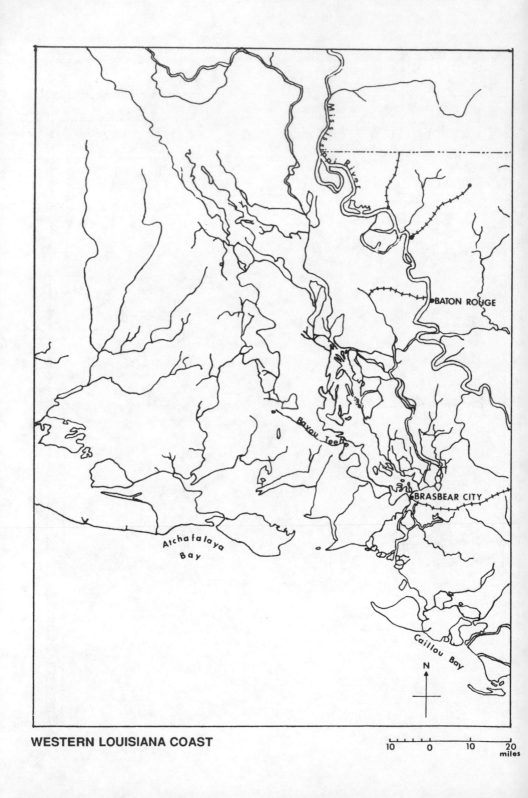

**WESTERN LOUISIANA COAST**

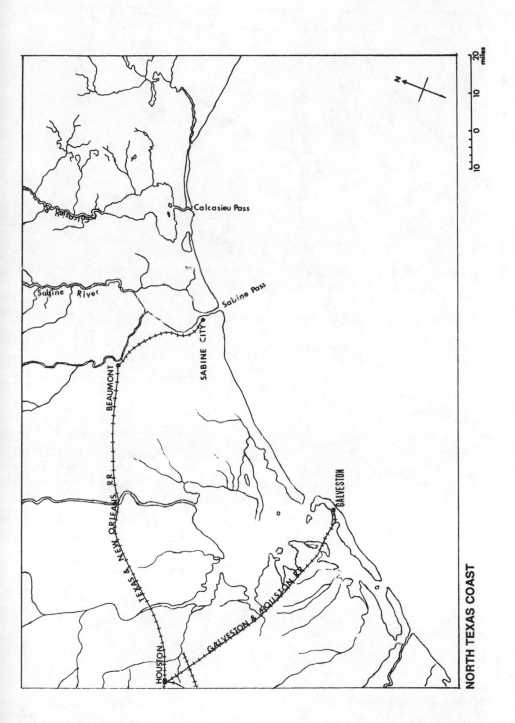

NORTH TEXAS COAST

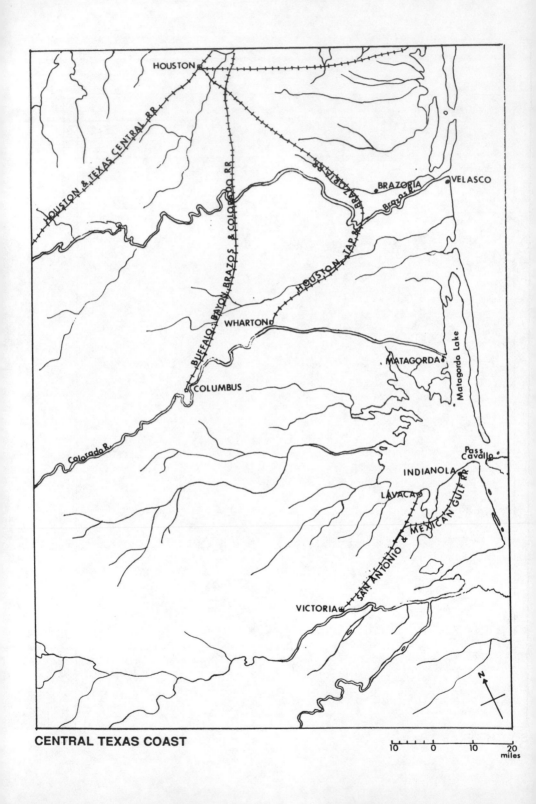

HOUSTON

HOUSTON & TEXAS CENTRAL RR.

BRAZORIA RR.

BRAZORIA

VELASCO

Brazos R.

BUFFALO BAYOU, BRAZOS & COLORADO RR.

HOUSTON TAP RR.

WHARTON

Matagorda Lake

MATAGORDA

COLUMBUS

Colorado R.

Pass Cavallo

INDIANOLA

SAN ANTONIO & MEXICAN GULF RR.

LAVACA

VICTORIA

N

**CENTRAL TEXAS COAST**

10    0    10    20
                miles

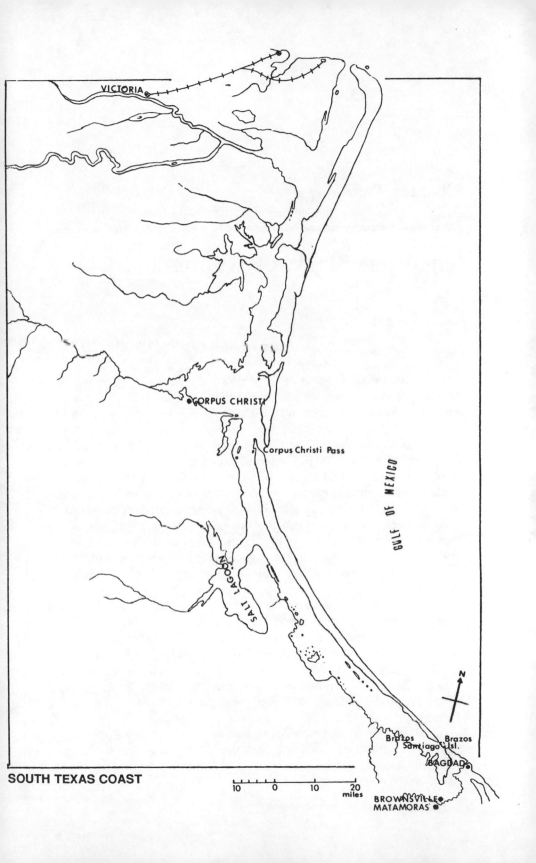

VICTORIA

CORPUS CHRISTI

Corpus Christi Pass

GULF OF MEXICO

SALT LAGOON

N

Brazos
Santiago Isl.
Brazos
Isl.

BAGDAD

BROWNSVILLE
MATAMORAS

SOUTH TEXAS COAST

10    0    10    20
miles

# Chapter Two

---

# The First Blockade Runners

Oftentimes the course of governmental actions is heavily influenced by private agencies and individuals; the Confederacy was no exception. Since the nation was without foreign recognition, it had to turn to established businesses for assistance in its overseas financial affairs. For aid in Europe the Confederacy employed John Fraser and Company, a decision that proved to be one of the most fateful of the war.

John Fraser and Company was a respected Charleston-based importing and exporting company. The firm had been established in the early nineteenth century by John Fraser, an immigrant from Scotland. In 1835 John Fraser retired from the business, leaving its affairs in the hands of his son John Augustus Fraser and his chief clerk George Alfred Trenholm. By the 1850s, the younger Fraser had dropped out of any active role in the firm, and Trenholm became the company's senior and directing partner.[1]

Under Trenholm's leadership the firm opened Fraser, Trenholm and Company in Liverpool and Trenholm Brothers in New York. The branches shared the same officers, though their division of profits varied from company to company. George Trenholm served as senior partner in all three companies while James T. Welsman headed the New York office, Charles K. Prioleau was president of Fraser, Trenholm and Company, and Theodore D. Wagner was president of John Fraser and Company.[2]

By 1860, Trenholm's companies were operating five sailing ships between Charleston, Liverpool, and New York, and were working to establish a direct steamship line between Charleston and Liverpool.

46

Trenholm had tremendous influence over Charleston's business circles, where he was regarded as the "master of local banking and cotton trade." The company also commanded an excellent reputation in England, where Trenholm had numerous business connections.[3]

Secession opened even greater business opportunities. Before the fighting broke out John Fraser and Company began negotiations to provide the Confederacy with steamship service to England. Trenholm and his partners also took advantage of the unsettled time before open combat by shipping arms from New York and Liverpool to Charleston. Some of the war supplies were gifts, such as a British-built Blakely rifle used in the bombardment of Fort Sumter, but for the most part they were sold to the state of South Carolina and later the Confederacy for excellent profits, giving Trenholm an idea of things to come.[4]

Once hostilities began and the blockade was established, the company closed down all active shipping. Like the rest of the South, Trenholm trusted that the power of cotton would soon force England to break the blockade. However, even though the Charleston partners publicly backed the cotton embargo, the company's Liverpool branch, with Trenholm's obvious approval, continued to negotiate for steamships and took on orders for imports from England. No matter what the outcome of the cotton embargo, Trenholm's companies would be prepared for all contingencies.[5]

Besides readying vessels for possible blockade running, Trenholm also offered the services of his Liverpool branch as financial agents for the Confederacy. For the standard commission of 1.5 percent, the Confederate Treasury could deposit specie or bonds with John Fraser and Company in Charleston, who would then send letters of credit for that amount to Fraser, Trenholm, and Company in Liverpool. Because of the excellent reputation of the firm, the letters of credit would be honored by banks in England, and cash could be obtained by Confederate agents operating overseas.[6]

The Confederacy was quick to accept Trenholm's offer. The use of the commercial house had many advantages. It allowed the South, at least for the time being, to keep its limited supply of specie at home, and kept the nation's cotton from being used as a basis of exchange, thus keeping the cotton embargo alive. The letters of credit sent to England via Trenholm's companies would give financial support to the nation's diplomatic missions and, most importantly, it would provide cash and credit for the purchase of badly needed war supplies.[7]

Of all items required by the Confederacy in 1861, military supplies were the most pressing. If Southern armies hoped to be able to turn back the numerically superior legions of the North they would have to be armed with the most efficient weapons of the time; however, at the start of the war only a few such arms existed in the Confederacy.

The problem of providing suitable armaments for the Confederate Army rested in the hands of the chief of the nation's fledgling Ordnance Bureau, Major Josiah C. Gorgas. A Northerner by birth, Gorgas, after his graduation from the West Point in 1841, had served in the United States Ordnance Bureau. In this duty, he had worked in nearly every arsenal in the nation and taken inspection tours of European arsenals and armories. While serving in the South he came to share the views of that section, and married the daughter of a former Alabama governor. His appointment as head of the Confederate Ordnance Bureau was an excellent one. Gorgas was a tireless worker with a remarkable talent for organization. He was a munition expert and was well acquainted with not only the arms situation of the Confederacy but also the vast potential of the North.[8]

The immediate problem facing Gorgas was equipping the 100,000-man army that the South was attempting to put in the field. Early inventories from his arsenals revealed the great weakness in Southern war supplies. The basic available infantry arm was the 69-caliber smoothbore musket, a weapon far outclassed by the North's Springfield rifle. There existed a severe gunpowder shortage, and the Southern artillery was heavily weighed toward siege and seacoast artillery with few modern field pieces available for service.[9]

Gorgas realized that the best answer to the Confederacy's needs lay with Southern-built munition complexes. The South contained large deposits of essential raw materials, and the great Tredegar Iron Works at Richmond could build the needed machinery. Potentially the new nation had the capacity to become self-sustaining in arms production, but it would be some time before the mineral wealth could be mined and factories completed.

Before putting his master plan to work, Gorgas had to deal with the immediate problem of arming the Southern soldiers, and until the factories were producing, military supplies would have to be procured outside the South. As information from his arsenals began to come in, Gorgas realized that the Ordnance Bureau would, at least for a while, have to "rely greatly on the introduction of articles of prime necessity through the blockaded ports." To direct the purchasing of foreign supplies, Gorgas sent Captain Caleb Huse to England. Huse had no detailed instructions, instead the captain was given wide discretionary powers to buy goods and ship them back to the Confederacy.[10]

Like Gorgas, Huse was not a native Southerner. Born in Massachusetts, he had attended West Point and graduated seventh in the class of 1851. Serving one year in the artillery corps, Huse returned to West Point to teach chemistry, mineralogy, and geology. During the years just prior to the war he served on various ordnance boards before retiring to teach at the University of Alabama. A capable and energetic worker, Huse was well qualified for the position of Confederate purchasing agent. However, unlike Gorgas, he was never able to remove the taint of his Yankee birth, and often it was only by the intervention of Gorgas that Huse was kept from being recalled.[11]

Leaving the South in mid-April, Captain Huse traveled north to New York, where he conferred with James Welsman of Trenholm Brothers and received money for his trip to England. Proceeding to Portland, Maine, Huse sailed to Liverpool, arriving May 10, 1861. He gained funds from Fraser, Trenholm and Company and immediately began to search the English market for Enfield rifles, a weapon whose performance matched the Springfield rifle. However, the market for the popular rifle, and for munitions in general, was flooded, and Huse had to contract such purchasing houses as Sinclair, Hamilton and Company, and S. Isaac, Campbell and Company to purchase the arms and supplies. Delivery would not be until late summer, and in the meantime Huse busied himself in searching out additional sources for supplies.[12]

A few weeks after his arrival in Liverpool, Huse was joined by agents representing the Confederate States Navy Department. Unlike the army, the navy had little to build upon. Though a comprehensive program was undertaken to develop a navy within the Confederacy, Secretary of the Navy Stephen Mallory, like Gorgas, realized that the quickest way to fill his department's needs was to make large purchases in Europe. To this end Mallory sent Captain James Bulloch to England to buy items ranging from letterhead stationery to ironclad warships.[13]

Bulloch, a former naval officer and commercial steamboat captain, arrived in Liverpool on June 4, 1861. Meeting with Huse and Prioleau, Bulloch adopted Huse's methods of hiring commercial agents to purchase his supplies. He then turned his attention to searching British shipyards for possible warships.[14]

While Huse and Bulloch were continuing their work, another Confederate agent, Major Edward C. Anderson, arrived in Liverpool. A well-known Georgia businessman, Anderson had served as an officer in the United States Navy and had twice been mayor of Savannah. A friend of Jefferson Davis, Anderson had traveled in early May to Montgomery, where he met with the Confederate president and Leroy Walker, the secretary of war. The Confederate authorities, worried by Huse's initial reports and wary of his Northern background, commissioned Anderson a major in the artillery and despatched him to England with the authority to replace Huse. However, if Huse was found to be doing his job, Anderson was then to assist him in securing supplies. Anderson's authority came directly from the secretary of war, and he was given *carte blanche* over all purchasing activities. As Anderson summed up his duties, he was "to be the Secretary of War in England."[15]

Sailing from Savannah on board the racing yacht *America*, now renamed *Camilla*, Anderson arrived at Queenstown on June 22, 1861. Hurrying to Liverpool he met with Huse and Bulloch and quickly realized that Huse was acting with the utmost competency. Within three days of his arrival, Anderson was working with the other agents purchasing supplies for the South.[16]

By late July the Confederates were receiving returns on their contracts. Warehouses across England were filling with supplies earmarked for the South; however, the agents were at a loss as to how to ship the goods. The Union blockade, coupled with a proclamation by Queen Victoria asking her subjects not to break a legally constituted blockade, had stifled all trade to the South. In desperation, Anderson and his associates turned to their financial agents Fraser, Trenholm and Company for help.[17]

The company was quick to reply, and on July 29, 1861, Charles Prioleau approached his fellow countrymen with a business proposition. Knowing their extreme difficulty in securing shipping, he offered Anderson part of the cargo space on board a steamer that Fraser, Trenholm and Company was readying for a run to the South. Even though Anerson considered the freight charges to be "high" he did agree, realizing that "it was that or nothing." Once the contract was signed, Anderson instructed Sinclair, Hamilton and Company to prepare the delivered goods for shipment.[18]

The vessel chosen to be the first steamer to challenge the blockade was the recently completed *Bermuda*, an iron-hulled, screw merchantman with a large carrying capacity. She was loaded with a cargo of private goods and Confederate munitions. Her master was Eugene L. Tessier, a Frenchman who before the war had commanded John Fraser and Company's sailing ship the *Emily St. Pierre*. Described by Anderson as a "determined little man," Tessier was just the captain to take the *Bermuda* through the blockade.[19]

The greater portion of the cargo belonged to Fraser, Trenholm and Company, supplies that the company planned to sell in the Confederacy for large profits. Shoes, blankets, dry goods, and drugs comprised the civilian side of the cargo. One report listed over 24,000 blankets and some 50,000 shoes as being on the vessel. The exact amount of military supplies put on board the *Bermuda* is unknown though the ship carried at least eighteen rifled field pieces, four heavy seacoast guns, 6,500 Enfield rifles, and 20,000 cartridges. The vessel also carried an unreported number of arms consigned to individuals who either planned to sell them to the highest bidder or were going to use the weapons to outfit military units. Among those utilizing space on board the *Bermuda* was Wade Hampton of South Carolina, who shipped in for his command 200 short Enfield rifles, 20,000 Enfield cartridges, and two 6-pound rifled field pieces.[20]

The *Bermuda* sailed on August 22, and made directly for Savannah, Georgia, arriving there via the main entrance of the river on September 18, 1861. Though there were Union ships in the vicinity, Tessier reported that no blockaders were sighted. The vessel's arrival had an immediate impact on the Confederacy. Army officers in Georgia and South Carolina vied with each other for control over the government arms, while Governor Joseph Brown of Georgia attempted to secure any private arms on the ship. Three thousand Enfields were seized by General Alexander R. Lawton in Savannah and put in the hands of Georgia regiments that were mustering for the war. The remaining small arms and field pieces were probably sent on to the Confederate army massing in northern Virginia.[21]

The balance of the *Bermuda*'s cargo was quickly purchased by both merchants and Confederate officials. The Quartermaster Department bought most of the shoes and cloth, though the quartermaster general complained bitterly that he had to pay Southern prices instead of English ones.

The ship remained at Savannah for over a month. While there, the Confederate War Department considered purchasing the vessel for its

own exclusive use. John Fraser and Company, representing their partners in England, willingly offered to sell the ship but, after considering
the matter, Secretary of War Judah Benjamin decided it would be better
to leave the shipping of goods in the hands of his European agents.[22]

On October 29, 1861, the *Bermuda*, loaded with some 2,000 bales of
cotton, cleared the Savannah River as easily as she had entered and
headed for England. Arriving in Liverpool in mid-November the vessel
discharged her cargo, which was sold on the struggling English cotton
market for a tremendous profit. As Thomas L. Dudley, the American
consul in Liverpool summed up the enterprise: "Prioleau made a fortune
by the *Bermuda* venture."[23]

The *Bermuda* not only brought an excellent return for her owners,
she also proved that steamers could reach Confederate ports. Until this
time, the only vessels used to break the blockade had been small
schooners whose impact on the Confederate war effort had been next to
nothing. The *Bermuda* also demonstrated that the so-called cotton embargo was a thing of the past and that immense profits could be made
from such ventures.

The example was not lost on the British merchants, and many began
to organize their own blockade-running firms. After the return of the
*Bermuda*, Dudley sadly reported to Seward that "English ship owners
are forming mutual associations for undertaking war risks. One in
London [Alexander Collie and Company] embracing to a great extent
the Kingdom, has already a capital of two millions sterling subscribed
for." Dudley also commented that other houses in Liverpool were
increasing their aid to the South and before long the North could expect
English-owned steamers to be challenging the blockade.[24]

Though a huge success for Fraser, Trenholm and Company, the
*Bermuda*'s run to the Confederacy did not satisfy everyone. Anderson
was not only displeased with the shipping rates dictated to him by
Prioleau, but purchasing officers in the Confederacy were outraged by
the huge prices over invoice that John Fraser and Company demanded
for their goods. Trenholm's companies defended themselves by pointing to the high risk they were taking in sending a vessel through the
blockade and, if captured, the government only lost their portion of the
cargo, whereas the shippers would lose not only their cargo but the
ship—and any future income from the vessel.

Even so, Anderson and his fellow agents felt such arrangements
were not advantageous to the Confederacy. Not only were the costs too

high, but they feared putting too much dependence on private companies for the delivery of vital munitions and other needed material. Private companies, no matter how patriotic, had to operate cost-effective enterprises to stay in business. In such cases Anderson feared that the interests of the Confederacy would be neglected for that of the company; something the new nation could ill afford.[25]

Before the *Bermuda* had even returned to England, Anderson and Bulloch received despatches from Richmond informing them that their government planned to put an army of 500,000 men into the field. More requisitions for funds would be soon arriving in England. The agents were to spare no expense in purchasing arms and accoutrements. Cannons, powder, and rifles were needed. If rifles were not available, then the agents had permission to purchase smoothbore guns, and even flintlocks if necessary.[26]

Purchasing operations were increased, but again there was no immediate solution to the problem of shipping the supplies. In early September, Prioleau again approached Anderson with offers to ship another cargo of goods to the South, but this time Anderson considered the charge to be "so extortionate . . . that it amounted very nearly to prohibition." Taking matters into their own hands, the Confederates decided to secure their own vessel. Two English agents were hired, and within two weeks, using funds provided by Bulloch, the iron-hulled screw steamer *Fingal* was purchased.

Extreme measures were taken to conceal the ship's mission from Union agents. The *Fingal* was registered in the name of a British citizen, and arrangements were made to load her via a chartered steamer, thus keeping Confederate supplies off the easily watched railroads. Just before she was ready to take on cargo, a mock sale was arranged to Bulloch's assistant John Low, who was then placed on trains and kept traveling across the countryside to avoid contact with Federal spies or inquiring English officials.

By October 8, 1861, Low was in Greenock watching the final loading of the *Fingal*. Her cargo consisted of about 11,000 rifles, mostly Enfields, 24,000 pounds of gunpowder, 500,000 cartridges, over a million percussion caps, two Blakely cannons, two smaller artillery pieces plus blankets, sabers, and drugs. All of the small arms were consigned to the Confederacy except for about 2,000 rifles owned by the states of Georgia and Louisiana. By her Bill of Entry the *Fingal's* cargo contained:

| Amount of Goods | Value |
|---|---|
| 410 boxes rifles | |
| 23 barrels rifles | |
| 236 casks rifles | 11,340 rifles £42,666 |
| 1,091 cases rifles | |
| 1 trunk rifles | |
| 60 pistols | 210 |
| 24,100 pounds gunpowder | 805 |
| 499,000 cartridges | 1,195 |
| 550,000 percussion caps | 162 |
| Apparel | 600 |
| Apothecary wares | 80 |
| 500 sabers | 350 |
| Leather | 200 |
| 4 pieces ordnance | 300 |
| 1½ tons of lead shot | 35 |
| 7 tons of shells | 929 |
| 230 swords | 230 |
| 9,982 yards of blankets | 1,240 |
| Total | £48,702 |

Besides carrying Low, the *Fingal* had on board both Anderson and Bulloch. Anderson felt his presence was no longer needed in England and was confident that Huse could handle the purchasing and shipping of arms, while Bulloch wanted to confer with Mallory over warship construction in Europe, and the potential use of cotton to fund the navy's European programs.

The *Fingal*'s voyage was far from uneventful. Before clearing English waters she ran down an Austrian brig. At Bermuda she took on a pilot from the Confederate warship *Nashville* who turned out to be a drunk with no knowledge of the entrances to Savannah; finally, with Anderson in charge, the *Fingal* slipped by a Union blockader and entered the Savannah River. Off Fort Pulaski the *Fingal* ran aground on obstructions, but she was now under the fort's guns and her valuable cargo secure.

Once freed, the steamer moved up the river and docked at Savannah. At least half the cargo was quickly despatched to Confederate armies in Tennessee, while the remainder was sent to Richmond for distribution. The two 4.5-inch Blakely guns were sent to Fort Pulaski, and the state arms were given out to troops mustering for the war. The Enfields on board the *Fingal* could arm ten to fifteen regiments, and were a great boost to the morale of the Confederacy as it showed the nation's soldiers that the government was working to give them modern and efficient arms.[27]

The significance of the *Fingal*'s run was fully appreciated by Anderson and Bulloch. Together they, with their companions in England, had outfitted an expedition that not only ran the blockade but had entered Savannah with a cargo exclusively for the Confederacy. They had eliminated the profit-gouging middlemen and presented the Southern government with a fine steamer that could be used repeatedly for the nation's benefit.

In order to keep this vital supply link open, both Anderson and Bulloch hurried to Richmond to report to their superiors. Anderson expected to find a government whose different bureaus were working together to supply the Confederate forces. Instead, he found just the opposite. Leroy Walker was no longer the secretary of war, and in his place Anderson discovered his old "messmate" George W. Randolph as the secretary of war-designate.

Randolph was pleased with Anderson's report and agreed that Huse, at least for the time being, was doing a good job in Europe, but when Anderson tried to convince Randolph to accompany him to see President Davis to discuss future blockade-running activities, he was dismayed to discover that Randolph was not on speaking terms with the president.[28]

Since the War Department was of little help, Anderson went to see Secretary of the Navy Mallory. Again, Anderson tried to push for an organized system of blockade running, suggesting that the navy form a flying squadron under John Newland Maffitt to assist in convoying blockade runners to the Southern shore. Unfortunately Mallory resented Anderson's interference in naval affairs and dismissed the ordnance officer with obvious "discourtesy."[29]

His assignment completed, the disillusioned Anderson returned to Savannah to serve on the staff of General Robert E. Lee. Anderson's departure as head of the government's foreign purchasing and shipping operations was a severe blow. An excellent administrator, he understood better than his companions the need of an efficient system to procure and ship goods to the Confederacy. He advocated the use of

Confederate vessels under Confederate officers to carry the needed goods to the South. But such a set-up would mean a sharing of authority across departmental lines, something the Southern government was not yet willing to do.[30]

Bulloch had better luck than his companion in discussing the future of blockade running with the secretary of the navy. Bulloch suggested that the *Fingal* be used only for the Navy Department. Pointing out to Mallory that the steamer had been purchased with Navy funds, Bulloch proposed to ship cotton and other goods to England, where they would be sold and the returns placed at the disposal of naval agents to purchase warships and other naval supplies. Such an arrangement would not only eliminate dependence on foreign shippers but also keep the *Fingal* firmly in the control of the Navy Department. Mallory quickly agreed to Bulloch's plan and sent him back to Savannah to load the *Fingal* with Navy cotton, but Bullock would never be able to take the vessel out of Savannah and he was forced to return to England on another, privately owned steamer.[31]

The *Fingal* would prove to be the last major government blockade-running venture for nearly a year. Against the advice of Anderson, the officials in Richmond allowed the war effort to become tied to private enterprise, trusting on profit and patriotism to supply their armies. The *Fingal* would be long remembered as a famed blockade runner, her name even eclipsing that of the *Bermuda*. However, she was destined to make only one run. Trapped at Savannah, she was eventually converted to an ironclad, and in June 1863, under the name *Atlanta*, she fell captive to the monitors *Nahant* and *Weehawken*.

Even with the successful runs of the *Bermuda* and *Fingal* in the fall of 1861, the Confederate government still waited for their King Cotton diplomacy to take effect. To aid in its acceptance, President Davis appointed James Mason and John Slidell as commissioners to England and France. The two went to Charleston, where they boarded the *Nashville* for passage to Europe. The use of the *Nashville* as a transatlantic carrier seemed a logical choice. The large sidewheeler, which had been seized after the fall of Fort Sumter, needed to be strengthened before she could adequately serve as a warship. The required work could not be done in Charleston, so it was decided to send her to England for alterations. At the same time the *Nashville* would also provide the proper vehicle for the Southern diplomats. They would arrive on a

Confederate naval vessel flying a Confederate flag, a dramatic event that
would not be missed by the foreign press.

However, the size of the *Nashville* restricted her to the main channel, which was well guarded by Union warships. Days turned to weeks
as the Confederates were frustrated in every escape attempt. During this
time, Mason noticed that the Federal warships gave little notice to the
small packets that operated within the harbor. Deciding that their
mission required prompt action, Mason and Slidell decided to hire one
of these steamers to run them to a nearby foreign port where passage
could be secured to Europe.[32]

The ship chosen was the sidewheeler *Gordon*. She proved to be an
excellent choice. A onetime privateer with a powerful engine, she was
offered to the commissioners for a charter fee of $10,000, or she could be
purchased for $62,000. Both amounts were considered too high, and
negotiations might have dragged on had not a third party entered into
the affair.[33]

In the *Gordon*, George Trenholm saw an opportunity to assist the
Confederate government and make a quick profit. Trenholm offered to
pay one-half of the charter fee for the privilege of using any available
cargo space. All parties agreed to the proposal, and by October 11, 1861,
the *Gordon*, now renamed *Theodora*, was ready for sea. Her commander
was Thomas Lockwood, who had taken the vessel on her earlier privateering expedition. Besides the diplomats, their aides, and Slidell's
family, the *Theodora* also carried Louis Mitchel Coxetter, who was
traveling to England under a false name. Coxetter, who, like Lockwood,
was one of the most knowledgeable captains on the coast, had been
hired by Trenholm to take command of a steam blockade runner that
was being outfitted in Liverpool.[34]

Shortly after one in the morning of October 12, the *Theodora* slipped
past Fort Sumter and under the cover of a rainstorm made for Nassau.
There Lockwood found no available transatlantic connections for his
passengers, so he sailed to Havana. Running low on fuel he stopped at
Cardenas, Cuba, for coal. Here Mason and Slidell debarked, going to
Havana by train. Once his bunkers were replenished, Lockwood continued to Havana, where Coxetter left the ship and a return cargo of
government and civilian supplies was placed on the *Theodora*. This
included some swords, pistols, lead, coffee, and 200,000 cigars. In late
October Lockwood left Havana and followed the Florida coastline until
he reached the intercoastal waterways off Georgia. He then guided the

*Theodora* through these protected waterways, arriving at Charleston on November 4, 1861.[35]

The *Theodora*'s voyage forecast the future of blockade running. Though she lacked a large cargo capacity, the vessel did prove the value of using fast, light-drafted steamers to run the blockade. While the larger *Nashville* was foiled from escaping, the little *Theodora* made a mockery of the blockade by using shallow and as yet unguarded channels. The blockade-running days of large steamers were drawing to a close. Soon the Northern blockade would be strong enough to stop nearly all ships with the size and draft of the *Bermuda* and *Nashville*.

Besides foreshadowing a change in vessels, the *Theodora* also began the use of intermediary ports for the shipping of supplies. Instead of employing large carriers coming directly from Europe, the little steamer proved the worth of transshipping goods from nearby ports onto ships more adept at avoiding blockaders. The *Theodora* used Havana, but other available ports were Nassau, Halifax, and St. George, Bermuda. As usual, John Fraser and Company was quick to pick up on such developments. Though Trenholm's firm did not immediately abandon their large vessels, it did begin to purchase smaller packets to shuttle between the nearby ports and the Confederacy.[36]

While Trenholm and his associates were improving their operations, the Confederacy began appointing agents to oversee the shipment of government goods. At first, Nassau and Havana were under the jurisdiction of Charles Helm, the Confederate consul in Cuba. However, it soon became apparent that Nassau required its own consul, and Louis C. Heyliger was despatched on the *Theodora* to serve as a special agent for the War Department. Heyliger arrived in Nassau in early December, finding in the harbor the merchantman *Gladiator*, a large steamer loaded with Confederate supplies.

The coming of the *Gladiator* had been expected. Despatched by Huse, she carried 20,240 Enfield rifles plus other munitions and goods. Her charter document called for the delivery of the cargo to a Southern port. It also contained a clause that obligated the Confederacy to purchase the vessel upon the demand of her captain.

At first, Heyliger hoped to run the *Gladiator* to the Confederacy, but these plans were canceled when Union cruisers arrived in and about the Bahamas. Any attempt by the heavily laden *Gladiator* to outrun the armed steamers was considered fruitless, and for the moment the Confederates were stalemated. To make matters worse, the captain of the

*Gladiator* tried to break his contract and return to England with the ship and cargo. Heyliger managed to stop this, but only by purchasing the *Gladiator*.[37]

The situation in Nassau might have continued if the ever present George Trenholm had not intervened. Learning of the stranded cargo, Trenholm contacted Secretary of the Treasury Memminger, offering to carry in the *Gladiator*'s cargo on his newly purchased steamers *Cecile* and *Carolina*. Memminger passed the letter on to Secretary of War Judah P. Benjamin, who approved Trenholm's plan.[38]

The exact details of the contract remain obscure; however, after a week of negotiations, it seems that Benjamin agreed to pay freight charges in proportion to the value of the vessel used to carry the cargo. The value of both ships was given at $65,000. If the entire cargo space of the *Carolina* and *Cecile* was employed, the cost to the Confederacy would be $130,000. If less than the full space was used, the charge would be reduced in relation to the amount of stowage area utilized. The actual arrangements of the runs were to be worked out in Nassau between Heyliger and Trenholm's agents Henry Adderley and Company.[39]

Both parties were concerned over where to land the supplies. Charleston was closely blockaded, and, with the Union occupation of Tybee Island, Savannah was out of the question. Benjamin suggested Wilmington, Georgetown, and Brunswick while John Fraser and Company put forward the obscure harbor of Mosquito Inlet at New Smyrna, Florida.[40]

The use of New Smyrna was probably recommended by Lieutenant John Newland Maffitt. At this time Maffitt was serving as a special naval aid to General Robert E. Lee along the Georgia, South Carolina, and east Florida coast. He assisted in the construction of batteries and river obstructions, and on occasion advised John Fraser and Company on blockade running. Maffitt was well qualified to give such advice. For fifteen years prior to the war he had served in the United States Coast Survey, where he gained extensive knowledge of the Southeast's harbors and channels. Trenholm considered his advice so invaluable that he suggested to Benjamin that Maffitt be furloughed from the navy and placed in charge of all blockade-running activities originating from Nassau. Trenholm even offered to give Maffitt command of the *Cecile*.[41]

While awaiting a reply from the government on Maffitt's status, the *Carolina*, now named *Kate*, arrived at Nassau. The packet was entrusted to the command of Thomas Lockwood, whose services had been hired by John Fraser and Company, forming a partnership that would last throughout the war. At Nassau, Heyliger immediately began loading the *Kate* with a portion of the *Gladiator*'s cargo. Heyliger hoped to lighten the *Gladiator* and thus increase her speed enough to enable her to run the blockade with the remaining munitions.

Placed in the *Kate*'s hold were 300 cases of Enfield rifles (6,000 rifles), 32 bales of blankets, 4 cases of surgical equipment, 94 boxes of mess tins, 15 cases of medicine, 1 barrel of medicine, 500 barrels of gunpowder, 514 boxes of cartridges, and 90 boxes of percussion caps. The next day she cleared for St. John's, New Brunswick, but in reality the *Kate* ran for Mosquito Inlet, a mere twenty-hour hours away.[42]

In preparation for the steamships, General Lee had the harbor fortified with a fieldwork mounting two guns. The *Kate* easily reached the unblockaded port and put her cargo ashore. Once landed, the goods were placed on wagons and carried to the St. John's River, where steamers transported the supplies to railroad connections at Jacksonville. From here the majority of the munitions were taken to northern Virginia.[43]

The off-loading decreased the *Gladiator*'s draft by nine feet, but Heyliger decided not to risk the larger ship. He now had the *Kate* and the *Cecile* to carry in the remaining supplies to New Smyrna. Under the supervision of Lieutenant Maffitt, who had arrived on the *Cecile*, the two vessels completed the delivery of the *Gladiator*'s cargo. Less than two weeks after the steamers had left the Florida harbor, Union forces occupied Jacksonville, and the Confederates evacuated New Smyrna.[44]

The delivery of the *Gladiator*'s cargo should have forewarned the Confederate leaders about the tenuousness of their overseas supply lines. Reliance on civilian contracts had nearly caused the loss of the *Gladiator*'s munitions. If Heyliger had not been present, the ship's captain may well have returned to England. Instead, Heyliger was able to buy the steamer and save its cargo, though delivery did require private help. To say that Heyliger was rescued by George Trenholm would be an overstatement. Though partially motivated by strong patriotic principles, Trenholm was still a businessman, and by placing the *Kate* and *Cecile* at the government's disposal, he was serving both the Confederacy and his company. The returns from transporting the government's goods, combined with the cotton taken to Nassau, easily covered the cost of the vessels and expenses. It also set a precedent for the Confederacy to rely on private shippers for the delivery of its munitions.

Secretary of War Benjamin and his successors either did not realize or ignored the hazards of this policy. It forced the Confederacy to pay extremely high freight costs for not only shipping goods from Europe but also for runs from the intermediate ports. It placed the nation at the mercy of private companies, which were not always as patriotic or helpful as Trenholm's firms. Unscrupulous civilian operators could break contracts, refuse to carry volatile munitions, and demand outrageous prices. However Benjamin remained unconcerned and, under his leadership, the South moved to total dependence on private shippers, while Confederate-owned blockade runners disappeared from the seas.[45]

By April 1862, the only legitimate Confederate cargo vessels were the *Gladiator* and the *Fingal*. The *Gladiator* remained in Confederate hands for only a brief period as, after her cargo was delivered, Benjamin instructed Heyliger to sell the *Gladiator* to John Fraser and Company. At Savannah, Bulloch had loaded the *Fingal* with Navy Department cotton and waited for months to escape out of Wassaw Sound. But with Union warships inside the sound, there was virtually no chance of escape, and eventually Bulloch returned to England out of Wilmington on the *Annie Childs* (formerly *North Carolina*), a John Fraser and Company vessel. For some time Mallory continued to hold out some hope that the *Fingal* would be able to escape, but in time her cotton was removed and sent to Charleston for shipment overseas, and the *Fingal* was converted into the ironclad *Atlanta*.[46]

Another vessel available to the Confederacy was the large sidewheeler *Nashville*. In November 1861 the *Nashville* had reached Liverpool, where it was hoped she could be renovated into a warship. However, the British held to a strict interpretation of their maritime law, and, not only was the *Nashville* kept from being rebuilt, the Confederates were denied arms and ammunition.

On February 3, 1862, the *Nashville* left English waters. Three weeks later she touched at Bermuda and then made for Beaufort, North Carolina. At daylight, February 28, she appeared off the port and approached the blockaders flying an American flag; then as she swept past the warships, the flag came down and the Confederate colors were run up.

The surprise coupled with the *Nashville*'s speed soon brought her to a safe anchorage inside the harbor.

The arrival of the *Nashville* gave the South a tremendous morale boost and was a great embarrassment to the North. However, her use as a warship was over, and since Mallory did not want to use her as a blockade runner, arrangements were made to sell her to John Fraser and Company. The firm agreed to take her, but since Beaufort was being threatened with imminent attack, they would not accept delivery at Beaufort. So to complete the deal the *Nashville* again ran past the Union blockaders and found refuge at Georgetown, South Carolina, where she was officially transferred to John Fraser and Company.[47]

With the disposal of the *Gladiator*, *Fingal*, and *Nashville*, the only potential blockade runner under government control was the *Theodora*, which had been purchased by the navy in December 1861 and renamed *Nassau*. Because of her great speed, the little ship was kept more as a despatch vessel than as a cargo ship. She was turned over to Lieutenant Maffitt, who renovated the *Nassau* and returned to Nassau with instructions from the War Department to take control over all vessels carrying government supplies. In this position he would assist Heyliger in routing blockade runners to the Confederacy. However, Maffitt was not allowed to begin his work.[48]

Shortly after his arrival, the English steamer *Oreto* came into Nassau. The *Oreto* had been built in England as a gunboat. On board was John Low, Commander Bulloch's aide. Low carried orders from Bulloch instructing Maffitt to take command of the *Oreto*. According to the orders, Maffitt was to outfit the *Oreto* as a commerce raider and "do something to illustrate the spirit and energy of our people and . . . repay upon the enemy some of the injuries his vastly superior force alone has enabled him to inflict on the Confederacy."[49]

Maffitt gladly accepted his new command, which took precedence over his instructions from the War Department. The day after meeting with Low, he gave up control of the *Nassau*, and wrote the secretary of war of his new position. In less than three months, after some legal difficulties with the British navy, Maffitt took the *Oreto* out of Nassau and turned her into the warship *Florida*.[50]

The appointment of Maffitt as commander of the *Oreto* clearly illustrated the difference of opinion between the Confederate War and Navy departments. The War Department wanted qualified naval officers to supervise and command vessels that carried Confederate supplies. On the other hand, Mallory took an indirect approach, placing his best officers on board commerce raiders, which he thought would draw blockaders away from the Southern ports, thus making it easier for runners to reach their destinations. Mallory's plan had merit, but in practice it failed to work. Those Union warships sent in search of Confederate raiders were, for the most part, large cruisers that would have been ineffective in guarding the shallow waters of the Southern coast.[51]

The lack of government-owned vessels to carry in munitions seemed of little concern to Confederate administrators. No attention was paid to the suggestions of subordinates like Anderson and Bulloch. Instead little effort went into controlling the South's vital overseas trade. Mallory continued to outfit commerce raiders while the secretaries of war, Randolph, Benjamin, and later Seddon, saw no reason to deviate from how the *Gladiator's* cargo was delivered. As a result, the secretaries were allowing John Fraser and Company and other private firms to take over the responsibility of delivering Confederate supplies.

The companies that gained most by the Confederate decision to rely on private shippers were those controlled by George A. Trenholm. Both John Fraser and Company in Charleston and the Liverpool-based Fraser, Trenholm and Company secured lucrative government contracts. Besides being paid for transporting Confederate supplies, the firms could employ any unused space for their goods and utilize the outward stowage for privately owned cotton. Such arrangements brought tremendous returns that often exceeded the cost of the vessel and its operating expenses.[52]

Even though the war was not yet a year old, blockade running was undergoing rapid transformation. The number of ports open to the trade had decreased. By spring 1862 Beaufort, North Carolina, Fernandina, Jacksonville, St. Augustine, and Brunswick were captured, and the approaches to Savannah effectively closed. Trenholm's firms met this challenge by bringing together at Nassau a small flotilla made up of the steamers *Kate, Cecile, Ella Warley, Nashville* (renamed *Thomas L. Wragg*), and the recently purchased *General Miramon*, now called the *Elizabeth*. From England came the *Cambria, Minho, Herald,* and *Leopard*. With these vessels, under experienced captains, Trenholm planned to benefit both the government and his companies.[53]

The focal point of the trade was the British colonial port of Nassau. Located on New Providence Island in the midst of the Bahamian archipelago, the small colonial capital was described as a "dusty pigeon hole somewhere in the colonial office." After the American Revolution numerous loyalists fled to the Bahamas, where many settled in Nassau. These "Conchs," as the white population of the islands was called, kept close family and cultural ties with their relatives in the Southern states.[54]

Nassau boasted a fine harbor formed by Hog Island lying parallel to the city. Open at both ends, the anchorage was well protected and the channel of excellent depth. For years before the war, Nassau had served as a minor naval base and coal depot for the Royal Navy. The town's commercial use had been limited, with only a few foreign vessels frequenting the port.[55]

The war in America ended this sleepy existence. Because of its proximity to the Southern coast, Nassau became the most popular port of entry and departure for vessels attempting to trade with the Confederacy. As it was located 500 miles from Savannah, 515 miles from Charleston, and 570 miles from Wilmington, steamers coming out of Nassau could make a one-way trip to the Confederacy in three days. For a round trip, a ship would consume about 160 to 180 tons of coal, less than what was needed for a similar run from Halifax, Bermuda, or Havana, thus saving more space for money-making cargo.[56]

Located in Nassau were a number of importing and exporting brokerage firms that assisted in the shipping of goods to and from the island. The largest of these was Henry Adderley and Company, which by 1862 counted the Confederacy among its clients. For a commission, the company handled all necessary transactions at Nassau. This included the transferring of cargoes, arrangements for dock and storage facilities, the providing of provisions and coal, and any other services required by their customers.[57]

Besides being the agents for the Confederacy, Henry Adderley and Company also served a large number of private firms including John Fraser and Company. Until the spring of 1862, transactions between the two firms were usually carried out by the captains of the blockade runners, but, as their business in Nassau grew, John Fraser and Company despatched its own agent to the islands to handle their affairs.

The man chosen for this position was Jean Baptiste Lafitte. Born in Augusta, Georgia, Jean Lafitte and his brother Charles had worked in Charleston before the war as shipping agents for the Savannah Steam Packet Company. When hostilities forced the company to close its doors, Jean Lafitte joined John Fraser and Company. Recognizing his talents and knowing his expertise in the shipping trade, Lafitte's new employers soon assigned him to their Nassau office.[58]

Besides overseeing the private goods shipped by John Fraser and Company, Lafitte assisted Heyliger with Confederate supplies. Heyliger met the goods sent by Huse and then placed them on board vessels provided by Lafitte, while all necessary brokerage duties were provided by Henry Adderley and Company.

This triumvirate worked closely together to insure that Confederate supplies received high priority as they passed through Nassau. In fact, the three were often thought to be one agency working exclusively for the Confederacy. However, this was not the case, and, even though, on occasion, Lafitte would handle Heyliger's duties when the latter was away from Nassau, each member was a separate interest working for his own superiors.

The agents were kept busy, as throughout the winter Captain Huse continued to purchase supplies and despatched them to Nassau on steamers and sailing ships. Besides the material he purchased in England, Huse achieved a major coup in Europe at the Vienna Arsenal, where he obtained 100,000 Austrian rifles, a large number of brass field pieces, knapsacks, swords, gunpowder, and other military equipment. These supplies were sent to Hamburg and Bremen, where Huse made arrangements to have them sent overseas.[59]

In directing the goods from England and the North Sea ports, Huse dealt with a number of shipping firms. The type of contract varied from company to company. Most of the shippers agreed to carry the goods to Nassau, where they would be turned over to the Confederate agents for transshipment to the South. A few of the contracts called for the delivery of cargoes to a Southern port, but these were exceptions.

Among the companies hired by Huse was the ever present Fraser, Trenholm and Company, which, with their partners in Charleston, was taking over, not only the running in of supplies from Nassau, but also the shipping of goods from Europe to the Bahamas. By the spring of 1862, Prioleau placed at Huse's disposal the steamers *Bermuda, Bahama, Gladiator,* and *Economist* plus numerous sailing ships to carry Confederate freight across the Atlantic. Any cargo space not hired by the Confederacy was used by Prioleau to ship private goods that would turn a handsome profit on the highly lucrative Southern market.[60]

Among the cargo vessels sent out by Fraser, Trenholm and Company was the former blockade runner *Bermuda*. Arriving at Bermuda on March 22, 1862, the steamer remained there for nearly a month. Why she stayed so long is unclear, though it seems likely that, when sent out from England, the steamer was under instructions to run the blockade as she had on her first voyage; but when she docked at Bermuda, agents of the company probably informed the vessel's captain C. Westendorf that the Union blockade was now too difficult for a vessel like the *Bermuda* to run through. After a month at Bermuda, the heavily laden steamer cleared the harbor and headed for Nassau, where her cargo could be placed on smaller vessels and sent into the Confederacy.[61]

Five days after leaving Bermuda, as she neared the Bahama Islands, the *Bermuda* fell in with the United States warship *Mercedita*, which ordered her to heave to. Union sailors came on board and searched the merchantman. Though she was legally cleared for Nassau and registered as a British vessel, the Federals found damning evidence in the ship's papers. As the commander of the *Mercedita* reported: "her log books show her to have run the blockade before. I found letters and orders from Charleston, S.C. for goods. Some of her lading is for Georgia." Her papers also included an instruction sheet for running the blcokade at Charleston, outlining signals that vessels approaching at night should use with the harbor forts. The vessel was seized and her capture upheld by the Federal prize court.[62]

The taking of the *Bermuda* and the resulting court ruling caused an immediate change in the methods of shipping goods to Nassau or any other neutral port near the Confederacy. No longer did the British flag provide immunity. By the court's decision, a ship could be stopped anywhere on the highs seas and seized if her papers gave any hint that the ultimate destination of her cargo was the Confederacy. Because of this ruling, some shippers backed off from carrying Southern-bound cargoes, but the majority merely repacked their goods and altered manifests to show Nassau as the freight's final destination.[63]

Besides causing a major change in the neutral ships, neutral goods doctrine, the capture of the *Bermuda* served as a severe blow to the immediate needs of the Confederacy. Not only were thousands of modern arms and equipment lost, but so were eight heavy pieces of rifled artillery intended for the defense of the remaining Confederate harbors. The pieces ranged in size from 5.5" Whitworth to mammoth

8.5″ Blakley guns, capable of damaging and possibly sinking Union ironclads.[64]

John Fraser and Company also suffered heavily by the capture of the *Bermuda*. At least two-thirds of her cargo was company goods bound for the Confederate market. Besides their cargo, the company also lost a valuable vessel from their fleet, one capable of carrying, not only goods from Europe, but also thousands of cotton bales back to Liverpool. However, the loss was far from a crippling one. With the success of their earlier ventures, and the prospect of even more successes, John Fraser and Company planned to recoup their losses with other ventures, especially those based on their blockade runners now coming together at Nassau.[65]

The firm learned about blockade running by way of trial and error. Some vessels were lost by mismanagement while the *Minho* and the *Cecile* were eventually sold for being too small. One vessel John Fraser and Company counted on for successful service was the recently purchased Confederate vessel *Nashville*. The ship was renamed the *Thomas L. Wragg*, and though it was acknowledged that her deep draft would be a problem, the company felt that the vessel's speed would enable her to run the blockade without too much difficulty. They were wrong. Out of four attempts to reach the South, the *Thomas L. Wragg* was twice turned away, and on one trip she ran aground in New Inlet, North Carolina, and had to be towed into the Cape Fear River. Finally, the *Thomas L. Wragg* made a trip to the unguarded Ossabaw Sound at the mouth of the Ogeechee River, south of Savannah. Here her cargo was removed by lighters and taken to the railroad for shipment to Savannah. Once unloaded, the steamer moved up the river past Fort McAllister.[66]

This was the *Thomas L. Wragg*'s last voyage as a blockade runner. John Fraser and Company, realizing their mistake in operating so large a vessel, sold her to a syndicate that converted her into a privateer. However, she never again went to sea as on February 28, 1863, while preparing to run out under the name *Rattlesnake*, she ran aground off Fort McAllister and was blown to pieces by the Union monitor *Montauk*.[67]

One reason that John Fraser and Company were willing to give up on the *Thomas L. Wragg*, besides her obvious defects, was that a new ship was being sent out from England. This was the onetime Dublin ferryboat *Herald*. Purchased by Prioleau, the *Herald* had a large cargo capacity, a low freeboard, and a loaded draft of only 10.5 feet. After her purchase she came to Liverpool, took on a cargo of artillery, shell and gunpowder and sailed for Bermuda. Onboard was Louis M. Coxetter, who had come out of the South on the *Theodora*, specifically to command the *Herald*. Coxetter took over the *Herald* at Bermuda and eventually ran her into Charleston.[68]

Coxetter and the *Herald* joined with Thomas Lockwood and the *Kate* to become the backbone of John Fraser and Company's blockade-running squadron. They also became Heyliger's main reliance in shipping government supplies. Both were very successful; however, the *Herald* never matched the impressive record of the little ten-year-old sidewheeler known as the *Kate*.[69]

Under Lockwood's command, the *Kate* became the workhorse for John Fraser and Company. Beginning in late April, Lockwood started the little steamer on a career that became so regular, she soon obtained the nickname "packet." The *Kate*'s ability to slip past blockaders became legendary; some observers credited the steamer with over forty violations of the blockade, though in reality the number was half that amount. Lockwood's favorite port of entry was Charleston, though he also made good use of Wilmington, and even once entered the "sealed" port of Savannah.[70]

On her trips through the blockade the *Kate* carried in thousands of small arms, hundreds of barrels of gunpowder, and tons of other vital munitions. The *Kate* was also entrusted with special cargoes. The Treasury Department used her to carry out gold destined for Captain Huse. Another time she brought in British-made iron plates for Confederate ironclads, and, in July 1862, she reportedly took into Charleston a complete and powerful steam engine destined for an ironclad ram.[71]

The *Kate* continued to be a thorn in the side of the Union blockaders throughout 1862. Though she was often sighted and occasionally chased, the Federal navy never had a clear opportunity to end her career. Instead her demise came in late November 1862 when, while running into Wilmington, she struck a snag in the Cape Fear River and sank. Her cargo was saved, but the *Kate* was a total loss. However, she had served her owners well, and profits from the *Kate* went into the purchasing of more blockade runners.[72]

The success of John Fraser and Company inspired imitators. As early as December 1861, Southern and English merchants and shippers, impressed by the huge returns Trenholm and his associates were receiving, began to form their own blockade-running companies.

One of these early Southern-based, blockade-running firms was the Importing and Exporting Company of South Carolina. Founded by a group of Charleston businessmen, the firm sold over one hundred shares of stock for a thousand dollars each. The largest shareholder in the company was its rival John Fraser and Company, which held nine and a half shares. No company officers were appointed; instead the day-to-day affairs were left to William C. Bee and Charles T. Mitchel, Charleston shipping and commission merchants who each owned two and one quarter shares. This arrangement was highly advantageous to the two merchants, especially Bee, who took the lead in running the company. In fact, his association became so prominent that the Importing and Exporting Company of South Carolina was often erroneously referred to as the "Bee Company."

Bee and Mitchel made certain that ships had outward and inward cargo, hired agents to handle brokerage duties in Nassau, and sold imported goods at private auctions in Charleston, which soon became known as "Bee Sales." For their work, they received a 5 percent commission on the value of all goods imported and exported and a 1 percent commission on profits received from the auction.[73]

In early April 1862, the company was ready to undertake its first venture. From the sale of stock, Bee and Mitchel purchased the steamer Cecile from John Fraser and Company, the schooner Edwin, and cargoes for the two ships. From John Fraser and Company they also secured the services of James Carlin to command the Cecile. Carlin had been the little sidewheeler's captain for a brief period before the war and was well acquainted with her.

The two vessels cleared Charleston in early April. Both arrived safely at Nassau, where they sold their cargo and took on return loads for both the company and the Confederate government. The government goods, quartermaster supplies of cloth, were loaded on the Cecile, which managed to slip back into Charleston harbor on April 28. The Edwin was not so fortunate and ran aground near the mouth of the harbor. The schooner was wrecked, but most of her cargo was saved and, together with the goods off the Cecile, were auctioned off in Charleston.[74]

The initial venture of the Importing and Exporting Company of South Carolina was a tremendous financial success. From the sale of the cotton and other produce the firm received about $18,000; another $25,000 came from the Confederacy for freight charges, and over $65,000 was gained at the auction. With a gross profit of over $100,000, the company easily met its expenses, covered the loss of the *Edwin*, and paid a commission of about $5,000 to Mitchel and Bee.

Not bothering to replace the *Edwin*, the company immediately readied the *Cecile* for another voyage. Again Carlin guided the vessel on a successful round trip, bringing back over 2,000 Enfield rifles for the Ordnance Bureau plus a large private cargo. As on the first run, the company saw a return of at least $100,000. However, they were not to be as fortunate on their next attempt.

On her third trip out of Charleston the *Cecile* arrived safely in Nassau during the first week of June, and unloaded a cargo of cotton worth over $23,000. Taking on a valuable return cargo she sailed for Charleston. On June 18, before clearing the Bahama Islands, she struck a rock in the Abaco Reef. The vessel was a total loss. A portion of her cargo was saved by professional Bahamian salvagers who eagerly resold the Confederate goods to Heyliger for an exorbitant price.[75]

The loss of the *Cecile* momentarily ended the blockade running of the Importing and Exporting Company of South Carolina. A stock dividend of $850 per share was paid in late June and, though it did not repay the initial investment made by the company's backers, it was merely a sign of things to come. The organizers of the company had no intention of stopping their blockade-running ventures. The remaining capital, minus the $99,025 paid out in dividends, was swiftly put to use to purchase newer, faster, and larger vessels to run the blockade.[76]

Other endeavors organized along the Southeast coast in 1862 were not as successful as those of the Importing and Exporting Company of South Carolina. Most of these operations were doomed from the start because of their use of inadequate vessels. Trying to turn a quick profit, entrepreneurs were willing to employ any available steam vessel to run the blockade. One speculator went so far as to offer $75,000 for the steamer *St. Marys*, which was lying underwater in the St. Johns River. Another business tried to base a venture around the thirty-year-old sidewheeler *William Seabrook*. Such haphazard operations made little if any money and did nothing to support the Confederate war effort.[77]

Along with the Confederate-based operations, English firms entered blockade running in early 1862. These companies were usually organized by shipping firms that contracted with Captain Huse to carry Confederate munitions into the South. But even though these attempts were well financed and supplied with good steamers, they underestimated the Union blockade and often failed.

One of the first British companies to challenge the blockade was owned and operated by Zachariah C. Pearson, a merchant, ship owner, and mayor of Hull. Loading his vessels in England with supplies provided by Huse, Pearson sent them to the Confederacy. Between May 4 and August 4, 1862, seven of his vessels attempted to break the blockade; six were captured, and the seventh, the *Modern Greece*, ran aground off Fort Fisher. Before the year was out Pearson and Company was forced to declare bankruptcy.[78]

Another attempt by English merchants to break the blockade was undertaken by Thomas Sterling Begbie, a London shipping merchant, and Peter Denny, senior partner of Denny and Company, a prominent shipbuilding firm located at Dumbarton on the Clyde River. During the spring of 1862 the two joined to sponsor, as a blockade runner, Denny's recently completed steamer *Memphis*.[79]

The *Memphis* had been built for use as a merchant vessel, and had a cargo capacity of 52,760 cubic feet. As manager of the vessel, Begbie chartered the *Memphis* to English speculators for three months at £2,500 per month. The charterers insured the vessel for £26,000 and loaded her at Liverpool with a cargo made up largely of Confederate munitions. Begbie was quite confident that the *Memphis* would be a successful blockade runner, as he wrote Denny that "she should be the best afloat for her trade."[80]

The *Memphis* cleared Liverpool on May 10, 1862. While approaching Nassau she was stopped and inspected by the Union gunboat *Quaker City*. The owners of the *Memphis*, aware of the fate of the *Bermuda*, had made sure that all manifests and papers were in order, and she was allowed to proceed. A month later, she sailed for Charleston, arriving off the port on the evening of June 22, 1862. Following instructions, probably given to the *Memphis* in Nassau, the vessel showed a red light as she approached Forts Moultrie and Sumter. The signal was returned, and the vessel slipped past the blockaders, but before entering the harbor she ran aground. In the darkness Fort Sumter opened fire on the stranded blockade runner. The red light was again shown, and the firing stopped.[81]

At dawn the *Memphis* was still aground. Union warships spied the vessel and began shelling her at long range. With a cargo that contained 112,000 pounds of gunpowder the *Memphis* was a loaded bomb requiring only a spark to set her off. For the entire day of June 23, Confederate soldiers on board flats from Sullivan's Island hurried to remove the gunpowder before a shell found its mark. Finally, by 5:00 P.M., the lightened vessel was towed by two steam tugs into the harbor. Miraculously not one Union shell had struck the ship.[82]

The following week the *Memphis* discharged her remaining cargo, which included 11,000 small arms, a million percussion caps, twenty-five tons of lead, medicine, bagging, leather, and cloth. Once the goods were ashore, the *Memphis* quickly loaded 1,446 bales of cotton and dashed out of Charleston on the evening of June 29, but before she could reach Nassau, she fell in with the Union gunboat *Magnolia* and was captured.[83]

These early losses of the British companies were due to the type of ships employed. Like many of the early Southern steamers, they were too large to challenge the blockade. With proper vessels, captains, crew, and luck, a blockade-running company could expect to make high returns on their investment, but there were risks. From September 1861 through December 1862, about 105 attempts were made to run the blockade. Seventy-seven were successful. Such figures encouraged speculators; however, while the success rate seemed high, of the thirty-six vessels that undertook runs, twenty-eight were captured or lost. Yet even with the loss of so many ships, the lure of profit kept the business going.[84]

While high profits increased the number of blockade runners, that did not mean that Confederate supplies were being delivered. With private companies so caught up in their own returns, Heyliger found it impossible to despatch to the South all the Confederate goods arriving at Nassau. From existing manifests it seems that, at best, he would acquire only two-thirds of a vessel's freight, and this usually came from the "patriotic" John Fraser and Company. With no government vessels at his disposal and the reluctance of most companies to turn over the majority of their cargo space, Heyliger had an increasingly difficult time meeting the demands of the Confederate armed forces.

By the end of the year, a logjam had been created at Nassau, with Confederate war material gathering in warehouses and piling up on the wharves. It was estimated that close to 200,000 small arms were delivered to Nassau in 1862, and less than one-half of these reached the Confederacy before the year was out. Such a ratio could probably be applied to all munitions and war supplies that came into Nassau, meaning that Southern armies fought their battles with at least one-half of their potential equipment in Nassau.[85]

It was painfully obvious to Confederate officials in the West Indies and the Confederacy that the delivery rate of goods was far too low. Dependence on private companies was not working. To help ease the situation, the nation's leaders were forced to undertake new contracts and operations to create a more efficient supply system.

# Chapter Three

# New Orleans: Lost Opportunity

New Orleans was the largest cotton port in the world, serving as the focal point for the tremendous commerce that funneled down the Mississippi valley. Served by hundreds of merchantmen, its volume of trade was greater than the combined commerce of all other Southern ports. New Orleans should have been the South's most important blockade-running port; however, only a handful of the city's numerous steamers ever reached the open sea.[1]

Unlike the Southeastern seaports, New Orleans was the home port of a large number of coastal steamships that could be converted into excellent blockade runners. Built for the shallow Gulf waters, these sidewheelers resembled British coastal packets. They had powerful walking-beam engines, shallow drafts, and large stowage capacity. Properly managed, the New Orleans-based steamers could have conducted an active blockade-running trade, but interference by Confederate and state authorities kept the steamship companies from using their vessels.

In 1861, there were two major steamship firms operating in the Gulf of Mexico. The New Orleans-Mobile Mail Company was operated by Robert Geddes, a New Orleans resident. Geddes ran the sidewheelers *Alabama, California, Cuba, Florida,* and *Oregon* on daily excursions between New Orleans and Mobile by way of Lake Pontchartrain and the Mississippi Sound. All were large vessels of good speed and light draft, and could easily have been altered to increase their cargo capacity. But the *Oregon* and *Florida* (later renamed *Selma*) were confiscated and converted into gunboats, whereas the *Alabama, California,* and *Cuba* were impressed by the War Department for use as transports in the Mississippi Sound.[2]

The major steamship company, and the one in the best position to originate a blockade-running trade was Charles Morgan's Southern Steamship Company of New Orleans. The firm operated fifteen large coastal vessels and had port facilities in New Orleans, Brashear City, Sabine Pass, Galveston, and Indianola. The company also had commercial contacts in Havana, Vera Cruz, and Tampico. But the company was never able to serve the Confederacy.

Early in the war, the company lost two of its vessels. At Galveston, the *General Rusk* was taken over by Texas officials and later turned over to the War Department for service as a harbor patrol boat. The *Suwanee* was seized in late May 1861 by Union naval authorities at Key West. Other losses followed. They included the *William G. Hewes, Tennessee, Texas,* and *Orizaba,* all impressed by the state of Louisiana in April 1861. These vessels were eventually released, but two months later a naval review board was inspecting another four of the company's vessels for possible conversion to gunboats.[3]

The company probably would have survived had it not been connected with the New York financier Charles Morgan. Morgan had founded the Southern Steamship Company and for years was its major stockholder. Just before the outbreak of hostilities, Morgan transferred his controlling interest to his son-in-law Israel Harris, a native of New Orleans, who hoped to use the breakup of the Union to his advantage. However, Harris was unable to convince Southern officials that he would work for the new government. The association with Morgan was too strong, and eventually Harris was forced to sell off to private speculators the vessels not seized by the military. This prevented the Confederacy from using the services of their largest and best-equipped steamship company. As warships the steamers were practically useless, and those that became blockade runners could have been put to more efficient use if they had remained under the control of a single owner. Though no longer in active business, Harris did continue a court battle that eventually ruled, in the summer of 1862, that he, and not Morgan, was the owner of the Southern Steamship Company. But by then it was far too late for the firm to assist the Confederacy.[4]

Throughout the first few months of the war the lack of cooperation between private, state, and government interests wrecked all attempts to send steam blockade runners out of New Orleans. Little was done until

October 1861, when Charles J. Helm assumed the post of Confederate consul in Havana. An excellent choice for this important position, Helm was a Kentuckian by birth, and had served for nearly three years as the United States consul in Cuba. At the start of the war, he resigned his position and returned to the South. Davis quickly appointed him commissioner to the West Indies, but before returning to Cuba, Helm went to England, where he conferred with Huse and Anderson regarding the purchase and shipment of military goods to the South. He then went on to Havana, where he renewed his old associations and gained the confidence and friendship of the Spanish authorities.[5]

Havana was 540 miles from the mouth of the Mississippi River, 500 miles from St. Marks, 590 miles from Mobile, and 850 miles from Galveston. Its large deep-water harbor could handle vessels of any size. In 1860 more than 2,000 vessels, nearly 700,000 tons of shipping, arrived at the port. Of these, over 1,600 had come from the United States, most coming from Southern ports. Besides the city's commercial links to the South, many Cubans were sympathetic to the Confederacy because they feared repercussions in their own slave population should the North win the war. Helm felt confident that a strong blockade-running trade could be established between Havana and New Orleans, and he immediately began to encourage such a development.[6]

By early November, Helm had begun to stockpile equipment. He reported that shoes and cloth could be purchased in Cuba, but arms and powder of good quality had to be shipped from England. Helm suggested that a depot be established in Havana to store supplies until shipment to the South could be arranged. He also asked that vessels be despatched from the Confederacy to receive the goods he had already acquired. However, shipments from Helm would not be the first sent into the Confederacy from Cuba; the initial vessels to run the blockade in the Gulf were private ventures that by-passed Helm. They were designed to gain profits by selling supplies to the hard-pressed defenders of New Orleans.[7]

The man who these first blockade runners dealt with was General Mansfield Lovell, President Davis's personal choice for the command of New Orleans. Arriving in October 1861, Lovell found himself in a very difficult position. The forts protecting the city were without modern artillery, many of his troops lacked proper equipment, and powder was in such short supply that his artillery could sustain a battle for no longer than one hour.

Lovell, like his counterparts on the East Coast had to initially depend on profit-minded private entrepreneurs to outfit his command. Though these merchants had lost many of their best vessels to the military, they still retained a number of older and smaller steamers for use as blockade runners. Among these were the thirty-seven-year-old sidewheeler *C. Vanderbilt*, the former Mexican warship *General Miramon*, and the small *Victoria*, a onetime Southern Steamship Company vessel. All had such light drafts that they could use the shallow bayous and bays that connected New Orleans to the Gulf of Mexico.

The first of these steamers to run the blockade was the *C. Vanderbilt*. The onetime Hudson River packet escaped to Havana about November 28, 1861. In the next two months she was followed by the *General Miramon* and the *Victoria*. The *C. Vanderbilt* and *Victoria* probably made their runs from the mouth of the Mississippi River while the *General Miramon* came out of Lake Pontchartrain.

All three steamers returned safely to the Confederacy, though none made a direct run back to New Orleans. The *C. Vanderbilt* arrived at Sabine Pass, Texas, while the *General Miramon* came into Grand Caillou Bayou. The *Victoria*, after escaping from Union gunboats, found safe refuge under the guns of Fort Livingston in Barataria Bay. Together, the vessels brought in about 130,000 pounds of powder and over 500 muskets. Lovell purchased the supplies, but the price was so high he decided to no longer depend on the open market. He ordered the construction of three powder mills and signed a number of shipping contracts. His first three agreements retained three vessels, the *Tennessee*, *Florida*, and *Magnolia*. The large screw steamer *Tennessee* was to sail to Havre, France, for saltpeter while the *Florida* and *Magnolia* were to run to Havana for the munitions being held by Helm.[8]

For their escape, the three vessels dropped down to Pass a L'Outre and, on the foggy morning of February 19, they tried to run out of the river. The *Magnolia*, the swiftest of the three, dashed out first, and was immediately pursued by the steam sloop *Brooklyn* and gunboat *Mercedita*. Chased eastward for three hours the *Magnolia* nearly made good her escape, but as she neared Mobile she was sighted and cut off by the blockader *South Carolina*. With capture inevitable, the crew rigged the boilers for explosion, set the ship on fire, and fled. Union boarding parties arrived after one boiler exploded, but managed to put out the fires and save the vessel from further damage.

Since the *Magnolia* had cleared the way, the screw-propelled *Florida* had no trouble slipping out of the river, and reaching Havana. The *Tennessee* was not so fortunate. The deep-drafted ship, heavily laden with cotton bales destined for sale in France, was unable to cross the bar, and without towboats to pull her through the mud, the *Tennessee* was forced to remain.[9]

Undaunted, Lovell chartered additional vessels at Sabine City, Brashear City, and Lake Pontchartrain. Success was mixed. Some escaped, others fell captive, while two, including the old *C. Vanderbilt*, were lost in storms. Those ships that did survive the trip to Havana preferred to return to isolated ports of entry than risk the heavily guarded Mississippi River passes.[10]

The use of these harbors often resulted in a safe arrival. However, it gave Lovell long and vulnerable supply lines. Cargoes landed at Brashear City were shipped to New Orleans by way of the New Orleans-Opelousas and Great Western Railroad. Supplies coming into Sabine City had to be taken by railroad to Beaumont, Texas, then carried overland in wagons to New Iberia, Louisiana, where steamboats carried the goods down Bayou Teche to Brashear City for transportation by rail to New Orleans. Blockade runners also arrived at Grand Caillou Bay and Barataria Bay, Louisiana. Munitions landed at these shallow harbors were transshipped onto light-drafted schooners and taken into New Orleans by way of connecting bayous and canals.[11]

This supply arrangement, though workable, was far from ideal. There were inevitable delays. Vessels had to wait for weeks to unload their goods and take on return cargoes. None of the sites were adequately guarded, and Lovell, already hard pressed to defend the main approaches to New Orleans, felt it would be only a matter of time before Union expeditions began to strike at his poorly protected supply lines. However, in early March, when vessels of the Union Gulf-Blockading Squadron under Flag Officer David G. Farragut, entered the Passes of the Mississippi delta, the Confederates were forced to depend on these periphery harbors.[12]

The entrance of the Union flotilla into the Mississippi ended all opportunities for additional steamers to escape the city. Among those vessels trapped were the *Tennessee* and the *William H. Webb*. The *Tennessee* would have been an excellent transport between Cuba and Europe, while the *William H. Webb*, considered the fastest steamer built in the United States, had the potential to become the war's best blockade runner. However, neither would see any service.[13]

With the mouth of the river closed, Lovell was forced to make new arrangements with the owners of vessels at Brashear City and Sabine Pass. Between mid-March and April 15, the steamers *Austin*, *Arizona*, *William G. Hewes*, and *Atlantic* cleared Brashear City, and the *Matagorda* sailed from Sabine Pass. Unfortunately for the defenders of New Orleans, none of these vessels were able to return in time to give aid to the beleaguered city. During this critical period only one vessel, the *Florida*, managed to return.[14]

After her successful trip to Havana, the *Florida* took on a cargo that included 2,500 rifles and 60,000 pounds of powder. Since the screw steamer had operated before the war between New Orleans and Apalachicola, her captain returned the *Florida* to the familiar waters of the Florida Panhandle. In early March, the vessel entered St. Andrews Bay, a sheltered anchorage between Pensacola and Apalachicola. Here, with the assistance of the army, the cargo was landed. The arms were owned by the Confederacy and were assigned to Florida troops and the forces around Pensacola.

The powder was privately owned and was offered to the Confederacy at two dollars a pound. The price was considered extortionate, especially since the military had been responsible for landing the cargo. But the powder was badly needed, and the price was met. Twenty thousand pounds was sent to Mobile, while the rest was shipped to Columbus, Kentucky. However, this position was evacuated by the Confederates on March 9, and the powder was rerouted to New Orleans.

Because of her location in the isolated bay, it took over a month for the *Florida* to take on a return cargo of cotton. Just before she was to sail, her presence was reported to the Union blockaders, and on April 6 a small boat expedition captured the vessel. The Federals, finding it impossible to bring the ship out on their own, managed to bribe the *Florida*'s pilot and engineers to take the ship out of the harbor.[15]

Even though the loss of the *Florida* further reduced the number of blockade runners available to the Confederacy, most of the powder from the steamer eventually reached New Orleans, but more was needed. In Havana, Helm readied a number of vessels. The goods were anxiously awaited by Lovell and his subordinates since it was obvious that the

Union fleet was preparing for action against Forts St. Philip and Jackson, the South's main defense positions on the Mississippi River.

On April 18, 1862, while the people of New Orleans were attending Good Friday services, Union mortar boats began to shell Fort Jackson. For five days Farragut waited as the thirteen-inch mortars pounded the Confederate stronghold. The bombardment failed to neutralize the Confederate guns, and the Union flag officer decided to run past the forts. Before dawn, on April 24, in a spectacular action, Farragut's squadron passed the Southern defenses and captured New Orleans.[16]

With the fall of New Orleans the nation lost, not only its largest and most industrialized city, but also its greatest port. New Orleans, with its command over the Gulf coast, could have served as the nation's main blockade-running port, controlling trade as far west as Sabine Pass and eastward to the Mississippi Sound. With the inlets properly guarded and supported by light-drafted gunboats, the Union Navy would have been hard-pressed to restrict vessels from reaching New Orleans. However, the city fell before an effective system was put into place; and, during the short period it was in Confederate hands, the New Orleans area saw only twenty steamers clear and a mere five arrive. The city's potential as a blockade-running port was never fulfilled and, on its capture, the Confederacy lost a tremendous and irreplaceable resource.[17]

The fall of New Orleans caused a disruption in Gulf blockade running. The capture of the city necessitated the evacuation of Confederate garrisons at Lake Pontchartrain, Barataria Bay, and Brashear City. Farragut's victory, coupled with the need of troops elsewhere, convinced the Confederates that they could no longer hold onto Pensacola, and on May 10 they evacuated the city. In addition to these losses, the port facilities of Cedar Key and Appalachicola were destroyed by Union naval expeditions. The Southerners were fortunate in that the majority of their best steamers had escaped to Cuba before the fall of New Orleans. These eight vessels were under contract to return to New Orleans, but once their home port had been taken, they remained in Havana to await further developments.[18]

The only major harbors in the Gulf of Mexico left to the Confederacy east of the Mississippi River were those of St. Marks and Mobile. St. Marks was at best a secondary port for steam-blockade runners. However, in the spring of 1862, the town was frequented by the small Spanish steamer *Havana*, which carried in coffee, dry goods, cigars, and lead in exchange for a few hundred bales of cotton. The

*Havana*'s career lasted only a few months. In early June, while moving along the Florida coast, the little blockade runner was trapped by the gunboat *Somerset* in Deadman's Bay, where she was burned by her crew to prevent her capture.

While St. Marks sufficed for small ships, the Alabama port of Mobile, with its deep-channeled and well-protected harbor, stood out as the logical successor to New Orleans. During the first year of the war the port's marine trade had been under the influence of New Orleans. Shipping that came to Mobile mainly consisted of small schooners and steamers moving between the city and Lake Pontchartrain through the Mississippi Sound. However, once New Orleans had fallen, this intercourse ended, and Mobile developed its own overseas markets.[19]

At first Mobile had only a few steamers for use as blockade runners, and the only ones to have any success were the *Cuba* and *Matagorda*, which was now under British registry and named *Alice*. The vessels were operated by local stock companies and well suited for blockade running, unlike the steamer *Ann*, the first foreign-owned vessel to test the blockade at Mobile.[20]

The *Ann* was a large screw steamer owned by the English firm Z. C. Pearson and Company. She arrived in Havana loaded with munitions in the spring of 1862. The company had planned to sell her cargo, but Pearson's agents were unable to find a buyer for her high-priced goods. As a result it was decided to run the vessel into Mobile.

On the night of June 29, the *Ann* attempted to slip past the blockaders by running in from the east along Mobile Point. As she neared Fort Morgan, the heavily laden steamer ran hard aground. Word of her predicament was quickly sent to the Confederate garrison and the next morning the steamer *Crescent*, under the protection of the guns of Fort Morgan, began to remove her cargo. Late that afternoon, the towboat *Dick Keys* arrived to try and pull the lightened *Ann* into the harbor. However, as the *Dick Keys* moved toward the stranded blockade runner, the Union gunboat *Kanawha* appeared, and the crew of the *Ann* quickly abandoned ship. The captain of the *Dick Keys* picked up the sailors and, not wishing to come under fire from the Union warship, hurried back to Fort Morgan.

The action of the crew and the *Dick Keys* infuriated the commander of Fort Morgan, Colonel W. L. Powell, and immediately Powell despatched soldiers in two small boats to take charge of the *Ann*. However, by now the *Ann* was drifting out to sea, and when the men boarded the vessel they discovered that the boiler fires had gone out, and, with the *Kanawha* threatening, they had no time to rekindle them.

Arrangements were quickly made to scuttle the vessel and, once carried out, the ship was again abandoned. However, the Confederates had not reckoned with the *Ann*'s water-tight compartments and, though they had flooded one of them, the vessel stayed afloat and was captured by the *Kanawha*.

Even though they had managed to save some 30,000 pounds of gunpowder and 400 muskets, all of which were taken by Colonel Powell for the defense of Fort Morgan, the Confederates left on board the *Ann* a large amount of valuable supplies. It was reported that 70,000 pounds of powder, additional muskets, and quantities of citric acid, paper, coffee, tea, and cartridge boxes were abandoned to the Federals, all extremely important to the Confederacy.[21]

Along with the loss of the *Ann*, Mobile suffered another blow to its blockade-running trade in the late summer of 1862. It was during this time that Captain John Newland Maffitt and the commerce raider *Florida* appeared in the Gulf. After the *Florida* had been released by the court in Nassau, Maffitt had taken the vessel to a small key in the Bahamas Islands, where he rendezvoused with a schooner that carried the vessel's armament. The guns were transferred, but Maffitt did not have enough men to complete his outfitting. Increasing his problems, Maffitt and his crew were stricken with yellow fever. The disease became so virulent that Maffitt had to put into Cardennas and later Havana, Cuba, to care for his men. At Havana, Maffitt learned that Union warships would soon be arriving off the Cuban port, and, not wishing to be trapped, he decided to sail for Mobile.

On September 4, with only a handful of his crew fit for duty, Maffitt approached the entrance of Mobile Bay in broad daylight. To confuse the blockaders Maffitt flew a British ensign over his vessel. Thinking the *Florida* was a British gunboat, the Union warships pulled close to the stranger and attempted to hail, but Maffitt did not stop. A shot was fired across the bow of the *Florida*, and at this point Maffitt ran up the Confederate flag and made a dash for the harbor. Somehow the *Florida* survived a heavy barrage of fire from three Union gunboats and safely entered the bay. For the next four months the *Florida* remained in Mobile. During this time her crew was brought up to full strength, and she was properly outfitted. Maffitt's feat of running the *Florida* into Mobile was a great embarrassment to the Union Navy and caused a great sensation throughout the North and South; however, in terms of material gain, the South proved to be the loser. The presence of the *Florida* led to an increase in the blockade off Mobile, causing blockade running to virtually come to an end for the remainder of the year.[22]

Between September 4, 1862, and the end of the year, not one steam blockade runner entered Mobile, and only two, the *Cuba* and *Alice*, ran out. During this period, the city had very little outside trade except by schooners, which added little to the Confederate war effort. While the *Florida* remained at Mobile the important seaport was closed to all steam blockade runners.[23]

While Mobile struggled to develop an overseas trade, the Confederate ports west of the Mississippi saw even less activity. Goods sent overland to Texas were often commandeered by local commanders before they crossed the Mississippi, and if supplies did arrive they were usually months in coming. It soon became obvious to Brigadier General Paul Octave Hebert, commander of the Department of Texas, that a better supply line was required, and he looked for relief from Mexico and Cuba.[24]

One of Hebert's first moves was to direct his chief quartermaster Major T. S. Moise to convert the gunboat *General Rusk* into a blockade runner. An iron-hulled steamer, the *General Rusk* was an excellent choice for this mission. Owned before the war by the Southern Steamship Company, the vessel could easily navigate the shallow Texas waters. Hebert's choice of commander for the venture, however, was a poor one.

Major Moise, seeing an opportunity to make a large personal profit, entered into a contract with a group of businessmen headed by Nelson Clements, a prominent Galveston merchant. The agreement called for Moise to transfer ownership of the steamer to the civilians who, for the right of shipping out their own cotton, would operate the vessel and bring in Confederate military supplies. The merchants put up a $50,000 bond, which they would forfeit if the *General Rusk* was lost, but this covered only one-third of the vessel's value. In reality, Moise and his associates were taking very little risk on a venture that could prove highly profitable.[25]

On June 5, 1862, the *General Rusk* cleared Galveston with a load of cotton and safely arrived at Havana. There, with the aid of George Wigg, the vessel was transferred to the British flag and renamed the *Blanche*. Returning in August, the steamer delivered munitions to Indianola, and a month later, after taking on cotton, she moved out of Matagorda Bay for Havana.

The *Blanche* had no difficulty in escaping from the Texas port and stopped at La Mulata on Cuba's western coast for fuel. She then proceeded along the coastline for Havana but, before reaching her destination, the *Blanche* was sighted by the Union gunboat *Montgomery*. The warship immediately gave chase, and its captain, the aggressive Commander Charles Hunter, drove the blockade runner into Spanish waters, where the *Blanche* ran hard aground. Hunter quickly sent in two small boats. When the Union sailors arrived they found on board a Spanish official who had raised the Spanish flag over the British flag. The Federals disregarded the Spaniard's authority, and when no cargo manifests or ownership papers were found they claimed the *Blanche* as a prize; however, before anything could be done, the vessel burst into flames, forcing all to abandon ship.

The chase and destruction of the *Blanche* caused an international incident. Spanish authorities were furious over Hunter's intrusion and immediately despatched warships in search of the *Montgomery*, but Hunter had long since left Cuban waters. Reparations were demanded, and Northern authorities, not wishing to anger the Spanish, paid over $200,000 for the *Blanche* and her cargo and dismissed Commander Hunter from the navy.

The matter did not end here. Both Confederate authorities and Major Moise's civilian partners attempted to claim the reparations. This revealed Moise's arrangements. During the resulting investigation it was discovered that Moise had recently purchased a $25,000 home in Alexandria, Louisiana. He was court-martialed and dismissed from service, while in Spain, Confederate diplomats managed to have the Spanish authorities defer a decision on reparations until the war had ended.[26]

Shortly after the burning of the *Blanche*, the remaining steam blockade runners in the western Gulf were either captured or destroyed, and on September 21 Union gunboats crossed the bar on the Sabine River and forced the evacuation of Sabine City. A little more than a week later, the Union blockading squadron off Galveston moved into the interior of the bay, and the Confederates abandoned the city. The squadrons lacked infantry support and did not occupy Sabine City or Galveston. However, the presence of vessels within the bays ended all blockade running activity.[27]

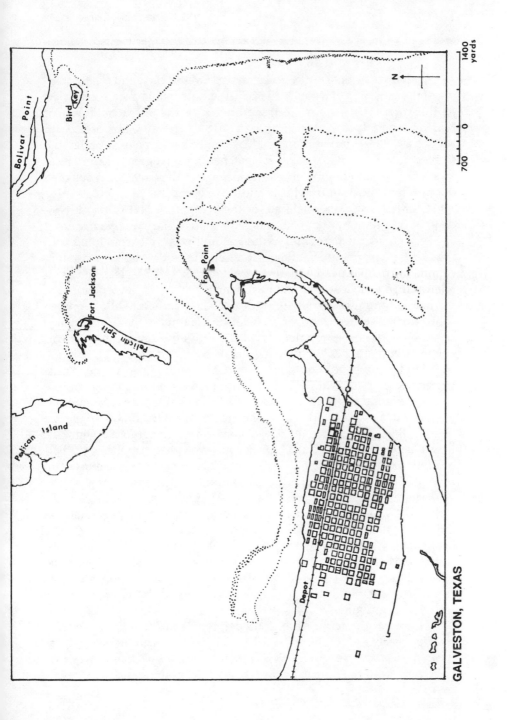

**GALVESTON, TEXAS**

With the evacuation of Galveston and Sabine City, and the tightening of the blockade off Matagorda Bay, the only viable port of entry left to the trans-Mississippi Confederates was the Mexican town of Matamoras. Early in the war, Southern officials viewed their border with Mexico as a large importation site. To open this avenue of supplies, the Confederate State Department despatched Juan Augustin Quintero to Monterey, Mexico, in June of 1861, to arrange trade agreements between the northern Mexican provinces and the Confederacy.[28]

Quintero was well qualified for the position. A New Orleans resident, he had been born in Cuba and educated at Harvard. He had lived in Mexico for some time prior to the war and was well acquainted with the country's fragmented political situation. His initial task was to secure supplies from Santiago Vidaurri, governor of the Mexican states of Nuevo Leon and Coahuila. Vidaurri, who was virtually independent of the Juarez central government in Mexico City, agreed to allow private contractors to sell lead, copper, powder, and leather to the Confederacy; however, Vidaurri would not export modern arms, and Quintero was able to secure only 200 antiquated muskets.[29]

Besides the goods contracted for at Monterey, Quintero also convinced Secretary of War Benjamin to use Matamoras as a landing place for Confederate supplies coming from Europe and Cuba. Matamoras was not a deep-water port. Vessels had to anchor at the mouth of the Rio Grande, thirty miles from the city, transferring their cargoes by lighters. It was a slow process, but Quintero believed that supplies could be brought to Matamoras and then sent by ferry across the river to Brownsville, Texas, and distributed to Southern troops.

Benjamin agreed, directed a purchasing agent to Matamoras, and contracted with Nelson Clements, a Texas businessman who held an interest in the *Blanche*, to ship supplies to the Mexican port. By the agreement, Clements was to provide 20,000 rifles, 5,000 pistols, 5,000 sabers plus large quantities of shoes and dry goods. For his work, Clements was to be paid 100 percent over his invoice on all items received at Matamoras. The payment was to be made in cotton, valued at thirty cents a pound.[30]

However, the immediate Confederate use of Matamoras was denied for nearly a year. The state of Tamaulipas, in which the seaport was located, was the site of a bloody confrontation between two rival governors, both claiming to be the rightful ruler of the state. The struggle

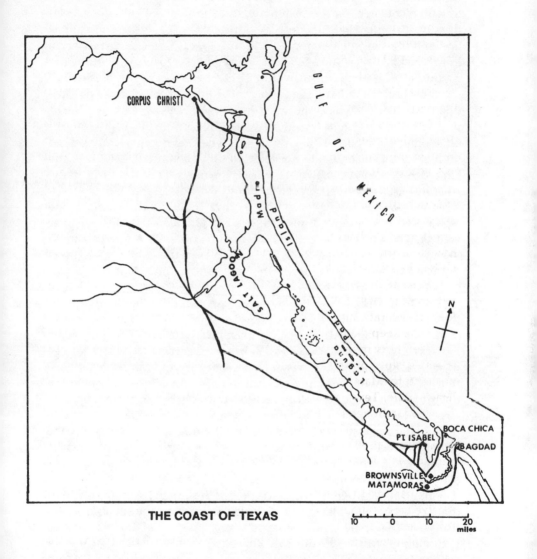

**THE COAST OF TEXAS**

centered around Matamoras, which suffered through a siege, thus cutting off all outside commerce. Finally, in February 1862, after months of fighting, President Juarez ordered Vidaurri to take charge of Tamaulipas and end the siege at Matamoras. Vidaurri gladly obeyed, and by early March he had driven the two warring governors into Texas, opening the route that the South hoped would circumvent the Union blockade.[31]

The use of the Rio Grande to outflank the blockade was not lost upon Northern naval authorities; however, they were in a difficult position to do anything about it. By a provision in the 1848 treaty of Guadalupe Hidalgo, the Rio Grande was a neutral river which could not be blockaded for one mile north or south of its mouth by either the United States or Mexico. Even so, the Union navy did post vessels off the river in hopes that their presence would discourage trade.[32]

On February 1, 1862, Captain S. Swarthout, in command of the sloop *Portsmouth*, sighted north of the Rio Grande the British steamer *Labuan*. The *Labuan* was being loaded with cotton by a small steamer. When Swarthout moved the *Portsmouth* closer, the lighter, which was flying a Confederate flag, fled to the Texas shore. Since Matamoras was still under siege, Swarthout correctly reasoned that the cotton had to be coming from Texas. When the boarding party found evidence to confirm this, Swarthout seized the vessel and sent her north to a prize court.

In the resulting court case the *Labuan* was released. The court ruled that, even though the steamer had Texas cotton on board, her anchorage in neutral waters made her safe from seizure. As long as vessels remained in this area, Union warships could not interfere. However, the decision did not stop Federal gunboats from stopping and examining the papers of all vessels they found between Cuba and Matamoras. These harrassing tactics proved successful in slowing the trade, and in the spring of 1862 a British officer on duty off the northern coast of Mexico lamented that the constant searching of merchantmen was causing a "stagnation to the trade of neutrals with Matamoras."[33]

Besides this interference on the port of the Union Navy, the Confederate trade through Matamoras was also stymied by the situation along the Texas-Mexican border. Transportation in and out of Brownsville was extremely expensive and difficult. Bandits roamed both sides of the river raiding wagon trains and disrupting trade. In April, less than one month after he had taken over Tamaulipas, Vidaurri placed a tariff on all goods shipped into Texas and out to sea. This was added to the normal fees of tonnage, harbor and custom house dues that were paid to the Mexican central government. These extra charges resulted in a price of thirty-five to forty dollars for shipping one bale of cotton at Matamoras; merchants in the Mexican town were offering only thirty-eight dollars per bale. With little or no profit available, most cotton merchants refused to sell their product until prices went up.[34]

What little trading went on was often carried out by New York merchants who traded specifically for cotton and were willing to pay higher prices than foreign businessmen. This trade, however, did nothing to support the Confederate war effort, and until the price of cotton went up there would be little help coming to the Confederacy through Matamoras.[35]

By the fall of 1862 large-scale blockade running carried out by steamers in the Gulf was at a standstill. Increased vigilance off Mobile due to the presence of the *Florida* kept that port closed to nearly all marine commerce, and St. Marks saw no activity after the runs by the *Havana*. In Texas, the positioning of Union gunboats inside the bars at Galveston and Sabine City stopped all trade, and the price wars in the Matamoras-Brownsville area kept that loophole from effectively serving the Confederacy. For the remainder of 1862, no steamer reached a Gulf port, thus closing a huge section of the Southern coastline from providing any support to the war effort.[36]

# Chapter Four

# King Cotton: A Tottering Throne

By the fall of 1862, the Confederate armed forces were becoming increasingly dependent on imported supplies. Resources were steadily dwindling. Critical losses of New Orleans, Memphis, Nashville, and large areas of Tennessee cut deeply into the South's ability to become self-sufficient. The nation was facing growing shortages in food, cloth, leather, raw materials, and munitions.[1]

Gorgas tried to release his bureau from dependence on imported supplies. His massive construction program resulted in munition plants throughout the South. Gorgas felt confident that, when completed, these factories could supply the Confederate armies. However, he soon realized that the South's lifeline to Europe could never be severed.[2]

Small arms production never reached adequate levels. The central armory building at Macon was completed, but its machinery was still under construction in England. Gorgas planned to fabricate 50,000 to 60,000 weapons a year, but actual output fell well below this level. Until July 1863, less than 40,000 rifles were made while nearly 200,000 were imported. For the rest of the war imports would outnumber home production two to one.

The manufacturing of powder was another critical area. A powder works was established at Augusta. Its output could supply the Confederate armies, but the majority of the essential ingredient—potassium nitrate, commonly referred to as saltpeter—had to be imported. Even though the Nitre and Mining Bureau did yeoman work in locating Southern sources for saltpeter, three-fourths of the compound came from overseas.[3]

Imports of other goods either remained the same or increased. Shipments of lead, percussion caps, and cartridges continued through the blockade as well as great quantities of iron, steel, and copper. Gorgas also found it necessary to bring in supplies of leather for cartridge boxes, harnesses, and other accoutrements.[4]

Besides the Ordnance Bureau other War Department sections increased their importations. The Medical Bureau relied heavily on imported drugs to meet its growing needs. The Quartermaster Bureau was forced to run in shoes, blankets, and material for uniforms.[5]

Another division that required imports was the Commissary Bureau. By November 1862, Colonel Lucius Northrop reported that the supply of beef available for the Eastern armies was nearly exhausted. The small number of cattle that did cross the Mississippi River went to forces in Tennessee and Mississippi, with little meat reaching the soldiers east of the Alleghenies. The bureau turned to pork, but Northrop felt that beef had to be provided, and soon he began the importation of beef rations for the Eastern armies.[6]

These shortages experienced by the various bureaus made obvious the fact that the Confederate supply system needed assistance. The requirements of the armies had grown to such proportions that home production and the present level of blockade running could not meet the demand. Efforts were made to expand home production, but for the moment, the South's main reliance for supplies would have to be on blockade running.

At first, all of the War Department bureaus employed Huse to purchase their needs. The supplies were met in Nassau by Heyliger, who placed the goods on blockade runners. The job was not an easy one. Some private carriers demanded $900 in advance for one ton of cargo space, more than twice the previous charge. Communication with Richmond was haphazard, and Heyliger had to guess what supplies were required. His first priorities were gunpowder and arms. He often held back artillery and other bulky material in order to ship munitions, shoes, leather, blankets, and woolens.[7]

Heyliger dealt with a number of firms and found the best rates from Southern companies. Unfortunately he also had to purchase space on British vessels whose owners drove hard bargains. Even though these companies often sympathized with the South, their main motivating factor was profit. If roles had been reversed, most would just as eagerly have served the other side and run cargoes to Boston and New York.

While Heyliger struggled in Nassau with private concerns, Huse continued his work. Nearly singlehandedly, he was providing the Southern armies with essential war materials. Up to February 1863, Huse had purchased over 180,000 stands of arms, of which nearly 165,000 were rifles. He had also acquired 129 cannon, over 4 million cartridges, 10 million percussion caps, half a million pounds of powder and numerous supplies for the Quartermaster and Medical bureaus. The expense was considerable. The supplies cost £1,186,472.19s.3d (nearly 3 million gold dollars), and Huse only had one-half that amount. Unless some of the debt could be paid off, British firms would be reluctant to continue their dealings with the Confederacy.[8]

Until the fall of 1862, Huse's funds had come from letters of credit drawn on specie shipped to Fraser, Trenholm and Company and bills of exchange that were bought by the Treasury Department and sent to their overseas agents. However, by the end of 1862, both methods had ceased to be a viable form of exchange. Huse had expended the supply of specie, which had been collected under the $15 million loan of February 28, 1861, and the premiums on the bills of exchange had jumped from the 9.5 percent at the start of the war to 200 percent by January 1863, thus virtually prohibiting their use.[9]

With their finances in Europe in a state of collapse and their creditors demanding payment, the Confederate government needed to establish a dependable form of credit. The crisis forced a reexamination of their long-cherished belief in King Cotton. Until this time the Southern leaders, still hoping for English intervention, had refused to use cotton in their financial schemes. Only a small amount of privately owned cotton and 428 bales owned by the Confederate Navy had reached Europe, a supply insufficient to meet the need of English manufacturers. However, even though Great Britain was suffering through a severe depression in her textile industries, her government refused to go to war for cotton.

That England would not intervene for cotton was a rude shock. During the fall of 1862, Edwin DeLeon, a Confederate agent to France, called the English cowards and selfish, for refusing to challenge the Union Navy. DeLeon wrote Benjamin that England "recognizes now the truth that 'Cotton is King' although like other kings he may be driven from his throne by Revolution and she seeks to wield his spectre, as well as that of the sea, which the North disputes with her."[10]

Northern agents in Europe also reported that the Confederate policy of King Cotton was failing. Thomas Dudley, the United States Liverpool consul, wrote Seward that the need of cotton was far outweighed by the growing strength of the United States Navy. Dudley observed that "Nothing will tend more to ward off and cause the nations of Europe to stand aloof from this contest than a large increase in our Navy of Iron Clad Ships. They fear the monitors . . . It is *fear* and not *love* that will prevent interference."[11]

King Cotton had failed, and with it the South's most influential foreign affairs policy collapsed. President Davis and his advisors could no longer plan on English intervention. Cotton's use as an instrument of foreign policy was ended, but its full value as a medium of exchange was just beginning.

The cotton held by the Confederacy had come from the three produce acts of 1861. These acts, or loans, were primarily designed to aid the financially disrupted cotton planters and to circulate bonds bearing 8 percent interest over twenty years. These bonds could be used for investment or currency, and with them Treasury agents purchased over 400,000 bales of cotton and other products such as turpentine and rosin. Initially, Secretary of Treasury Memminger viewed the government-owned cotton as a "white elephant," but by the fall of 1862 his opinion had changed.[12]

As already noted, the Confederacy's first use of cotton had occurred when the Navy Department attempted to ship cotton on board the *Fingal*. The cargo eventually traveled on the *Economist* to England, where it was sold by Fraser, Trenholm and Company. The profits were credited to the Navy Department for use by Bulloch and other naval agents.

Following this lead, Secretary of Navy Mallory despatched additional agents with the authority to pledge cotton for the construction of warships. These representatives found British financiers very cooperative and, by the summer of 1862, deals were struck that allowed the South to use cotton certificates or bonds to purchase vessels. These bonds could be held for their interest or redeemed in the South for cotton at a rate of 8 cents a pound, which was three to four times less than the current English price.

Mallory's use of cotton bonds set a precedent, and soon Confederate authorities decided to try a larger and more comprehensive use of their cotton reserves. To carry this out, Huse and Slidell were sent to Paris to negotiate a foreign loan with Erlanger and Company, a French banking house. An agreement was reached which called for a £3 million loan, from which the Confederacy planned to finance its purchasing of war materials. The twenty-year bonds were to bear 7 percent interest semiannually, and were redeemable biannually at one-fortieth of their face value. However, what made the bonds attractive was that arrangements could be made to exchange them in the Confederacy for cotton at six pence (about twelve cents) per pound.[13]

When word of the foreign loan reached the European financial circles, Southern agents found credit easier to obtain, and purchasing operations were resumed. On March 19, 1863, the books were opened to subscription. The initial reaction was favorable, giving the Confederates cause to expect a solid return. In reality the loan provided about $7 million, for which the South pledged nearly $45 million worth of cotton. However, as unbalanced as this may seem, the loan did have the positive effect of providing the nation's purchasing agents with money and credit. In addition, because the bonds could be exchanged for cotton, the loan also gave rise to a number of private blockade-running ventures.[14]

The high rate of subscription received by the Erlanger loan was based on many factors, including a desire for cotton by British speculators, genuine sympathy to the Southern cause, and a belief on the part of British financiers that if the Union should win the war, the Lincoln government would assume the Confederate debt. Such rumors were encouraged by Mason, who assured English merchants that all obligations would be honored no matter who won. Dudley reported that such beliefs were strongly held in Liverpool. He reported to Seward: "As strange as it may seem, these people here who are aiding the Rebels and taken or purchased these bonds think if worse comes, and the Union is restored that the United States Government will assume the payment of their bonds." These beliefs were incredulous to Dudley, but he had to admit that the Erlanger loan and other cotton bonds were having a positive effect on Confederate purchasing operations.[15]

While most Confederate officials favored the partnership between the private sector and government, there was one notable exception in the person of Josiah Gorgas, the chief of the Ordnance Bureau. Gorgas never approved of the South's reliance on private enterprise. Guns, powder, and other war materials were too valuable to be left in the hands of profit-minded shippers. Instead, Gorgas wanted to place his bureau's foreign supplies on government-owned vessels and, working with new Secretary of War James Seddon, Gorgas made arrangements to establish his own line of blockade runners.

During the fall of 1862, Gorgas despatched Major Norman S. Walker to England to confer with Huse. Walker carried with him two million dollars' worth of Confederate bonds. The bonds were probably cotton bonds, which Huse used to reduce his indebtedness and purchase for the Ordnance Bureau a number of light-drafted steamers. After meeting with Huse and delivering the bonds, Walker proceeded to Bermuda, where he became the bureau's resident disbursing agent. At Bermuda he was to work with S. G. Porter, an Ordnance Bureau official and ship captain and John T. Bourne, a native Bermudian who handled wharfage duties for numerous private companies, including John Fraser and Company. Later, Major Smith Stansbury arrived and took charge of the South's ordnance depot. Gorgas also wanted assistance from the Navy Department, but Mallory continued to keep his operations separate. The only support received from the Navy was the occasional use of furloughed officers to command the blockade runners.[16]

The base for these operations was the Bermuda port of St. George. Until 1860, St. George had been a stopover for vessels crossing the Atlantic. Located on the island of St. George, the port had the advantage of being located closer to the open sea than Bermuda's other port: Hamilton. Its harbor was one of good depth, being nearly landlocked with water as clear as crystal.[17]

At the beginning of the American Civil War, the town was used mainly as a coaling site by blockade runners heading for Nassau, and few runs originated from the port. Bermuda's main drawback to blockade running was its distance from the Confederate coast. It was 674 miles to Wilmington and 772 to Charleston from St. George versus 570 and 515 from Nassau. This extra distance caused blockade runners to carry an extra two-day supply of coal and, since most private companies preferred not to use valuable cargo space for coal, Bermuda was rarely used by these firms.

It was probably this lack of competition for the port's facilities that initially attracted Gorgas to St. George. Other advantages included the fact that Union warships could not cruise off Bermuda as they did Nassau. The Federal base of Key West was only a day's steaming time from Nassau, while Bermuda was 700 to 800 miles from the nearest Union coaling station. St. George was also championed by John Tory

Bourne, a native commission merchant. Bourne encouraged the Confederacy by pointing out that the port could handle vessels drawing up to 20 feet and had excellent coaling facilities. He also offered a disbursement fee of 2.5 percent versus the 5 percent charged by other merchants in Bermuda and Nassau.[18]

During the late fall and early winter of 1862–1863 Huse purchased three steamers for the Ordnance Bureau. These were the *Columbia*, *Eugenie*, and *Merrimac*—all iron-hulled sidewheelers of light draft and good speed. As planned, the vessels were to operate between St. George and Wilmington, carrying in supplies and taking out bureau-owned cotton. All profits were to go to Huse's account with Fraser, Trenholm and Company.

The focal point for the trade coming out of St. George was Wilmington, North Carolina. Gorgas probably chose this port over Charleston because, as yet, it had not attracted the large number of blockade runners that so burdened Charleston's facilities. Wilmington also had the advantage of two well-guarded inlets and excellent railroad communications. In charge of the blockade-running operation, Gorgas placed his brother-in-law Major Thomas L. Bayne. Bayne's duty was to supervise the landing and distribution of incoming cargo and the purchase and loading of government cotton. Such work involved considerable labor and coordination. Since the majority of the government-owned cotton obtained under the produce loans had already been earmarked for use with cotton certificates or promised for the redemption of the Erlanger loan, there was little left for the Ordnance Bureau. In order to supply Gorgas's blockade runners, Secretary of the Treasury Memminger allowed his purchasing agents to work for the Ordnance Bureau. Cotton bought by these agents would be paid for by the Treasury Department funds allocated to the Ordnance Bureau. It was a difficult and complicated system, but Bayne managed to make it work.[19]

The Ordnance Bureau's depot at Wilmington was under the direct command of James M. Sexias. His role was to supervise the landing and shipping of supplies, to keep a supply of coal on hand, and handle all wharfage matters. Though badly strapped for time and resources, both Sexias and Bayne were prepared when the bureau's blockade runners began to run to the Confederacy.[20]

The first of the three steamers to be fitted out was the Clyde River ferryboat *Columbia*. She was renamed *Cornubia* and, in accordance with British law, cleared Glasgow with British registry and a British captain.

She arrived in Bermuda on December 3, 1862, and ten days later made her first successful run into Wilmington.[21]

The second vessel purchased by Huse was the *Merrimac*, an extremely fast sidewheeler. In buying the vessel, the Confederacy was solving a long-standing problem. The *Merrimac* had been owned by Z. C. Pearson and Company, who had accepted a Confederate contract to bring in a cargo that included three 8-inch Blakely rifled cannon and 1,100 barrels of gunpowder. Pearson was to receive payment on delivery of the goods.

The *Merrimac* and her valuable cargo arrived at St. George on September 5, 1862, enroute from London to Nassau. Before she could continue her voyage, Pearson and Company declared bankruptcy and their creditors seized the *Merrimac*. Southern agents were unable to separate their cargo from the impounded steamer and, as a result, Huse found it necessary to purchase the vessel and her cargo for £7,000. Once in the hands of the Confederacy, the *Merrimac* was made ready for sea and on April 13, 1863, under the command of S. G. Porter, ran into Wilmington. The three Blakely guns, each capable of firing a 170-pound projectile, were divided up, one going to Vicksburg and the remaining two being kept for the defense of Wilmington. One was placed at Fort Fisher at New Inlet while the other was positioned at Fort Caswell at Old Inlet.

The *Merrimac* never again went to sea for the Ordnance Bureau. Though she had been an extremely fast vessel, reported to have made eighteen knots on her trials, her engines became fouled, and Gorgas sold her to private interests.[22]

The final vessel purchased by Huse for the Ordnance Bureau was the newly constructed *Eugenie*. Like the *Cornubia*, the *Eugenie* retained British registry and was commanded by British captains. However, when the contracts of the Englishmen expired in the summer of 1863, Gorgas replaced them with naval officers and reregistered the steamers as Confederate merchantmen. Lieutenant Richard N. Gayle took over the *Cornubia*, and Lieutenant Joseph Fry assumed command of the *Eugenie*.[23]

Unlike private vessels, the *Cornubia* and her consorts were under strict regulations. No passengers or private freight were allowed on board without approval from Sexias. For the *Cornubia*, Lieutenant Gayle had to examine all ship papers and present his cargo manifest to the War Department agents immediately on his arrival at Bermuda or

Wilmington. Gayle was also responsible for hiring engineers who had the all-important duty of caring for the ship's powerful yet highly sensitive engines.

Even though serving on a government vessel, Gayle and his crew received special pay. The officers signed on for six months, and salaries ran for that entire term, even if the vessel was captured. One-half of the salary would be paid in Bermuda before the start of the run. The bonus, or bounty, for successful completion of a voyage could be paid, at the discretion of the War Department, in either Bermuda or Wilmington. The officer and crew of the vessels were paid in gold, though Sexias reserved the right to pay the bounty in Confederate currency. The scale called for the following wage and bonus, per round trip.

| Rank | Wage | Bonus |
| --- | --- | --- |
| First Officer | $200 | $200 |
| Second Officer | 100 | 80 |
| Third Officer | 60 | 50 |
| Purser | 60 | 60 |
| Quartermaster | 50 | 40 |
| Boatswain | 50 | 50 |
| Seaman | 40 | 40 |
| First Engineer | 300 | 200 |
| Second Engineer | 150 | 100 |
| Third Engineer | 100 | 80 |
| Fourth Engineer | 80 | 70 |
| Fireman | 50 | 50 |
| Trimmers | 40 | 40 |
| Engineer Storekeeper | 25 | 25 |
| Chief Steward | 60 | 60 |
| Second Steward | 40 | 40 |
| Chief Cook | 50 | 50 |
| Second Cook | 40 | 40 |
| Waiters | 25 | 25 |
| Mess Boys | 25 | 25 |
| Pilot | 300 | 100[24] |

Under Gayle, the *Cornubia* became renowned for her ability to run the blockade. During her career, the steamer acquired the nickname

*Lady Davis*, which often confused observers. Many prominent passengers ran the blockade on the *Cornubia* including the banished United States Congressman Clement Laird Vallandigham, who was carried to Bermuda in late June, 1863.[25]

While the *Cornubia* was compiling the most successful record of any Ordnance Bureau vessel, a fourth steamer, the steel screw steamer *Phantom*, was added to the bureau's squadron. Built for Fraser, Trenholm and Company, the *Phantom* had been completed in early 1863, and immediately despatched to Bermuda under the command of Eugene L. Tessier, the same captain who had taken the *Bermuda* to Savannah in September 1861. From Bermuda, the sleek steamer ran into Wilmington, where Trenholm offered the vessel to the Confederacy. Purchased by the Ordnance Bureau, the *Phantom* was placed under the command of S. G. Porter, who guided her back to Bermuda to join the other government-owned runners.[26]

The most famous of the Ordnance vessels was the fast Clyde River sidewheeler *Giraffe*, which the War Department renamed *Robert E. Lee*. The vessel was not purchased with the intention of joining the squadron brought together by Gorgas but, through a combination of circumstances, she eventually joined the Confederate service.

The *Giraffe* was the central feature in a scheme originated by Benjamin F. Ficklin, a Treasury Department agent, who was responsible for the purchasing and delivery of engraving supplies from England. Ficklin proposed to Secretary of Treasury Memminger that he be allowed to go to England with a naval officer, purchase a steamer, load it with Treasury and War Department supplies, and run it to the South. Ficklin assured Memminger that he had the perfect vessel in mind for the mission, the fast sidewheel packet *Giraffe*. The two-year-old vessel had operated between Glasgow and Belfast, but had lost money and had recently been put up for sale by her owners. Ficklin thought the steamer could be easily obtained and, once the voyage was completed, he requested permission to purchase the vessel for his own use.[27]

Memminger approved the plan, and by the late summer 1862 Ficklin and naval lieutenant John Wilkinson were in London negotiating for the *Giraffe* with Alexander Collie. Collie, a British businessman who was outfitting his own blockade-running company, at first refused to sell the vessel but finally gave in to overtures from Wilkinson, and sold the *Giraffe* for £32,000, with the provision that the ship not be resold to private interests. Wilkinson, unaware of Ficklin's arrangement with

Memminger, agreed, and soon converted the *Giraffe* from a luxury ferryboat to a blockade runner.

By November 1862, the *Giraffe* was ready. On board were a number of munitions, lithographic equipment, and twenty-six lithographers hired by Ficklin for the Treasury Department. Wilkinson accompanied the *Giraffe* to Nassau, where he took command of the vessel. Ficklin returned on a passenger steamer via New York, and from there he planned to make his way south, slip through the Union lines to Richmond, and begin his negotiations to buy the *Giraffe*.

After assuming command, Wilkinson took the *Giraffe* out of Nassau on December 27, 1862, and headed toward the South Carolina coast. As he approached Charleston, he found the weather too thick, and made for Wilmington. As the *Giraffe* neared Old Inlet, a blockader was sighted patrolling the coastline. Wilkinson edged the *Giraffe* close to shore and waited until nightfall. In the cover of darkness, he slipped his vessel past the Union warship and made for Old Inlet. The *Giraffe* passed through the blockaders at full speed without being sighted, but before reaching safety she crashed headlong into the "Lump," a sandy knoll two or three miles outside the bar. The impact of the collision knocked the entire crew off their feet, but the vessel was unharmed. Wilkinson sent the lithographers ashore in a small boat while he and his crew struggled to free the steamer. By using a kedge (an iron anchor) attached to the stern hawser and working the paddlewheels, Wilkinson slowly freed the blockade runner. The hawser line was cut, and the *Giraffe* dashed into the Cape Fear River, arriving off Smithville just before midnight on December 29, 1862.

The *Giraffe* proceeded to Wilmington and was unloaded while Wilkinson awaited further orders. By this time Ficklin had made his way back to the Confederacy and was ready to claim the *Giraffe*. Memminger, who was probably unaware of the full agreement with Collie, favored selling the vessel to Ficklin, but the War Department refused to give up its interest and took control of the steamer, foiling Ficklin's plans. Turned over to Gorgas, the ship was given a Confederate registry and renamed the *Robert E. Lee*. Lieutenant Wilkinson was retained as her commander, and in late January took the vessel out of Wilmington, completing the first of five round trips.[28]

While the Ordnance Bureau developed its own line of blockade runners, other War Department bureaus also found it necessary to increase their imports from England. Until this time, Caleb Huse had made random purchases for all bureaus. However, it soon became apparent that additional agents were needed, and in December 1862 Quartermaster General Abraham C. Myers despatched Major J. B. Ferguson, Jr. to Europe to serve as his bureau's purchasing agent.

At about the same time that Ferguson was sent to Europe, Secretary of War James A. Seddon entered into a loose agreement with Captain William G. Crenshaw for the establishment of a line of blockade runners. Crenshaw, an artillery officer and an established Richmond merchant, was to go to England and enter into a partnership with a British mercantile house for the purpose of securing and shipping goods to the Confederacy. Crenshaw was authorized to purchase or build the needed vessels; he and his partners would be allocated one-fourth of the cargo space on the ships; their goods would be free from all import duties, and they would receive a 2.5 percent commission on the purchasing of supplies, ships, and sale of Confederate cotton. The remaining profits from the cotton would then go to procure cargoes and pay expenses. Both the War and Navy departments made plans to use Crenshaw's steamers. The exact details of the contract were left in the hands of James Mason, who would work them out once Crenshaw arrived in England. The plan had merit in that it provided more vessels for the South, but it tied the government to a private enterprise run by profit-minded civilians. It also entrusted Mason with the negotiation of a contract that protected the government's interests, something the diplomat had difficulty accomplishing.[29]

On arriving in London, Crenshaw found a willing partner in Alexander Collie, the head of Collie and Company, the firm that sold the *Giraffe* to the Confederacy. Crenshaw contacted Mason and by mid-March the two Virginians had signed an agreement with Collie. By the terms of the contract, the Confederacy was obliged to pay three-quarters of the cost of the steamers, with Crenshaw and Collie paying only one-eighth each. The cargo space was distributed with one-half going to the War Department, one-fourth to the Navy Department and one-fourth to Crenshaw and Collie. The pact was done without the knowledge of Huse or Slidell, who were in France working on the Erlanger loan.

With Collie's assistance, Crenshaw purchased excellent vessels for the venture. His English partner directed him to John and William Dudgeon of London, who were builders of the experimental, iron-hulled, twin-screw steamers. Collie had already purchased one of these sleek vessels, the *Flora*, and her sister the *Kate* was doing quite well for another blockade-running company. Crenshaw was so impressed that he bought from Collie the contract of the next vessel, the *Hebe*, and put in an order for three additional ships. The *Hebe* would be finished by April 6, and would be followed at one-month intervals by her three sisters, the *Dee*, *Ceres*, and *Vesta*. The four steamers cost £14,000 each, less 1 percent brokerage fee. Crenshaw, and Collie also took a 2½ percent commission from the transaction.

Though the four ships were sisters, their speeds varied. The *Hebe* was guaranteed at 14½ knots, the *Dee*, to be finished by May 6, was guaranteed at 13½ knots, while the following two, the *Ceres* and the *Vesta*, were to be completed by June 30 and July 15 with a promised speed of 15 knots. The twin screws were a new style of merchantmen. Built of iron, they were fast, maneuverable, compact vessels. By reversing one screw and running the other forward, the ships could actually turn as if on a pivot. Such ability was highly valued by captains who suddenly found a Union warship in their path. However, the vessels did have a deeper draft than sidewheelers because of the depth of water needed to efficiently operate their screws. Paddlewheelers also obtained a greater speed in less time, giving them the ability to dash past blockaders, and sidewheelers could free themselves from sandbars faster than twin screws by working their paddlewheels in a rocking motion. Still, the *Hebe* and her sisters were remarkable vessels and blockade running would be the twin screw's first great test.

Besides the four twin screws, Crenshaw also purchased the large iron-hulled paddlewheel steamer *Venus*. With the *Venus*, and the soon-to-be completed *Hebe*, Crenshaw planned to begin loading in mid-April the goods purchased by Major Ferguson. To prepare for the arrival of these vessels, and increase his profits, Crenshaw was allowed to name his brother James as agent for both the incoming Confederate and private supplies. It was also requested that the Navy Department provide the vessels with commanders but, even though they would carry naval supplies, Mallory refused to release any active officers.[30]

When Gorgas learned of the Crenshaw and Collie contract, he immediately lobbied against it. Though he could not stop its implementation, he did keep James Crenshaw from controlling War Department supplies at Wilmington. Gorgas correctly viewed such activities as direct competition to his line of blockade runners, and this time he managed to head off any serious problems. However, while he dealt effectively with the situation in the Confederacy, he could do little to assist his overseas agent, who was coming under attack from William Crenshaw and his European backers.[31]

In early April, after Crenshaw and Collie had begun their activities, an uninformed Captain Huse returned to discover Crenshaw demanding ordnance and medical supplies for his vessels. Huse was stunned, especially since he had recently placed three steamers into service specifically for that purpose. Huse refused, and also declined to sanction purchases by Crenshaw and Collie for these bureaus, preferring instead to keep it all in the hands of his agents, S. Isaac, Campbell and Company.

Disturbed by Huse's attitude, Crenshaw tried to bypass Gorgas's agent by urging Seddon to make him and Collie purchasing agents for the Ordnance and Medical bureaus. While awaiting a reply, Crenshaw continued to accept orders for 5,000 tons of meat and 6,000 tons of armor from the Commissary Bureau and the Navy Department. At the same time, he ordered a fifth twin screw from Dudgeon. By the end of May, 1863 Crenshaw had accumulated for the Confederacy a debt of £115,334 and, as yet, had not delivered a cargo.

To pay part of this debt, Crenshaw demanded funding from Huse, but was refused. Huse, who had spent months trimming his own debt and reviving Confederate credit, declined to share any of his funds. Outraged, Crenshaw, with fellow Virginians Ferguson and Mason, lobbied for Huse's removal. Even though he was backed by Gorgas, Erlanger and Slidell, Huse was in a precarious position. Complicating matters was his alliance with S. Isaac, Campbell and Company, a firm with a reputation of scandal dating from the Crimean War. Unknown to Huse, the firm was carrying out unethical bookkeeping while purchasing Confederate goods.

Seddon, alarmed by the troubles in Europe, separated Huse and Crenshaw by directing Huse to deal only with medical and ordnance supplies while Crenshaw was given control over quartermaster and commissary goods. The secretary of war also asked Colin J. McRae, the Confederacy's chief agent for the Erlanger loan, to investigate the charges against Huse.

Crenshaw, unsatisfied with the compromise, threatened to end his contract, but eventually he accepted Seddon's conditions. To reduce his debt, Crenshaw sold the fifth twin screw to Collie. Then, by using funds from the Quartermaster and Commissary bureaus and the Navy Department, he continued his work.[32]

The Crenshaw and Collie contract would not be the last to interfere with Confederate-operated blockade runners and purchasing operations. Instead of expanding Gorgas's venture, Seddon continued to deal with private shippers. The eventual result of these partnerships would be increased competition in England, the West Indies, and Southern ports, causing interdepartmental rivalries within the Confederate government for agents, ships, crews, captains, coal, cotton, and supplies. An octopus was growing with its tentacles becoming even more entangled, and it would take a wiser man than Seddon to disentangle them.

While the War Department struggled to meet its needs, the Navy Department added its presence to the already complicated scene. Though it was the logical service to undertake the importing of supplies, and had achieved some success with the *Fingal*, the navy had shown little interest in blockade running. Instead, throughout 1862, Mallory and Bulloch placed their overseas efforts into the building of commerce raiders, ironclads, and marine engines. It was not until their funds ran low that the navy returned to blockade running.

To meet their expenses Mallory directed Bulloch and his aide Commander Matthew F. Maury to purchase a fast vessel in Europe for running cotton out of the South. At the same time, Mallory ordered two naval steamers, the *Stono* at Charleston and the *Oconee* at Savannah, converted to blockade runners. Neither of the vessels had any luck. In June 1863, the *Stono*, the onetime Union gunboat *Isaac Smith*, crashed aground in the breakwater off Fort Moultrie while two months later the *Oconee* was lost in a storm after escaping from the Savannah River.[33]

The loss of the *Stono* and the *Oconee* delayed Mallory's plans to finance his operations in England, but by midsummer he received word that his agents had found a suitable blockade runner. The vessel chosen by Bulloch and Maury was the twin screw *Coquette*, which they purchased for £10,000 in cash and £14,000 in cotton. The cotton, some 1,100 bales, would be carried out on the vessel's first run. After this, all outward cotton would go to Bulloch's account. The *Coquette*, built by Hoby and Son of Renfrew, was larger than the twin screws built by Dudgeon for Crenshaw and Collie. She had a ten-foot draft, and was capable of carrying over 1,000 bales of cotton. Her speed was "guaranteed" at 15 knots, though after rigorous testing, it was found to be 13.5 knots.

Bulloch planned to have the *Coquette* in service before the year was out. On her first run she would carry a steam engine destined for an ironclad. Profits would go to purchase two more blockade runners. Only then, with three vessels, did Bulloch feel he could receive enough cotton to finance his overseas work.[34]

Though important to the naval program, Mallory's operations were small and rarely interfered with the War Department. However, as the war progressed, and the need for overseas supplies increased, the central government soon found competition coming from state governments, who entered the trade in order to help their citizens and soldiers.

Among the first to enter the blockade running arena was the state of North Carolina. Early in the war the state legislature requested and received from the Confederate government funds that normally would have been used to purchase clothing for North Carolina troops serving with the army. The state then used the money to buy raw materials that were turned into uniforms by North Carolina's growing textile industry. However, by the end of 1862, the state was facing a severe shortage of leather, cotton, and wool thread. The crisis was such that the state's Adjutant General James G. Martin suggested to Governor Henry Toole Clark that a blockade runner be purchased to bring in the needed material from England. Clark felt that he did not have the authority for such action, but his successor, Zebulon Baird Vance, was not so timid, and less than one month after taking office Vance was ready to sponsor a blockade runner.[35]

The state issued $1,500,000 cotton bonds which Vance despatched to England in the custody of John White and Thomas Crossan. The two were to purchase material for North Carolina soldiers, especially shoes and blankets, and a blockade runner. The bonds carried by White and Crossman paid 7 percent annually starting July 1, 1863. The interest could be collected in Manchester, England, or the bonds could be redeemed for cotton in North Carolina. To gain the cotton, a bond holder had to give sixty-day notice to the North Carolina commissioners in England, who would then arrange to have the cotton waiting at Wilmington. A £100 bond was worth twelve bales of cotton, each weighing at least 400 pounds. The exchange was roughly 4 pence a pound, a better bargain than the Confederate bonds.[36]

Vance and Martin had chosen their agents carefully, giving each a specific role. John White, an established dry goods merchant, was in charge of purchasing and shipping supplies. Thomas Crossan, a former lieutenant in the Confederate Navy who had commanded the gunboat *Winslow* at the battle of New Berne, was in charge of choosing and outfitting the blockade runner. On reaching England, the two entered into a business agreement with the ever present Alexander Collie, who took the North Carolina bonds as collateral and established a line of credit with which White and Crossan were able to purchase their supplies and a steamer.

The vessel chosen by Crossan was the iron-hulled sidewheeler *Lord Clyde*. Built during the summer of 1862 by Caird and Company of Glasgow, the packet operated for six months between Dublin and Glasgow before being sold to North Carolina for $175,000 or £35,000. Less than one month later, the steamer was loaded with supplies and on her way to Bermuda under the command of Joannes Wylie.

On June 28, 1863, Wylie safely brought the *Lord Clyde*, loaded with dry goods, shoes, and cotton cards, into the Cape Fear River. The cloth was sent to Raleigh, where state-operated factories turned it into blankets and uniforms. The cotton cards were distributed to households throughout the state for turning cotton into thread. The thread could then be used by the families and the surplus taken by the state for uniform production.

At Wilmington, the *Lord Clyde*'s registry was changed, and she was renamed the *Advance*, a name that would often be confused with the ship's sponsor, Governor Zebulon Vance. People often tried to match the name of the steamer with that of the governor, but she was referred to in all correspondence and official port records as the *Advance*, and it was under this name that she became one of the war's most successful blockade runners.

The use of the *Advance* by the state of North Carolina was a bold step by Governor Vance. The operation proved highly successful, but it did cause problems between the state and central government. Both were in direct competition for the purchasing of cotton, space on railroads, dock facilities in Bermuda and Wilmington, and even in the mining of coal in North Carolina. In Europe, agents contended with each other for quartermaster supplies, and their bonds competed for the money of European financiers. However, the greatest competition to North Carolina and the Confederacy did not come from each other, but from the private businesses that operated highly lucrative blockade-running firms that cut deeply into the government run ventures.[37]

# Chapter Five

# Time for Champagne Cocktails

Profits and patriotism were the two most powerful motivating elements in blockade running. Without profits, blockade running would not have existed; few entrepreneurs would have operated vessels on patriotism alone. For this reason the Confederacy did not restrict private ventures. Beginning in late 1862, this laxity resulted in a tremendous increase in civilian-operated blockade runners.

Lured by the prospects of huge returns on their investments, individuals and firms from England, Canada, Cuba, the Confederacy, and even the United States began to enter the trade. These concerns ranged in size from single-ship ventures to large stockholding companies. The larger companies operated, not only blockade runners, but also added to the profits with cargo vessels that carried merchandise to and from the West Indies.[1]

The most important element in these undertakings was a vessel capable of running the blockade. By mid-1862, the predominant blockade runner on the East Coast was the steamer. Only during the first months of the conflict did large sailing ships try to run the blockade, and this was only for outward runs as their owners refused to risk their vessels a second time against steam warships. After June 1862, under forty sailing ships, all schooners and sloops, tried to clear Charleston. Their total cargoes amounted to less than 1,000 bales of cotton. The data for sailing ships leaving Wilmington would be similar.

The mainstay of the trade was the steam-propelled blockade runner. At the beginning of the war, companies were able to employ nearly any size steamer and expect a reasonable chance of success. However, as the blockade tightened, they were forced to adopt the use of light-drafted ships. Twin-screw, single-screw, and paddlewheel steamers were employed, but most companies utilized sidewheelers. Single propellers required extra depth at the stern, thus restricting their use in many shallow channels. For the most part, firms looked for light-drafted paddlewheelers, while a few experimented with the new twin screws.

The preferred paddlewheel steamers were those built after a style first perfected on the Clyde River in Scotland. These rakish packets, often referred to as "Clyde Steamers," combined long iron hulls, narrow beams, powerful engines, and light drafts for tremendous speeds. By 1860, the sidewheelers had gained widespread use on the Clyde and Mersey rivers and on the coasts of Ireland and England. The potential of these vessels as blockade runners was first recognized by Fraser, Trenholm and Company in early 1862, when they purchased the *Herald* from the Dublin and Glasgow Steam Packet Company. She was the first Clyde steamer to be taken into the trade. Less than one year later, the docks of Liverpool and Glasgow were filled with similar packets undergoing the conversion to blockade runners.

After being purchased, the vessels were altered. Staterooms were removed and stowage capacity increased. On some vessels, telescopic smokestacks were employed so they could be lowered while running the blockade. Masts and spars were reduced to a minimum, with some masts being placed on hinges or in sockets so they could be removed when not in use. The vessels were painted a light gray or bluish green and stocked with smokeless anthracite coal.[2]

Once the vessel was readied, the companies hired experienced officers and crews. The sailors were, for the most part, English or Irish. Even the crews of the Southern-based companies had a large percentage of foreigners, as before the war many of the sailors in the Southern states were recent immigrants or had been hired off European merchantmen. Also, because the native sailors were eligible for conscription into the Confederate Army, many were either drafted, joined the Confederate Navy, or changed their citizenship. The latter was very popular with the Southern sailors who served on blockade runners as when captured, foreign sailors were detained only a few weeks, while Confederate seamen were sent to Northern prison camps where survival was a daily struggle. One such sailor was Sidney C. Lanier, the future poet and literary figure. Captured on board the blockade runner *Lucy*, he was sent to Point Lookout prison on the coast of Maryland. Though exchanged three months later, Lanier emaciated to a near skeleton and developed tuberculosis.

The persons most sought after by blockade running companies were Southern steamboat captains. These men, with their knowledge of the shoreline, were highly prized as they could serve as both captains and pilots. Captains, such as Louis M. Coxetter, James Carlin, and the Lockwood brothers, all commanded large salaries, and were often the cause of bidding wars between companies. All four began their block-ade-running careers with John Fraser and Company, but only Thomas Lockwood remained with the firm. Both Coxetter and Robert Lockwood switched to the Chicora Importing and Exporting Company by the second year of the war, while Carlin became an early participant in the Importing and Exporting Company of South Carolina.

Carlin's experiences were typical of a blockade runner. In 1862 he commanded the *Cecile* until she was wrecked in the Bahamas. While waiting for the company to purchase new vessels, he briefly captained Alexander Collie's *Ruby*. He returned to the Importing and Exporting Company of South Carolina in April 1863 to command the *Ella and Annie*. Later that year, he operated the firm's steamer *Alice* before going to England to assist the company in constructing and outfitting additional blockade runners.

Besides paying their commanders' high salaries, owners of block-ade-running companies counted on patriotism to encourage the South-ern-born captains to take greater risks to deliver their cargo than a foreigner. If captured, the captains, like the native crewmen, were sent to prison camps. However, the commanders were usually sent to either Fort Lafayette in New York harbor or Fort Warren at Boston, sites that, though barren and desolate, were more hospitable than Point Lookout.[3]

When Southern captains were not available, companies easily filled their vacancies with English civilian captains and furloughed naval officers. Many, such as Augustus Charles Hobart-Hampden and William N. W. Hewett, who were officers of the Royal Navy, and the civilians A. O. Stone and Jonathon Steele came to the trade for high profits and adventure. They became very adept at running vessels through the blockade and, in time, gained their own reputations. If captured, the Englishmen had little to fear. At best, Northern authorities could detain them for testimony at the prize courts. This would usually last only a few weeks, and if they were held longer, the local British consul would force their release. Once free from Northern authorities the sailors would often return to Nassau or Bermuda to rejoin the trade.[4]

Because of the physical danger of running the blockade, a romantic atmosphere developed around the men who worked the trade. The sailors involved were seen as daredevils who sought life-and-death adventures while taking their frail vessels through a gauntlet of Union warships. In actuality, there was little danger in challenging the blockade. The fast, low-lying steamers had all the advantages of speed and surprise over the blockaders. Their arrivals off the coast were timed so to coincide with nightfall, and, whenever possible, with a new moon or when the moon had set. While running through the blockade, the ships were guided by lights placed and maintained by the Confederate Signal Corps that revealed the location of channels. Only a chance observance by a blockader would cause alarm, and even then the possibility of being struck by a shell was slight. The vessels were difficult targets, and when discovered they would send up signal rockets to confuse the warships. Even when trapped, the crew was rarely in danger, because the Federals preferred to capture the vessel and gain the prize money than destroy it.

Runs out of Southern ports were even safer than inward voyages. Before coming out, runners would gain detailed information on the location of the Union blockaders from Confederate lookouts. By using this information, commanders would chart their outward dashes so to avoid the main line of blockaders. For the year 1863, out of nearly 170 attempts only 11 ships were lost trying to clear Wilmington and Charleston, while 36 were lost in over 200 tries to enter the ports.[5]

The most dangerous time for blockade runners was during daylight hours while steaming to and from the Southern coast. If they were sighted by a Union blockader, it became a test of speed and durability, and even though the Union Navy placed its fastest cruisers around the Bahamas and in the Gulf Stream, the blockade runners usually outran their opponents or kept the chase up until nightfall, when they disappeared into the darkness.[6]

The officers and sailors of blockade runners received excellent wages for their service. The men were paid in gold at a set salary that varied from company to company. One half of the gold was paid at the start of the run, and the balance on completion of the voyage. Salaries from private companies were much higher than Confederate wages, as seen by the following pay scale of the *Venus*, a Crenshaw and Collie vessel. For each trip the crew received:

| Rank           | Wage    |
| -------------- | ------- |
| Captain        | $5,000  |
| First Officer  | $1,250  |
| Second Officer | $750    |
| Third Officer  | $750    |
| Chief Engineer | $2,500  |
| Crew           | $250    |
| Pilot          | $3,500  |

The entire payroll for the *Venus* was about $25,000, versus $5,000 for a Confederate ordnance vessel. As an added incentive, the owners of private blockade runners often allowed their officers to carry goods for themselves, which supplemented their income by thousands of dollars.

The combination of quality captains, crews, and ships with profit-minded businessmen, gave rise to a number of ventures both in the Confederacy and Great Britain. Those organizing in England had the advantage of direct access to a large and innovative shipbuilding community and sources of marketable goods. These factors gave the British firms a head start on their Southern counterparts, but they could not always guarantee success.[7]

Among the first, and least successful, of the British-based ventures was the Navigation Company of Liverpool. The firm despatched a total of six steamers to Nassau, where they were controlled by George Wigg. Wigg, an Englishman who had been a cotton merchant in New Orleans before the war, now found a lucrative business in managing blockade runners. However, even Wigg's expertise could not change the luck of blockade runners.

Ill fortune constantly hung over the vessels of the Navigation Company. Two were captured, three ran aground off the Southern coast and one, the *Iona*, was run down in the Clyde River while preparing for her transatlantic voyage. The most renowned vessel owned by the firm was the medium-sized, iron, screw merchantman *Georgiana*, though her history hardly merits fame.[8]

The *Georgiana* made an unlikely blockade runner. She was not very fast and a deep draft limited the vessel to main channels. Because of this, some Federal authorities suspected that she was destined for use as a privateer. While loading in Liverpool, the Union consul Thomas Dudley carefully investigated the vessel and reported her to be too frail for a warship. He felt her only purpose was to run the blockade.

The matter should have ended there, but when the *Georgiana* reached Nassau on March 2, 1863, she had two small guns mounted on deck. The cannons, taken from the ship's cargo, were of no use, and were little more than theatrics on the part of the *Georgiana*'s captain. But they did catch the attention of the highly excitable Union consul at Nassau, James Samuel Whitney, who claimed the *Georgiana* would be coverted to a privateer on her arrival in the South. Whitney did convince British authorities to investigate the *Georgiana* and, like Dudley, the British officials found nothing unusual.

With the *Georgiana* free from any controversy, George Wigg quickly prepared her for a run to the South. On March 15, she cleared Nassau and three days later approached Charleston, trying to enter the harbor via Maffitt's channel. Sighted by the Union blockaders, the *Georgiana* was chased aground off Long Island. Federal sailors boarded the stranded steamer and found her abandoned, scuttled, and hard aground. Unable to free their prize the sailors reluctantly set the wreck on fire.[9]

While the Navigation Company was losing its vessels, two more British firms, Alexander Collie and Company of Manchester and Edward Lawrence and Company of Liverpool, joined the trade. Collie, with the backing of numerous wealthy Englishmen, had entered the business in late 1862, and by February 1863 the first of his steamers were running the blockade. Results were so good that Collie was able to add two more ships before the year was out. These vessels were operated independently of the Crenshaw contract and were initially handled by George Wigg.[10]

Another major British blockade-running firm to become active in 1863 was the Anglo-Confederate Trading Company, a venture organized by members of Edward Lawrence and Company, a large Liverpool-based shipping concern. The group first tried to enter the trade during the summer of 1862, when, believing reports that any steamer could run the blockade, they purchased the old "second hand cattle boat," the *Despatch*. She was loaded with munitions and cloth and sent out to the Bahamas with Thomas Taylor as her super cargo. In July 1862 the vessel reached Nassau, where Taylor learned that she was too slow and heavily laden to run the blockade. Taylor then sold his cargo in Nassau and returned with the *Despatch* to England, where a steamer was being built by his backers specifically for running the blockade.[11]

The vessel under construction at Liverpool was the steel-hulled sidewheeler *Banshee*. The ship was built from the keel up as a blockade runner. She measured 220′ × 20′ × 12′, had a flat bottom, four water-tight compartments and was made out of steel plates one-third of an inch thick. Her draft was only 8 feet. In January 1863, the *Banshee* responded splendidly during her trials. On board were numerous ship-pers and merchants, including representatives from Fraser, Trenholm and Company.

In April 1863, the *Banshee* became the first steel vessel to cross the Atlantic, a feat accomplished with a great deal of luck. Her plates were too thin and badly fitted, causing the ship to leak. The *Banshee*'s engines were discovered to be too powerful for her frail frame, causing her ribs to buckle and rivets to crumble. Still, she managed to survive the voyage and arrived in Nassau on April 20, 1863.

For the next two weeks Taylor went about preparing the *Banshee* for its first run through the blockade. The masts were taken down to the lower sections, which were arranged as lookout stations. The entire vessel was painted a dull white, a color proven to be best for near invisibility at night. Taylor was fortunate in securing the services of an experienced crew, a fearless captain in the Englishman Jonathon Steele, and a knowledgeable Wilmington pilot in Tom Burroughs.[12]

On May 9, 1863, with Taylor on board, Steele took the *Banshee* out of Nassau and headed for Wilmington. The vessel never reached her prescribed speed of 13 knots, and instead made only 9, which was hardly enough to outrun a Union cruiser. Because of this, Taylor kept lookouts constantly posted and avoided any suspicious vessels. After a voyage of three days the *Banshee* came off the coast, just north of New Inlet. With Burroughs giving directions, Captain Steele maneuvered the *Banshee* along the shore and through the cordon of gunboats. At daybreak, just as the vessel passed Fort Fisher, she was sighted and fired on by warships. However, by now the *Banshee* was under the protection of Fort Fisher, whose guns kept off the Union vessels as the blockade runner slipped into the river. Taylor was elated by the run. He immedi-ately declared a celebration with champagne cocktails instead of whis-kies and sodas.[13]

Taylor did not keep the *Banshee* in Wilmington very long. Within five days he had discharged his cargo and taken on a load of tobacco and cotton. Under the steady hands of Burroughs and Steele, the vessel weaved her way through the blockade and back to Nassau. Profits from the round trip were extremely lucrative. For the inward voyage, Taylor had received £50 per ton for carrying Confederate war material, and he reported a profit on the outward cargo of at least £32,000. The run easily paid for the building of the *Banshee,* and every subsequent trip brought even greater returns to her owners.[14]

The English firms were sympathetic to the Southern cause, though there could be no doubt that their participation in blockade running came from a desire for profits. Southern firms also viewed blockade running as a money-making venture, but, they realized that their survival as businesses depended on a Confederate victory. For this reason, a strong streak of patriotism ran through their operation, one that, to some extent, would temper their hunger for profits.

One such firm was the Importing and Exporting Company of South Carolina. The backers of this company had been so encouraged by the success of their first steamer, the *Cecile,* that an additional sale of stock was authorized, and once $200,000 had been accumulated the company began new operations.

The firm was now run by a president and four directors. William C. Bee was elected the company's first president, while such people as William Ravenel, W. P. Magrath, Benjamin Mordecai, C. T. Mitchel, E. L. Kerrison, and Theodore Jervey served at different times as board members.

The company's operations differed little from its previous manner. Bee and Mitchel continued to run the business, taking orders from merchants and individuals for the importation of certain goods. Bee also kept up the practice of running in articles that the company sold at their public auction, the so-called Bee Sales. The outward cargoes consisted of cotton purchased for the company by Benjamin Mordecai and W. W. Garrand at Columbus and T. N. Johnson at Augusta, Georgia. The company continued its working relationship with the Confederate government, offering priority to inward Confederate freight.[15]

With their initial outlay, the firm purchased the former Southern Steamship Company vessel the *William G. Hewes* at Havana and the sidewheelers *Sirius* and *Orion* at West Hartlepool, England. The vessels were brought to Nassau and renamed the *Ella and Annie, Alice* and *Fannie,* respectively. In early April the *Ella and Annie,* under the command of James Carlin, made her first run into Charleston. Less than two months later she was joined by the two English sister ships. Together the three ships would make 52 trips through the blockade.

The ability of their vessels to slip in and out of the Confederacy made the company one of the war's most successful blockade-running businesses. While owned by the Importing and Exporting Company of South Carolina, the *Ella and Annie* accounted for 8 runs through the blockade. She could carry up to 1,300 bales of cotton, which when combined with her inward cargo, meant a profit of about $200,000 per round trip. The *Alice* and *Fannie*, which averaged 925 bales of cotton per trip brought a profit of over $100,000 per circuit. During its existence, the company paid out dividends of $9,000 Confederate and £120 per share.[16]

Besides the Importing and Exporting Company of South Carolina, another successful Charleston blockade-running firm was the Chicora Importing and Exporting Company of South Carolina. The president of the Chicora Company was the Charleston merchant Archibald Johnson, and among the company's backers were George W. Williams, a leading Charleston banker, and Theodore Wagner, one of Trenholm's partners in John Fraser and Company.

Though not incorporated until December 1863, the firm began operations in September 1862 when it purchased the steamer *Herald* from John Fraser and Company. Renamed *Antonica*, the vessel became so successful that, by early 1863, the Chicora Company was able to purchase the large English iron paddlewheel steamer *Havelock*. After her initial run into Charleston in February 1863, she was reregistered as the *General Beauregard*, and placed under the command of Louis Coxetter, who started the vessel on a long and highly profitable career.[17]

While the new Southern firms kept close watch on their profits they realized that their success depended upon a strong and eventually victorious Confederacy. To this end, they often opened their cargo holds to government supplies at reduced rates. Both the South Carolina and Chicora companies carried in such items as iron plates, small arms, acids, gunpowder, and submarine cable for use with underwater mines. Unlike the European blockade runners, these firms would often carry dangerous explosive materials. However, it should be noted that the companies did not lose money on these shipments.

Even though the new and reorganized Southern and European firms were very successful and added the element of competition to the trade, no blockade-running company could compare to John Fraser and Company. By 1863, the Charleston partners had exported over 18,000 bales of cotton, which sold for at least £900,000 ($2,160,000 in gold). With their profits, the firm purchased additional vessels, cotton, merchandise, and some six million dollars' worth of Confederate bonds. They also bought, chartered, and built cargo ships to carry supplies across the Atlantic.[18]

By the spring of 1863, John Fraser and Company was operating a number of vessels specifically chosen for blockade running. They provided the firm with high returns, and even though all of the steamers were lost or sold to rival firms by the end of the year, the company was able to use the profits to replace them with ships specially built for blockade running.[19]

One of the finest vessels ever used by Trenholm's companies was the steamer *Douglas*, which was renamed the *Margaret and Jessie*. The wooden sidewheeler had been built in 1855 by Robert Napier at Glasgow, Scotland, and was reputed to be the fastest vessel in English waters. In November 1862, she was purchased for £24,000 and converted into a blockade runner. Under the command of Captain William Wilson, the swift sidewheeler made five trips through the blockade in the first half of 1862, four to Charleston and one to Wilmington. On these trips, Captain Wilson had no difficulty eluding the blockaders, so, as he prepared to clear Charleston on the night of May 27, he had no reason to believe that this voyage would be any different.[20]

At midnight, the *Margaret and Jessie* moved out of the harbor and successfully passed through the line of blockaders. By daylight the ship was in open sea heading for Nassau. Captain Wilson did not push his vessel as she was low on fuel and her boilers were fouled. On the second day, lookouts spotted bearing down on them the Union warship *Rhode Island*. Wilson quickly put on all possible speed, even employing sails as he attempted to outrun the Union vessel.

The *Rhode Island* gained on the *Margaret and Jessie* and, as they neared the Bahamas, the warship began to fire on the fleeing vessel. At first, the shells fell short, but soon they found the range. One shell entered the ship and ripped through a boiler. Captain Wilson, fearing for the safety of his crew and passengers, beached the *Margaret and Jessie* off Eleuthera Island and ordered the vessel evacuated. The *Rhode Island*, seeing that the blockade runner had been hit, and in British waters, stopped its pursuit and stood off for some time before sending in a small boat. The sailors were under strict orders not to board the vessel, but merely to report on its condition and identity.

Meanwhile on shore, the crew and passengers of the *Margaret and Jessie* were surrounded by a gang of black wreckers who made their living by scavenging grounded vessels. When they realized that the

Figure 1. The *Calhoun* as a prewar packet running between New Orleans and Mobile. (*Sketch by Wendell P. Wass, from a private collection*)

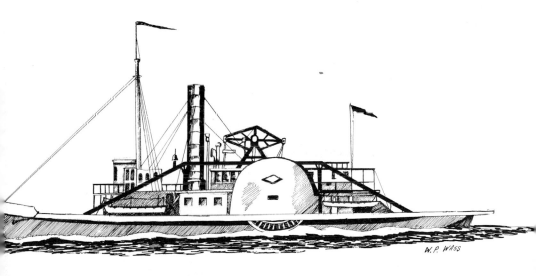

Figure 2. The *Calhoun* after her conversion to a blockade runner. (*Sketch by Wendell P. Wass, from a private collection*)

Figure 3. Josiah Gorgas, Chief of the Confederate Ordnance Bureau. It was his task to supply arms and ammunition to the Southern armies. (*Library of Congress*)

Figure 4. George A. Trenholm, Charleston businessman who came to control the war's two largest blockade-running companies. He resigned from these firms in July 1864 to become the Confederate Secretary of the Treasury. (*Courtesy of the Confederate Museum, Charleston*)

Figure 5. Thomas Lockwood, commander of blockade runners; his success was so great that he became known as the "Father of the Trade." He captained the *Theodora*, *Kate*, *Elizabeth* and the *Colonel Lamb*. (*Courtesy of the Confederate Museum, Charleston*)

Figure 6. Robert Lockwood, pilot and captain of blockade runners; he was captured while commander of the *Margaret and Jessie*. (*Courtesy of the Confederate Museum, Charleston*)

Figure 7. John Julius Guthrie, commander of the *Advance* between October 1863 and March 1864. (*Courtesy of the Confederate Naval Museum, Columbus, Georgia*)

Figure 8. Frank N. Bonneau, fearless commander of the *Ella and Annie*, when trapped by the Union gunboat *Niphon*, Bonneau tried to run down the Union warship. (*Courtesy of the Confederate Museum, Charleston*)

Figure 9. John Newland Maffitt, officer in the Confederate Navy; Maffitt's knowledge of the coast caused him to be assigned to a number of blockade runners. Though best known as the commander of the commerce raider *Florida*, he was also captain of the blockade runners *Theodora* and *Owl*. *(From a private collection)*

Figure 10. W. F. Adair, highly successful commander of the *Antonica*; he guided the vessel on seven trips through the blockade before being captured in December 1863. *(Courtesy of the Confederate Museum, Charleston)*

Figure 11. E. T. "Ned" Burriss, pilot of the *Wando (Let Her Rip)*. *(From a private collection)*

Figure 12. Alexander G. Swasey, captain of the early blockade runner *Ella Warley* from January 1862 until her capture on April 25, 1862. *(From a private collection)*

Figure 13. The *Aries,* an early blockade runner that employed hinged masts. She was captured on her third trip and converted into a U.S. Navy gunboat. (*U.S. Navy Photograph*)

Figure 14. The *Denbigh,* running out of Mobile Bay. The blockade runner made twenty-six trips through the blockade to Mobile and Galveston before running aground in Galveston Harbor in May 1865. She was the war's second most successful blockade runner. (*From a private collection*)

*Blockade Runner "Little Hattie."*

Figure 15. The *Little Hattie*, operated by the Importing and Exporting Company of Georgia, she made five round trips through the blockade between June 1864 and February 1865. (*Courtesy of the Maritime Museum of the Atlantic, Halifax, Canada, N–13641*)

Figure 16. The *Armstrong*, owned by Crenshaw and Company, she carried in vital supplies of meat to the Confederacy during the final months of 1864. (*Courtesy of the Maritime Museum of the Atlantic, Halifax, Canada, N–13642*)

Figure 17. The *Tallahassee*, onetime twin screw blockade runner *Atalanta*, at Halifax, Nova Scotia, August 18, 1864. She was purchased by the C.S. Navy and served as a privateer under the names *Tallahassee* and *Olustee*. She ended her career as a government-run blockade runner appropriately named *Chameleon*. (*Courtesy of the Maritime Museum of the Atlantic, Halifax, Canada, N–4959*)

Figure 18. The *Whisper*, built in 1864; she arrived in time only to make one trip through the blockade. (*From a private collection*)

Figure 19. The *Lizzie*, built in 1864; she was designed to operate in the shallow waters of the Gulf of Mexico. (*London Illustrated News*)

The "Fox."
Bound to Nassau from Liverpool. Put into Cork to fill up coals April 26th and sailed April 27th 1864. Arrived at Nassau May 23rd.

Figure 20. The *Fox*; the steel-hulled vessel made eight round trips to Charleston in 1864 before going to the Gulf and making one round trip to Galveston. (*U.S. Navy Photograph*)

Union warship was not going to interfere, the blacks raced out to the stranded ship in small boats and began throwing bales of cotton overboard, many of them, in order to guard their new possessions, rode the bobbing bales through the surf.

Word of the vessel's fate was sent to Nassau, but before Heyliger could arrive, the *Margaret and Jessie* was towed to Nassau by professional salvagers. Heyliger did gather up depositions to prove that the *Rhode Island* had violated British waters. He hoped to influence public opinion and possibly encourage the British naval squadron to sweep the patrolling Union warships away from the Bahamas. Heyliger's attempts to make the issue an international incident came to naught, as the Bahamian authorities ignored the event. Though angered at the British indifference, Heyliger had little time to reflect on the matter, as he soon learned that the salvagers of the *Margaret and Jessie* laid claim to the vessel by right of salvage, and only through his lobbying was the blockade runner returned to her original owners.[21]

The *Margaret and Jessie* was easily repaired and a new boiler installed, but John Fraser and Company decided it best to sell the steamer. In early June, the ship was purchased by the Importing and Exporting Company of South Carolina. Her name was retained, and she continued her successful career in the capable hands of Captain Robert Lockwood.[22]

By the fall of 1863, only the *Elizabeth*, under the command of Thomas Lockwood, remained in active use for John Fraser and Company. A few new vessels were on order in England, but for the most part, the company was moving away from operating blockade runners. Prioleau, viewing the trade from Liverpool, considered the day of sure profits from running vessels through the blockade to be over. Though he was unable to convince his Charleston partners to turn exclusively to the shipping of goods from England, he did gain a curtailment in the firm's outfitting of blockade runners. However, when needed, Prioleau did continue to assist the war effort by arranging special runs with steamers loaded with specific Confederate cargoes.[23]

By 1863, important Confederate contracts for specialized English manufactured goods were being completed and ready for shipment. These items, which included machinery for the making of small arms, molds for artillery shells, heavy artillery, and marine engines for warships were too valuable to be sent to Bermuda or Nassau and reshipped on blockade runners. If any parts were lost during transshipping it would take months for replacements to be made. Instead, the government decided to hire Fraser, Trenholm and Company to send the goods from England directly to the South.

The first of these ventures centered around the *Princess Royal*, an iron screw steamer chosen to run marine engines to the Confederacy. These engines were badly needed by the Southern Navy to outfit its ironclads. Until this time, engines for the Confederate ironclads were usually taken from prewar steamers and rarely were efficient enough to power the warships. The Tredegar Iron Works was capable of turning out engines, but was hard pressed with other war-related work to meet the navy's needs. A marine engine works was under construction at Columbus, Georgia but, until it was finished, the majority of the navy's engines would have to come from steamers or overseas.

On board the *Princess Royal* were placed two pairs of horizontal, direct-acting steam engines, complete with boilers and propellers rated at 180 and 110 nominal horsepower. They were apparently destined for ironclads being built at Charleston. Also on board were 600 barrels of gunpowder, six 70-pound Whitworth cannons, 930 steel-headed Whitworth shells, 35 tons of projectile steel, a machine for molding and planing shot and shell for the guns, 1,500 ounces of quinine, plus quantities of leather, shoes, wire, files, screws, cast iron, coffee, tea, clothing, and 25 cases of paper, a total value of £78,808.

In mid-January, after a long and difficult voyage, the *Princess Royal* arrived at St. George, Bermuda. Though only two years old and having a draft of eleven feet, the vessel was considered by the U.S. Bermuda consul to be too slow and heavily laden to run the blockade. However, her owners believed she could, and before the month ended she cleared for Charleston.

At 3:15 on the morning of January 29, 1863, with her captain sick in his cabin, the *Princess Royal* made her approach. As she neared the harbor, she was sighted by the schooner *G. W. Blunt*, which opened fire and signaled the rest of the squadron. This action alerted the steamer *Unadilla*, which soon forced the *Princess Royal* aground. Boarding parties were sent out, but before they reached the stranded vessel the captain, pilot, a number of her passengers and crew left the ship. Found on board the stranded vessel were a few British sailors and a machinist who had accompanied the vessel to instruct the Confederates in the operation of the Whitworth machinery. Using tow lines, Union warships freed the blockade runner and since the blockading squadron was short on sailors, the Federal commander hired the Englishmen to take the *Princess Royal* north to a prize court.[24]

Though the *Princess Royal* operation had ended in failure, the Confederate government and Fraser, Trenholm and Company again entered into a joint venture four months later. This time the cargo was to consist of two 12.75-inch Blakely rifled cannon, each weighing over 27 tons. The Blakelys had been purchased by Huse and were intended for coastal defense, especially against enemy ironclads. The cargo consisted, not only of the two rifled tubes, but two iron carriages, cranes for loading the guns, 150 solid shots, each weighing 650 pounds, and 50 shells weighing 450 pounds each. To ship the material, Fraser, Trenholm and Company decided to use the recently purchased *Gibraltar*, a vessel that was already well known to the Union Navy.[25]

The *Gibraltar* was the third name given to the screw packet *Havana*. She had originally been fitted out at New Orleans by Lieutenant Semmes as the cruiser *Sumter*. After escaping from New Orleans, the warship operated against Northern merchantmen for seven months, capturing eighteen vessels. On January 4, 1862, Semmes took his vessel into Cadiz, Spain, for badly needed repairs. However, the authorities refused to allow the ship to stay longer than two weeks, forcing Semmes to take the *Sumter* to Gibraltar, where she was effectively blockaded by Union warships.

With his vessel in need of an extensive overhaul, and trapped by a superior force, Semmes disbanded his crew and proceeded to England, where he was given command of the recently completed *Alabama*. After her armaments were removed the *Sumter* was sold to Fraser, Trenholm and Company. She was then taken to Liverpool and converted back to a merchantman. After renovation, Prioleau probably would have sold the vessel to a British concern. However, with the arrival of the Blakelys, he saw a way to regain some money and assist the Confederacy. Prioleau proposed to Huse that the Confederacy buy back the *Gibraltar* and use her to deliver the rifled cannons. Huse quickly agreed and then left England, leaving the entire affair in Prioleau's hands.

Because of her past, the *Gibraltar* came under close observation by Consul Thomas Dudley. At first Dudley thought she was being strengthened to return to duty as a commerce raider, but actually she was being readied to carry the mammoth Blakely guns. Since the cannons were too large to fit below decks, special harnesses were built to hold them upright in the cargo hatches, making it look as if the vessel had three smokestacks.

When Dudley realized that the *Gibraltar* was not being outfitted as a warship, he suspected that the guns were destined for the Confederate ironclad rams that were being completed at the Laird yards. Since it would be a violation of British law if the ironclads were armed in England, Dudley thought they would rendezvous with the *Gibraltar* for their armament in some isolated harbor, much like what had been done with the CSS *Florida*. Dudley tried to have the Liverpool port authorities stop the *Gibraltar* from clearing, but the vessel's papers were in order, and she was allowed to sail.[26]

The *Gibraltar* cleared on July 3, 1863, under the command of Captain E. C. Reid, and before the month was over she slipped into the Cape Fear River via New Inlet. The guns were immediately called for by General Beauregard at Charleston and, by the end of September, positions for the Blakelys were readied on the city's battery, where they remained for the rest of the war, never to fire a shot in anger.[27]

Such assistance to the war effort by private blockade-running companies was not uncommon, especially by the Charleston-based firms. However, as much as the Confederate officials appreciated this assistance, the private sector continued to hamper the overall ability of the government to use blockade running for its own advantage and to stabilize its economy. Nonmilitary articles carried in by private vessels were sold on the Southern market at extremely high prices, fueling inflation. The government did not attempt to control the type of goods coming in, and valuable cargo space was given over to such luxury items as liquors, carpets, furniture, and jewelry, which brought a high return in the South.

Besides vying for cargo space, private companies competed with the government for use of railroads, warehouses, pilots, and coal. In order to keep their operations away from the growing private sector, the Ordnance Bureau concentrated its efforts at Wilmington, leaving Charleston almost exclusively in the hands of private shippers. For a short time, this arrangement helped ease some of the problem, however, as the year 1863 continued, so would the problems between the government and the private shippers.

# Chapter Six

---

# Charleston and Wilmington: Gateways to the South

In the fall of 1863, Jefferson Davis made his first trip to Charleston since 1850, when he had attended the funeral of John C. Calhoun. This time Davis was in the port city to test the morale of the South Carolinians. Speaking from the portico of City Hall, he urged the citizens to sacrifice even more for the cause. He confidently predicted that Charlestonians would leave their city in ruins than allow the Federals any spoils of war. The inspired crowd picked up on this and shouted back at the president; "Ruins! Ruins!" It was an arrogant boast, nor did those present realize the truth of the spontaneous chant, not only with regard to Charleston, but to every city that served as a major blockade-running port.

Throughout the first two years of war, Charleston had suffered little. The mix of old established families with young aggressive merchants had served the port well. Using the conflict to their advantage, the profit-minded entrepreneurs imported goods that were eagerly purchased by the wealthy citizens. These patrons of blockade running purchased china, liquors, furniture, carpets, cigars, and of course Charleston's favorite wine, Madeira.

By early 1863 the war had little affect on those with money. For a price, any luxury could be brought through the blockade, even if it meant that certain war material was left behind in Nassau or Bermuda. However, many in the city did not have the cash or credit to afford even a meager life-style. These less affluent people were hit hardest by

121

spiraling inflation. The first to feel the pinch were the lower classes, but in time the middle class also found it difficult to keep up with the cost of living. Those who could fled inland, where food was somewhat more available, but many could not leave. Those left behind were often families headed by widows or women whose husbands were serving in the armies. Unable to meet the expenses of the port cities, they were forced to survive on charity, stealing, and prostitution.

Cities of great contrast resulted; seacoast towns contained wealthy reminders of the Old South, young entrepreneurs, and sailors who lived the fast life and often spoke with an English accent; the military, guarding the vital lifelines to Europe; and those who could not afford to leave, who lived on the benevolence of the rich, or off the passion of the foreigners and sailors.

Charleston was large enough that the usual wartime activities infesting a seaport did not readily influence day-to-day activities. The shippers were restricted to the Cooper River side of the peninsula where the city's main docks and warehouses were located. Here the companies carried out their business, and, for the first two years of the war, the lifeblood of the Confederacy flowed.

The city served as the home port for the majority of the South's blockade-running companies. The cry of auctioneers was a familiar sound along the wharves as the firms vied for the remaining Southern wealth. The docks were crowded with sleek blockade runners, which shared space with army transports and the ungainly ironclads. At one point the river was so congested that the ironclad *Chicora* rammed the blockade runner *Alice* as the latter was pulling away from the dock. The collision ripped a gash beneath the *Alice*'s waterline, flooding her rear compartment. The heavily loaded blockade runner rushed back to the pier, where her cotton bales were removed and the hole brought above the waterline.

Even so, accidents like that were few and, more important, escapes numerous. For the first years of the war, Charleston so dominated the blockade-running trade that Thomas Dudley wrote from Liverpool claiming that its capture would be regarded as the deathblow to the rebellion, and do more to discourage those who were aiding the South with supplies and money than any other event. The authorities in Washington needed little prodding to organize an expedition against Charleston. Both the Army and Navy, embarrassed over their earlier failures to take the city, were eager to redeem themselves and, by May

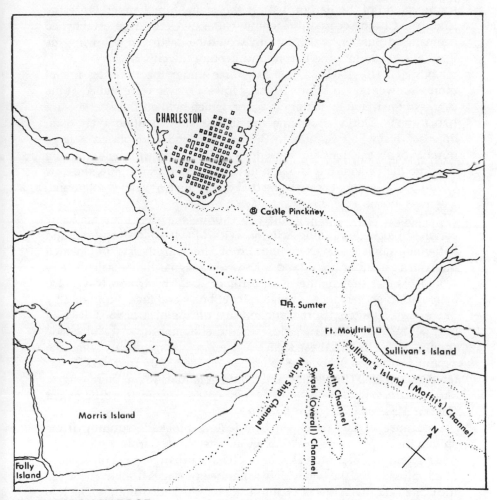

**CHARLESTON HARBOR**

not to scale

1863, meetings were underway to formulate a joint attack. The plans called for a quick seizure of Morris Island, a barrier island located on the southern end of the harbor just off the main ship channel. Once the island had been secured, breaching batteries were to be established against Fort Sumter, which in turn would be destroyed, allowing the ironclads to run into the harbor and capture the city.[1]

On July 10, 1863, an infantry force under the covering fire of monitors swept on to Morris Island. However, they were stalled at the center of the island by Battery Wagner, which held off the attackers for two months. During this time the Confederates shifted their main defenses from Fort Sumter to Sullivan's Island and placed a large number of obstructions and torpedoes in the entrance of the harbor. By the time the Federal forces had pounded Sumter into rubble, the new Confederate works were so strong that the Union Navy never attempted a serious attack.

Though the campaign failed to capture the city, it dramatically curtailed blockade-running activity. With Morris Island captured and batteries established on Cummings Point, Union artillerists could watch Sullivan's Island at night, and whenever a signal light flashed, they would blanket the channel with artillery fire. The Union Navy also increased its surveillance. At night picket boats and tugs, supported by one or two monitors, were stationed just off the obstructions, leaving only a small, shallow area close to the shoreline open to blockade runners. The effect of these tactics was telling. From July 10, when the assault first began, through September 18, 1863, only four vessels entered and cleared Charleston, and from September 18 on, there was no blockade-running activity until March 4, 1864, when the dredgeboat *General Moultrie* cleared for Nassau.[2]

Because of the attack on Charleston, blockade-running firms shifted their operations to Wilmington. The North Carolina port could not compare to Charleston as a commercial or urban center, but, because of its railroads and the two widely separated passages from the ocean to the Cape Fear River, it was a natural site for blockade running. The two entrances and escape routes caused the Union Navy to split its block-aders into two squadrons that could not support each other. This division of strength made it easier for runners to enter the river. In time, Wilmington became the most important blockade-running port of the Confederacy, a distinction the city found as a mixed blessing.

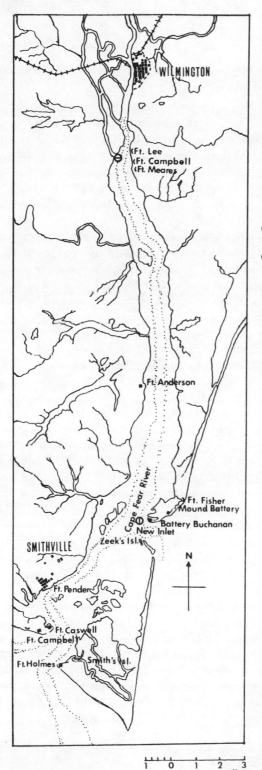

**WILMINGTON and the CAPE FEAR RIVER**

Θ Obstructions

Ⓘ Wreck of the RALEIGH

Wilmington discovered the perils of blockade running early in the war while the city was still serving as a secondary port. During the late summer of 1862 the sidewheeler *Kate* arrived at the city docks heavily laden with supplies from Nassau. Since the *Kate* was among the first ships to use the city, her arrival was met with great excitement, especially by the merchants, who envisioned large profits from selling her cargo. However, besides her goods, the *Kate* off-loaded the deadly scourge of yellow fever.

Unknown to the townspeople, members of the *Kate*'s crew were infected with the disease, which was soon transmitted by mosquitos to area residents. The first to contract the disease was Lewis Swarzman, a German emigrant who sold coal and wood to steamers. His office was near the wharf used by the *Kate*, and the blockade runner had been one of his clients.

His death on September 9 caused little concern among the populace as it was thought to be jaundice, but over the next few days physicians began reporting a number of fevers. Still, no one seriously thought it could be yellow fever. Wilmington was just too far north for the disease to take hold.

The citizens of the town continued to ignore the warning signs for another week. The local paper admitted that there had been a few cases, but assured their readers that an epidemic was impossible. However, just for precaution, a number of citizens began burning rosin in an attempt to stop further spread of the presumably air-transmitted disease. The precautions were in vain and by mid-September yellow fever was raging throughout the city.

The disease struck all classes. Civilian and military, black and white, child and adult became infected. All activity ceased save that of the doctor, minister, and undertaker. The paper closed down, as did most businesses. The military stopped its operations at the armory and removed its men from the city. People tried to flee, but were turned back by other North Carolina communities, forcing the population to ride out the sickness in Wilmington.

Certain brave individuals continued to bring food to the city while others carried lumber—to build coffins. Aid came from other coastal communities, especially Charleston, which despatched both military and civilian doctors and nurses. The medical assistance helped ease the suffering but, since no one knew the cause, much less the cure for yellow fever, there was little anyone could do to arrest the disease.

In the midst of the epidemic the *Kate* returned with another cargo. Port authorities, fearing an attack on the ship and her crew by the populace, wisely kept her presence a secret. The *Kate* remained below the city and was off-loaded by lighters.

Even if the citizens had known of the *Kate*'s presence, they were in no position to do anything. By early October there were 395 new cases and 40 deaths. The temperatures continued to hover around 80 degrees, unseasonably hot, even for Wilmington. The city was a ghost town with the only outside activity being funerals, and then only when coffins were available.

In October, the temperatures began to moderate, but rather than easing the situation, the cooler temperatures made those already sick even worse. People were now dying, not only from yellow fever, but also pneumonia.

However, while the cold weather increased the sufferings of the ill, it did, eventually, end the spread of new cases. By early November the situation brightened, and work notices were posted, calling people to return to their jobs. On November 11, the Wilmington *Daily News* returned to publication, announcing that "Our streets begin to look lively once more; people are coming back in and seem glad to get back." Also on the eleventh, the *Kate* successfully ran into Old Inlet and began to move upstream; but before venturing too far, the frail steamer ran onto a snag and sank.

The loss of the *Kate* was hardly noticed in Wilmington, and those who knew probably did not regret her sinking. The disease carried to Wilmington by the blockade runner had caused over 1,500 cases of yellow fever, killing over 700 in the town and another 100 in the countryside—over 15 percent of the town's population. The epidemic left such an impression that the civil authorities vowed it would not happen again.[3]

Almost as soon as the ravages of the yellow fever had subsided, the first blockade runners of the Ordnance Bureau began arriving at the North Carolina port. These vessels had been directed to Wilmington by Gorgas, who was attracted to the port because of its lack of traffic. With almost exclusive use of the town's dock facilities and railroads, Gorgas's agents were able to keep up a productive trade that in four months accounted for 60,000 modern rifles, hundreds of thousands of cartridges and percussion caps, immense quantities of saltpeter, and other needed materials.

From Wilmington, the government supplies were shipped via rail-roads to factories and distribution points. Saltpeter went to the powder mill in Augusta. Equipment ready for immediate use was divided be-tween the War Department depots in Richmond and Augusta. From these points it was distributed to the eastern and western armies.[4]

The presence of the Ordnance Bureau's vessels did little to disturb the seaport. The vessels were efficiently run, and their crews kept under tight supervision. They were vital to the well-being of the armies, and everything connected with them was well organized.

Gorgas and his coworkers did not keep Wilmington to themselves for long. Slowly, as private concerns began to realize the advantages of the dual-entrance port, blockade running increased. By June 1863, the weekly number of steamers coming into Wilmington equaled that of Charleston, and then, when the South Carolina port came under attack, Wilmington inherited the entire East Coast trade. With the increased traffic Wilmington suffered under new problems which many consid-ered as ruinous to the onetime sleepy river town as the yellow fever plague.

Like other ports, Wilmington gained little from the supplies being unloaded at its wharves; most went inland. As a result, goods grew scarce, and prices went up. Speculation became rampant, adding to the spiraling costs of goods. The railroads became dominated by private shippers, who not only outbid the government agents for space, but also bought up inward rail space for cotton, which kept out shipments of food and other necessities.

Wilmington also suffered under the accompanying invasion of personnel involved in wartime shipping, many of which the city's prewar population found distasteful and disruptive. Before the war Wilmington had prided itself on its attempts to bring civilization to an otherwise out-of-the-way, undistinguished seaport. Besides the classic façades of their churches and impressive Southern homes, the city boasted a town hall that possessed a large theater run by a local Thalian Association. Throughout the war the actors managed to keep up their productions, but this attempt at culture was one of the few holdouts as Wilmington's life-style collapsed under the seamier aspects of the trade.

In time, Wilmington became overrun with the crews of private blockade runners. Unlike the Confederate sailors, these civilians had no

military regulations governing their actions. They were found throughout the city with large amounts of money to spend on whatever enter-
tainment they wanted, and in a short time all types of pleasures were
available in the city.

Those with the most money, both in gold and Confederate currency, were the young British captains. These men, with their well-cut
clothes and foreign accents, looked out of place in Wilmington, where
they more resembled young cadets than sea captains, but in this case,
looks were deceiving. They took to their positions with great zeal.
Successful runs lined their pockets with currency, which they freely
spent. A few residents compared the Englishmen to exuberant college
students, who were part of a tightly bound fraternity, but many considered them to be bluff, coarse, and vulgar.

Their companies set up boarding houses in Wilmington where the
men lived a life of constant parties and pleasure, entertaining themselves by hiring musicians and handsome quadroon women. One such
establishment, housing the employees of Collie and Company, soon
gained a reputation of sin and degradation. The constant parties and
visitation of prostitutes made it the scandal of the town. As such activity
increased, many towns people left, and in time the port became one
large cantonment for the crews of the blockade runners, speculators, and
camp followers. As one visitor noted, Wilmington was the "meanest"
place in the Confederacy.[5]

The presence of these sailors and their consorts was a necessary
evil. The sailors were needed to man the blockade runners, which
brought the supplies so vital to the existence of the Confederacy. After
June 1863, the steamers coming into Wilmington represented the single
most important element in the Confederate supply system.

Guarding this vital gateway was an elaborate system of fortifica-
tion, which the Confederates continually improved and extended. The
commander of Wilmington's defenses was Brigadier General Henry
Chase Whiting. By reputation and experience, a better officer would
have been hard to find. His credentials as an engineer were impeccable.
Whiting had graduated first in the West Point class of 1845, with the
highest marks ever registered by a cadet. Immediately assigned to the
Corps of Engineers, Whiting spent the next fifteen years working on
masonry fortifications on the Atlantic, Gulf, and Pacific coasts.

On the secession of the lower South, Whiting followed his native state of Mississippi into the service of the Confederacy. Given a commission, he went to Charleston to assist in the construction of fortifications against Fort Sumter. Later, he served at the first battle of Bull Run, commanded a division at Fair Oaks, and served under Stonewall Jackson during the Seven Days' Battle. Though he distinguished himself in Virginia, he never received a promotion, an oversight for which Whiting held Jefferson Davis personally responsible.

In November 1862, Whiting accepted a transfer to Wilmington, where his engineering skill was badly needed. A brusque and demanding officer, he nevertheless inspired great loyalty in his troops, who affectionately referred to the handsome and elegant officer as "Uncle Billy." However, he was not as well loved by the townspeople and those involved in blockade running, whom he treated with a heavy hand. Whiting was also fond of drink, and rumors of heavy drinking had followed him from Virginia; but it rarely interfered with his work, and in time Wilmington became one of the best-defended ports in the world.

The fortifications commanded by Whiting had, by 1863, grown into extensive lines of batteries that, not only kept the Union fleet from entering the river, but also gave blockade runners valuable cover fire. The works at Old Inlet were centered around Fort Caswell, an old-style masonry fort that had been converted into an earthwork. Stretching down the coast, to the west of Caswell were massive earthworks guarding the approaches to the inlet. Across the channel on Smith's Island was Fort Holmes, a smaller earthwork whose guns assisted in forming a cross fire over Old Inlet.

Fort Fisher and Battery Buchanan guarded New Inlet. Located on the tip of Federal Point, Buchanan's four heavy guns swept the mouth of the inlet, while a mile to the north Fort Fisher protected the main approach route to New Inlet. Most vessels coming into New Inlet would steam far to the north, then turn back and sail south along the coast. Once through the blockading squadron, the ships would come under the protection of Fisher, whose guns kept the Union warships away from the shore. From this point on, only a lucky, long-range shot could stop the blockade runner, and even then, a disabled vessel was easily cared for as no Union gunboat would dare risk Fort Fisher's firepower.[6]

The commander of Fort Fisher was the active and industrious Colonel William Lamb, who proudly proclaimed after the war that he had built a work capable of withstanding "the heaviest fire of any guns in the American Navy." A journalist by profession, Lamb had arrived in Wilmington in September 1861. His work on defenses near the city so impressed his superiors that on July 4, 1862, he was assigned to command the defenses on Federal Point. There he found a collection of scattered earthworks hardly capable of withstanding an attack, but in a year's time he turned them into Fort Fisher, the largest earthwork of the war.[7]

Never satisfied with his work, Lamb constantly strove to improve the defensive capabilities of Fisher. He was unable to obtain the Blakely cannons, but he did gain the use of numerous British rifles and the highly effective Confederate-made Brooke rifles. To assist any stranded blockade runners north of the Fort, Lamb organized a flying battery that included Whitworth field pieces. The British-made breech-loading Whitworths could accurately fire a solid shot up to four miles, which easily kept off the light Union gunboats.

For his tireless efforts Lamb received favors and gifts from the owners and commanders of blockade runners. Many of the "presents" were military supplies, including pieces of artillery. Lamb and his wife also entertained captains of blockade runners at their cottage inside Fort Fisher. At these gatherings, over a social glass, Lamb would often convince his guests to bring needed equipment that otherwise would be held up at Nassau.[8]

While Lamb improved the defenses on Federal Point, Whiting worked to control affairs about the city. In September 1863 he issued eleven regulations that dealt directly with blockade running. Restrictions were placed on all passengers leaving the South, and operators were required to produce a complete crew and cargo list before clearing. A curfew was also placed on all sailors, with only their officers being allowed in the city after 9:00 P.M.[9]

Additional regulations were added by the city authorities to control yellow fever. When the season for the disease returned in 1863, all vessels arriving at the port underwent a mandatory two-week quarantine. The policy elicited a strong reaction from Confederate officials because it impaired the flow of supplies. A compromise was worked out that allowed ships from ports with no fever to forego the quarantine, while the others were unloaded onto Army-operated lighters. Once this was done the ships were cleaned, ventilated, and whitewashed. The precautions were effective; Wilmington managed to escape a second yellow fever epidemic.[10]

Even though Confederate-owned vessels sailed from Bermuda to Wilmington, Nassau still remained the number one jumping off point for blockade runners. During 1863, some 164 steamers cleared Nassau for the South whereas only 53 departed Bermuda. Private companies remained reluctant to switch their base of operations to the more distant Bermuda unless heavily compensated by Heyliger, something the Confederate agent refused to do.

Instead, Heyliger continued to purchase cargo space on steamers coming out of Nassau. This practice forced the Confederacy to divide their incoming munitions between the two ports. This, coupled with the private goods arriving at Nassau from Europe, made the port one of the busiest in the world. Not only were supplies flowing in from across the ocean, but also a large number of New York shippers were sending nonmilitary supplies that eventually found their way to the Confederacy. Northern officials attempted to stop this trade by forcing shippers trading in Nassau to put up a bond that would be forfeited if their cargoes were found going on blockade runners. However, since the goods were sold to middlemen or merchants who warehoused the items, they were mixed with other supplies, making it nearly impossible to prove their destination.[11]

Because of the amount of activity in the Bahamas, the Union Navy kept a flying squadron constantly in motion off the islands searching for blockade runners and cargo vessels whose papers were not in order. The harassment of incoming vessels did little to stop the trade. Most blockade runners were able to outrun the larger and slower warships, while the merchant vessels were well prepared for any searches. However, on occasion stopping an incoming vessel would result in a prize.

One such case centered around the British bark *Springbok*, which was stopped on February 3, 1863, by the warship *Sonoma* some 150-200 miles east of Nassau. On boarding the vessel, the Union sailors found the *Springbok* to be under charter by Thomas Sterling Begbie and carrying a cargo owned by S. Isaac, Campbell and Company. The cargo was consigned for delivery in Nassau, but the vessel carried no cargo manifest, so the commander of the *Sonoma* seized the *Springbok* and sent her north to a prize court.

On inspection of the *Springbok*'s hold, it was discovered that among her cargo were articles obviously destined for the Confederacy. These included 45,000 naval buttons and 150,000 army buttons, all marked with Confederate insignias, seven bales of army cloth, and 20 bales of

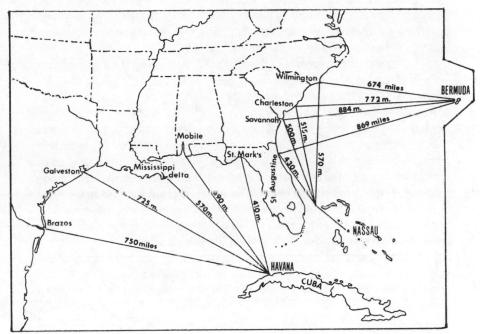

**CONFEDERATE PORTS**
DISTANCES TO HAVANA, NASSAU & BERMUDA

not to scale

Because of the Union attacks against the coast, by 1863 steam blockade runners were limited to using the ports of Wilmington, Charleston, Mobile, and Galveston, with a small trade carried on at St. Marks. For the most part, vessels coming out of Bermuda ran to Wilmington, while steamers from Nassau employed both Wilmington and Charleston. The majority of supplies landed at Charleston and Wilmington were shipped by rail to either Augusta, the main depot for the Western armies, or Richmond, the Eastern depot. Goods coming to Mobile were usually sent by rail to Augusta or via steamship to Selma. Imports at Galveston were sent to Houston by rail and steamship.

gray cloth. The court upheld the seizure and condemned the *Springbok*. This, coupled with the strong naval presence off the Bahamas, served notice to all involved in blockade running that the Federal Navy was doing all that it could to curtail the trade.[12]

The harrassing activities of the Union Navy outraged Heyliger, who now feared that the enemy would soon be taking all ships that attempted to reach Nassau, including the all-important colliers. He, therefore, made numerous complaints to the British authorities, but received no satisfaction. He wrote Judah Benjamin in early April 1863: "Such is the condition of things to which we are exposed without apparently a remedy. It is certainly not to be sought for in the spoiled indifference of the Government of Great Britain." Nor did Heyliger reserve his complaints for only the British. He also commented that St. Thomas, in the Virgin Islands, which was being used as a coaling base for Union vessels, was "simply a Yankee port," and that "Danish neutrality is another word for downright hostility" to the Confederacy.[13]

Much of Heyliger's anger probably came from the frustration of his position; even though there were now more vessels running the blockade than ever before, the needs of the Confederacy were threatening to outstrip the ability of the blockade runners to deliver the necessary supplies. In mid-July, Heyliger received news of the South's defeats at Vicksburg and Gettysburg. This, coupled with the material-consuming siege of Charleston, increased the demand for supplies. Even with the line of ordnance vessels and the establishment of a depot in Bermuda, Heyliger still had to purchase goods in Nassau, then buy as much private stowage space as possible to deliver the War Department's supplies. From the middle of July until the end of August, he contracted for space on at least nineteen steamers and sent into Wilmington large quantities of tin, lead, percussion caps, and rifles, all needed to supplement the munitions being shipped by Major Walker from Bermuda.[14]

Confederate operations at St. George, Bermuda, were well under way by the summer of 1863. Under the direction of Walker, Stansbury, and Bourne, the Ordnance Bureau vessels, by August 30, had made twenty-one runs into Wilmington carrying immense amounts of military equipment. Walker, however, like Heyliger, found himself forced to hire space on a private vessels to assist in the delivery of munitions. Among the vessels employed by Walker were Taylor's *Banshee*, and the North Carolina-owned *Advance*.

The problem of maintaining a constant flow of supplies from Bermuda resulted, not only from a lack of ships, but from general problems with the port's facilities. Even though Bourne had assured his clients that St. George would be an excellent harbor, he had not reckoned with the size of the operations and the number of vessels that soon came to the port. It was difficult to keep a supply of coal on hand, and Stansbury was constantly worried that he would not have enough fuel for the government vessels. The turn-around time in St. George was longer than at Nassau, and sometimes a vessel would lose "a moon." If goods for a blockade runner were in different warehouses the ship had to transfer wharves to be loaded. Only vessels drawing twelve feet could reach the docks; the rest had to be loaded or unloaded in the harbor by lighters. There were only four customs officials at the port and, since one had to be present at all transfers of cargoes, valuable time was often wasted waiting for one to appear.

Stansbury also complained that there was no room to inspect munitions as they arrived from Europe, and he feared he was wasting valuable space with useless or damaged goods. The Confederate authorities were well aware of the difficulties faced by their agents and, though they could do nothing about the facilities in St. George or sweep away the Union vessels that cruised off the Bahamas, they did attempt to add to the number of vessels run by the Ordnance Bureau, some even coming from the North.[15]

One of the more curious vessels to become a Confederate blockade runner was the paddlewheel steamer *Ella*. What made this little steamer unique was that she had been built in Brooklyn, New York, with the obvious intention of being used to run the blockade. In July 1863, her owner, Werner Foss, brought the *Ella* to Bermuda, where he offered her to the Confederacy. Bayne forwarded the proposition onto Seddon, who approved the acquisition of the ship and, by the first of November, the *Ella* joined the Confederate service.[16]

Another vessel put to use by the Confederacy was the *Ella and Annie*. In August 1863, the swift vessel was chartered from the Importing and Exporting Company of South Carolina to run badly needed munitions to the Trans-Mississippi Department. The *Ella and Annie* retained her civilian crew and her commander, Captain Frank N. Bonneau.

In August, Bonneau brought the steamer to Bermuda, where Stansbury loaded her with arms and munitions. By early September she was ready to sail, but Bonneau was no where to be found. Word eventually reached Stansbury that the captain was ill, but the Confederate agent knew full well that Bonneau was in Hamilton with a woman that had accompanied him from Nassau. Finally on September 9, Stansbury got Bonneau away from the "magnet which distracted him from his duty," and put the *Ella and Annie* out to sea. However, once out of Bermuda waters, the blockade runner was sighted by a Union cruiser and chased back to port. Two days later Bonneau again headed the *Ella and Annie* out of St. George, but this time the vessel was caught in a severe gale that tore off both her paddle boxes. Somehow Bonneau managed to return to Hamilton, where she underwent repairs for over a month.[17]

The difficulties of the *Ella and Annie* may well have been a forewarning to the Confederacy. Until the late summer of 1863, their blockade runners enjoyed an incredible rate of success. However, in mid-August, just as the South was beginning to replace the supplies lost at Vicksburg and Gettysburg, their luck began to run out.

Among the first vessels lost were those operated under the Crenshaw and Collie contract. By mid-June 1863 both the *Hebe* and the *Venus* were running in needed quartermaster and commissary supplies. In Wilmington, James Crenshaw met the steamers and handled all necessary wharfage duties. While doing so, the abrasive Crenshaw gained the hostility of many of the town's remaining citizens, among them Mary Ann Buie, the leading sponsor for the city's relief organizations. Miss Buie received the majority of her subscriptions from the operators and officers of blockade runners. Most were quite generous, but Crenshaw was not, and Miss Buie publicly stated that she hoped that Crenshaw's next vessel would be lost.[18]

Up to this time, Crenshaw's ships had enjoyed complete success in running the blockade, but, with Miss Buie's curse, their fortunes changed. The very next Crenshaw vessel that headed for Wilmington, the *Hebe*, was chased ashore and destroyed off New Inlet. Still, Crenshaw ignored Miss Buie and her relief fund, so again, she prayed for the destruction of his next steamer. Three days after the demise of the *Hebe*, the large sidewheeler *Venus* was driven aground and broken up.

Besides incurring the wrath of Miss Buie, the Crenshaw brothers also managed to lose the confidence of their British partner. As Collie wrote Mason after the loss of the *Hebe* and *Venus*:

I regret very much to say that I fear the Crenshaw contract will not work out. The hitch is owing entirely to a nasty *jealous* spirit which is not credible to those who indulge in it. It is *supposed* that my people in Bermuda & Wilmington do what they can to injure the Crenshaw steamers—as if *my own* clerks would have any interest in injuring my own property. I regret that I did not claim control over these steamers, as the management which is entirely in Crenshaw's hands in Wilmington has been far from good: and I do not hesitate to affirm that the *Venus* had been lost solely through this.

Collie went on to report that he would continue his partnership with the Crenshaw brothers only in the operation of the *Dee, Ceres,* and *Vesta.* He refused to build any new vessels for the contract, though he did offer to provide the Confederacy steamers from his other company.[19]

Despite these setbacks, the Crenshaws continued their operation. The *Dee* made three successful round trips to Wilmington in late 1863. She was later joined by the *Ceres* and *Vesta.* However, Miss Buie's anathema still clung like destiny to Colonel Crenshaw. On December 6, 1863, the *Ceres,* on her first attempt to reach Wilmington, ran aground off Old Inlet and was captured. A month later the *Vesta,* also on her maiden voyage, ran ashore and was set afire by her crew. The *Dee* did not survive much longer; on February 6, 1864, the last of Crenshaw and Collie vessels was lost off Masonboro Inlet, thus ending the partnership and the contract with the Confederacy.[20]

Besides the quick demise of the Crenshaw and Collie steamer line, the War Department also suffered a series of losses to their own vessels and to private ships on which they usually purchased cargo space. These losses were due to a combination of bad luck, poor seamanship, and the fact that the Union blockaders off Wilmington were adopting new tactics and adding faster vessels to intercept the blockade runners.

For the first part of 1863, the vessels of the Federal North Atlantic Blockading Squadron were too few in number to keep a tight watch on the entrances to the Cape Fear River. From January through July 1863, only seven steamers had been captured out of the nearly one hundred that attempted to clear or enter the port. However, beginning in the late summer, because of the addition of more and faster vessels, the blockaders were able to increase their vigilance, not only directly off the inlets, but also along the coastline north and south of the entrances. The results were soon felt by the blockade runners.[21]

Among the first vessels to be lost by the Confederacy was the sidewheeler *Eugenie*. In early September 1862, under the command of Lieutenant Joseph Fry, the steamer eluded Union warships, but as she passed Fort Fisher, the *Eugenie* slammed into a sandbar. The guns of the fort protected the vessel until she was brought into the river. The *Eugenie*'s iron hull was mangled, and even though makeshift repairs allowed her to escape to Nassau three months later, her days as a blockade runner were over.[22]

The next vessel lost to the Confederacy was the *Phantom*. On the morning of September 23, Captain S. G. Porter guided the screw blockade runner toward New Inlet and through the ring of blockaders. However, at daylight Porter sighted the powerful Union warship *Connecticut* bearing down on him. Realizing he was being overhauled, Porter turned the *Phantom* back toward the shoreline, where he beached his vessel, set her afire, and fled to the mainland.[23]

Three days after the *Phantom* was destroyed, the *Elizabeth*, trying to make Old Inlet, ran ashore off Lockwood Folly Inlet. Finding her hard aground and surrounded by blockaders, Captain Thomas Lockwood burned his ship. The removal from service of these vessels cut heavily into the available Confederate cargo space, and kept needed supplies in the islands.[24]

From the destruction of the *Elizabeth* in late September through October the Confederacy had a brief respite in the loss of vessels. During this period important ordnance supplies needed to restock the depleted Confederate armies arrived at Wilmington on such blockade runners as the *Antonica, Banshee, General Beauregard, Hansa, Alice,* and *Fannie*. However, after October, the South was hit with devastating losses.

On October 13, 1863, the *Margaret and Jessie* cleared Nassau for another run to Wilmington. Since her encounter with the *Rhode Island*, the fast blockade runner had made four more round trips to the Confederacy, all under the command of Captain Robert Lockwood. Because of her high success rate there was little reason to believe that this trip would be any different. Four days out from the Bahamas, Lockwood guided the *Margaret and Jessie* toward New Inlet, but before he could reach the safety of Fort Fisher the blockade runner was sighted by the gunboats *Niphon* and *Howquah*, which immediately moved to capture her.

Lockwood, seeing his path cut off, turned his craft out to sea. All night he ran the vessel from the Union ships, losing the *Howquah* though not the *Niphon*. At daybreak the blockade runner was sighted by the gunboats *Keystone State* and *Nansemond* and the Army transport *Fulton*. All three joined the pursuit and by 11:30 A.M. the *Nansemond* was within cannon range and began firing on the fleeing vessel. Although rough seas soon forced the *Nansemond* to slow her speed, the larger *Fulton* cut through the waves and forced the *Margaret and Jessie* to surrender. She was taken north, condemned, purchased by the Union Navy, and converted to the gunboat *Gettysburg*.[25]

On the day that the *Margaret and Jessie* was captured, three other renowned blockade runners were preparing to clear St. George harbor. They were the *Ella and Annie*, *Cornubia*, and *Robert E. Lee*. These three vessels had accounted for forty-one runs through the blockade and were responsible for carrying in vast quantities of munitions. The *Cornubia* was the only one of the trio that had been active in October. The *Ella and Annie* had been undergoing repairs, while the *Robert E. Lee* had undertaken a clandestine mission to Halifax, Canada.[26]

The secret project separated a successful team. Under the command of Lieutenant Wilkinson, the *Robert E. Lee* had made thirteen trips through the blockade. Because of his success and the resulting fame, Wilkinson was chosen to take part in an attempt to free Confederate prisoners held at Johnson Island, Ohio, in Lake Erie. Twenty-six officers were to run out of Wilmington on the *Robert E. Lee* along with a full cargo of cotton. At Halifax the cotton would be sold, with the proceeds going to finance the expedition.

On October 10, 1863, the *Robert E. Lee* cleared Wilmington. Once in the open sea, Wilkinson ran up the American flag and headed for Halifax. Numerous vessels were sighted, but none challenged the blockade runner. Wilkinson left the ship at Halifax, turning her over to John Knox.

In late October, Knox brought the ship back to Bermuda, where he took on a cargo of munitions. On November 5, in company with the *Ella and Annie* she cleared St. George. A few hours later the *Cornubia* followed her consorts out of the harbor.[27]

Even though the *Cornubia* had left five hours behind the other vessels, she was the first to reach the Southern coast. About midnight, November 7, Lieutenant Gayle guided her toward New Inlet, steaming from the north along the coastline. Near Masonboro Inlet the *Cornubia* was sighted by the *James Adger*, which sent up a signal rocket and gave chase. The blockader *Niphon*, attracted by the rocket, stood in along the shoreline. Soon the *Cornubia* came into sight and Gayle, seeing he was trapped, ran the vessel aground. The two Union gunboats quickly moved in and captured Gayle and his crew before they could escape. The *Cornubia* was undamaged and, while the *Niphon* shelled the beach to keep off Confederate pickets, the *James Adger* attached a hawser to the stranded blockade runner and pulled her out to sea.[28]

The following morning, about 6:00 A.M. the *James Adger*, back at her post after putting a prize crew on board the *Cornubia*, sighted a steamer north of Fort Fisher near Bogue Inlet. The gunboat gave chase and in less than one hour came within range and opened fire on the blockade runner. At 7:30, the unidentified vessel, which later proved to be the *Robert E. Lee*, hove to and surrendered.[29]

While the *James Adger* was pursuing the *Robert E. Lee*, the *Ella and Annie* began her run toward New Inlet. Off Masonboro Inlet, Captain Bonneau sighted the Union gunboat *Niphon* standing between him and Fort Fisher. Unlike the other commanders, Bonneau refused to surrender or ground his vessel, and challenged the *Niphon* to a test of nerve. Bonneau put on all possible speed and drove the *Ella and Annie* straight at the Union vessel.

The *Niphon*, a much smaller vessel than the blockade runner, was positioned with her bow pointing toward the beach. Upon seeing the intention of the *Ella and Annie*, the captain of the *Niphon* turned his ship sharply to the starboard to avoid the direct impact of the collision. The gunboat responded quickly, and the *Ella and Annie* crashed into the *Niphon*'s fore rigging. The convergence caused the ships to swing alongside. The warship opened with canister and sent over boarders. After a brief engagement the *Ella and Annie*'s crew was overpowered.[30]

The capture of these three vessels was a devastating blow to Confederate blockade running. In less than forty-eight hours three of the best blockade runners had been lost. All of the steamers were taken north, condemned at prize courts, and purchased by the Union Navy. They soon returned to the Southern coast as gunboats. The *Cornubia* retained her name while the *Ella and Annie* became the *Malvern*, and the *Robert E. Lee* was taken into the Federal Navy as the *Fort Donelson*.[31]

The night after the *Robert E. Lee* and the *Ella and Annie* were captured, and before Admiral Samuel P. Lee had written north to Gideon Welles about the prizes, a fourth steamer fell into the hands of the Union squadron. At 7:15 A.M. on November 10, the *Howquah* spotted a blockade runner thirteen miles north of Fort Fisher making for New

Inlet. The Union gunboat gave chase and, when her first shot "glanced against the gallows frame of her engine," the blockade runner surrendered. The *Howquah* discovered that her prize was the little *Ella*, making her first run to Wilmington. The vessel was sent north and would later return as the gunboat *Philippi*.[32]

Less than two weeks later another blow fell on the Confederate lifeline. On the morning of November 21, the *Banshee* was sighted by the army transport *Fulton*, which was transporting troops from Hilton Head to New York City. The powerful steamer, which had captured the *Margaret and Jessie* on her last trip north, quickly gave chase. She was later joined in the pursuit by the gunboat *Grand Gulf* and, after a chase of two and a half hours, the combined shelling of the Federal vessels forced the *Banshee* to surrender. The *Fulton* was the first to reach the blockade runner and immediately put a prize crew on board. Though Thomas Taylor was not on the *Banshee* on this run, Captain Steele and his entire crew were taken prisoner. The *Fulton* attached a hawser to the *Banshee* and towed her prize north, the second in less than two weeks. The *Banshee*, like those vessels taken before her, became a Union warship.[33]

By December, the Confederacy had lost all the blockade runners operated by the Ordnance Bureau and a large number of the private vessels that they had depended upon to deliver goods. Two vessels that did remain were the *General Beauregard* and the *Antonica*, both operated by the Chicora Importing and Exporting Company, but before the year was out these two would also be gone. The *General Beauregard* was the first of the two former Glasgow-to-Dublin ferry boats to be lost. On the evening of December 11, 1863, while heading for New Inlet, she was driven aground and wrecked by the *Howquah*.[34]

Nine days later the *Antonica*, under the command of W. F. Adair, approached Old Inlet south of Fort Caswell. On his first try Adair spotted two vessels and turned out to sea. He then came in again by Lockwood Folly Inlet, but was sighted and had to move off. For his third approach Adair tried to slip the *Antonica* past a Union blockader near Smith's Island, but this time he beached the steamer on a sand bar. Adair realized that the blockade runner was hopelessly aground, and he ordered the vessel abandoned, but it was too late. The Union gunboat *Governor Buckingham* had sighted the *Antonica* trying to pass inside of her and had moved to intercept the fleeing ship. A few well-placed shots convinced Adair and his men to surrender. For the next few days the Union squadron attempted to free the *Antonica*, but to no avail, and she was destroyed by the pounding sea. The destruction of the *Antonica* ended the career of one of the war's most successful blockade runners. The vessel had compiled twenty-four runs through the blockade, a record that would not be broken until the final months of the war.[35]

The loss of these blockade runners could not have occurred at a worse time. Defeats at Gettysburg and Vicksburg caused a tremendous demand for more munitions and a falling off in the subscription of the Erlanger loan. By August, the bonds were 20 percent to 36 percent below discount. Southern finances in Europe were again in shambles. To help revive Confederate credit and replace the military equipment lost in Pennsylvania and Mississippi, Secretary of War Seddon took a bold and unprecedented step. In August 1863, he directed the commanders of Wilmington, Charleston, and Mobile to take over from the blockade runners one-half of their outward cargo space. Liberal compensation was offered but, if the owners refused, the port commanders were to seize the ships. Seddon wrote: "We must use for this purpose all vessels suitable for evading the blockade now in our ports, and unless satisfactory arrangements can be made with the assent of the owners, we have no alternative but to resort to impressment." By September, blockade runners were taking on Confederate cotton, though they were not always loaded with the prescribed amount as Confederate agents were still having a difficult time securing rail space.[36]

While Seddon was working to ship cotton from the South, his agents in Europe were striving to improve their operations. Colin J. McRae's investigation of Major Huse soon cleared the purchasing agent of any wrongdoing, though McRae did halt all dealings with S. Isaac, Campbell and Company, whom he suspected of deliberately overcharging the Confederacy.[37]

In his investigation of Confederate finances in Europe, McRae became acutely aware of their unstable and haphazard nature. In October, shocked by what he considered reckless financial practices ruinous to Confederate credit, McRae suggested to Memminger that all contracts calling for profits or commissions be annulled; that one person be placed in charge of Confederate finances in Europe and under him would serve the Navy and War Department agents; that the government take control over all exports, and that all cotton and tobacco in the South be impressed by the government and used to finance the war effort. McRae's ideas were not new. The seizing of cotton had been advocated by some politicians since the start of the war. In June of 1863, Slidell had written Benjamin outlining a similar plan. However, not until the military setbacks of July 1863, did the Confederacy act.[38]

In fact, before McRae's despatch had reached the Confederacy, President Davis and his cabinet had agreed to centralize its European purchasing operations. With the president's approval Seddon ordered McRae to take charge of all Confederate securities deposited with Fraser, Trenholm and Company. McRae was instructed to distribute the funds to the various purchasing agents he saw fit. In effect, McRae became the South's European secretary of the treasury.

The decision was an excellent one. McRae soon ended the discord and confusion and began to work out an efficient system for purchasing and shipping supplies. McRae would also become instrumental in an additional plan to further increase government control over blockade running.[39]

# Chapter Seven

# The Confederacy Takes Control

It would take time before the reorganization of Confederate European finances and impressment of cargo space could effect the war effort. By 1864, Confederate fortunes were at a new low. In Virginia, Lee's army was regrouping after a devastating loss of men and supplies at Gettysburg. The conditions were so bad that a number of soldiers deserted the army, taking arms and accouterments. The situation of the western army was little better. In the November 1863 rout at Chattanooga, the men left behind thousands of arms and other valuable equipment, all of which would have to be replaced before the unit could again become a viable fighting force. Reports circulated that the armies favored peace, and many soldiers were greatly concerned over the condition of their families.[1]

Besides the heavy losses in battle, Confederate forces also suffered from growing shortages of food and supplies. Through attrition and the loss of territory, the South had to turn more and more to imports to outfit and feed its men. Such items as leather, cloth, and meat were in short supply. Gorgas was soon forced to substitute cotton cloth for leather in the manufacture of cartridge boxes and haversacks. The experiment was successful, but shoes and harnesses could not be made from cotton cloth and leather had to be imported.[2]

The problems of procuring meat continued to haunt the Confederates throughout 1864. To supply the soldiers, the Commissary Bureau turned to large-scale overseas purchases. In November 1863, contracts were signed with companies, including a new firm headed by William Crenshaw, for the importation of three million pounds of bacon. The problem was so acute that General Robert E. Lee asked permission to trade cotton and tobacco for meat through the Northern lines. Seddon agreed, and a limited exchange was started. However, this was only a stopgap measure. If the Confederacy was to survive, it needed an enlarged and dependable blockade-running system.[3]

The required steamers were available. By late 1863, the shipyards along the Mersey and Clyde rivers were turning out new iron and steel vessels specifically designed for blockade running. These new ships, built from the keel up, were based on the design of the *Banshee*, but on the whole, were stronger, faster steamers constructed with large stowage space and small silhouettes. The vessels were a cross between the narrow sleek lines of the *Banshee* and the larger, more seaworthy Clyde ferryboats that had dominated the trade in 1863.

English shipbuilders had discovered that a narrow beam could increase a vessel's speed only a certain extent before it caused structural weakness. It also restricted the size of engines and carrying capacity. Shipwrights turned away from the extreme narrow beams and returned to building sturdier vessels with larger power plants and stowage areas. Such steamers were nearing completion during the winter of 1863–1864, and their increased cargo space would help ease the loss of freight space demanded by the Confederate War Department.[4]

The program initiated by Seddon to impress cargo space on private blockade runners had begun slowly. There was confusion over the government's authority, especially in regard to vessels under contract to the Confederacy and those owned by the states. Bayne and his agents had a difficult time supplying enough government cotton to make up one-third to one-half of the outward cargo. There was also an outpouring of criticism from foreign shippers and their Southern partners over the infringement of their business rights. However, most Confederate officials saw that government control was necessary.

In early February, the Confederate Congress showed its approval by passing a bill that allowed President Davis to regulate all foreign commerce. The bill gave Davis total control over the exportation of cotton, tobacco, military and naval stores, rice, sugar, and molasses. It also prohibited the importation of many luxury items that were taking up valuable space in the blockade runners. Forbidden imports included all brandy and spirits, carpets and rugs, carriages and carriage parts, furniture, marble, wallpaper, bricks, coconuts, gems, antiques, and coin collections. The bill went into effect on March 1, by which time Davis and his cabinet members had developed a comprehensive program to control blockade running.[5]

The second bill, formulated by Davis, Memminger, Benjamin, and Seddon, was passed on March 5, 1864, and set additional regulations. The bill required all operators and shippers to make a declaration giving the names of the vessel's owners, officers, crew, passengers, port of destination, and the quantity and value of the cargo before leaving a Southern port. Those blockade runners using cotton bonds or under contract to the Confederacy would not have their cargo space confiscated, but all other vessels were liable to have one-half of their inward and outward stowage taken by the government. For carrying Confederate produce the operators received 5 pence per pound while goods brought in from the islands were paid for at £25 per ton. If a carrier desired, he could take out two-thirds of his cargo on government account at 6 pence per pound.[6]

The regulations were a compromise between the Confederate government and the civilian businessman. The South needed the space to supply McRae with cotton and for the importation of supplies. Lenient rates for bonding and freight were offered, and at the same time the Confederate leaders were guaranteeing inward cargoes for the armed forces and goods for the relief of the civilian population.

The regulations, however, were far from perfect. The Confederacy still had to honor the existing unfavorable contracts. The bill also allowed shippers to circumvent the new arrangement by using cotton bonds purchased in Europe; nor did the bill cover state-operated vessels. All of these points would come to haunt the government, but, if nothing more, the South finally had a set of rules from which it could work.

British operators quickly reacted against the new regulations. A clerk for one of the companies wrote that "The blockade runners swear that they will not bring in a single cargo under the present arrangement viz one-half of the cargo. It is unjust and extortionate. If the Govt. does not prove successful in running its own steamers it will suffer rather than gain by such a regulation."[7]

However, for all their protests, the British operators did not remove their vessels from service. While the number of attempts that occurred in February—about twenty-nine—were reduced to twelve in March and eleven in April, seven of the vessels that accounted for the attempts in February were either captured or destroyed and two others, the *Hansa* and the *Index*, were retired. Before long the foreign owners grudgingly accepted the regulations and worked with the Confederate authorities to deliver Southern supplies.[8]

To enforce the regulations the War Department upgraded Major Bayne's office. In early March, Bayne was promoted to lieutenant colonel and placed in charge of the Bureau of Foreign Supplies. Since the majority of the cotton obtained under the produce loans had been promised in various cotton bonds and certificates, the Confederate Congress appropriated twenty million dollars to buy additional cotton, tobacco, and naval stores. Bayne was to use these items to pay off debts and open new contracts. Any surplus cotton would be shipped overseas for the purchase of supplies. To enforce the regulations, bureau agents were placed at the main Confederate ports east of the Mississippi. J. M. Sexias remained in charge of Wilmington while James D. Aiken took over at Charleston, A. B. Noyes at St. Marks, and John Scott at Mobile.[9]

The cotton shipped by the agents was received either by Walker in Bermuda, Heyliger in Nassau, or Helm in Havana. From these points the staple was sent on to Fraser, Trenholm and Company in Liverpool, where it was sold and the proceeds turned over to McRae. To illustrate, 100 bales of cotton carried out of Wilmington in the summer of 1864 on the *Banshee (II)*, were sold at Liverpool for £4616.10.10. The expenses, which included freight costs, dockage, wharfage, and insurance fees, cost £1695.17.9 This gave the Confederacy a net profit of £2821.1.3, or about $14,137 in gold or $311,000 in Confederate currency.[10]

This profit was used to purchase supplies for the armed forces. However, the Quartermaster Bureau, now under Brigadier General Alexander R. Lawton, who had replaced Myers, could not wait for goods sent from England. Instead, Lawton had his funds returned to the West Indies in the form of drafts on Fraser, Trenholm and Company. Here his agents purchased necessary items that were on hand in the islands and shipped them to the South. These transactions were carried out by Majors Norman S. Walker in Bermuda and Richard P. Waller in Nassau and were made at considerable expense; but Lawton, knowing the needs of the Confederate armies, saw no other choice.[11]

In order to avoid such transactions as Lawton's, Southern leaders decided to establish a line of steamers exclusively owned and operated by the War Department. To achieve this, McRae opened negotiations in early April 1864 with the Mercantile Trading Company of England, which was operated by Edwin Pinchback Stringer and Edward Pembroke, both strong Southern supporters. The negotiations dragged on throughout the month until finally McRae, feeling that their demands were too high, broke off the talks. He then turned to Charles Prioleau and Fraser, Trenholm and Company for assistance and, as usual, found the firm ready to help the Confederacy.

Fraser, Trenholm and Company agreed to furnish the Confederacy with eight steamers. The contract for two, the *Bat* and the *Owl*, which were under construction for Fraser, Trenholm and Company, were transferred to the government. Prioleau also agreed to pay for two vessels that Bulloch had ordered, the *Stag* and the *Deer*. Four were to be built by Jones, Quiggin and Company, while four more were to be constructed by Laird and Sons with all work supervised by Bulloch.

The steamers were to be operated by Fraser, Trenholm and Company, until purchased by the Confederacy from the sale of Confederate cotton. To pay for the ships, one-half of the outward cotton would be given to Prioleau's firm until the value of the vessel, plus a 20 percent commission, had been covered. At this time the blockade runners would be turned over to the Confederacy, which, if it desired, could keep the civilian crews, or replace them with naval personnel. The *Owl* and *Bat* would be finished in August while the following six were to be completed two at a time in November and December 1864 and April 1865.

For additional vessels, McRae was directed by Prioleau to the John K. Gilliat and Company of London, a banking establishment that served the Confederacy throughout the war. From Gilliat, McRae contracted for six additional steamers. Before work began he deposited three million dollars in Erlanger cotton bonds with a margin of 25 percent to cover a £150,000 advance demanded by the firm. Once this was completed Gilliat placed an order with Jones, Quiggin and Company for the ships. The delivery date was set for December 1864. As in the agreement with Fraser, Trenholm and Company, Gilliat would handle the sale of produce, for a 5 percent commission, plus other incentives. One-half of the cotton brought out would go toward the payment of the steamers and, once paid off, the Confederacy would become their sole operators. The vessels paid for by the two companies were:

**Blockade Runners Paid for by Fraser, Trenholm and Company**[12]

| Name | Builder | Dimensions | Burden |
|------|---------|-----------|--------|
| Owl | Jones, Quiggin and Co. | 230' x 26' x 10'6" | 771 tons |
| Bat | Jones, Quiggin and Co. | 230' x 26' x 10'6" | 771 tons |
| Stag[a] | Jones, Quiggin and Co. | 230' x 26' x 10'6" | 771 tons |

| | | | |
|---|---|---|---|
| Deer[b] | Jones, Quiggin and Co. | 230' x 26' x 10'6" | 771 tons |
| Lark | Laird and Sons | 210' x 26' x 10' | 552 tons |
| Wren | Laird and Sons | 210' x 26' x 10' | 552 tons |
| Albatross | Laird and Sons | 240' x 30' x 13' | 1063 tons |
| Penguin | Laird and Sons | 240' x 30' x 13' | 1063 tons |

### Paid for by Gilliat and Company

| | | | |
|---|---|---|---|
| Rosine | Jones, Quiggin and Co. | 270' x 33' x 15' | 1391 tons |
| Ruby | Jones, Quiggin and Co. | 270' x 33' x 15' | 1391 tons |
| Widgeon | Jones, Quiggin and Co. | 225' x 24' x 11' | 645 tons |
| Curlew | Jones, Quiggin and Co. | 225' x 24' x 11' | 645 tons |
| Snipe | Jones, Quiggin and Co. | 225' x 24' x 11' | 645 tons |
| Plover | Jones, Quiggin and Co. | 225' x 24' x 11' | 645 tons |

[a] Subcontracted to Bowdler, Chaffer and Company
[b] Subcontracted to W. H. Potter and Company

The vessels, all sidewheelers, were among the final generation of blockade runners, varying in size to meet their specific function. The four largest ships, 240 feet or longer, could carry over 1,000 bales of cotton while the *Owl, Bat, Stag,* and *Deer* carried 800 bales at a draft of 7 feet 6 inches and a speed of 13 knots. The six smaller steamers were built for eventual use in the Gulf of Mexico. The *Lark* and *Wren,* the smallest of the ships, were designed for use in isolated harbors. They could take 350 bales at a draft of 5 feet, and 500 bales at a draft of 6 feet.[13]

It would take time for the first of these vessels to arrive on the Southern coast, and even longer before they would be totally in the hands of the Confederacy. In order to keep up a flow of supplies during the interim, McRae, Bayne, and other officials entered into various short-term contracts. The agreement with Crenshaw was continued, and McRae advanced the Richmond businessman £140,000 to keep his venture running. At this time, Crenshaw and his new associates had three blockade runners in operation with two more under construction. Though the ships continued to carry quartermaster and commissary goods that were needed by the Confederacy, McRae still felt that the contract should be renegotiated to make it more favorable to the South.[14]

McRae also entered into a new contract with Collie and Company for the importation of £200,000 worth of quartermaster, ordnance, and medical supplies. The agreement called for Collie to provide four steamers and to buy materials valued at £150,000 for the Quartermaster Bureau and £50,000 for the Ordnance and Medical bureaus. The purchases were to be made under the supervision of Major Ferguson and Captain Huse, and delivered within the next six months. Collie was to receive 50 percent over invoice plus expenses. He was to be paid in cotton at 6 pence a pound. At these rates, Collie could sell his cotton in Liverpool for a gross profit of over £800,000. To cover his expenses in Europe, Collie was permitted to take out one-tenth of the cargo space on his own account. As a final provision, the Confederacy also agreed not to draft Collie's Southern employees.

Collie planned to employ his newest steamers for this contract. They were the *Falcon, Flamingo, Condor,* and *Ptarmigan,* all built by Randolph, Elder and Company. Considered by many to be the finest blockade runners built, the iron-hulled sidewheelers were 270 feet long and had a draft of about 8 feet. Built for tremendous speed, the ships had a very distinctive silhouette of three funnels running down the hull in front of the wheelhouse. Collie believed that there were no blockade runners superior to these steamers.[15]

Along with the contracts made by McRae in Europe, Bayne also approved a number of agreements to ease shortages within the Confederacy. Bayne made two pacts, one with W. H. Peet, Rodney F. McDonald, and Thomas A. Harris, for the delivery of quartermaster, ordnance, and nitre and mining supplies, while the other, signed with Power and Low and Company of Wilmington, provided the delivery of meat for the Commissary Department. Neither Power and Low nor Peet and his associates owned their own blockade runners, so they contracted with British shipping companies to provide the needed steamers. Peet and his partners hired E. P. Stringer's Mercantile Trading Company while Power and Low entered into a partnership with the Anglo-Confederate Trading Company, a branch of Edward Lawrence and Company of Liverpool. Since Lawrence and Company had vessels already in operation, Power and Low were able to begin the delivery of meat within a very short time. The contract with Peet, however, would take much longer, because as yet, the Mercantile Trading Company had no ships.[16]

Besides negotiating the additional contracts, Bayne also undertook the task of keeping his bureau operating. He faced many problems. The cotton supply on the Atlantic seacoast was extremely limited. There were only 14,000 bales of government cotton east of Alabama, and much of this was scattered on isolated plantations. To ease the situation Bayne directed blockade runners using Confederate cotton bonds to Gulf ports, where government cotton was more plentiful. In this way, Bayne tried to keep Wilmington for Confederate vessels, and those under government contract.

In spite of many difficulties, Bayne's bureau began to show positive results. By April 1864, vessels carrying large supplies of meat, shoes, blankets, and military equipment began to arrive along with the first deliveries of machinery for the armory at Macon and submarine cable for use in torpedoes.[17]

From England, McRae reported positive results. By July, the Confederate agent wrote Seddon that the South's European finances were beginning to firm up and that credit was now easier to secure. On July 4, 1864, he wrote to Secretary of War Seddon: "Our credit begins to grow stronger and by proper management will soon be available for all our wants." McRae urged Seddon not to be swayed from pressures to modify the regulations and asked that no new contracts be signed, as the first of the Confederate-owned vessels would soon be ready to run the blockade.[18]

Two weeks later, an important change took place within the Confederate cabinet that strengthened the position of those backing a Confederate line of blockade runners. Christopher Memminger, long under attack for his financial policies, resigned as secretary of treasury, and was replaced by George Alfred Trenholm. The new appointment came at a time when Trenholm's experience in shipping and finances was needed to keep the South from breaking away from the new regulations.

After resigning from his firms, Trenholm quickly took steps to keep the government operations going. To the new secretary of the treasury, the most vital element for the survival of the Confederacy was the importation of foreign munitions. If the South was to be defeated, he did not want it to be because the soldiers were not properly equipped. The task ahead of him was a difficult one. Bayne estimated that £1,491,000 of foreign supplies were immediately needed. To pay for this, Trenholm concluded that he would have to ship 6,000 bales of cotton over the next six months on at least fifteen steamers per week. At this time such a task was impossible. Besides the lack of government-controlled vessels, the South was also tied to contracts that took away the majority of their cotton. Up to August 12, 1864, only 1,672 bales went out to McRae for the "general credit of the Treasury," while 962 bales went to Collie and

Company, 1,943 to Crenshaw and Company, and 953 for freight charges. Trenholm believed the payment to Collie was justified as it covered supplies actually arriving, but much of the cotton going to Crenshaw was being put into the construction of vessels and not the delivery of goods. To help keep up the purchases of supplies Trenholm sent McRae three million dollars' worth of Confederate bonds for use as collateral until more cotton could be delivered.[19]

Along with the problem of keeping up a flow of exchange to McRae, Trenholm also had to provide Bayne with funds to purchase cotton within the South. Problems arose over citizens' reluctance to sell their cotton for bonds, and with the railroads still shipping private cotton ahead of the government's. Trenholm felt the South's greatest enemy was the selfishness and apathy of the Confederate people. As he wrote to a Treasury Department agent in Augusta, Georgia: "If we break down under such circumstances it will be our fault and we deserve nobody's compassion or sympathy."[20]

While the War Department was attempting to put together a workable system, the Navy Department kept up independent operations. The cotton was badly needed in order to fund the Navy's ambitious foreign construction program. In all, the Navy was attempting to build five ironclads, five large commerce raiders, twelve torpedo boats, and engines for Southern-built ironclads and torpedo boats. For such a program thousands of bales of cotton were needed.[21]

To deliver this required exchange, Mallory and his associates considered a number of options, from converting existing warships to building blockade runners in England. However, the Navy found it best to employ two vessels that were already under departmental control. These were the *Juno* at Charleston, and the *Coquette*, which was still outfitting in England.

The *Juno*, originally a privately operated blockade runner, had been impressed at Charleston in 1863, and later purchased by the Navy. Her use as a warship was extremely limited and, by the spring of 1864, she was returned to service as a blockade runner.

On March 9, 1864, the little sidewheeler, now named *Helen*, slipped out of Charleston with 220 bales of navy cotton. She was under the command of Lieutenant Philip Porcher and had on board a crew of twenty-two men and eight officers, including Acting Master Charles D. Tucker, son of the commander of the Charleston Naval Squadron, Commander John R. Tucker.

Once clear of the harbor, the *Helen* ran into heavy weather. Around 10:00 A.M. on the second day a leak was discovered. To lighten the vessel Porcher tossed sixty bales of cotton overboard and continued running the pumps, but the storm soon reached gale proportions, and the *Helen* was fighting for her life. By 2:00 P.M., the pumps could no longer keep the water out, and the engine room flooded. Sails were set, but the strain amidships from the water-logged cotton and the pressure of the water broke the vessel in two. The bow section sank immediately while the stern remained afloat long enough to allow Porcher and some of the crew to launch a lifeboat; however, it immediately capsized. Only engineer J. Harry Dent and pilot William Burke managed to survive. Clinging to wreckage, they were discovered the next day by the schooner *Petrel*, which was attracted to the scene by the floating cotton bales. The two men were taken aboard the sailing ship and carried to Nassau.[22]

The loss of the *Helen* left the navy with only the twin-screw steamer *Coquette*, but even this vessel had a difficult time starting her career. The ship, under Lieutenant Randolph Carter, had arrived in Bermuda with its cargo of a marine engine on November 19, 1863. While there, Carter cleaned the vessel, painted her a lead color and cut the masts down to eighteen inches above the scarfs. Carter cleared the *Coquette* for Wilmington on December 13, 1863; but, on the first day out, a cylinder blew, and he had to return to port.

For nearly three months, the *Coquette* remained in St. George harbor until a replacement cylinder arrived from England. Finally, on March 3, 1864, the *Coquette* again made for Wilmington and five days later, while attempting to enter Old Inlet, she ran aground on the bar. The tug *Equator* pulled the blockade runner off, but in doing so the *Coquette* mangled her port propellor. The vessel was towed to Wilmington, where the marine engine was finally delivered.

The *Coquette*'s propellor was repaired and, after taking on navy-owned cotton, Lieutenant Carter successfully guided her back to Bermuda. The steamer continued to be plagued by bad luck; while anchored in St. George harbor she became fouled with the British warship *Vesuvius* and received a large gash in her stern, resulting in extensive repairs. Finally her luck changed and, between May 9 and July 11, 1864, she made five trips through the blockade, carrying out thousands of bales of cotton. Her naval career ended in July 1864, when deposits of silt in her tubes reduced her speed to such an extent that Mallory ordered her sold. She was put on the market for £16,000 and was purchased by a group of Richmond merchants headed by the onetime Treasury agent, Benjamin F. Ficklin, and Joseph R. Anderson, president of the Tredegar Iron Works.[23]

In July 1864, while the *Coquette* was being sold, the Navy impressed two blockade runners for an elaborate plan to free prisoners from a Union camp inside Chesapeake Bay. By this point in the war, the South were desperately short of men, and a raid against the Union prison at Point Lookout, Maryland, was seen as a way to fill the depleted ranks. The post was located in Chesapeake Bay on the north side of the mouth of the Potomac River on the tip of a peninsula formed by the Patuxent and the Potomac rivers. The plan, which originated at the headquarters of General Robert E. Lee, was the brainchild of Lee's aide Colonel James Taylor Wood, who held commissions in both the army and navy. Wood formulated the idea along with naval lieutenant John Wilkinson, who had returned from Canada, and Lee's son Major General George Washington Custis Lee. The plan called for a coordinated land and naval assault on Point Lookout with Brigadier General Bradley T. Johnson's calvary providing support from the land side.

The operation began on July 2, 1864, when a force of about 200 marines and sailors moved from Drewry's Bluff and Richmond to Wilmington. There, they joined men from the Wilmington squadron on board two impressed blockade runners, the *Florie* and *Let Her Be*. The *Florie* was owned by the Importing and Exporting Company of Georgia, while the *Let Her Be*, soon to be renamed *Chicora*, was operated by the Chicora Importing and Exporting Company. They were both new, powerful steamers well suited for the mission.

On July 10, the steamers anchored off Smithville. The *Let Her Be*, under the command of Colonel, now Commander Wood, was armed with a 20-pound Parrott and a 12-pound Napoleon. The *Florie* had a similar armament and was commanded by Lieutenant William H. Ward. Lieutenant Wilkinson accompanied Ward on the *Florie*. That night, the two vessels moved into New Inlet, but before passing into the open sea a signal from Fort Fisher ordered the steamers back. Wood went ashore and found a message from Richmond warning him that knowledge of the expedition may have leaked to the enemy. Wood was undaunted and prepared his ships to go out on the following night. However, before they could leave, an order from Jefferson Davis arrived calling the operation off. Within a week the crews returned to their squadrons, and the vessels were back in the hands of their owners.[24]

Though the expedition had come to naught, it did show that the Navy needed vessels that could be used on such operations. This, plus the desire to send out an additional commerce raider, caused the navy to acquire the blockade runner *Atalanta* in late July 1864. Originally built as an English Channel ferry on the Dover to Calais run, the fast twin screw had been purchased as a blockade runner by E. P. Stringer's Mercantile Trading Company. The *Atalanta* made three round trips to Wilmington before being purchased by the Confederacy. On obtaining the vessel, the South converted her to a gunboat and placed her under Commander John Taylor Wood.

On August 6, 1864, Wood took the steamer, now named *Tallahassee*, out of Wilmington on a nineteen-day cruise along the northern coast. While on the raid he destroyed twenty-six vessels and captured and bonded another seven. The *Tallahassee* returned to Wilmington on August 26, and took up duty as a guard boat, though she could easily return to sea as a commerce raider or a blockade runner at any time.[25]

Throughout 1864, Wilmington remained firmly in the grasp of General Whiting's regulations. During the winter, Whiting ordered all vessels clearing the Cape Fear River to report to either Fort Fisher or Caswell for inspection before receiving permission to sail. Later, rules governing the use of signalmen and pilots were added. Men from the signal corps were assigned to assist the vessels in contacting stations along the coast. They worked at a set rate, and often doubled as the ship's purser, which added even more gold to their pay.

The civilian pilots were also placed under strict military control. A register was made from which pilots were assigned to vessels. Captains could request specific pilots, and usually Whiting would comply. A pilot who went out had to return on the vessel he had sailed on, or, if it was not coming back, return to the South within a specific time. If they did not, the pilots were considered deserters. The men continued to receive an excellent rate of pay, though their wages could no longer exceed that paid to pilots of government-run vessels. Some of the men were stationed in the islands to bring in vessels while others served only on outward runs. The most-prized individuals were those who could handle both ends of the trade.[26]

Although Whiting was the main authority in Wilmington, he had to share responsibility for the defense of the port with the small, poorly equipped naval contingent under Flag Officer William F. Lynch. Besides guarding the water approached to the city and assisting blockade runners, the navy was in charge of overseeing the interests of the Navy Department. When the War Department could not make up their allotted space on a blockade runner, the navy could place their cotton on board the vessel.

Such situations often occurred, and in February 1864, the War Department did not have cotton available for the *Hansa* and the *Alice*. Before the steamers cleared, naval officials attempted to place their cotton on the vessels. The operators of the runners balked, and Lynch, deciding not to press the issue at this time, released the ships on the condition that they would take out one-half of their cargo for the navy on their next run. The two ships returned to Wilmington later in the month, and when they tried to leave without naval cotton, Lynch asked Whiting to detain them. The *Alice* was stopped, but not the *Hansa*, so Lynch, under orders from Mallory, took charge of the vessel and had the *Hansa* anchored next to the ironclad *North Carolina*.

Whiting was outraged by the seizure as he considered it to be an attack on his authority. The next morning, March 9, Whiting sent the *Cape Fear* (formerly *Flora*), with a battalion of soldiers to the *Hansa* and took over the vessel, ejecting Lynch's marine guard. Whiting returned the blockade runner to her original wharf and, in order to keep the navy from moving the *Hansa* a second time, placed soldiers on the gangplanks of the naval ships with orders to keep the sailors from boarding their vessels. Since the men of the Wilmington squadron spent their evenings ashore, this action by Whiting kept the sailors from manning their own warships. The action caused an immediate response from Lynch, who, as one observer reported, "came upon the ground, and attempting to board one of his own vessels, was challenged by a sentinel, and might have been shot, had not the intrepid old man put aside the brute's musket with his walking cane and awed him with a look of command." Once on board his flagship, the *Yadkin*, Lynch had the boat tow the *North Carolina* to a position off the *Hansa*. Tensions were high, and Whiting telegraphed Seddon demanding that Lynch be removed from command.

Arbitration over the incident occurred in Richmond where both Seddon and Mallory worked to solve the embarrassing situation. Mallory accepted responsibility for Lynch's actions, and Seddon ordered the

*Hansa* turned over to the Navy. A number of observers claimed that Whiting had been drunk when the incident occurred. However, whatever the case, it revealed the deep animosity between the two services.[27]

To help ease matters in Wilmington, Mallory directed Lieutenant Wilkinson to serve as a liaison officer between Whiting and Lynch. Wilkinson was given command over seventy men. Their duties included setting up lights along the coast, inspection of blockade runners, aiding stranded vessels, and enforcement of all other government regulations. Mallory also instructed Wilkinson to do all in his "power to secure harmony of action" between the "military authorities."[28]

While the Confederacy continued to smooth out their operations, Governor Vance of North Carolina worked to improve the efficiency of his blockade-running business. Throughout the fall of 1863, the *Advance* continued its successful career. Through January 1, 1864, the vessel had evaded the blockade eight times. On one run, the *Advance* carried in 1,700 heavy blankets, 2,000 pairs of shoes, 30,000 yards of flannel, 5,000 pairs of socks, 96 dozen wool and cotton cards plus bagging and rope for the shipping of cotton. Besides operating the *Advance*, the state impressed every wool and cotton factory within North Carolina to turn out cloth for uniforms. Any surplus goods were sold to the Confederacy at a "minimum price."[29]

The arrangements made by Vance showed excellent results. They kept North Carolina troops well equipped, and the state even made a profit on the items sold to the Confederacy. By the end of 1863, Vance had in transit some 40,000 blankets, 40,000 pairs of shoes, large quantities of army cloth, 112,000 pairs of cotton cards, machinery to retool the state's wool and cotton factories, and a large supply of bacon. However, Vance feared that Wilmington would be taken before the *Advance* could deliver the supplies. To provide additional steamers the governor sold off one-half interest in the *Advance* to Power, Low and Company. Then, using the money from the sale of state cotton bonds Vance purchased one-fourth interest in four of Alexander Collie's steamers.

Even though Vance proved to be a meddling and bothersome partner, the arrangement worked quite well. Collie and his backers received North Carolina cotton and Vance received his supplies. By February 1864, Vance wrote Collie, proudly proclaiming that the North Carolina troops were now better equipped and clothed than at any time in the war.

The greatest challenge to Vance's venture did not come from the Union blockade, but rather from Confederate authorities who demanded that the North Carolina vessels comply with the government regulations. As long as the *Advance* had been owned entirely by the state, the War Department did not interfere, but when Vance sold off a portion of his interests, the Confederacy claimed space on both the *Advance* and the Collie steamers.

At first Vance tried to fight these stipulations, but Seddon remained firm. Both South Carolina and Virginia, which held part interests in steamers, had agreed to the regulations, and Seddon demanded that North Carolina do likewise. Vance threatened to remove his ships from service, but he soon realized that his protests and threats were falling on deaf ears, and he grudgingly complied with Seddon's orders.[30]

Another state that ran afoul of the new regulations was Georgia, which had an arrangement with the Importing and Exporting Company of Georgia for the shipping of state-owned goods. The firm had been organized during the summer of 1863 by Gazaway B. Lamar, who revamped his company following advice from John Fraser and Company. Before the year was out, Lamar formed a partnership with the Liverpool-based Henry Lafone. Together they ordered six blockade runners and purchased the sailing ship *Storm King* to ferry goods across the Atlantic.

In the Confederacy, Lamar placed his steamers under a charter from Georgia Governor Joseph Brown. This gave priority to Georgian cotton and goods. Any unused space was taken by the company. Lamar also tried to interest the governor of Florida in his line, but the offer was rejected.[31]

The first vessel sent out by Lafone was the tiny steamer *Little Ada*. Barely over 100 feet in length, the ship had an extremely light draft, which allowed her to enter the Santee River, South Carolina, in February 1864. Here she off-loaded her cargo and took on Georgian cotton via the town of McClellanville. However, before she could sail, the War Department demanded one-half of the *Little Ada*'s cargo capacity for Confederate cotton. Lamar and Governor Brown refused, but the War Department would not back down, and a battery of artillery was despatched to keep the vessel in the Santee River.

While the arguments continued, the presence of the *Little Ada* was reported to Union blockaders. A small boat expedition was organized from the warship *Winona* and, in the early morning of March 25, 1864, one gig and two cutters, carrying twenty-seven sailors, moved up the river toward the *Little Ada*. The crew of the blockade runner spotted the approaching Union sailors and attempted to flee, but were overtaken and returned to the vessel.

The Federals tried to steam the *Little Ada* out the river, but were thwarted by the Confederate artillery arriving from McClellanville. An attempt to burn the ship failed, and the Federals abandoned the blockade runner and her crew, and returned to the *Winona*.

The *Little Ada* remained in the Santee River for the next three months, blockaded, not only by the Union Navy but also Confederate troops. Finally, in late May, Lamar and Brown bowed to the inevitable and agreed to comply with the Confederate regulations. One-hundred and forty-seven bales of Georgia cotton were removed and replaced with War Department cotton. Although she was released by the army, the *Little Ada* still had to escape from the closely guarded Santee River. For three more weeks the vessel waited. In mid-June, during a heavy gale, she slipped past the *Winona* and escaped to Nassau, where the 295 bales of cotton were sold for £8016.8.7. The proceeds were then divided between the Confederacy and her owners. A few weeks later the *Little Ada* cleared Nassau for another run to the South, but on this trip she was sighted approaching Wilmington and captured.[32]

The next company vessel to run the blockade was the sleek, new sidewheeler *Lilian*. On board was John Newland Maffitt, former commander of the CSS *Florida*. After escaping from Mobile on January 16, 1863, Maffitt had taken the commerce raider on a successful career before coming to Brest, France, for repairs in early August 1863. While there Maffitt was compelled to give up command because of health problems. He recuperated in England and, in May 1864, Maffitt took passage for the Confederacy on the *Lilian*. Upon reaching Bermuda, Maffitt was offered command of the *Lilian*. He accepted and, on June 1, took the steamer out of St. George and ran the blockade into Wilmington. A few days after arriving Maffitt was assigned to the ironclad *Albemarle*, while the *Lilian* returned to Bermuda.

After completing her first round trip the *Lilian* was turned over to Captain Daniel H. Martin, who had commanded the *Little Ada* on her voyage to the Santee River. Martin made a successful round trip in July 1864, and in late August Martin prepared for another run. As the *Lilian* cleared St. George, the purser paid the crew its customary bounty

money. Once this had been done the firemen struck work and demanded to be put ashore. For a moment the mutinous firemen held the
upper hand, but the *Lilian*'s officers hailed the passing *Storm King* for aid.
With help from their consort the mutiny was subdued after a short
struggle and the troublesome crewmen placed in irons. The firemen
were then given a choice of imprisonment or work, and in a short time
the men were back at their stations.

The *Lilian* proceeded, and as she neared the Southern shoreline she
was sighted by the warship *Shenandoah*. Rough weather kept the *Shenandoah*'s cannoneers from accurate fire, but her powerful engines kept
her close. In the midst of the chase one of the *Lilian*'s boilers collapsed,
cutting her speed by one-third. Again the firemen refused to work, but
Captain Martin, fortified by a bottle of brandy in one hand and revolver
in the other, ordered them back under the threat of death.

The chase continued with shells exploding all around the *Lilian*.
The *Shenandoah* was slowly forcing the blockade runner closer to the
shoreline. Martin, fearing that his vessel would soon be aground, ordered the lifeboats readied and burned the mailbag. However, the *Lilian*
was saved by darkness, when she slipped away from her pursuer.

The *Lilian* continued on toward New Inlet, but because of her
crippled boiler, was unable to reach the port before sunrise. When dawn
came she was off Masonboro Inlet moving south. At any moment the
crew expected to be discovered but, because of her sandy paint color, the
blockade runner blended with the sand dunes. She soon passed Fort
Fisher and entered New Inlet. Once on the Cape Fear River the *Lilian*
steamed toward Wilmington.

Not all dangers were behind the *Lilian*. As she passed Fort Anderson, one of Wilmington's interior defenses, two shots were fired at the
blockade runner, one crashing through the rigging. The cannon fire was
a gentle reminder to Captain Martin, who had failed to stop for inspection. Finally, the *Lilian* reached Wilmington and unloaded her cargo.
Martin then discharged the mutinous firemen and made arrangements
to repair the boiler.

By August 22, the *Lilian*, loaded with some 1,200 cotton bales, was
ready to leave Wilmington. Before she was released by Confederate
authorities, the ship underwent a rigid search for stowaways. Long poles
were inserted between the bales and the vessel was fumigated to flush
out anyone hiding amidst the cargo. Once completed, the *Lilian* eased
down river. About 10:00 P.M. she slipped over the bar at Old Inlet and

headed toward the inner line of blockaders. She was sighted by a Union barge, which set off rockets and tried to board the *Lilian*. The attempt failed, and the blockade runner continued through the warships under a hail of fire.

Daylight found the vessel cruising toward Bermuda, but around 10:00 A.M. the lookout reported two ships following her. All possible speed was put on, and by noon the ship was outstripping one of her pursuers, but the other ship continued to gain ground. To help increase his speed Martin ordered cotton bales thrown over the side, but still the Union ship came, and soon shells began to fall around the *Lilian*. The two vessels were sailing at over 15 knots an hour, and to the amazement of the men on the blockade runner the Union ship kept closing. Finally a shell ripped into the starboard bow of the *Lilian* below the waterline. An attempt was made to fill the hole with blankets, but it did not work, and Martin stopped his engines and surrendered his vessel. The swift pursuer turned out to be the gunboat *Gettysburg*, the one-time blockade runner *Margaret and Jessie*. The prize crew pumped the water out of the *Lilian* and took her to Beaufort, North Carolina. She was condemned at a prize court and purchased by the Union Navy, eventually returning off Wilmington as a Federal gunboat.[33]

Even with the loss of such vessels as the *Lilian*, private companies continued to expand their ventures. Only a few individuals actually removed their vessels from service when the new regulations came into effect, and they were quickly replaced by the remaining firms. Profit levels were kept up by lucrative contracts with the War Department, states, and the employment of new and larger steamers. By doing this, such businesses as Collie and Company, Crenshaw and Company, E. P. Stringer's Mercantile Company and Edward Lawrence's Anglo-Confederate Trading Company were tying themselves even closer to the fortunes of the Confederacy.

The firms realized that their future profits depended on a Confederate victory. If the South lost, most companies would be devastated. Some tried to console their investors with the hope that, even if the Confederacy perished, the North would take over its foreign debts and obligations. Such views were strongly held by Alexander Collie, whereas others, notably Edward Lawrence and Company, worked hard to retrieve as much cotton as possible before the conflict ended. To achieve this, Lawrence and Company provided their agent, Thomas Taylor, with additional vessels.

Taylor's new blockade runners were the fast, iron paddlewheel steamers *Will of the Wisp*, *Wild Dayrell*, and *Tristram Shandy*. Unfortunately for Taylor the *Wild Davrell* and *Tristram Shandy* had short and undistinguished careers, leaving him to depend on the often unreliable *Will of the Wisp*.[34]

The *Will of the Wisp* had arrived in Bermuda in December 1863, but she leaked badly, and Taylor was forced to send the steamer to Halifax for repairs. However, the Canadian iron workers could do little to correct the grossly incompetent workmanship that had gone into the vessel's construction. The *Will of the Wisp*'s only redeeming quality was her powerful engines, which could propel the ship at speeds upwards of 17 knots and still keep her pumps running. On arriving at Nassau from Halifax, the ship was leaking so heavily that her commander, Captain P. Capper, ordered the streamer beached until further repairs could be done. These were finished by early April and, with Taylor on board, the ship began her maiden run.

While steaming toward Wilmington the *Will of the Wisp* hit bad weather, which slowed her progress enough to cause her to arrive off New Inlet just as dawn was breaking. With the squall becoming worse, Taylor and Capper decided to risk the fire of the blockaders rather than try to weather a storm in a leaky vessel. Finding a gap between two Union warships, the *Will of the Wisp* made a dash for New Inlet. With her engines nearly pulling loose from her hull, the vessel sped on under a rain of shells, some striking the ship. One shot ripped off the flagstaff while another tore through the forehold. This hole was plugged with blankets and the *Will of the Wisp* soon came under the protective fire of Fort Fisher.

Once safe, the *Will of the Wisp* entered New Inlet, but she failed to respond to her wheel and crashed aground on a sand bar. The entire vessel was shaken, and new leaks appeared. Taylor, fearing that his ship would break apart, ordered the deck cargo thrown overboard until the vessel was free and able to enter the river.

Additional repairs were made at Wilmington and, in late March, Capper and Taylor took the vessel out for a return trip. Once past the bar, and in the midst of Union gunboats the chief engineer informed his superiors that water was already gathering in the engine room. At the same time, wood stored near the smokestack burst into flames revealing the fleeing ship's location. Under fire, Capper skillfully maneuvered the runner past the blockaders and into the night.

Although safe from Union warships, the *Will of the Wisp* was not free from danger. Her pumps could not keep the water from gaining, four of her eight furnaces were extinguished and her speed fell to under five knots. The cotton piled on deck was thrown overboard, and for a time the lightened ship gained on the water and the crew was able to restart the fires. The struggle went on for nearly three days, until finally, on March 28, the *Will of the Wisp* limped into Nassau. She anchored in shallow water and within twenty minutes was resting on the bottom.[35]

Eventually Taylor raised the *Will of the Wisp*, and returned the ill-constructed vessel to duty. With her pumps in constant use, she turned in excellent service. In late August she carried in two 12-pound Whitworth rifles, a gift from Taylor's company to the Confederacy. The guns were soon put to use by the defenders of Wilmington. Before being sold by Taylor in October 1864, the *Will of the Wisp* made a total of six round trips through the blockade.[36]

Like the owners of the *Will of the Wisp*, the Charleston-based blockade-running companies also increased their operations. Continuing to use Wilmington as their main port of entry, many of the companies kept an eye on affairs around Charleston, hoping to reopen trade at their home port. The first firm to break the stalemate was the Palmetto Importing and Exporting Company, which outfitted the old dredge boat *General Moultrie*. In early March 1864, with 163 bales of cotton, the small steamer successfully escaped to Nassau. She never returned to the South and some months later was sold in Nassau, where she returned to work as a dredge boat.[37]

The significance of the *General Moultrie*'s run was that she proved Charleston could again be used as a port of entry, and soon companies were willing to risk larger blockade runners on trips to Charleston.

The first firm to renew regular business at Charleston was the Charleston Importing and Exporting Company, which operated the paddlewheel steamer *Syren*. A fast, well-constructed vessel, the *Syren* began her career in November 1863, when she ran from Nassau to Wilmington. Before the war ended, the steamer would make a total of thirty-three runs through the blockade, the most of any blockade runner. She owed much of her success to her daring captains and pilots who disdained the usual cautions taken by most blockade runners. The *Syren* would run the blockade at any time, not waiting for a new moon, or proper weather conditions. During one point in her career she reportedly made three round trips to Charleston while other blockade runners, awaiting a new moon, never left port.

The *Syren* was so successful that the company found it unnecessary to purchase any other vessels. By the end of the war, the Charleston Importing and Exporting Company had not only paid back its investors but also gave them a 100 percent profit over their initial investment. In the fall of 1864 a single share of the firm's stock, which originally sold at $1,000, commanded over $3,000.[38]

The Chicora Importing and Exporting Company also did quite well. The company repaid its stockholders' initial investments through dividends, but payments were with inflation-riddled Confederate Treasury notes and bonds. Individual shares of stock also rose in value, some going as high as $10,250 per share. The firm's good fortune came from its new steamers, the *Let Her Be* and *Let Her Rip,* which became the *Chicora* and *Wando.* The two would eventually account for eighteen trips through the blockade.[39]

The Importing and Exporting Company of South Carolina also continued its impressive record throughout the spring and summer of 1864. Its two vessels, the *Alice* and the *Fannie,* turned in tremendous performances, and, between the two, some forty-four trips were made through the blockade. The resulting profits were used to pay expenses, buy Confederate bonds and additional steamers. The construction of new blockade runners was supervised by Captain James Carlin, who for the moment gave up his blockade-running career to work with English shipwrights.

At first Carlin had a difficult time finding someone to build the company's vessels. In January 1864, he undertook a tour of English shipyards. Many were so busy building blockade runners that they refused to take on new contracts. A firm at Hull could not promise delivery under a year, and Carlin was unsatisfied with the work being done at most Clyde River yards. One of the few shipbuilders that did impress Carlin was Denny and Company of Dumbarton, Scotland. By early February, Carlin reported that he had contracted with Denny for three sidewheelers, the *Ella, Caroline,* and *Emily.*

The ships were supposed to be finished in time to replace the worn *Alice* and *Fannie,* but the toil of blockade running forced the company to send the *Fannie* back to Liverpool in late May 1864, before the new vessels were completed. The *Alice* remained in service for two more months before being relieved by the first of the Denny vessels, the *Ella,* which arrived in Bermuda on July 2, 1864.[40]

While most firms expanded their operations, John Fraser and Company began to cut back its activities. During the fall and winter of 1863, the firm operated only two vessels. Prioleau planned to put two more superblockade runners into serivce by the end of 1864, but he considered any more involvement to be a waste of money. He tried to convince his Charleston partners that the day of sure returns was over. Too many blockade runners were now falling victim to Union warships, and with the current cost of steamers, Prioleau saw no need to continue. Instead, he wanted the firms to work exclusively as commission brokers for the Confederacy and other companies, and to speculate in the construction of blockade runners. He did send five recently completed steamers to Nassau, where he hoped Lafitte would sell them to other firms. But instead, following instructions from Charleston, Lafitte incorporated them into the company's line of steamers. For the moment, Prioleau's fears seemed unfounded as the new ships made thirty-six runs through the blockade with only one being captured.

The two supersteamers that Prioleau had ordered specifically for the firm were the sidewheelers *Hope* and *Colonel Lamb*. Both were nearly 280 feet in length with a registered tonnage of 800, almost three times the capacity of most blockade runners. The *Hope* was ready by July 1864, while the *Colonel Lamb*, constructed under the careful supervision of Thomas Lockwood, would follow two months later.[41]

Vessels like the *Hope* and *Colonel Lamb* were needed as, by the fall of 1864, blockade running served an even greater role in the Confederate war effort. With the loss of more territory containing industrial and raw material sites, the South had no choice but to increase its dependence on the fast, powerful vessels that ran into the nation's remaining ports. Besides the loss of vital territory, the Confederacy was also feeling the tremendous strain of Grant's application of constant pressure on all fronts. No longer did the South's armies have the luxury of resupplying after campaigns; instead campaigns, especially on the Richmond and Atlanta fronts, were continuous, exhausting both men and supplies. The replacement for much of the material had to come from overseas, and the result of this was a long supply line stretching from the ports to the armies.

Even so, the system worked. Hard-pressed Confederate agents were successful in delivering suppliers. All of the bureau chiefs seemed to feel that the main problem of supply was not the availability of equipment but the ability of the Confederacy to deliver the goods to the front. Food, clothing, shoes, and munitions were being turned out in factories and imported in adequate numbers; the question remaining was one of transportation, especially for units that broke away from their established supply lines. However, over this aspect of supply those in charge of blockade running had little control.

All three of the major War Department bureaus relied on blockade running. From March 1864 through the fall of the year, the Ordnance Bureau brought in some 4,700 Austrian rifles, 22,000 Enfield rifles, well over a million pounds of saltpeter, over 3,500 pigs of lead, bales of leather, bundles of steel, sheets and pigs of copper, chemicals, and other finished metals. The Subsistence Bureau continued to secure a large portion of its meat requirements from overseas. Throughout the summer, the bureau managed to keep the Army of Northern Virginia supplied with meat coming in almost exclusively at Wilmington. Though the bureau rarely had the luxury of a large stockpile, it did keep up a continuous supply of tinned beef, bacon, and dried fish to the soldiers. Fragmented reports mention that the Quartermaster Bureau also kept its obligations through heavy reliance on blockade running. From March though September 1864, Lawton's Bureau brought in over 290,000 pairs of shoes, 275,000 blankets, and large quantities of cloth and finished uniforms, all desperately needed by the Confederate forces.

These deliveries were made until the fall of 1864 on private blockade runners operating under the new government regulations. Soon, with the completion of their vessels, Seddon, Trenholm, and McRae hoped to increased the flow of supplies and ship out enough cotton to meet the nation's financial obligations. For such an undertaking, not only would they have to employ the ports of Charleston and Wilmington, but also the Gulf ports.[42]

# Chapter Eight

# Failures in the Gulf

Throughout the war, the volume of blockade running in the Gulf never equaled that of the East Coast. There were a number of reasons for this situation. Primary among them was the fall of New Orleans. On its capture the city's merchants, unlike the shippers at Charleston, were unable to shift their trade to another port; when New Orleans fell, so did its blockade-running ventures.

Any new attempts would have to deal with harbors that had shallow bars and channels. Blockade runners had to have a draft of no more than twelve feet and ideally under ten. Since the vessels had to be smaller, voyages were not as profitable as those on the East Coast. Additionally, English shippers preferred using the British colonies of Bermuda and Nassau over Spanish-controlled Havana. The few Spanish-Cuban merchants who entered the trade lacked the commercial or cultural ties with the South, and did not have a well-developed shipping industry behind them.

Government policy also favored the East Coast ports. Since cotton bonds allowed merchants to pick their port of entry, most chose those located in the Southeast. This forced the government to honor the bonds by bringing massive shipments of cotton from Mississippi, Alabama, and west Georgia to Charleston and Wilmington, tying up valuable railroad space and wearing out both track and rolling stock. Not until early 1864 did the Confederacy make any attempt to force shippers to the cotton-rich Gulf ports.[1]

After New Orleans was captured, the ports of Mobile and Galveston became the region's primary ports, and St. Marks and Sabine

City served as secondary entry sites. However, by the fall of 1862, none had enjoyed much success. St. Marks was too isolated for most shippers, and Mobile was under tight blockade because of the presence of the *Florida*. Hence, all blockade running had been stifled. In Texas, both Galveston and Sabine City had Union flotillas inside their harbors, which cut off all water-borne trade.

The Texas situation was the first to change. On New Year's Eve 1862, Major General John Magruder sent a mixed force of Confederate infantry and cotton-clad gunboats against the Federals. Before 1863 was a day old, Magruder had captured the Union garrison and the sidewheel gunboat *Harriet Lane*, forced the destruction of the Northern flagship, and regained control of Galveston and its harbor.[2]

Nearly three weeks later, the Confederates repeated their successful tactics at Sabine Pass. This time, two small river steamers fell in with two blockading sailing ships. In a short, sharp fight, the two outclassed schooners were captured, and another site for blockade running was opened on the Texas coast.

While these events were occurring in the western Gulf, Lieutenant John Newland Maffitt was readying the warship *Florida* for a run out of Mobile. During the commerce raider's four-month stay, she had been properly outfitted and her crew brought up to strength. By January, Maffitt was ready for sea, and steamed the *Florida* to the head of the bay to await an opportunity to run the blockade. Her appearance off Fort Morgan caused the Northern squadron to make immediate preparations. The blockaders formed a semicircle off the mouth of the harbor with the gunboat *Pembina* near the bar. It was the responsibility of the *Pembina* to send up a signal when the *Florida* ran out, at which time the squadron's two swiftest vessels, the *R. R. Cuyler* and *Oneida*, were to give chase.

At 2:00 A.M., January 16, with storms threatening, Maffitt stood the *Florida* out of Mobile Bay and over the bar. She was seen by the *Pembina*, which raised a red light to signal the rest of the squadron, and then steamed after the *Florida*. The *R. R. Cuyler* also gave chase, but the *Oneida* missed the signal and remained at anchor. The *Pembina* and the *R. R. Cuyler* followed the Confederate warship throughout the night, battling a strong gale.

By morning the slower *Pembina* had dropped out of the hunt, but the *R. R. Cuyler*, an extremely fast though frail converted merchantman, continued on. She gained on the *Florida* during the daylight hours and, by twilight, was nearly ready to open with her bow gun when darkness came and the *Florida* slipped away.[3]

The escape of the *Florida* was a tremendous embarrassment to the Union Navy, though it would have been difficult to stop the vessel because of the lack of fast blockaders and heavy weather. Farragut's command was badly overextended with duties along the coast and on the Mississippi River. If this was not enough trouble, Farragut also had to contend with the presence of the commerce raider *Alabama*, which had recently appeared off Texas, sinking the converted merchantman *Hatteras* near Galveston. Such conditions gave blockade runners better opportunities, but the Confederacy and the merchants in Havana were in a poor position to take advantage of the situation.[4]

Unlike the East Coast, the Gulf did not have a large number of steam vessels available for service as blockade runners. Most of the Southern-owned packets had been lost or removed from the trade on the fall of New Orleans, and few British or Spanish vessels appeared to take their place. Instead, most of the trade that went on in early 1863 was carried by small schooners that did little to contribute to the Confederate war effort. Only the sidewheelers *Cuba* and *Alice* operated during this period, and they could not come close to handling the volume of trade the South needed from Havana.[5]

Ships coming from Havana to Mobile or St. Marks could use two routes. The quickest and most direct was to run straight across the Gulf. This circuit could be attempted only by the swiftest steamers because it placed the blockade runner on open sea, vulnerable to attack by Federal warships. The other course took vessels east from Havana along the Cuban coast before cutting north across the Florida Straits. If they successfully passed this heavily patrolled stretch of water, the ships would cruise up the western side of the Florida peninsula, using the many small bays and rivers as daytime hiding places. At some of these spots, such as the Suwannee River, Bayport, and Tampa Bay, small cargoes of cotton could be obtained; however, the best profits were made at St. Marks and Mobile. The danger of using this approach was being caught by the Union East Gulf Blockading Squadron, which constantly swept through the bays and sounds.

If the blockade runners survived the trip to Mobile, they had their choice of three entrances into the harbor. The least-used channel was that of Grant's Pass on the western side of the bay. The passage was guarded by Fort Powell, a small earthwork built on Tower Island just south of the channel. Grant's Pass, however, could be used only by blockade runners that first managed to slip into the Mississippi Sound. Since the entrances to the sound were shallow and closely watched by Union gunboats, only the most desperate seamen would try this route.

The main channel into Mobile Bay entered the harbor between Dauphin Island on the west and Mobile Point to the east. Here were situated the main Confederate fortifications. On Dauphin Island was Fort Gaines, a weak brickwork whose guns barely covered the western edge of the main channel. Across from Dauphin Island was Fort Morgan, a large masonry fort that served as the primary bastion of Mobile's defense. Its guns not only swept the main channel but also covered the smaller Swash channel that ran in from the southeast along Mobile Point, joining the main channel just outside the bay. In front of Morgan the Confederates placed a line of obstructions that narrowed the harbor's entrance to 100 yards. It was through this narrow passage, guarded by the fort's heaviest guns, that the blockaders ran. Like Fort Fisher, the garrison of Fort Morgan contained sections of light artillery that were kept ready to supply blockade runners that ran aground near the fort.

Both Gaines and Morgan were isolated works that could be easily cut off. The land defenses were dependent on the Navy and vessels of the Quartermaster Bureau to keep communications open with Mobile, located some ninety miles away. Because of this, the main harbor defense rested with the naval squadron which, at least on paper, was one of the strongest in the South. Besides three wooden gunboats, the Confederacy planned to put into service a total of nine ironclads to guard the bay. However, only one, the *Tennessee*, would be at the mouth of the harbor when the Union attack came. In the end, blockade runners would have to depend on the widely spaced fortifications to keep Mobile open.[6]

After the escape of the *Florida*, it took time for a blockade-running system to develop at Mobile. While Helm continued to stockpile munitions in Havana, officials at Mobile began to hire steamers for runs to Cuba. Two were the prewar coasting packets *Cuba* and *Alabama*; however, the majority of the contracted ships were flat-bottomed river steamers from the Tombigbee-Alabama River system. These vessels were not designed for use on the open sea, but their carrying capacity of hundreds of bales of cotton overruled any objections to their unseaworthiness.[7]

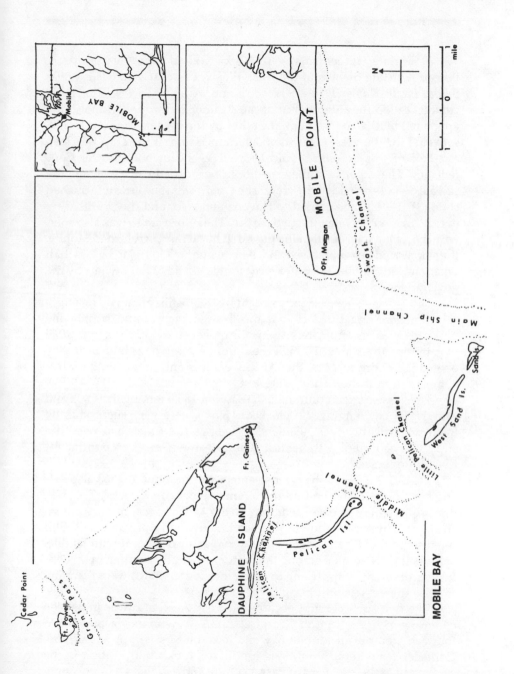

MOBILE BAY

MOBILE POINT

Ft. Morgan

Swash Channel

Main Ship Channel

Sand Is.

West Sand Is.

Little Pelican Channel

Pelican Channel

Middle Channel

Pelican Isl.

Ft. Gaines

DAUPHINE ISLAND

Pelican Channel

Grant Pass

Ft. Powell

Cedar Point

MOBILE BAY

Mobile

N

mile

0

At Mobile, agreements were worked out by the Quartermaster Bureau with the owners of the *Alice Vivian, Crescent, Kate Dale, James Battle, Lizzie Davis, Planter, Warrior,* and *William Bagley.* The basic contract called for an appraisal of the steamer by two individuals, one appointed by the government, the other by the owners of the vessel. A set value for the vessel was then determined and, if the ship was lost, one-half of this amount would be paid to the owners by the Confederacy. The expense of the expeditions was equally shared while the private owners provided the crew. The Quartermaster Bureau furnished cotton that would be carried to Havana and sold, and the profits were evenly divided between the two parties. The return cargo was also split, with the government half being provided by Helm. On return to Mobile, the ship would be reappraised and, if her value was found to be less than when she left Mobile, the difference would be paid to her owners by the government.[8]

The contracts were eagerly sought by steamship owners. The greatest attraction was the fact that the Confederacy would supply the outward cargo of cotton, thus saving the owners the expense and trouble of gathering the staple. Though their profits were not as high as if they owned the entire cargoes, their risks were less and they would receive compensation if their ships were lost.

The vessels began running in late spring 1863, joining the *Cuba* and *Alabama* in challenging the blockade. None were very successful. By September all the river steamers, as well as the *Cuba,* had been destroyed or captured, with the fast Union steamer *DeSoto* accounting for five of the losses.[9]

Besides the use of the river steamers, the summer of 1863 also saw another Confederate method to gain new blockade runners. This was the use of small boat expeditions to go out and capture Northern steamers. These raids operated much like the early privateers. A captured ship would be condemned and sold at a prize court with its cash value being distributed among the captors. It was blockading in reverse. Instead of taking ships trying to enter, the Confederates were planning to seize the vessels and bring them to port.

The first such attempt occurred in early April and was under the command of Acting Master George C. Andrews, who took a launch and fourteen men out of Mobile Bay and into the Mississippi Sound. The Confederates entered the Mississippi River, took up a position in the swamps near the coal yard at Pass á l'Outre and awaited an opportunity to capture a steamer. Their chance came on the evening of April 12, when the sidewheeler *Fox* arrived at the coal yard. The *Fox*, which had been taken at New Orleans on the city's fall to Farragut and was being used as a despatch vessel, anchored at the wharf, where its civilian crew prepared to spend the night. Around 2:00 A.M. Andrews led his men out of the swamp and onto the vessel. The crew of the *Fox* gave no resistance, and joined their captors in taking the steamer out of the river. By flying the American flag Andrews sailed the *Fox* to Mobile and ran her past the blockaders into the bay.

Once in port the *Fox* was condemned and sold with the prize money going to Andrews and his men. The *Fox* was purchased by a J. L. Harris, who renamed her the *Fanny* and contracted with the Quartermaster Bureau to use the vessel as a blockade runner. It was a role well suited for the fast sidewheeler as she originally had been the *A. J. Whitmore*, a blockade runner that served the South before the fall of New Orleans.[10]

The *Fanny* went on to make two round trips to Havana and, with the prewar coastal packet *Alabama*, was the most successful of the runners operating out of Mobile. By late August 1863, the two vessels were in Havana and ready for return runs to Mobile.

The *Alabama* left the Cuban port at 8:00 A.M. on September 7, 1864. Under Captain J. Hopkins, the vessel steamed along the coast of Cuba, and then turned north and during the night moved through the Florida Straits. The next morning the *Alabama* was sighted by the Union warship *San Jacinto*, which immediately bore down on the blockade runner. Hopkins turned his vessel to the west and outran his pursuer. He kept on until the *San Jacinto* was out of sight, then turned back to his original course.

The next morning another blockader was sighted coming at the *Alabama* from the east, and again Hopkins turned his ship to the west. This time the blockade runner could not lose the warship, and the chase went on throughout the daylight hours. Finally at nightfall Hopkins lost his pursuer by changing direction and hiding along the shoreline.

When morning came, Hopkins moved toward Mobile, but the *San Jacinto* soon appeared on the horizon. Hopkins pushed his vessel in an attempt to outrun the Union ship, but a second blockader appeared, cutting him off from Mobile. Without hesitation Hopkins hauled about. Before long the blockade runner neared the chain of islands that formed the Mississippi Sound. Hopkins hoped to lose the *San Jacinto* by entering one of the narrow, shallow passes that led into the sound but, as he directed the *Alabama* toward the northern point of Chandeleur Island, a steamer stood out. Again he changed course, this time making for the Horn Island Pass, but another Union ship, the *Tennessee*, was spotted, and Hopkins veered off.

On closer observation, Hopkins realized that the steamer he had seen coming out of Chandeleur Pass was his consort, the *Fanny*, also being chased by an enemy warship. With the entrance now open Hopkins turned the *Alabama* back toward the pass. With the *San Jacinto* shelling his vessel, Hopkins ordered cargo tossed overboard in an effort to increase speed. He first disposed of the cannon powder, which was followed by the deck cargo and a portion of the supplies stored below decks. This gave the *Alabama* enough speed to enter the pass ahead of her pursuers. The *San Jacinto* stopped, but the *Tennessee* slowly followed. While the Union ship struggled through the narrow pass, Hopkins ordered more speed, but before she could reach deeper water the *Alabama* ran aground, and was easily captured by the blockader *Eugenie* coming into the pass from the Union base on Ship Island.

While the *Alabama* was attempting to elude the Union blockaders, the *Fanny* tried to make her escape. She managed to evade the *Tennessee*, which later joined the chase of the *Alabama*, and work her way back into the sound. However, she was again sighted and eventually run down off Pascagoula by a trio of gunboats. To avoid capture the captain of the *Fanny* ran her aground and fired his vessel as he and the crew escaped to shore.[11]

The loss of the *Fanny* and *Alabama*, coupled with the capture of the remaining river steamers, nearly ended the Mobile's blockade-running activities. By the end of September 1863, some of the few remaining vessels began to turn their attention to the less-guarded port of St. Marks, Florida.[12]

Only small ships could use St. Marks. Their size allowed them to hide in bays and sounds along the Florida coast and navigate the shallow St. Marks River. However, their survival rate was poor and only one, the *Little Lilly*, made more than two round trips—the Brooklyn, New York-constructed steamer was able to complete five round trips before being captured.[13]

Another notorious vessel using St. Marks at this time, which had one of the most unusual careers of any blockade runner, was the small tug *Union*. Originally built in 1861 at Philadelphia, she had a brief career in Galveston Bay before escaping to Havana. She was reportedly owned by Nelson Clements, who sold her to Marie Avendans, a Havana businessman. In mid-May 1861 Avendans cleared the *Union* for Matamoras, but just as she passed out of Cuban waters she fell captive to the Federal warship *Huntsville* and was sent to the prize court at Key West for condemnation. Lawyers for Avendans contended that the ship had been going to Matamoras for use as a tug, but this argument was dismissed, and the steamer was condemned and sold to new owners.

By September 1863, the *Union*, now called the *Rosita*, reappeared in the Gulf and began operating between Havana and St. Marks. Because of her small size, the *Rosita* was well suited for use in the region's shallow waters. She was able to make at least two round trips between September 1863 and January 1864 before being caught by the U.S. transport *Western Metropolis*. The vessel again went through the condemnation procedures at Key West and by June 1864 was back in Havana under the name *Carolina*.[14]

By the time the *Rosita* was captured, the Federal East Gulf Blockading Squadron was ending the trade at St. Marks. In early 1864, the squadron was reinforced by a number of light-drafted steamers including the former blockade runners *Alabama*, *Nita*, and *Eugenie*. With the assistance of these vessels, the St. Marks trade was effectively ended. Even though Confederate officials in Richmond and England frequently proposed the use of St. Marks as a port of entry, no independent operators would again send their steamers to the Florida port. From February 1864 to the end of the war St. Marks would cease to serve steam blockade runners.[15]

With St. Marks closed off, blockade running in the eastern Gulf was concentrated in Mobile. This trade might have remained a haphazard, secondary affair if crowded conditions along the Atlantic coast and government incentives had not caused shippers to establish new links with Mobile. Those who came to the Alabama port soon discovered that, not only was turn-around time faster at Mobile but, in order to free Wilmington for government cotton and supplies, the Confederacy placed no restrictions on vessels using cotton bonds.

One of the first ventures to come to Mobile was a coalition between the H. O. Brewer and Company of Mobile, J. H. Shroeder and Company of Manchester, England, and Erlanger and Company of Paris. Together, they formed the European Trading Company and planned to make exclusive use of Mobile. The partnership had all the necessary ingredients for a successful business. H. O. Brewer and Company, an active commission merchant firm, had long been connected with blockade running out of Mobile. Shroeder and Company, a banking firm, handled the Erlanger loan in England, while Erlanger and Company, sponsors of the Confederate foreign loan, controlled a number of cotton bonds. The bonds obliged the Confederacy to deliver cotton to Mobile, where the firm found little competition.[16]

The first vessel employed by the European Trading Company was the small iron-hulled sidewheeler *Denbigh*. Built by Laird and Sons in 1860, she was well suited for use in the Gulf, measuring 182' × 22' × 8'7" and having a draft of only 9 feet. Arriving in Havana in late December 1863, the *Denbigh* ran to Mobile the following month. She took on a full cargo of about 500 bales of cotton, all purchased with Erlanger bonds. During the night of January 31, 1864, the *Denbigh* attempted to escape but ran hard aground a mile east of Fort Morgan, about 100 yards offshore. To protect the stranded runner, soldiers were sent on board and light artillery stationed on the beach. For four days the *Denbigh* suffered under constant long-range shelling from the block-aders until she was lightened enough to be towed into the bay. A few days later, after one hundred cotton bales were removed, the *Denbigh* escaped to Havana. This was the first of seven round trips the *Denbigh* would make between Mobile and Cuba. Her runs became so regular that the blockaders referred to her as "the packet."[17]

When news of the *Denbigh*'s run and use of Erlanger bonds reached Liverpool, a wave of excitement swept through the city's business section. Since the fall of 1863, blockade runners using bonds at Wilmington had been forced to take on one-half of their outward cargo for the Confederacy. No such restrictions had been placed on the *Denbigh*, and she carried a full cargo of private cotton. Such a policy encouraged the use of Mobile by private shippers and caused a new run on the Erlanger bonds. Their revival not only provided McRae with additional funds, but helped Trenholm when he began sounding out the European market for another foreign loan.[18]

The vessels coming to the Gulf in 1864 were steamers chosen for their ability to carry large amounts of cargo on very shallow drafts. Some, like the *Denbigh*, were converted merchantmen, while others were built specifically for the trade. At Havana these new vessels joined the *Denbigh*, *Alice*, and the *Austin* (now named *Donegal*) in providing service to Mobile. Each company had its own agents in Havana. Some hired Cuban firms while the Albion Trading Company and European

Trading Company employed the experienced blockade-runner agent George Wigg.

A large portion of the blockade runner's inward cargoes was supplied by Helm, who paid a generous rate for stowage. The Confederate agent sent in large quantities of ordnance, commissary, and quartermaster goods, and though the volume never reached that of Wilmington, during the summer of 1864, Mobile became an important center for government imports.[19]

The new steamers coming out of Havana were well served by a number of capable commanders and pilots. In their own area of operations the best Gulf captains were as well known as their eastern counterparts, and most disturbing to the Union officials, a number of them were Northerners. Captains Godfrey of the *Denbigh*, Bernard of the *Lavinia*, and William Smith of the *Austin* were from Maine while Barry Pendleton of the *Virgin* was a New Jersey native. Experienced pilots for the blockade runners were provided from the large pool of native fishermen who lived along Mobile Bay. These locals were well acquainted with the channels and shoals about the coast and, for substantial salaries, were quite willing to challenge the blockade.[20]

In 1864, there were at least 22 attempts by steamers to reach Mobile; of these 19 were successful. No vessel was taken coming out of the port. Mobile, however, was far from an open port. The Union squadron controlled the Mississippi Sound, thus cutting off Grant's Pass as an escape route, and the squadron kept tight control over Mobile's main channel. This forced blockade runners to use Swash Channel, which ran along Mobile Point. The entrance was narrow and tricky to navigate. Many vessels ran aground and were forced to jettison some of their cargo in order to enter the bay. Among the ships that ran ashore were the *Donegal* and *Denbigh* in April and the *Mary* in May 1864. All were saved by the heavy guns of Fort Morgan, which protected the vessels until they were freed.[21]

Blockade running at Mobile continued to grow from the spring of 1864 through the summer. More steamers came from Europe and New York, and the Confederate government laid plans to shift some of their steamers onto the Havana to Mobile run. To try and stop the blockade runners, the Union squadron increased the number of fast, light-draft warships patrolling Mobile's entrances, many of which were former blockade runners.

One of the first casualties due to the tightened blockade was the *Donegal*, the old New Orleans-based *Austin*, which had returned to service in January 1864. By June, the iron sidewheeler had made four round trips to Mobile and one to Galveston. In the first week of June, the *Donegal* cleared Havana and steamed for Mobile. By 1:30 A.M. Captain William Smith had guided his ship just off Mobile Point, but before he could reach the protection of Fort Morgan, he was sighted by the warship *Metacomet*. The blockader fired her guns and set up a rocket to alert the rest of the squadron.[22]

Smith quickly turned the *Donegal* out to sea. The commander of the *Metacomet* tried to follow but in the darkness lost his quarry. The Union captain then guessed the *Donegal*'s route and steamed southeast into the Gulf. At daylight the *Donegal* was again sighted, and the chase resumed. Within a half hour the *Metacomet* ran down the blockade runner. The *Donegal* was brought back off Mobile and anchored in sight of the Confederate works next to the Federal flagship, so the Southerners could see that the blockade runner had been captured.[23]

Another victim of the blockade's increased vigilance was the *Ivanhoe*, an iron paddlewheel steamer that had been recently completed in Greenock by John Scott and Sons. Coming out of Havana in late June she tried to slip into the harbor by way of Swash Channel, but was sighted by the gunboat *Glasgow*, the former blockade runner *Eugenie*. The Union warship signaled the rest of the squadron and opened fire on the *Ivanhoe*, forcing the ship aground about a mile east of Fort Morgan and forty to fifty yards off shore.

The *Glasgow* was driven away by fire from Fort Morgan, whose gunners at first suspected that a general attack was underway. When the *Ivanhoe*'s fate was discovered, the commander of Fort Morgan, Brigadier General Richard Lucian Page, sent out a section of artillery with a 30-pound Parrott and a company of infantry to protect the derelict. The soldiers reached the *Ivanhoe* and began to remove her cargo, but at daybreak they had to leave the ship and hide in the sandhills while the Parrott dueled with Union warships.

For the next few days, the blockaders constantly shelled the *Ivanhoe* while the Southerners worked at night removing her cargo. By July 4, the majority of her goods had been taken off, and the *Ivanhoe* remained relatively undamaged from the Union gunfire.

After five days of ineffective shelling, Farragut sent in a small boat expedition that managed to set the ship on fire before the Confederates drove them off. But only the vessel's woodwork burned, leaving her hull and machinery intact, allowing General Page to send out working parties to dismantle the blockade runner's engines.

Throughout July the Confederates worked at removing the *Ivanhoe*'s machinery, and by the end of the month the work was completed. A plan was then formulated to tow the damaged hull into the harbor; however, the Union presence off the port had increased, and General Page had to call off all efforts to save the *Ivanhoe* and prepare for an impending attack.[24]

Mobile had long been a prize coveted by Rear Admiral Farragut. He first wanted to seize the port just after the capture of New Orleans, but the Union Naval Department remained committed to the clearing of the Mississippi River valley, and Mobile had to wait. Later the assault on Mobile took second place to operations in Texas. It was not until the summer of 1864 that Farragut was permitted to proceed with definite preparations for an advance on Mobile.[25]

By mid-July the Federal squadron was nearly ready, save for the arrival of monitors from the East Coast and the Mississippi River. While Farragut waited for these warships, a number of blockade runners slipped in and out of Mobile. From June through July, the *Heroine, Alice, Denbigh, Mary,* and *Virgin* arrived, but only the *Denbigh* and *Alice* escaped.[26]

The last blockade runner to reach the city was the *Red Gauntlet*, a sister ship of the ill-fated *Ivanhoe*. She entered the bay on the morning of August 4 and two days later docked at Mobile. Among her cargo for the Confederacy were 25,000 pounds of lead, 63 sacks of coffee, 33 barrels of beef, 4 cases of harness leather, and 2 cases of stationery. She, like the other blockade runners still at the city, would never have a chance to escape. On August 5, 1864, Farragut took his assault force of 18 ships past Fort Morgan and into the bay. There the Union squadron defeated the Confederate naval contingent, captured the ironclad *Tennessee*, and took control of the upper regions of the harbor. Fort Powell at Grant's Pass was evacuated and on the sixth, Fort Gaines on Dauphin Island surrendered. Sixteen days later, after withstanding a heavy land and sea bombardment, General Page surrendered Fort Morgan.[27]

Trapped at Mobile were the blockade runners *Heroine, Mary, Virgin,* and *Red Gauntlet*. Since most operators thought that blockade running at Mobile was over, the runners were sold or chartered to the Army and put to use as transports. However, there were a few individuals who still believed that a vessel could run past the Union squadron inside Mobile harbor. Among these were the operators of the steamer *Heroine*. The fast sidewheeler was owned by John Fraser and Company and under the command of David Vincent. Early in her career she had made two successful runs to Wilmington before shifting her base to Havana in April 1864 to carry munitions under a charter with the Ordnance Bureau. Vincent, not wishing to abandon his vessel, volunteered to take her past the Union fleet. The *Heroine* was readied, but military authorities eventually put an end to the foolhardy idea. Vincent and his crew were paid off, and many returned to the East Coast, where they joined blockade runners coming into Wilmington.[28]

At Mobile, the trapped blockade runners worked about the waterfront. They assisted the Confederate engineers in building new defenses and obstructions to resist future Federal attacks. Still, there were those who thought an escape was possible. One of these was Lieutenant Joseph Fry, who had arrived from the East in January 1865 to assist with Mobile's defense. After reviewing the situation, the onetime commander of the *Eugenie* and *Agnes E. Fry* requested an opportunity to take out the *Red Gauntlet*. Fry suggested that the recently finished torpedo boat, *St. Patrick* be used to attack the Union squadron, and, in the confusion, Fry planned to escape in the *Red Gauntlet*. The plan was never carried out, and though the *St. Patrick* did venture out in an unsuccessful attack in late January, the *Red Gauntlet* never left port. Renewed Union assaults eventually forced Mobile's evacuation on April 12, 1865. The *Heroine* was captured at the city while the *Red Gauntlet*, *Virgin*, and *Mary* fled up the Tombigbee to Gainesville, where they later surrendered.[29]

The fall of Mobile was not as severe a blow to the Confederate war effort as might be expected. It never ranked close to Wilmington or even Charleston as a port of entry, and it was only as an afterthought that the Confederacy promoted its use. Since the beginning of the war about 36 steamers entered Mobile and another 44 cleared, while Wilmington had 286 clearances and Charleston 114.

Mobile was a minor part of Bayne's operations. Even so, the opportunity for its use was there throughout the war. Farragut's forces were too overextended to properly watch the port. Whereas the Union ships could catch the converted river boats, they did poorly with the fast, foreign-built steamers. However, by the time the European runners arrived, it was too late for the Confederacy to take complete advantage of the situation.[30]

Why Mobile was never fully utilized by the Confederacy was because of its policy of noninterference with private blockade running. By allowing the operators to choose their ports of entry, the government caused the burden of the trade to fall on Wilmington instead of distributing it between the East and Gulf coasts. Supplies for both the Eastern and Western armies arrived at Wilmington, then had to be routed to Western depots. While at the same time, Western cotton came to Wilmington for exportation.

The wear on the railroads and other logistical problems so encumbered the Confederate supply system that bottlenecks occurred all along the line, with the greatest strain falling on Wilmington. Mobile was in a position to relieve the transportation problems. By using its railroad and steamship lines, Mobile could have become the major supply center for the Western armies. But without government incentives or regulations, English shippers preferred to use Nassau and Bermuda, which allowed them to employ larger and more profitable vessels than could be operated in the Gulf. Though the opportunity existed, neither Bayne, Gorgas, nor Helm was willing to make more than a minimum effort to develop Mobile into a blockade-running port until new regulations, intended to ease the burden on Wilmington, went into effect. Even then, only a fraction of the trade shifted to the Gulf. However, in a backhanded way, the one-port policy worked, as when Mobile was closed, the flow of supplies was not substantially interrupted, and for five more months the Confederate lifeline was kept open at Wilmington.

After the fall of Mobile, the Gulf blockade runners did not relocate in Nassau or Bermuda, but remained in Havana and looked toward the Texas coast for new ports of entry. However, the Texas coast had unique problems that hampered the trade. Even though the coast contained numerous sites for blockade runners, communications were lacking. After the fall of New Orleans, rail connections to the Eastern states ran from Monroe, Louisiana, to Vicksburg, Mississippi. However links between Monroe and Texas depended on slow wagon trains, which took weeks to complete the journey.[31]

While transportation difficulties remained the major reason against the importation of supplies into Texas, a second factor was the Confederate's inability to properly defend the region's harbors. Few major shippers were willing to risk their vessels at ports that could be captured at any time. Even Galveston was too weakly defended for most operators and, after the harbor was recaptured and defenses readied, only one steamer, the *Alice*, used the port in 1863. Blockade-running activity was mainly limited to schooners, which made quick profits for their owners, but did very little to assist the Confederate war effort.[32]

For the first part of the war the majority of the munitions used in the Trans-Mississippi area came from Confederate arsenals east of the Mississippi, with a small amount of arms and equipment coming from Mexico. Large amounts of this equipment went east in 1861 and later in early 1862 when Confederate troops were transferred across the Mississippi. To make up for this, Gorgas sent some 34,000 small arms and two million rounds to the Western states between September 1862 and March 1863, but most of these supplies were used up during campaigns in Arkansas and Louisiana, leaving the region in constant need of additional munitions.[33]

Besides the arms problem, the Trans-Mississippi area was wrongly viewed by the rest of the Confederacy as a supplier of beef and other foodstuffs. Attempts to send beef across the Mississippi River were very haphazard. There was no continuous supply link, and those cattle that did make it rarely left the state of Mississippi. Besides this, transportation was so poor west of the Mississippi that the Confederates had difficulty providing meat for their own men, much less feeding the Eastern troops. Other items sent east included molasses and salt. Molasses was used by the Subsistence Bureau, which traded it for more substantial foodstuffs, and the salt was used for curing and preserving meat.[34]

While New Orleans remained in Confederate hands, the Trans-Mississippi Department was able to receive military supplies via the city's vast transportation system, but once the port was taken, officials in Texas and western Louisiana were forced to look elsewhere for munitions. Among the first to realize the region's dilemma were General Magruder and his quartermaster Major Simon Hart. Together, they entered into a contract with Nelson Clements of Galveston for the importation of arms, dry goods, and other supplies to Matamoras. Magruder and Hart also attempted to buy cotton for use in obtaining supplies, but they constantly found themselves being outbidded by private speculators, who dominated the cotton trade. Later, the officers attempted to control the trade by licensing, but this was struck down by authorities in Richmond. Because of these setbacks, the military considered impressing cotton, but decided against taking such extreme measures until their new commander arrived.[35]

On March 7, 1863, Lieutenant General Edmund Kirby Smith reached Alexandria, Louisiana, to take command of the Trans-Mississippi Department. The general was dismayed at what he found. His army was poorly clothed, armed, and fed. Realizing that relief could not be had from the East, Kirby Smith turned to importations. There were three avenues for overseas or foreign supplies. One possibility was to acquire goods from licensed Northern merchants at Shreveport. This trade had been authorized by Lincoln and the Treasury Department to provide cotton for the depressed Northern mills. At first all types of supplies, including some arms, arrived by this route but, in time, the Union commander at New Orleans, Major General Nathaniel Banks, tightened security, and the trade became an exchange of hard currency for cotton. This stopped valuable supplies from arriving at Shreveport, but it did add needed funds to Kirby Smith's war chest.

A second route readied by Kirby Smith was the use of blockade runners; however, in this area, he had few options. Kirby Smith ordered the captured *Harriet Lane* prepared as a department-run blockade runner and organized agents to control all trade coming into coastal cities; but in 1863 and early 1864 there were few steam blockade runners coming to Texas. Instead, there were only schooners and sloops operating in the western Gulf. Most of the small sailing craft ran out of Galveston and were, for the most part, individually owned. Few made more than one outward run; nearly half were captured, and over 60 percent ran to either a Mexican port, Belize, Honduras, or Kingston, Jamaica. Only those going to Havana could pick up Confederate munitions, and most did not. Of some seventy sailing ships that attempted to clear Galveston between January 1863 and March 1864, under a dozen ever returned. A supply system based on these ships was extremely tenuous, but until private steamers could be lured to Galveston, the Confederate commanders in Texas had little choice but to employ the little vessels as best they could.[36]

The final supply source open to Kirby Smith was the Mexican town of Matamoras. The port had the great advantage of not being blockaded, but the expense of shipping goods to and from the Mexican town was tremendous. By the time one purchased cotton, paid transportation fees, import and export duties, the staple ended up costing thirty-six cents a pound at Matamoras versus six cents a pound at Galveston. This discouraged many private speculators but, since the military was not out for profit, Kirby Smith hoped that he could employ the Matamoras loophole to some advantage.

But the task was not an easy one. In order to gain cotton for shipment from Matamoras, Kirby Smith had to resort to impressment. Owners were paid at a set rate, one that was well below the market value. This action caused a severe reaction, and soon the military found itself in a cotton price war with the state of Texas which, in order to protect its citizens, began buying up cotton at a more reasonable rate. The conflict between the civil and military leaders went on for sixteen months until the Texas governor, Pendleton Murrah, realized that his tactics were severely hindering the outfitting of Confederate soldiers, agreed to accept the military's management over the cotton trade.

Besides the difficulties with Murrah, Kirby Smith encountered a number of other problems over the use of Matamoras. The logistics were terrible. If the wagon trains survived the bandits, Indians, and the two and a half months on the trail, the shippers still had to deal with warring Mexican factions and the advancing French. Rarely did any munitions make this return trip to Texas. Of all the articles ordered under the Clements contract, only the dry goods and shoes arrived in Texas intact; the rest of the goods became the property of the Mexican Army, the French Army, and various Mexican irregulars.[37]

Another inteference came from the harassing tactics of the Union blockaders. Merchantmen overtaken in the open sea were still subject to inspection, and any ships found on the Texas side of the Rio Grande were seized. Most vessels stopped on the way to Matamoras carried legitimate papers and were allowed to continue, but one that did not escape the blockade was the British steamer *Peterhoff*, which was stopped on February 25, 1863, off St. Thomas by the warship *Vanderbilt*.

Though the inspecting Union sailors found the *Peterhoff*'s papers in order, they discovered that the cargo included gray blankets, boots, horseshoes, nails, and other items that a member of the *Peterhoff*'s crew claimed were to be landed at Brownsville. On the basis of this evidence the vessel was seized and sent to New York, where she was condemned and purchased by the Union Navy.

The seizure caused some difficulties with Great Britain, because when taking the ship, the Navy had interfered with the delivery of British mail. Parliament did not react kindly to the mail situation, and

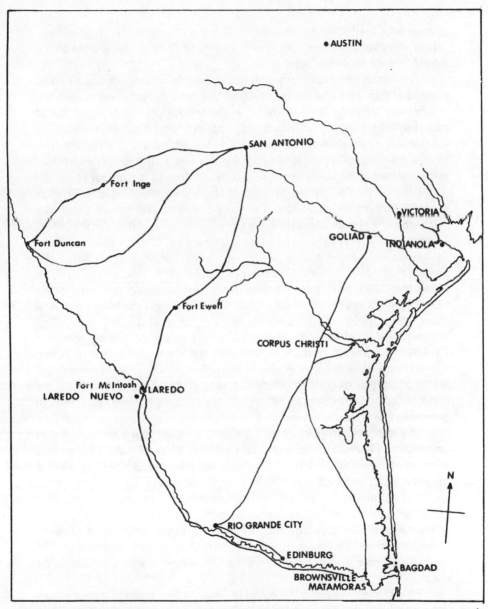

**OVERLAND ROUTES FROM MEXICO TO TEXAS**

not to scale

censure was forthcoming from the British government, but any confrontation was avoided when the mail bags were delivered unopened to the British consul in New York.

The owners of the *Peterhoff* appealed the decision of the prize court after the war, and the United States Supreme Court overturned the lower court's ruling. It was ruled that the testimony of one sailor could not disqualify legally certified ship papers, and that there was no substantial proof that the goods were to be landed at Brownsville. The *Peterhoff*'s owners were reimbursed for the cargo and vessel,which had subsequently been sunk near Wilmington while in Northern service.[38]

Even with the presence of the Union warships, Kirby Smith's greatest difficulties remained the logistical and command problems centering on the Brownsville-Matamoras connection. Besides interference by the French and Mexicans, there were rumors that his commander and quartermaster in Brownsville were stealing from the government and turning their backs on falsified invoices. Then, in November 1863, a Union expedition seized Brownsville. For the next six months only a small, unreliable trade was kept open via Monterey, and even when the Federals withdrew from Brownsville, Kirby Smith and his associates had to work in the midst of an ever confusing Mexican Civil War, which continually cut the supply lines from Mexico to Texas.

By the end of the war, it was evident that the use of Matamoras did little to aid the overall Confederate war effort. The majority of the exported cotton was owned by private speculators and was not used to purchase Confederate munitions.

The military supplies received were, for the most part, dry goods and shoes. Heavy equipment could not be brought into Matamoras because of the difficulty of shipping it to San Antonio. Some powder and finished cloth arrived from Monterrey but, because of the constant threat of seizure by the French or the Mexicans, importation of arms and ammunition was negligible. To escape the problems surrounding the Matamoras trade, Confederate officials in Texas and Havana were forced to make arrangements to deliver all types of military goods, especially arms and ammunition, to Galveston via steam blockade runners.[39]

To establish connections with Havana, Kirby Smith planned to use the recently converted *Harriet Lane*. In September 1863, he gained two more steamers, the *Clifton* and *Sachem*, which were captured during an unsuccessful Federal attack on Sabine Pass. However, none of the ships ventured out under militray control; instead they were sold to private shippers who, in early 1864, prepared them to run the blockade.[40]

The first of the trio to run out was the *Clifton*, which on the night of March 20, 1864, tried to slip through the narrow channel at Sabine Pass. As she crossed the bar, the sidewheeler ran aground and, to prevent capture, she was fired by her crew. The next morning her burned-out hull was discovered by the Union blockaders. The *Clifton*'s consort, the old screw-steamer *Sachem*, reportedly renamed *Clarinda*, probably escaped to Mexico later in the year.[41]

A few miles west of Sabine Pass, the Union Navy kept up a tight watch over Galveston Bay. However, they were unable to completely cut off the use of the shallow Southwest Channel that ran along Galveston Island. During April 1864, the steamers *Isabel*, *Susanna*, *Alice*, and *Donegal* arrived by this passage. Of these vessles, only the *Alice* had any serious difficulty reaching Galveston. In early February the steamer attempted to run into the bay but was driven off and instead entered the Brazos River. There, she took on a load of cotton, but the cargo so increased her draft she was unable to cross the bar. The cotton was unloaded and sent to Galveston. The *Alice* then escaped from the Brazos and steamed northeast into Galveston Bay to regain her cargo.[42]

However, escape from Galveston was somewhat more difficult. The Union squadron of six steamers, was mainly concerned in keeping the *Harriet Lane*, now renamed *Lavinia*, in port; however, their vigilance hindered the movement of other blockade runners. Believing that the deep-drafted *Lavinia* would be restricted to the main channel, the Federals placed their most powerful vessels at that passage. If any ships sighted the *Lavinia* a prearranged signal would be given and pursuit immediately undertaken by the blockaders' fastest steamers.

The Southerners foiled the Union plan by lightening the *Lavinia* and sending her with the *Alice* and *Isabel* through the Southwest Channel. At about 9:00 P.M., April 30, with the *Lavinia* in the lead, the three steamers stood out of the harbor and into the open sea. The only Union ship watching the passage was the screw gunboat *Katahdin*, under the command of Lieutenant Commander John Irwin. The night was exceptionally dark, and when Irwin first spotted the *Lavinia* he did not recognize her as the *Harriet Lane*, so he did not send up a signal to alert the other warships. Instead Irwin followed, but soon lost sight of the blockade runner. Irwin continued on, sighted the *Alice* and opened fire, but the shells missed their target, and again Irwin lost contact.

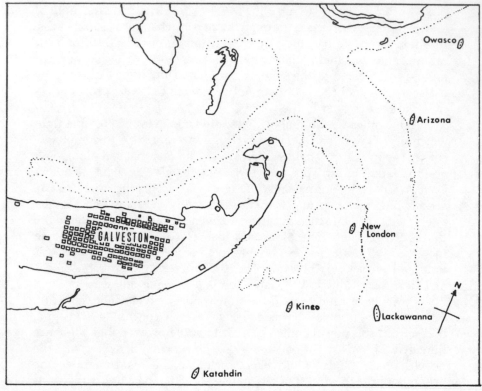

**BLOCKADING VESSELS OFF GALVESTON—APRIL 30, 1864**

not to scale

When daylight arrived, Irwin spotted the three blockade runners. He first chased the *Lavinia*, but the *Katahdin* was low on fuel and with boiler pressure dropping Irwin had to depend on his sails for added speed. When the commander of the *Lavinia* saw this he turned his vessel into the wind, forcing Irwin to pull in his sails. Irwin then turned toward the slower *Alice*. He hoped to capture the blockade runner, replenish his coal supply, then chase the *Lavinia* with both vessels. However, the commander of the *Alice*, John P. Smith, also turned his ship into the wind requiring Irwin to again drop his sails. Throughout the day the *Katahdin*, by burning coal, firewood, loose lumber, tar, and pork, gained on the *Alice*, and by afternoon began to shell the blockade runner. The gunboat fired over 100 shots, but none found their mark.

Captain Smith was also pushing his ship to the limit. Some 250 to 300 bales of cotton were thrown overboard, helping to increase the *Alice*'s speed. All day the bockade runner ran to the east forcing the *Katahdin* to fight a strong head wind. At nightfall the *Alice* turned north and lost her pursuer off Bayou Mermentau, east of Sabine Pass, by hiding along the shoreline. Irwin searched for the runner, then moved out into the Gulf in the vain hope of finding the *Alice* the next morning.

Although Smith had successfully escaped capture, the strain of the chase had caused his engines to break down. The crew worked throughout the night repairing the ship, and by morning the *Alice* began limping toward Havana. Smith eventually reached the protection of Spanish waters, but not before he burned the *Alice*'s upper deck.[43]

The escape of the *Lavinia* along with the *Alice* and *Isabel* was quite embarrassing for the Union Navy, though by no means the only embarrassment suffered by the Federals during the month of May. On May 6, the same day the blockade runners from Galveston reached Havana, the former blockade runner *Granite City*, now a Union gunboat, and the small steamer *Wave* were surprised in the Calcasieu River, Louisiana, by a force of Confederate infantry and field artillery. The two vessels fought bravely but, caught in a narrow river and unable to maneuver, were forced to surrender. The *Wave* was taken for use as a transport while the *Granite City* was repaired and returned to her old role as a blockade runner.[44]

The North regained some of its prestige three weeks later when the *Isabel* was sighted by the Union steamer *Admiral* about 30 miles off Galveston. This was the *Isabel*'s first run back to the Texas port since her escape with the *Lavinia* and *Alice*, but this time she was not so fortunate. The *Admiral* was a fast, powerful merchantman that had been converted into an armed cargo ship. When she sighted the *Isabel*, the *Admiral* was on her way to supply the Federal vessels off the Texas coast, but quickly turned and gave chase. The *Isabel* fled back toward Cuba, and soon reached a speed of over fourteen knots; but it was not enough, and after a chase of six hours, the *Admiral* pulled alongside the *Isabel*. The blockade runner still refused to surrender, and two broadsides had to be unleashed before she stopped.

A prize crew was placed on board, and the damaged *Isabel* was sent back to New Orleans. On entering the river, she was stopped by the quarantine officer at Southwest Pass and was still there three days later when the *Admiral* returned to New Orleans. The *Isabel* was taking in water and, not wishing to lose a valuable prize, the commander of the *Admiral* hauled the blockade runner onto the river bank by connecting hawsers to trees, but during the night the *Isabel* broke loose and sank.[45]

As she was one of only a few available vessels, the loss of the *Isabel* cut deeply into the Confederate ability to send munitions to Galveston. The *Alice* was already out of action for weeks while undergoing repairs, and the *Lavinia* was deemed too large for use in the Gulf. Two ships that were employed during the spring of 1864 were the *Susanna* and the *Carolina*. The two were old hands at blockade running. The *Susanna* had originally been the *Mail*, a British-built blockade runner that had been taken in October 1863 on her first run from Havana. Sent north, she had been condemned and sold, only to return to the Gulf, where she again became a blockade runner. The *Carolina* was operating under her third name, having formerly been the *Union* and the *Rosita*.

By June 1864, the two ships had combined for four runs into Galveston. The *Susanna* would continue a successful career, but the *Carolina*, after delivering 1,100 Enfield rifles, ran aground in early July 1864 and was destroyed while trying to escape from Galveston.[46]

The destruction of the *Carolina* left only the *Susanna* and the repaired *Alice*. They were joined in late August by the *Denbigh*, whose owners put her on the Galveston run shortly after the fall of Mobile Bay. By good fortune the *Denbigh* had not been trapped at the Alabama port. However, the loss of the other, British-built steamers that were caught at Mobile greatly hindered Helm's ability to utilize Galveston, as only one steamer, the *Zephine*, would come to the Gulf that fall to take up blockade running. The Confederates in Texas would have to depend upon the *Susanna*, *Alice*, *Denbigh*, and *Zephine* for the bulk of their munitions until December, when events on the East Coast would alter the situation.[47]

# Chapter Nine

# The Lifeline Is Cut

The summer of 1864 had seen a rise in the Confederacy's overseas credit. The combined effects of the new trade regulations and the successful defense of Atlanta and Richmond had caused the Confederate loan to reach a new high, allowing McRae to increase his purchases. By September huge quantities of goods were arriving in the West Indies.[1]

This period of increased credit was short-lived, as military reverses took their toll, returning the South's finances onto precarious ground. In late September, Consul Dudley reported that when word of the fall of Atlanta and the capture of Mobile harbor reached Liverpool it "produced in the commercial world almost a panic." The Erlanger loan fell 20 percent, and the price of cotton decreased. McRae managed to continue operations because of the arrival in England of government cotton, but the reduction in his credit rating forced him to be very prudent.[2]

Besides the problems in England, the South was having a difficult time delivering goods that had accumulated in the West Indies. By late summer, yellow fever was rampant in Bermuda and Nassau. Ships at Bermuda were quarantined for twenty-one days, while officials at Wilmington, still remembering the epidemic of 1862, refused to allow a vessel from the islands to approach the city unless it had been quarantined for thirty days. Such procedures increased the time for a round trip from two weeks to six or eight weeks.[3]

In order to avoid the quarantine, some shippers shifted their base of operations to Halifax, Nova Scotia. Throughout the war, the Canadian port was a popular shipping point between England and Nassau, Bermuda, and Havana. It was also one of the few ports where iron-hulled blockade runners could receive extensive repairs. For the first three years of the war, blockade runners coming out of the Great Lakes and the St. Lawrence River, and those crossing the North Atlantic from England, came to Halifax for refueling, but none had ever used the city as a site from which to run the blockade.

However, during the late summer of 1864, there was an attempt at Halifax to establish a depot for running supplies into the Confederacy. With vessels coming to the city to avoid the lengthy quarantine at Nassau and Bermuda, the shipping firm of Wier and Company offered their services to blockade runners, and a wharf and warehouse were made ready to transfer cargoes. These activities were carefully watched by the U.S. consul, who feared the city would become a major shipping point. His concerns were unwarranted. In all there were less than a dozen round trips between Halifax and Wilmington. Because of exposure to the turbulent North Atlantic seas, many vessels required repairs after their extended voyages. Also, the ships lost valuable cargo space because of the extra coal required to make the run, and the departure of every ship was wired ahead to Federal naval bases by the Northern consul.

Because of these factors, Halifax never developed into a large-scale blockade-running port. At best, Halifax served as a site for the funneling of supplies to Nassau, Bermuda, and Havana and as a major repair station. When cooler weather came, almost all of the blockade runners were again routed through Nassau and Bermuda.[4]

Among those who suffered because of the delays caused by disease in the islands were the Confederate Quartermaster Bureau and the Bureaus of Ordnance and Subsistence. Of all War Departments divisions, these three bureaus were the most dependent upon blockade running. Throughout the summer they had been able to meet the needs of the Confederate armies but, with winter coming, the bureau chiefs were concerned over their ability to continue, especially under the relentless pressure of the Union armies. All realized that they would have to increase their reliance on blockade running.

The section most tied to blockade running became the Subsistence Bureau. By late summer the problem of provisions had become critical. The Army of Northern Virginia and the forces in the Southeast were receiving nearly all of their meat from overseas. The supply of beef and bacon was enough to feed the soldiers, but rarely could the bureau stockpile more than a month's requirements. Because most shippers refused to carry the bulky, space-consuming meat containers, the bureau had to depend on agreements with Crenshaw and Company and Power, Low and Company for most of their shipments.

These two firms were the South's major source of meat throughout the fall of 1864. The pact with Power, Low and Company proved to be the better of the two contracts, as it employed blockade runners operated by Thomas Taylor. By using the *Will of the Wisp* and three recently completed steamers, the *Wild Rover, Night Hawk*, and *Banshee (II)*, Taylor provided a continuous, though somewhat tenuous, supply of meat.[5]

The pride of Taylor's little squadron was the *Banshee (II)*, a powerful steel-hulled paddlewheel steamer built by Aitken and Mansel. The ship was a vast improvement over her namesake. She was larger, stronger, and a better sea boat, one of the best examples of the final generation of blockade runners. She combined the speed and light draft of the *Banshee (I)* with the strength and carrying capacity of the larger Clyde River ferryboats.[6]

One of Taylor's vessels that had poor luck was the *Night Hawk*. In late September, under Captain Uriah F. Smiley, the *Night Hawk* cleared Bermuda for Wilmington with Taylor on board. Taylor noted that the captain and crew were new to the trade and that his pilot was unsure of himself. Around 11:00 P.M. on September 29, the vessel made for Old Inlet but, not trusting his pilot's knowledge of the approach, Taylor ordered the vessel to New Inlet, where he believed he could guide the *Night Hawk* through the blockade.

As the vessel made for New Inlet she was spotted by gunboat *Niphon*, which immediately gave chase and forced the *Night Hawk* aground. The commander of the *Niphon* then despatched a cutter under Acting Ensign E. N. Semon to take charge of the wreck. Before the Federals could reach the *Night Hawk*, the pilot, signalman, and four sailors escaped in a small boat. The Northerners fired a ragged volley at the fleeing men but missed, and instead wounded Taylor and two men on the *Night Hawk*.

Semon and his men boarded the blockade runner and quickly determined that it would be impossible to free the vessel. Setting the ship on fire, Semon directed Smiley and Taylor to follow the Federal sailors back to the *Niphon*. Smiley and twenty-three of his crew did transfer to the Union warship, but Taylor and about thirteen men remained on board. Taylor tried to convince the men to put out the fire.

However, his offer to pay £50 per man failed to secure any cooperation, and Taylor reluctantly joined the men in fleeing to shore in a damaged lifeboat.

On reaching the beach, Taylor found that Colonel Lamb had sent volunteers from Fort Fisher's garrison to aid the stranded blockade runner. The soldiers managed to extinguish the fire. After having his wound treated, Taylor returned to the *Night Hawk* and found the woodwork burned away but the engines intact. He immediately began to formulate plans to salvage the vessel.[7]

While Taylor's remaining vessels continued to carry in the bulk of the meat, Crenshaw and Company did manage to place a few vessels into service. One of these was the *Armstrong*, a recently completed paddlewheel steamer that made five successful trips through the blockade. The ship, however was poorly constructed, and her engines constantly caused damage to the ship's framework.

In October the *Armstrong* was commanded by Michael P. Usina, one of the youngest men to command a blockade runner. His reputation was based not only on his successful career, but also on his pet dog Tinker, a little terrier that served both as the ship's ratter and good-luck charm. On this trip to Wilmington, Usina ran into heavy weather that so damaged the *Armstrong* that he had to anchor her in Little River Inlet for repairs.

While in the river, the vessel was hailed by a group of men on shore. Usina despatched a small boat which soon returned with six ragtag and disgruntled Union soldiers. The men had recently escaped from the Confederate prison camp at Florence and had made their way to the coast in hopes of meeting a blockader, but instead they met a blockade runner.

Usina and his crew worked to repair the *Armstrong* while keeping a careful watch for Union warships. Several blockaders passed the damaged vessel, but they apparently mistook the *Armstrong* for one of their own ships as no hostile move was made. By nightfall, Usina had his vessel ready and by 11:00 P.M., he guided her into Old Inlet and under the guns of Fort Caswell.

Usina's good fortune held for the balance of the war. When he gave up command of the *Armstrong*, he was offered $500 in gold for his dog Tinker, but he refused to give up his good-luck charm.[8]

Besides the contracts with Crenshaw and Power, Low and Company, Northrup instructed his assistant Major Frank G. Ruffin to buy meat in the West Indies that would be shipped in via individual contracts with anyone willing to carry Confederate supplies. The actual purchasing agents were Walker and Heyliger, who then made the necessary delivery arrangements. The meat they purchased was, for the most part, from the Northern states. The United States consul in Nassau reported that "enormous quantities of American provisions" were constantly arriving in the Bahamas. Some came directly from Boston and New York in foreign ships while Northern ships "touched" at Canadian ports and then proceeded to the West Indies. In Liverpool, Dudley reported that beef packaged in Cleveland and pork from Cincinnati were coming into the English port and then reshipped to Bermuda.

These individual contracts, which paid shippers profits of about 350 percent for each round trip, helped ease the provision crisis. Later, when combined with the unexpected regularity of Crenshaw's steamers in the final months of 1864, the South was able to keep up a steady flow of meat through December.[9]

The Ordnance Bureau also continued its use of European imports. Gorgas had hoped that domestic production would alleviate his dependence on foreign supplies, but soon realized this was not to be. There were many reasons for the failure. The nation lacked the skilled laborers, and those that did exist were often drafted into the army. There was continuous pressure by the Union armies against important commercial-industrial centers; the fall of Atlanta had cost the bureau valuable time as the city's factories had to be dismantled and moved to Selma and Macon. The hardest blow suffered by Gorgas came in October 1864, when the blockade runner *Ella* arrived in Wilmington with the first load of machinery for the armory at Macon. The two main power engines were too small, and it would be months before replacements could arrive.

In October, Gorgas reported to Secretary of War Seddon that 20,000 small arms were in transit from Europe, another 50,000 were on order, and he intended to have Huse purchase an additional 50,000. Gorgas also noted that the Confederate supply of powder, though adequate for the moment, was entirely dependent on the importation of saltpeter. The South's supply of lead was precarious as the mines of Wytheville, Virginia, were the nation's only supply of lead. The balance had to come from abroad or be "gleaned" from battlefields. Besides this, the production of artillery required large imports of copper and iron.

From October 1864 to January 1865, the Ordnance Bureau imported nearly 50,000 rifles and carbines, over 400,000 pounds of lead, great quantities of copper, tin, and a vast supply of saltpeter. These items, plus chemicals and other goods needed for the production of munitions kept the Southern armies properly equipped.[10]

While the Subsistence and Ordnance bureaus were increasing their use of the blockade runners, the Quartermaster Bureau managed to reduce some of its dependence on the trade. Lawton's office successfully manufactured summer uniforms and socks from cotton. This reduced the need of foreign dry goods, and dispensed with Major Waller's mass purchases in Nassau from private merchants. However the arrival of cold weather would end the use of cotton uniforms, and the bureau would have to secure woolen goods from Europe. In late September, Lawton ordered Ferguson to buy wool and flannel cloth, gray cloth instead of blue for trousers, blankets and a cheap serviceable hat.[11]

Along with the importation of finished goods, Lawton arranged for shipment of machinery for the manufacture of blankets and shoes. To make certain the machines reached the South, he had more than one set purchase and gave instructions for them to come in on separate vessels. In this way, he hoped at least one of each would make it through the blockade. However, it was not until late fall that the first piece of machinery would be sent from England.

From April to November 1864 Lawton's bureau brought in enough supplies to outfit the Confederate soldiers through the last year of the war. Blockade runners carried into Wilmington and Charleston at least 400,000 pairs of shoes and 300,000 blankets along with vast amounts of uniform material. The shoes and blankets were immediately sent to depots for distribution, while the cloth was sent to factories to be cut and sewn into uniforms. Actual delivery of the supplies depended on the Confederacy's ability to keep its internal lines of communication open.[12]

The supplies brought in for the Ordnance and Quartermaster bureaus reached the South via two shipping firms, Collie and Company and Edwin P. Stringer's Mercantile Trading Company. For the delivery of his goods, Collie employed his "three stackers," vessels he considered to be the fastest in the trade. One of these steamers, the *Condor*, found herself, on her maiden voyage, entrusted with more than Quartermaster supplies.

After leaving England, the *Condor* made port at Halifax, arriving there in early September 1864. While there she was closely watched by the Federal consul, who quickly reported to his superiors that the *Condor* was more than the normal blockade runner. Her commander was William Nathan Wrighte Hewett, a captain in the British Navy. On leave, Hewett was using the name Samuel S. Ridge. Among the passengers were two Confederate agents, James P. Holcombe, a onetime spy returning from Canada, and the infamous Rose O'Neal Greenhow, who had revealed the North's plans for the First Bull Run Campaign to General Beauregard.

Mrs. Greenhow had just completed a year in England, where she had written a book and been active in Confederate affairs. Deciding to return to the South, she carried $2,000 in gold sovereigns, the proceeds from her book, which she planned to donate to Southern relief funds. She was also entrusted with a set of despatches from Mason to Secretary of State Benjamin.

In late September, Hewett guided the *Condor* out of Halifax harbor. Immediately word of her sailing was telegraphed to Washington by the Union consul. The steamer arrived off New Inlet in the early hours of October 1. She slipped through the outer line of blockaders, but was sighted near the bar by the ever present *Niphon*. Under fire from the warship, Hewett pushed on toward New Inlet, but as the *Condor* neared the safety of the passage, a ship's silhouette loomed ahead, and the pilot turned the vessel hard to the starboard, running the *Condor* aground. The vessel the pilot had turned to avoid was not a Union warship, but the grounded blockade runner *Night Hawk*.

The position of the *Condor* was precarious. If she could survive the pounding of the waves and the shells of the *Niphon*, she might be freed by the morning tide. But Mrs. Greenhow would not wait and demanded to be put ashore. Attempts to dissuade her were fruitless. A small boat was launched, and she with Holcombe, the pilot, and two seamen, tried to reach shore through the heavy surf. The small boat capsized and, although the four men survived, Mrs. Greenhow, weighted down by her gold, drowned. Her body was discovered the following day by Thomas Taylor, who was still at Fort Fisher supervising the salvage of the *Night Hawk*. The gold was not with the body. It was later learned that a sentry had found her, removed the gold, and pushed her body back into the surf. Once the soldier learned the circumstances, he returned the gold to Colonel Lamb. Mrs. Greenhow's body was taken to Wilmington, where she was buried with full military honors.

Those remaining on the *Condor* had no trouble escaping the next day once the heavy seas had subsided. Hewett had hoped to save his vessel, but the hard pounding had crushed her hull. However, the turbulent seas that destroyed the *Condor* assisted in saving her consort the *Night Hawk*, as the waves carried the burned-out hull over the shoals and onto the beach. Taylor immediately hired several hundred slaves, who pumped out the vessel and repaired the battered hull. By attaching cables onto the hull, Taylor, with the use of nearly three hundred slaves, pulled the *Night Hawk* into a small body of water between the beach and the shoal. At high tide she floated free, steam was raised, and she sailed into the river. The vessel was taken to Wilmington, where extensive repairs were started.[13]

Taylor continued to employ his other vessels to carry government supplies; however, both Bayne and Trenholm hoped that they could soon turn the majority of the trade over to the vessels being constructed by Fraser, Trenholm and Company and Gilliat and Company. By September, the first of these vessels, the *Owl*, was ready for service; however, there was confusion over her status and, when she arrived at Wilmington later in the month, naval officials tried to take over the ship.

The *Owl*'s commander Matthew J. Butcher refused, rightfully contending it violated the agreement with Prioleau. Butcher was allowed to take his vessel to Bermuda, but on the *Owl*'s next trip to Wilmington, the Navy intended to give the ship to commander John Maffitt. A disgusted Butcher sailed to Bermuda, and turned the *Owl* over to the Confederate agent. He then planned to return to Liverpool but, before he could do so, he contracted yellow fever and died.

The seizure of the *Owl* caused a severe reaction in England. Such a move placed the private companies in an extremely awkward position. If the Navy operated the ships without changing their registry, they were breaking British law. This made the vessels liable to seizure, and, since the *Owl* was registered in Prioleau's name, he could be fined and imprisoned.

When Bulloch learned of the events in Wilmington, he correctly surmised that Mallory was confusing the blockade runners with the warships Bulloch was building in England. He quickly wrote Mallory, pointing out that the *Owl* and her sisters were constructed as blockade runners, not warships, and strongly urged his chief not to seize any more vessels. Bulloch's letter had its desired effect. Whereas the *Owl*, with a new registry, remained in Confederate Navy hands, she was retained as a blockade runner, and none of the following ships were seized.[14]

The *Owl* went on to a successful career under Maffitt's command, but her sister the *Bat* was not as lucky, and was taken on her first run. The captors of the *Bat* were very impressed with their prize. She was the finest blockade runner captured up to that time, and was a forewarning of the new steamers that would soon be challenging the blockade.[15]

While the Confederacy awaited the completion of the rest of the *Owl*'s sisters, Bulloch worked to complete his European program. Arrangements were made to begin the shipping of torpedo boat engines, a power plant for an ironclad ram, and the completion of twin-screw gunboats. None of these ventures proved successful, though Bulloch did manage, with the assistance of the steamer *Laurel*, to put to sea the commerce raider *Shenandoah*. The *Laurel*, after outfitting the cruiser, went on to Nassau to take up blockade running, eventually operating under the name *Confederate States*.[16]

While Bulloch worked in Europe, Confederate naval authorities in the South purchased the blockade runner *Edith* for use as a commerce raider. Originally owned by Collie and Company, the *Edith* had compiled nine trips through the blockade before her sale to the Navy Department. The *Edith* was similar to the *Tallahassee*, the former blockade runner that the Navy had converted into a warship earlier in the year. Though smaller, the *Edith* was also an iron-hulled, twin-screw steamer built by John and William Dudgeon of London. In September 1864, the Confederates equipped the *Edith* with three guns and commissioned her the CSS *Chickamauga*.

The Union Navy, aware of the vessels, took extra precautions to keep them from escaping. As warships, the *Tallahassee* and *Chickamauga* were of little value. Their raids could not affect the overall war effort, but their escape and resulting attacks on merchantmen would be very embarrassing and could cause heavy losses to the North's maritime commerce. In order to keep the makeshift gunboats in port, the Federals placed additional steamers off Wilmington. The increase in blockaders did not contain the warships, but they did capture a number of blockade runners, including three of the five vessels carrying supplies for North Carolina. The losses were a severe blow to Governor Vance's plans, and to add insult to injury, the pride of the fleet, the *Advance*, was among the lost runners.[17]

Disaster signs had foreshadowed the *Advance*'s final run. In early September, while under the command of Joannes Wyllie, she was foiled in numerous escape attempts. Later she was accidentally rammed by the *Old Dominion*. Repaired, the *Advance* again attempted to run out; but her draft was too deep, and Wyllie had to remove her deck cargo.

Finally, on September 9, Wyllie guided the *Advance* out of New Inlet. As the vessel crossed the bar, she was fired on by the *Britannia*, but the shells missed, and by morning the *Advance* was running northward away from Wilmington. It appeared that her luck had returned, but later in the morning Wyllie spotted a pursuing Union vessel.

The ship was the *Santiago de Cuba*, one of the North's swiftest blockaders. The warship had been on its way to Hampton Roads for coal when it sighted the smoke from the *Advance*. The chase continued all day. The *Santiago de Cuba* slowly gained on the *Advance*. At about 8:00 P.M., the Union ship came in range and opened fire. Wyllie, realizing the inevitable, stopped his ship and surrendered.

The Federals found 410 bales of cotton and a few barrels of turpentine on the *Advance*. She was sent north, condemned, and purchased by the Union Navy. Renamed the *Frolic*, the steamer was strengthened, armed, and returned to the waters off Wilmington to hunt for her onetime consorts.[18]

The capture of the *Advance* caused severe repercussions in Raleigh, Wilmington, and Richmond. Vance and Whiting blamed the loss of the vessel on two factors, the lack of hard coal and the presence of the commerce raiders at Wilmington. They contended that the tightened blockade was causing severe difficulties for blockade runners. By now, almost no vessels were passing through the blockade without being seen, and few passed without being fired on.

Vance and Whiting demanded that the *Tallahassee* and *Chickamauga* be disarmed and converted to transports or blockade runners. Davis and Seddon turned the matter over to Secretary of the Navy Mallory, who refused to dismantle his warships. Mallory believed that his cruisers would hinder Northern coastal trade, raise the cost of Northern marine insurance, and cause the withdrawal of blockaders from Wilmington to pursue the raiders.

In the end, Vance and Whiting proved to be correct. Between September 1 and December 10, the period when the Federals increased their blockade, out of 96 attempts, 16 ships were captured or destroyed, a 20 percent loss, while in the previous three months out of 111 attempts only 11 vessels were lost, or a 10 percent rate. In the meantime, Mallory's ships only inconvenienced Northern shippers and did nothing substantial for the war effort.[19]

Whereas Vance and Whiting were correct regarding the commerce raiders, their concern over the lack of hard coal was not justified. In order to avoid using North Carolina coal, which was often of mixed quality, most blockade runners carried enough coal for a round trip. Some firms stockpiled coal in Wilmington, but this placed their fuel in a position where it could be seized by the military. Blockade runners stocked both hard and soft coal. The hard coal, being more efficient and smokeless, was used during the actual running of the blockade when low visibility and quick bursts of speed were required. Soft coal was used on the open sea, since most blockade runners could usually outrun warships even when using the soft coal.

After the *Advance* was captured, Governor Vance claimed that his vessel had been lost due to the navy's seizure of state-owned hard coal for the *Chickamauga* and *Tallahassee*. The accusation was false, but Vance continued to make the charge until the end of the war. As it was, the *Advance* was lost nearly two months before the Navy began impounding coal.

The problems over the coal supply were slight in comparison to the tightening of the Wilmington blockade. Some vessels changed to Charleston, where Union activity had somewhat diminished, but the majority of the blockade runners continued to risk the Wilmington run as the North kept up their watch on the commerce raiders.[20]

By late October, the two converted blockade runners were ready to undertake short cruises against Northern merchantmen. Lieutenant William H. Ward commanded the *Tallahassee*, now named *Olustee*, while Lieutenant John Wilkinson was in charge of the *Chickamauga*. On October 28, Wilkinson ran the *Chickamauga* out of Old Inlet and, though fired on, the vessel passed through the blockade unharmed.[21]

The next evening the *Olustee* escaped. Seen coming out of Old Inlet, she received some damage, but continued on to raid commerce off the Delaware Capes. Since neither ship was recognized, some days passed before the Federal squadron learned of the raiders' escape. No vessels were despatched north, instead the tight security net was kept off Wilmington, taking additional blockade runners while the Northern warships waited for the commerce raiders to return.

As the Federals continued their vigilance, the raiders took thirteen prizes off the northeastern coast. After ten days the ships ran short of fuel and began to move toward their home port. On November 6, while steaming south off Cape Charles, the *Olustee* was sighted by the gunboat *Sassacus*. The resulting chase continued all day, and only at nightfall was Ward able to evade the warship. The next morning, while continuing south, the raider was detected by the gunboats *Lilian*, *Montgomery*, and *Quaker City*. After four hours of pursuit the Union gunboats closed the gap and began to shell the *Olustee*. Ward ran up the Confederate ensign and returned fire. None of the vessels were hit, and the *Olustee* managed to keep ahead her pursuers until 5:30 P.M., when she escaped into a fog bank.

Ward's troubles were still not over. The *Sassacus*, after her unsuccessful chase of the raider, continued on and warned the Wilmington blockaders about the approaching *Olustee*. The Union warships increased their watch off both inlets, but on the night of November 8 Ward guided the *Olustee* into New Inlet.[22]

Wilkinson did not take the *Chickamauga* directly to Wilmington; instead he sailed to Bermuda, where he refueled for the return run. Leaving on November 15, he made for Wilmington. Four days later Wilkinson was guiding his ship toward New Inlet. The night was so foggy that landmarks could not be seen. Stopping his vessel above Fort Fisher, Wilkinson waited as the fog cleared. Union gunboats, sighting the *Chickamauga*, slowly approached what they thought to be a stranded blockade runner. Wilkinson opened fire and with the fog lifting made for the inlet. With supporting fire from Fort Fisher, he brought the *Chickamauga* safely into the river.

Though both vessels had carried out successful raids, Wilkinson immediately went to Richmond to argue against the use of commerce raiders. Pointing out that the makeshift gunboats resulted in a tightened blockade that denied the South needed supplies, Wilkinson urged their removal from service. His opinion was accepted, and he returned to Wilmington with orders to convert one of the raiders back to a blockade runner. Since the *Chickamauga* was known to British authorities in Bermuda as a gunboat, Wilkinson renovated the *Olustee*. Because of her conversion Wilkinson decided to give the vessel a new and appropriate name—the *Chameleon*.[23]

Wilkinson intended the *Chameleon* to join other government-owned blockade runners. But, as yet, few of these had reached the West

Indies. Private vessels continued to bring in the bulk of the Confederate supplies along with large amounts of private goods. From Liverpool, Dudley reported that though some of the smaller ventures had been discouraged by the Confederate regulations, the remaining firms were more than making up for lost business. In the late summer of 1864, he informed Seward that the trade at Liverpool and Glasgow was "as brisk as ever."

In later despatches Dudley described the vast building projects in the shipyards on the Clyde and Mersey rivers. A new fleet of iron- and steel-hulled vessels was being constructed. Many of these ships were designed to carry upwards of 1,500 bales of cotton. With such a capacity, the blockade runners could give the Confederacy one-half of their cargo space and still make a profit that would recover their initial investment.[24]

These immense profits were shared by a diminishing number of blockade runners. By the fall of 1864, attrition and the new regulations had eliminated the smaller firms and left about twelve to fifteen companies, of which five were controlled by English interests.

The two most prominent British firms were Edward Lawrence's Anglo-Confederate Trading Company and Collie and Company. Lawrence's firm was by far the most successful. Its ascendency was the result of the excellent work of Thomas Taylor, who kept up a high level of efficiency in the extremely competitive, high-risk field of blockade running. While good fortune played a large role in the company's high returns, Taylor worked hard in preparing his vessel and crew, leaving little to fate.

By the late fall of 1864, the Anglo-Confederate Trading Company had three operating vessels. The impaired *Will of the Wisp* had been sold in October, and the *Night Hawk* was still undergoing repairs in Wilmington. This left Taylor with the *Stormy Petrel, Banshee (II)*, and the *Wild Rover*. Of these three, only the *Stormy Petrel* would be lost, running aground December 7, 1864, near New Inlet. However, the *Banshee (II)* and the *Wild Rover* continued to make important runs in December and January.

Profits went toward outfitting additional ventures and paying dividends to their stockholders. Unlike other companies, Lawrence's firm did not reinvest all its returns into Confederate or state bonds; nor did it expand its working squadron beyond four runners at any one time. The company's good fortune was remarkable. The vessels supervised by Taylor made forty-nine successful trips out of fifty-eight attempts. One source reported that the company paid out two dividends in the fall of 1864 that amounted to 2,500 percent over the original cost of a share of stock.[25]

On the other hand, Collie and Company had fallen on hard times. Unlike the Anglo-Confederate Trading Company, Collie had greatly expanded his operations. Profits from his venture went into new vessels and North Carolina cotton bonds. Unfortunately, Collie's new steamers had a run of bad luck. Many were captured, and his prized three-stackers developed chronic mechanical problems, and not one made a run during the critical months of November and December 1864.

Though Collie kept up a strong faith in a Confederate victory, and in his ability to regain a profitable operation, he also depended on cotton bonds for security. Like many Englishmen, Collie believed that even if the North should win the war, the victors would honor the South's foreign commitments.[26]

Like their European counterparts, the Southern-owned blockade-running companies had mixed success in the final months of 1864. Many turned to newer and larger vessels while some of the firms, like Collie, believed that if the South lost, the North would honor existing contracts and respect private property. Also, faith was retained that, no matter what the war's outcome, the cotton market would remain at a boom level and profits would continue.[27]

While their competitors continued to enlarge their operations, John Fraser and Company retained its lead in blockade running, but as Prioleau predicted, a number of steamers were lost. By the end of 1864, only the *Fox* was active, and the firm was selling a number of its uncompleted steamers.

Two vessels that the company did not part with were the *Hope* and the *Colonel Lamb*. These ships represented the war's best blockade runners. Both were large, steel ships, described by Dudley as being "larger and superior to most that have been recently built." They measured 280′ × 35′ × 15′, and had a cargo capacity larger than other blockade runners.

The *Hope*'s captain was William C. Hammer, onetime commander of the *Annie Childs*. The vessel arrived safely at Wilmington in late July with a valuable cargo that included two 150-pound Armstrong cannons and two 12-pound Whitworth guns. Hammer returned the *Hope* to Nassau and quickly made preparations for another trip.

At about 1:00 A.M. on October 22, Hammer brought the *Hope* off Old Inlet, where she was sighted by the *Eolus*. Hammer tried to escape by running the *Hope* out to sea. For 65 miles the chase went on, but, just as the *Hope* was making good her escape, a steam pipe burst, and she was overtaken by the *Eolus*.

Shortly after the *Hope*'s capture, the *Colonel Lamb* arrived at Nassau to try her luck against the blockade. Though considered sisters, the *Colonel Lamb* had been altered to fit the requirements of her captain, Thomas Lockwood. Lockwood, nicknamed the "father of the trade" by his peers, had definite views on the *Colonel Lamb*'s construction and rigging. By the time he was finished, her cost had soared to £50,000, some £12,000 over the price of the *Hope*. Prioleau gave Lockwood full control and, when Bulloch complained about the vessel's upper works, the irrepressible Lockwood told the naval officer to mind his own business, stating that he knew more about ships than Bulloch. Prioleau did not interfere, but privately expressed concern that the *Colonel Lamb* was a costly experiment. As it turned out, Lockwood lived up to his reputation by successfully taking the *Colonel Lamb* into the Cape Fear River on November 29, 1864.[28]

By bringing their supplies to Wilmington, vessels like the *Hope* and *Colonel Lamb* were following the standard route taken by the majority of blockade runners operating in the waning months of 1864. Charleston had a slight revival in the latter part of 1864, but the bulk of supplies continued to flow through the North Carolina town. By the fall of 1864, Wilmington was one of the most important sites in the Confederacy. Through the port came arms, saltpeter, lead for bullets, iron, copper, and steel for the foundries, cloth for uniforms, food, shoes, and leather. Without the port of Wilmington, the South could not have properly supplied its armed forces.[29]

By 1864, leaders in the Union War Department began to realize just how important Wilmington was to the Southern war effort, but by this time the city's defenses were so strong that it would take a substantial force to guarantee victory. The Navy Department decided that the best mode of attack was a joint expedition against Fort Fisher. Once the fort was captured, warships could be sent through New Inlet, flanking the defenses at Old Inlet, and sealing the river. In August 1864, Secretary of Navy Welles and his assistant Gustavus Vasa Fox approached Lincoln and Secretary of War Stanton regarding an assault on Fort Fisher. The idea was well received, but the final decision lay with General Grant, who would have to provide the necessary troops.[30]

The commanding general was also receptive, but only if it required no more than 12,000 men and that someone more aggressive than the current naval commander off Wilmington, Rear Admiral Samuel P. Lee, be in charge of the naval contingent. The conditions were agreed to, and by November 1864 a force of 6,500 soldiers under Major General Benjamin Butler and over 50 vessels commanded by Rear Admiral David Dixon Porter, was assembled at Hampton Roads.

The expedition suffered numerous delays. One centered on outfitting a powder boat for use against Fort Fisher. The idea originated with Butler and was backed by Porter. It called for the conversion of the warship *Louisiana* into a floating bomb. Made to resemble a blockade runner, it was planned to detonate the ship off Fisher. It was thought that resulting explosion would level the fort.[31]

Besides waiting for the *Louisiana*, the expedition was slowed by other problems and did not appear off Cape Fear until December 19, 1864. The sighting of the fleet caused immediate activity among the blockade runners. While Colonel Lamb and General Whiting readied their defenses, several steamers prepared to clear the port. Before the attack got under way, the vessels *Colonel Lamb*, *Charlotte*, and *Owl* ran out of Old Inlet, and a fourth vessel, the *Talisman*, tried to escape from New Inlet, but in a storm she crashed onto the wreck of the ironclad *Raleigh* and returned to Wilmington for repairs.

The remaining blockade runners came under the eye of General Whiting, who tried to seize the vessels for use as block-ships at New Inlet. His commanding officer, General Braxton Bragg, turned down his request, refusing to allow the impounding of private property. Whiting then asked the Navy for the *Chickamauga* and the floating battery *Arctic*, but the Navy also turned him down. Whiting did gain the use of the blockade runners *Badger* and *Night Hawk* as transports, and the two steamers joined the *Cape Fear* in ferrying troops along the Cape Fear River.[32]

While the Confederates prepared their defenses, Porter and his vessels waited for the weather to clear. On December 23, the seas had calmed enough to send in the powder-ship *Louisiana*. The command of the altered warship was given to Commander Alexander C. Rhind, who, with a picked crew, was to run the ship as near Fort Fisher as possible before igniting the powder. Towed by the gunboat *Wilderness* until close to the beach, the *Louisiana* was cast loose and Rhind steamed her near the fort. As he moved along the shallows, Rhind spotted the blockade runner *Little Hattie* moving toward New Inlet. He quickly followed the ship, hoping that the *Louisiana* would be mistaken as a blockade runner. The ruse was successful.

When Rhind reached a point off Fort Fisher's northeast bastion, he stopped the engines and readied the explosives. The sea was rough and the night dark, but he was able to stop the *Louisiana* about 600 yards off the beach. He then ordered his crew away. Retaining two men, Rhind set the fuses and ignited a fire on the ship's deck in case the fuses failed. The three men then pulled away from the *Louisiana* and rejoined the rest of the crew aboard the *Wilderness.*

At about 2:00 A.M., the great explosion took place. It rocked the fleet and created a huge sulphur cloud. The only effect on the fort was to awaken the garrison. Colonel Lamb noted in his diary that "a blockader got aground near the fort, set fire to herself and blew up."[33]

When the morning reconnaissance revealed an undamaged fort, Porter commenced a two-day bombardment while Butler's troops went ashore. However, Butler and his commanders felt it too risky to assault Fisher, and by December 27 a disgusted Porter had removed the soldiers. Butler, his men, and transports returned to Hampton Roads, while Porter, determined to continue the attack, took his fleet to Beaufort, North Carolina.[34]

During the bombardment, the Confederate government-owned blockade runner *Stag* escaped from Old Inlet. About the same time, the *Virginia* and *Agnes E. Fry* tried to enter the river. The *Virginia* safely passed in, but the *Agnes E. Fry* was chased ashore below Fort Campbell. The commander of the vessel Lieutenant Joseph E. Fry managed to land his crew and passengers; and though there was some hope of salvaging the vessel's cargo and machinery, the operation was never carried out.

Whiting and Lamb had more important problems than the stripping of a derelict blockade runner. Both officers expected the attack to be renewed, as did their commander in chief General Robert E. Lee, who informed them that if Fisher fell, he would be unable to maintain his army. Whiting and Lamb realized the importance of their position and, during the next two weeks, furious preparations went on to ready their defenses.

At the same time, the operators of blockade runners, also realizing that the Federals would be returning, began sending their vessels out of

Wilmington. Between December 28 and January 2, seven ships, including the rebuilt *Night Hawk* and the damaged *Talisman*, escaped; but the unlucky *Talisman*, which had struck the wreck of the *Raleigh* less than two weeks earlier, ran into heavy seas and broke up. Her crew, including Clifford Lanier, brother of Sidney Lanier, was saved by a passing schooner and carried to Bermuda.

The last vessel to enter Wilmington was Thomas Taylor's *Wild Rover*. She was also the last blockade runner to leave the city, clearing on the night of January 2, 1865.[35]

The Federals were returning. After the first attempt, Porter wrote Secretary of Navy Welles, attacking Butler's role in the assault and promising better results if a new army commander was appointed. Welles relayed the messages to Grant, who complied with Porter's wishes and assigned Brigadier General Alfred H. Terry to lead a reinforced contingent in the next assault against Fort Fisher.

On January 12, 1865, the fleet again appeared off Fisher. This time the attack was carried out in an organized manner. The weather stayed clear, and Porter supplied a naval landing force to assist in the rush. The navy's bombardment dismounted the majority of the enemy's guns and paved the way for the land attack. The final assault came in midafternoon of January 15, and though the Southerners put up stubborn resistance, they were forced out of the fort and back to Battery Buchanan, where they surrendered.[36]

The fall of Fort Fisher allowed the Union gunboats to enter the Cape Fear River through New Inlet and cut off the defenses at Old Inlet. After Fisher's capture, the Confederate troops on Smith's Island were transferred to Smithville, where they joined the men from Forts Caswell and Campbell in retreating overland toward Wilmington. The presence of Federal vessels between Smithville and Wilmington forced the Confederates to destroy the *Cape Fear* near Fort Caswell. Around the same time, the blockade runner *North Heath*, which had been badly damaged while entering the river in October, was sunk as an obstruction just below Wilmington. The *Chickamauga* continued to serve in the defense of Wilmington until February 25, 1865, when, on the abandonment of the city, she was sunk in a vain attempt to block the Cape Fear River between Wilmington and Fayetteville.[37]

While the Confederates were evacuating Smithville and their other defenses at the mouth of the Cape Fear River, Commander Maffitt brought the *Owl* into Old Inlet and anchored his vessel off Fort Caswell.

Maffitt immediately realized that something was wrong when he
noticed that the signal lights were not lit. His suspicions were confirmed
when a launch from Smithville pulled alongside and informed him that
Fisher had been taken and the rest of the Cape Fear defenses were being
abandoned. Maffitt lingered only long enough for his pilot to visit his
family at Smithville, and on the pilot's return, the *Owl* ran out to sea.[38]

As the *Owl* moved away from Old Inlet, the runner *Rattlesnake*
approached New Inlet. Her commander M. P. Usina found the coastline
off Fort Fisher crowded with Federal ships, but none took notice of him.
Seeing unfamiliar campfires around Fisher, Usina quickly surmised that
the fort had fallen. He then managed to turn the *Rattlesnake* back to sea
and sail back unrecognized through the Union fleet.[39]

Before Maffitt and Usina could return and warn off other blockade
runners, three, the *Stag* and *Charlotte* in Old Inlet and the *Blenheim* in
New Inlet, were lured in by false signal lights set by the Federals and
captured. A fourth vessel, the *Chameleon* had better luck.[40]

The *Chameleon*, after being refitted by Wilkinson, had gone to
Bermuda in late December. While there, Wilkinson had to convince
doubting British authorities that the *Chameleon* was a legitimate blockade runner and not a privateer. Two vital weeks were lost; finally by
mid-January Wilkinson was off Fort Fisher, but on seeing no signals he
took the *Chameleon* back out to sea. The next night he again steamed into
New Inlet. This time Wilkinson spotted two Union gunboats coming
toward him. Most blockade runners would have been trapped; however,
by using the *Chameleon*'s twin screws, Wilkinson spun the ship on her
keel and escaped.[41]

While the *Chameleon* was moving away from Wilmington, the *Owl*
arrived and stopped a number of blockade runners from sailing. The
news of the fall of Fort Fisher had a severe reaction. The U.S. consul in
Bermuda reported that "Upon receit [sic] of the information by the *Owl*
business was nearly suspended, and had they known the Islands were to
sink in twenty-four hours, there could hardly have been greater conster-
nation; the blockade runners and their aiders feel their doom is sealed."

Since the majority of the trade from Bermuda had gone to
Wilmington, the closure of the Cape Fear River virtually ended the use of
St. George by the blockade runners. Those desiring to continue shifted
their base to Nassau, where ships were readied for runs to Charleston.[42]

Throughout the summer and fall of 1864, Charleston's trade had
enjoyed a small revival. The vessels that ran to the port were small and

privately owned, most being operated by firms based in the city. Among the most prosperous ships were John Fraser and Company's *Fox*, the Chicora Importing and Exporting Company's *Chicora*, the Steamship Druid Company's *Druid*, and the Charleston Importing and Exporting Company's immensely successful *Syren*. In 1864, these ships made twenty-four of the thirty-eight runs into Charleston. By the end of the year their example caused other firms to test the blockade off Charleston.[43]

After the closure of Wilmington, additional Federal warships arrived off Charleston, thus making it extremely difficult for blockade runners to use the port, but there remained a number of captains who, for profit and patriotism, were willing to risk the run. Among the vessels that managed to reach the port in January were the *Fox*, *Syren*, and *Chicora*. A fourth blockade runner coming into Charleston was the *G. T. Watson*, a light-drafted twin screw that had seen service earlier as the blockade runner *Kate*. After being seized off Wilmington in August 1863, the *Kate* had been condemned and sold to private interests. Her new owners took her to Havana in December 1864, and returned the ship to the blockade-running trade.

The majority of the vessels coming to Charleston carried private goods but, after Fisher's capture, Maffitt and Wilkinson made plans with Heyliger at Nassau to run government supplies into Charleston. However, their attempts during the month of February were foiled. The increased blockade stopped most ships trying to reach the port. One steamer, the *Rattlesnake*, ran aground while all others save the *Syren* were turned away.[44]

Charleston's importance remained only as long as its railroad connections were open. Shortly after the fall of Fort Fisher, Charleston's fate was sealed when General William T. Sherman's army moved into South Carolina and cut the railroads. Once this occurred, plans were immediately made to evacuate Charleston, and the blockade runners prepared to abandon the port.

The *Chicora* escaped on February 12, and two days later the *Celt*, a vessel built at Charleston during the war, made an attempt but ran aground off Fort Moultrie. On the sixteenth, the *Syren* entered Charleston harbor on her thirty-third trip, making the little sidewheeler the war's most successful blockade runner. The last ship to leave the port was the *G. T. Watson*, which pulled away from a flaming wharf on

February 17, the night the city was evacuated. Three days later she docked at Nassau with the news of Charleston's fall.

The morning after the Confederates left, Union soldiers and sailors entered the harbor in small boats and raced to the city. Sailors from the Federal tug *Gladiolus* found the abandoned *Syren* at a dock in the Ashley River. Though she was on fire, a group of blacks were trying to salvage her cargo. The Union sailors organized a fire brigade and, with the help of the blacks, managed to extinguish the fire. Saved and sent north, the *Syren*, the war's top blockade runner, eventually became a United States merchantman.[45]

As at Wilmington, the Union commanders maintained most of the harbor's signal lights. The ploy was successful; on the night after the evacuation, the unsuspecting blockade runner *Deer*, on her first attempt to reach the South, approached the port. She was commanded by Joannes Wyllie, who had captained the *Advance* on her last voyage. As he brought the *Deer* along Long Island, Wyllie noticed that the usual signal light on the northern end of Sullivan's Island was not lit; still he continued on and soon saw the light at Fort Beauregard, but as he passed through the channel the *Deer* ran hard aground. Union sailors from monitors stationed in the channel rowed out, and, much to Wyllie's embarrassment, took possession of the stranded steamer.[46]

After the capture of the *Deer* no other vessel tried to come into Charleston. The *G. T. Watson* had warned off any more ships from clearing Nassau. The evacuation of Charleston had the same effect in Nassau as the capture of Fort Fisher had on Bermuda. Offices were closed and goods sent back to Liverpool and New York. Within a week of Charleston's fall, the U.S. consul at Nassau informed Seward that "Blockade running from this port has ceased."[47]

While the fall of Charleston and Wilmington was a tremendous blow to the islands, it was devastating to the South. By the latter part of 1864, the Confederate armies were almost totally dependent on goods received through the blockade. While the lifeline to the islands had remained open, the Confederacy was able to refit the Western Army after its many defeats, and keep up a supply of necessities to Lee's army in the trenches around Petersburg and Richmond. After Hood's costly Atlanta campaign, the Army of Tennessee required over 58,000 pairs of shoes, 55,000 pairs of pants, 38,000 small arms, and 21,000 blankets. The War Department bureaus refitted the Army, but in January, after the disasters of Franklin and Nashville, the Army again needed huge amounts of supplies, especially quartermaster goods. Before the month was out, Lawton requisitioned for that Army 45,000 jackets, 100,000 pairs of pants, 100,000 pairs of shoes, 27,000 blankets, 60,000 shirts, and 108,000 pairs of drawers, supplies for only an army of 25,000.

The Army of Northern Virginia also received a large supply of quartermaster goods during the last six months of 1864. Lawton's bureau issued over 100,000 jackets, 140,000 pairs of pants, 167,000 pairs of shoes, 74,000 blankets, 4,800 overcoats, 170,000 pairs of drawers, and 150,000 cotton shirts. Some of the items came from domestic production, but even so, most of the cloth came through the blockade. These supplies were for an army that numbered only 72,000 and whose ranks were decreasing daily through desertion and losses in battle.

The ending of blockade running east of the Mississippi also stopped the work of the states of Georgia and North Carolina. Their arrangements had shown excellent results. In 1864, Georgia supplied its soldiers with 26,700 jackets, 28,000 pairs of pants, 37,000 pairs of shoes, 7,500 blankets, 24,000 shirts, 24,000 pairs of drawers, and 23,000 pairs of socks. North Carolina also shipped in large amounts of equipment, especially cloth that was made into uniforms. Because of their work the state's officials boasted that their soldiers were the best equipped in the army.

However, demands for quartermaster stores continued, and with the states out of the quartermaster business, Lawton filled the orders as best he could, but supplies of shoes, blankets, and jackets were dwindling. The end of winter would ease the requests, but without his European connections it would become impossible for Lawton to completely fill the necessary requisitions.[48]

The closing of the eastern seaports also severely taxed the resources of the Ordnance Bureau. During 1864, the bureau reported importing nearly 50,000 rifles, 1,700 pistols, and 4,700 carbines. Another 10,000 to 12,000 small arms were in the islands, and thousands more were on order in Europe. Home production was down and losses in battle up. The troops were well armed, but reserves were low, with only 5,600 rifles and 3,500 muskets in the arsenals. Ammunition was adequate, but the supply was heavily dependent on blockade running for lead, cartridge paper, and saltpeter. As with the Quartermaster Bureau, the Ordnance Bureau had enough supplies stockpiled that, when supplemented by domestic production, materials would be available for a few more months, but their vital supplies would eventually dry up.[49]

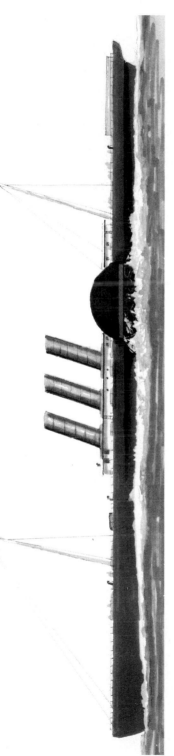

Figure 21. The *Flamingo*, one of the unique three-stackers operated by Collie and Company. Though considered by some to be the finest blockade runners, the *Flamingo* and her sisters suffered from chronic mechanical and structural difficulties. (*Painting by Wendell P. Wass, from a private collection*)

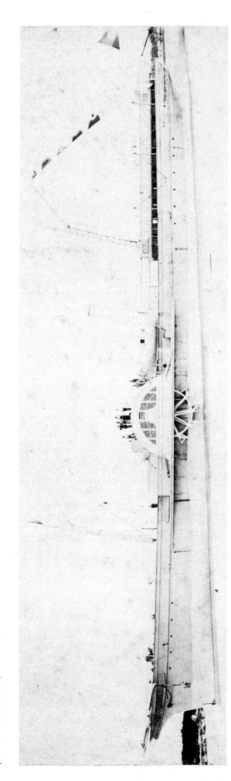

Figure 22. The *Advance*, aground for repairs in Nassau. The *Advance* was purchased and operated by the state of North Carolina. In the winter of 1863, the state sold off half of its interest in the vessel in order to gain shipping rights on additional blockade runners. (*From a private collection*)

Figure 23. The *Dee*, built in 1863; she was one of the twin screws that served Crenshaw and Collie and Company. The *Dee* made six trips through the blockade before being run aground off Wilmington. (*U.S. Army Military History Institute, Carlise, Pa.*)

Figure 24. Builders' model of the *Rosine*, largest of the fourteen blockade runners ordered by the Confederacy in the spring of 1864. She was unfinished at the war's end. (*From a private collection*)

Figure 25. A blockade runner eludes Union warships. Over seventy-five percent of all attempts of steamers to run the blockade were successful. (*From a private collection*)

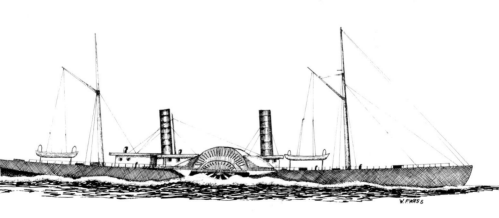

Figure 26. *Colonel Lamb,* built in 1864 for Fraser, Trenholm, and Company, she was outfitted by Thomas Lockwood. She was considered the final word in blockade runners. (*Sketch by Wendell P. Wass, from a private collection*)

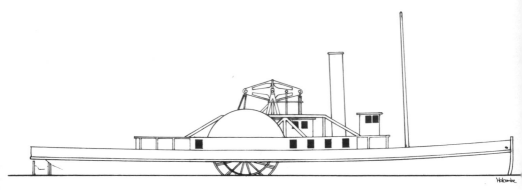

Figure 27. The *Kate*, constructed in 1852 for use as a coastal packet. She measured 165′ × 29′10″ × 10′4″ and made twenty runs through the blockade. (*Line drawing by Robert Holcombe from a private collection*)

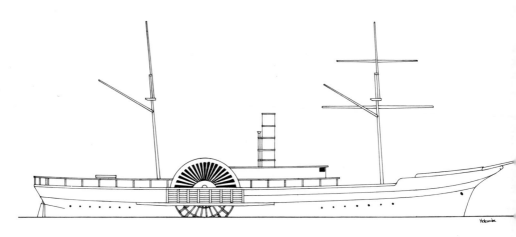

Figure 28. The *Nashville*, constructed in 1853 as an ocean-going liner. During the war she was renamed *Thomas L. Wragg* and *Rattlesnake*. She measured 216′ × 34′9″ × 22′ and made seven runs through the blockade. (*Line drawing by Robert Holcombe from a private collection*)

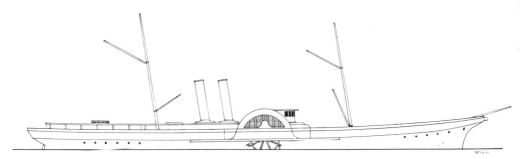

Figure 29: The *Advance,* constructed as a ferryboat in 1862; she was converted to a blockade runner in 1863. She measured 236′ × 26′ × 10′ and made seventeen trips through the blockade. (*Line drawing by Robert Holcombe from a private collection*)

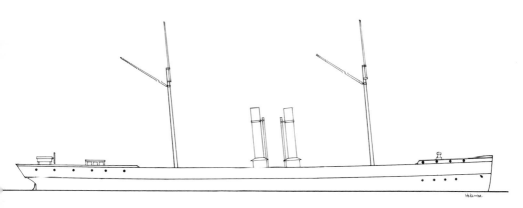

Figure 30. The *Atalanta,* constructed as a cross-channel ferryboat in 1863. She became a blockade runner in 1864, was purchased by the Confederacy and converted into a commerce raider. While in Confederate service she was named the *Tallahassee, Olustee,* and *Chameleon.* She measured 220′ × 24′ × 14′ and made twelve trips through the blockade. (*Line drawing by Robert Holcombe from a private collection*)

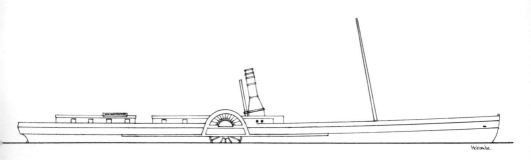

Figure 31. The *Denbigh,* constructed as a merchant steamer in 1860. She became a blockade runner in 1863. She measured 182' × 22' × 8.7' and made twenty-six trips through the blockade. (*Line drawing by Robert Holcombe from a private collection*)

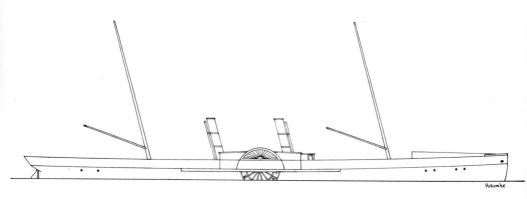

Figure 32. The *Banshee* (I), constructed as a blockade runner in 1862; she measured 214' × 20' × 8' and made fourteen trips through the blockade. (*Line drawing by Robert Holcombe from a private collection*)

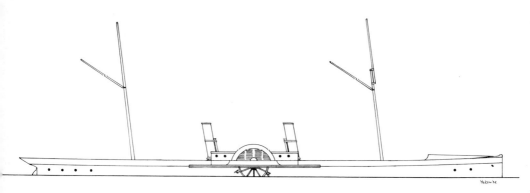

Figure 33. The *Will of the Wisp*, constructed as a blockade runner in 1863, she measured 210′ × 23′ × 10′ and made twelve trips through the blockade. (*Line drawing by Robert Holcombe from a private collection*)

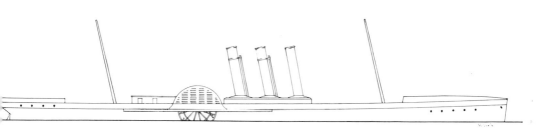

Figure 34. The *Flamingo*, constructed as a blockade runner in 1864; she measured 270′ × 24′ × 12′ and made two trips through the blockade. (*Line drawing by Robert Holcombe from a private collection*)

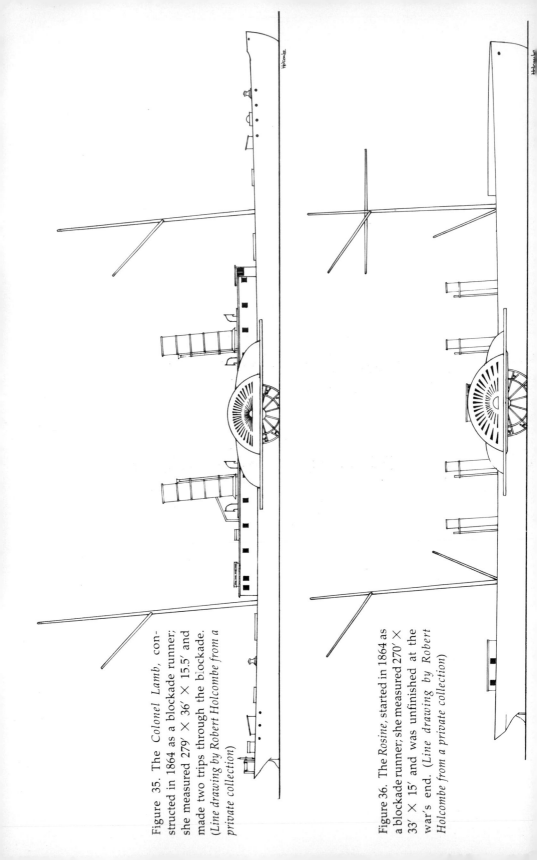

Figure 35. The *Colonel Lamb*, constructed in 1864 as a blockade runner; she measured 279′ × 36′ × 15.5′ and made two trips through the blockade. (*Line drawing by Robert Holcombe from a private collection*)

Figure 36. The *Rosine*, started in 1864 as a blockade runner; she measured 270′ × 33′ × 15′ and was unfinished at the war's end. (*Line drawing by Robert Holcombe from a private collection*)

The problem of food became critical after the fall of Charleston and Wilmington. The Army of Northern Virginia was nearly totally dependent on supplies received through the blockade, while the rest of the Southern forces east of the Mississippi had to scavenge for food. After the fall of Fort Fisher, the Army of Northern Virginia had only about a month's worth of rations while another two- to three-month supply was on railroads between Wilmington and Richmond. In time the army's food supply would be gone.[50]

The loss of the South's last two major Eastern seaports sealed the fate of the Confederacy's major armies. The Confederates had enough supplies for only three or four months and, after that, critical shortages of food, ammunition, powder, and shoes would occur. A quartermaster official remarked that nothing contributes more to the demoralization of an army than to leave it neglected, abandoned, and without rations. Governor Vance, who suspended his blockade running after the fall of Fort Fisher, summed up the situation in writing to John White: "It is bad enough, God knows."[51]

Those Confederate leaders involved in government blockade-running were well aware what the loss of Wilmington and Charleston would mean to the South. To keep his bureau in operation, Bayne tried to enlist both the Navy and War Departments' support in using Georgetown, St. Marks, and Apalachicola as entry sites for steamers, but little could be done. The ports were not adequately protected, and the narrow shallow channels limited the number of vessels that could use the ports.

In order to gain suitable blockade runners, Mallory directed Maffitt (Wilkinson's superior) to sell the *Chameleon* and buy a light-drafted vessel. If he was not able to sell the steamer, he was to send her back to England and turn her over to Bulloch. Maffitt, with the *Owl*, was to try and run supplies into an Eastern port. If this proved impossible, he was to join the light-drafted *Wren* and *Lark*, and open a supply line either at the small Florida Gulf ports or at Galveston.

Maffitt found no buyer for the *Chameleon*, and sent Wilkinson and the *Chameleon* back to Liverpool while he took the *Owl* from Nassau to Havana, where he joined the *Lark* and *Wren* for runs to Galveston. Before going to the Gulf, Maffitt made one more run to the North Carolina coast. On this trip, he sailed to Little River Inlet, North Carolina, where he dropped Thomas Conolly, an eccentric Irish member of Parliament, who was carrying despatches from Mason to Richmond. Maffitt then turned the *Owl* toward Havana, where he joined the war's last blockade runners in runs to Galveston.[52]

Few steam blockade runners had used Galveston before the fall of Wilmington and Charleston. Trade was hindered because of Galveston's exposed position, the difficulty in moving cotton to the city, uncertainty over Kirby Smith's acceptance of cotton bonds, and outbreaks of yellow fever. However, as long as profits existed, certain speculators would always overlook the port's handicaps.

One vessel that came to Galveston in 1864 was the steamer *Zephine*. Originally built by Harlan and Hollingsworth of Wilmington, Delaware, as the *Frances*, she was a powerful walking-beam sidewheeler. At Havana she was sold to blockade-running interests for $100,000 in gold, and given a British registry. Even with a payroll of over $36,000 in gold, the ship made money. On her first run in September 1864 she carried out over 1,000 bales of cotton, and turned a profit in excess of $300,000 in gold, more than enough to pay for the ship, the crew's wages, and the inward cargo.

Helm saw the *Zephine*'s success as proof that government-run blockade runners could use Galveston, and urged his superiors to send vessels and supplies to Havana. He also suggested that the government stockpile cotton at Galveston. As he saw it, "one hundred bales of cotton invested in supplies abroad save us at home a thousand." However, until the capture of the eastern ports, the government paid little attention to Helm's ideas.[53]

While waiting for the government to utilize Galveston, Confederate officials in Cuba and Texas became involved in a scheme to bring soldiers through the blockade. During 1864, General Magruder and his chief engineer Colonel Valery Sulakowski, a native of Poland, had approached Richmond with the idea of recruiting Polish exiles to aide the South. They suggested that offers of land and possibly slaves could induce large numbers of Poles, recently forced out of their homeland by the Russians, to come to Texas and form their own military units. Both Benjamin and Seddon approved the idea and, in the summer of 1864, Sulakowski went to Havana. From there he was to embark for Europe to raise a brigade of Poles and bring them back via Matamoras.

Instead of going through with the plan, Sulakowski turned himself in to Thomas Savage, the Union consul at Havana. Apparently he held a grievance against Jefferson Davis over a promotion. He offered his services to the surprised diplomat and volunteered to lead attacks against the Texas coast. Savage sent him to Key West to confer with the military authorities. The affair was reported to Seward, and a close watch was kept on European ports. Rumors concerning the recruitment of Poles continued throughout the war, but the plan never materialized and, by November 1864, Dudley reported that, as yet, no Poles had embarked from England.[54]

Besides watching for mercenaries, Savage also reported on the increasing blockade activity at Havana. By the end of the year, the two light-draft blockade runners the *Lark* and *Wren* made their appearance in Cuba. Built by Laird and Sons under the sponsorship of Fraser, Trenholm and Company, they were excellent examples of how shipbuilding had advanced since the beginning of the war. The two steel-hulled vessels measured 210' x 23' x 10'4", had a registered tonnage of 267 tons, and drew only 6 to 9 feet. Savage reported that the ships were superior to those heretofore used in the trade and suspected that they might be used as privateers. The vessels were not warships, and in January 1865 they joined the other blockade runners in running to Galveston.[55]

The blockade runners at Havana comprised an odd collection of ships ranging from the older *Lavinia* (formerly *Harriet Lane*) to the sleek, three-stacker *Ptarmigan*. Some were hastily converted merchantmen while others had been built specifically for the trade. Not all the blockade runners from Nassau and Bermuda were able to adapt to the Havana-Galveston run. Some did not have the coal capacity for the 8- to 10-day round trip, while others had too deep a draft to enter Galveston Bay. Among those that fell into the latter category were Thomas Lockwood's *Colonel Lamb* and Maffitt's *Owl*. Both eventually returned to England. Even those ships that could adapt were often unable to complete the run. Some were forced back by Federal warships while others miscalculated the amount of coal needed for the voyage. Those ships that did complete the run were faced with long layovers while waiting for return cargoes since both military and civilians were reluctant to stockpile cotton at the exposed town. Thomas Taylor, who came into the port during this time, found Galveston to be a "miserable little place with rotting wharves and little defense." He found General Magruder to be helpful, but the port was very inefficient and impracticable. Still, the lure of profits kept the trade alive.[56]

This desire for profit drew many speculators to the Gulf. One venture, originating from north of the United States, was based on the steamship *Acadia*, built by two Canadian businesmen for the sole purpose of running the blockade. She was constructed at Sorel, Quebec, on the St. Lawrence River, and measured 211' × 31'1" × 12'6". The ship was finished in late October and by December was on her way to Bermuda under command of Thomas Leach. Her cargo consisted of household items that were certain to earn a profit in the South. Among the supplies were porcelain commodes complete with a lead base and a brass flusher designed by Thomas Crapper. Also, the U.S. consul at Halifax reported that the *Acadia* had stopped there to take on a group of Confederate agents who supposedly were heading for the Pacific ocean for raids on Northern gold ships.

The *Acadia* arrived at Bermuda on December 12, 1865, then proceeded to Havana. From there she sailed for the Southern coast, and by early February was heading for Velasco, Texas. Captain Leach tried to find the Brazos River, but he ran the ship aground about ten miles east northeast of the river's entrance. The next morning, February 6, the warship *Virginia* sighted the grounded blockade runner. After shelling the *Acadia* for two hours, the Federals sent in a small boat to burn the vessel, but the surf was too rough, and the cutter was unable to reach the blockade runner. Later, the Confederates were able to salvage some of the cargo before the waves broke up the vessel.[57]

On the same day that the *Acadia* was destroyed, the blockade runner *Wren* tried to make Galveston Bay, but ran aground directly off the Gulf side of the city near Fort Point. Spotted by the blockading squadron, two Federal cutters with twenty-five men were sent in at nightfall to destroy her. As the Union sailors neared the blockade runner, the commander of the expedition decided that the *Wren* was too well protected by the fort's guns, and instead took his cutters just inside the harbor, where he captured two cotton-laden schooners and brought them safely out. Meanwhile, the *Wren* was able to land her cargo and, thus lightened, was able to extricate herself and slip into the bay.[58]

The *Will of the Wisp* was not as fortunate. The fast but unstable vessel had arrived in the Gulf under new ownership in November 1864. Two days after the *Wren* had gone aground, the *Will of the Wisp* tried to enter Galveston but was cut off by two Union gunboats. While trying to escape, she crashed into the shore about two miles from the harbor's entrance. The next morning the blockaders found the partially submerged vessel and made plans to burn it.

That night a small boat expedition was sent in and, once on board, the Federals found the ship hard aground and riddled by cannon fire. Her hull was broken, filled with water and sand, and the salvagable parts of her engines removed by the Confederates. The Union sailors considered burning the wheelboxes, but decided that it was unnecessary and returned to their vessels.[58]

Even with the loss of the *Acadia* and *Will of the Wisp*, operators continued to send ships to Galveston in an effort to take out as much cotton as possible before the Confederacy collapsed. From March to the end of May 1865, there were at least thirteen runs made to Galveston, some by such well-known ships as the *Banshee (II)* and the *Fox*.[60]

The blockade-running activity at Galveston had no effect on the war east of the Mississippi. After the fall of Wilmington and Charleston the North did not wait for the South to run out of supplies. Instead, pressure was kept up on all fronts to hasten the Confederate collapse. Besides the relentless advances of Sherman and Grant, attacks were made against Mobile and Wilmington, and General James Wilson's cavalry corps was sent into the industrial heartland of the South. By April 9, 1865, Lee's army was trapped at Appomattox Courthouse, and seventeen days later General Johnston surrendered the Army of Tennessee near Durham Station, North Carolina. Wilson's cavalry swept through Selma, Tuscaloosa, and Montgomery, Alabama, Columbus and Macon, Georgia, and by May 3, had occupied Augusta, Georgia. A week later, elements of Wilson's force captured Jefferson Davis outside Irwinsville, Georgia.

Even while the South was collapsing, certain Confederate officials refused to accept the inevitable and went to desperate lengths to challenge the blockade. One such venture centered around the *William H. Webb*, which by 1865 was an unarmed gunboat-ram laid up at Shreveport, Louisiana. Before the fall of Richmond, Secretary of Navy Mallory ordered Lieutenant Charles W. Read from the James River Squadron to take command of the *William H. Webb* and run her from the Red River past New Orleans and out to sea.

Read was just the man for such an operation. He had served as an officer on the ironclad *Arkansas* during her lopsided fights against the Union fleet at Vicksburg, spent some time on the *Florida* with Maffitt, and commanded a number of sailing ships while on a daring raid along the New England coast. He was eventually captured in Portland,

Maine's harbor while trying to seize the revenue cutter *Caleb Cushing*. Imprisoned at Fort Warren in Boston harbor, Read was eventually paroled and returned to duty with the James River Squadron. In October 1864, after three months at Richmond, he was ordered to Shreveport.

At Shreveport, Read readied the *William H. Webb* for duty as a commerce raider, arming the vessel with a 30-pound Parrott rifle, two 12-pound howitzers, and a number of spar torpedoes. He brought the ship down to the mouth of the Red River and on the night of April 23 took her past Union gunboats into the Mississippi.

The *William H. Webb*, capable of making twenty knots, sped past New Orleans around 1:00 P.M. on April 24. She was fired on, and two steamers gave chase; but Read knew he could outrun his pursuers. He had hoped to pass the forts at the mouth of the river at night, but twenty-five miles south of the city he found the screw sloop *Richmond* readied and cleared for action. It would have been suicide to continue as one broadside from the warship could easily crush the *William H. Webb*. Read ran his vessel aground, set it afire and fled with his crew into the swamps. Eventually Read and most of his men were captured. The fire consumed the *William H. Webb*, but her engines and much of her metal work were salvaged.[61]

Another Confederate vessel that nearly ran the blockade during the last months of the war was the French-built ironclad *Stonewall*. The ship, originally contracted for by Bulloch, had, like all the vessels ordered by the South in France, been held from delivery by orders of the French government. The ship's contract was then sold, and she was purchased by the Danish Navy; but by the time she was finished, the Danes had no use for her, and the ironclad was purchased by the Confederacy.

In December 1864, Captain Thomas Jefferson Page took command of the ironclad and the following month cleared Copenhagen. He rendezvoused off the coast of Brittany with the *City of Richmond*, a steamer owned by Crenshaw and Company that had been hired by Bulloch to carry men from the crews of the *Florida* and *Rappahannock* to the ironclad. Page then took the *Stonewall* to Spain, where he received an engineer off the Confederate naval vessel *Louisa Ann Fanny*. He then stopped in Portugal before turning toward Nassau.

The *Stonewall* reached Nassau on May 6, but did not enter the harbor. She continued on to Havana, arriving there on the eleventh. Rumors had the vessel leading a fleet of blockade runners to Galveston; another envisioned the ironclad steaming to the Florida coast to pick up

Jefferson Davis. Page was under orders from Bulloch to attack the Union base at Port Royal. However, Page realized that nothing could be accomplished by suicide runs, and even an attack against the Federals at Galveston would not be feasible since the *Stonewall*'s draft would not allow her to enter the Texas port. Finally, Page turned the vessel over to the Spanish authorities for $16,000 and used the money to pay off his crew. The Spanish later delivered the *Stonewall* to the Federals, who would in turn sell her to Japan.[62]

While these last-ditch efforts by the Confederate Navy continued, blockade runners were increasing their utilization of Galveston, but the trade never reached the level enjoyed by Wilmington or even Charleston. Still, through Helm's hard work and Magruder's efforts in Galveston, Kirby Smith received a large amount of valuable equipment that included some 10,000 small arms, powder, cartridge paper, uniforms, and even a battery of breech-loading Whitworth field pieces. These supplies, however, were not enough to keep the military functioning, and in May the commanders of the Trans-Mississippi Department were beginning to accept the inevitable.[63]

By mid-May, conditions were deteriorating all across the territory. Troops were deserting in such numbers that whole military organizations would disappear overnight. In Galveston, officers could no longer control their men, and wholesale looting broke out. Finally on May 22, Magruder, from his headquarters in Houston, ordered his commander in Galveston to arrange an armistice so that surrender negotiations could begin. The next day, while the Confederates were waiting for a reply, the *Denbigh*, which by now ranked second only to the *Syren* as the war's most successful blockade runner, ran into the harbor. However, this time luck was not with the little steamer, and she ran aground on Bird Key Spit. Her crew fled to the city, and the next morning Union gunboats shelled the stranded vessel and sent a small boat expedition to burn the wreck.

The following night the *Lark* slipped into the harbor. Her captain had managed to enter the bay even though none of the signal lights were lit. Once docked, the vessel was overrun and stripped by Confederate soldiers. When the soldiers left, the *Lark*, minus her cargo, proceeded to another wharf, where she picked up the *Denbigh*'s stranded crew and dashed out to sea. She was the last steam blockade runner to enter and leave the Confederacy. Nine days later Kirby Smith and Magruder went on board the warship *Fort Jackson*, anchored off Galveston, and surrendered the final remains of the Confederacy. On June 5, 1865, led by the former blockade runner *Cornubia*, a Union squadron entered Galveston, closing the Confederacy's last blockade-running port.[64]

# Chapter Ten

# The Final Ledger

On June 23, 1865, President Andrew Johnson officially ended the blockade. From the first run of the *Bermuda* to the *Lark*'s final escape from Galveston, just under 300 steamers tested the blockade. Out of approximately 1,300 attempts, over 1,000 were successful. The average lifetime of a blockade runner was just over four runs, or two round trips. Some 136 were captured and another 85 destroyed.

Reports of Federal consuls in the West Indies and Liverpool reveal that the amount of cotton carried out by all blockade runners amounted to no more than 350,000 bales with another 50,000 coming through Tampico and Matamoras. Of this, some 210,000 were carried out by steamers from the East Coast with another 30,000 transported by sailing ships. In the Gulf some 50,000 bales were shipped by steamers while 30,000 went out by sailing ships.

About 50,000 bales went to the account of the Confederacy, 45,000 were sent out by John Fraser and Company while 22,000 were shipped by the Importing and Exporting Company of South Carolina. Other firms such as the Importing and Exporting Company of Georgia, Collie and Company, the Anglo-Confederate Company, and the Chicora and Charleston Importing and Exporting Companies, transported about 10,000 bales apiece. Success in blockade running varied for each exporter, but all firms suffered with the collapse of the Confederacy.[1]

Several months before President Johnson declared the blockade over, merchants and shippers had begun to terminate their blockade-running businesses. Huge quantities of blankets, shoes, meat, dry goods, and munitions were returned to England along with many steamers.

Some of those vessels were such well-known blockade runners as the *Caroline, Alice, Fannie, Wild Rover, Old Dominion,* and the *Chameleon.* There were also thirteen recently completed blockade runners that never left England. Dudley reported that prices for munitions and the specially constructed vessels had plummeted and businessmen were desperately working to salvage some part of their investments.[2]

When the South collapsed, Confederate officials in England closed their operations, leaving their debts in the hands of Fraser, Trenholm and Company. The head of the firm, Charles K. Prioleau, was understandably perturbed by this. Not only did the Confederacy owe his company £170,000; it also left him with the responsibility of dealing with British merchants and the Federal government, which soon brought suit against his firm in an attempt to gain all Confederate property controlled by the company. Prioleau had planned to sell his Confederate holdings to recoup part of his losses. These assets consisted of some cotton, machinery, and a number of blockade runners. Any profits from the sale were to be applied toward the debt owed Fraser, Trenholm and Company and not to any other creditors.

The company attempted to quickly close its books on the Confederate account. Such action caused tremendous dismay among the British business community, which hoped to regain some of the money owed them by the Confederacy, but there was little left to meet these obligations. The South had never been able to accumulate enough funds in Liverpool to finance their European operations. Instead, Trenholm and McRae operated on a system of credit based on the promise of eventual payment in cotton. During the last six months of the war, Trenholm reported that cotton valued at $1,500,000 (gold) had been shipped to England, on which Confederate agents could purchase $45,000,000 (gold) worth of supplies. On this amount goods were ordered and inventories increased. When the Confederacy collapsed, the British merchants were without recourse. No funds were coming from Fraser, Trenholm and Company, and the United States government refused to accept the Southern debt. The North was not going to pay those that supplied an enemy and helped cause the death and wounding of so many Federal soldiers and sailors.

By closing their books on the Confederate debt, Fraser, Trenholm and Company did not endear themselves to the British business community, but it did solve one of the firm's problems. However, Prioleau and his associates still had to handle a financial crisis within their own firm.

From 1861 through 1863, Fraser, Trenholm and Company had received nearly 35,000 bales of cotton. A large amount of the proceeds from this cotton had been put into new vessels and Confederate bonds. During the last year of the war, another 10,000 bales arrived in Liverpool, profits from which were used to support the South's European ventures. Prioleau and his partners realized that the company's future was heavily dependent on a Confederate victory. If the South had won, the firm would have recouped its debts and become the new nation's premier transatlantic shipper. The Confederate defeat ended all such hopes and forced the company to find other means to solve its financial problems.

Fraser, Trenholm and Company's first step was reorganization. William L. Trenholm and James Welsman returned to the South, and James Armstrong, a native Englishman, joined Prioleau on the firm's board of directors. Those left in Liverpool had to deal with a difficult situation. The United States government continued to press its suit, thus keeping the firm from selling the Confederate property. The value of their vessels had dropped by two-thirds, and shipbuilders were demanding wartime prices for steamers still under construction. The company tried to make an out-of-court settlement with the United States, but this failed and in May 1867, Fraser Trenholm and Company was forced to declare bankruptcy.

When this occurred, the Federal government immediately moved against the Charleston-based John Fraser and Company in hopes of gaining redress for the Confederate property once held by their Liverpool partners. A bill of complaint was brought against the firm, claiming that it not only served as agents for the Confederacy but was also part of the Confederate Treasury Department. An investigation of the company's Liverpool account books was carried out in the hopes of proving a direct link between the Confederate Treasury Department and John Fraser and Company, but the search revealed little of consequence. In time the Federal agent in Liverpool, Samuel Duncan, reported that he found nothing to substantiate the claim.

While the Federal government was trying to connect John Fraser and Company to the Confederacy, other creditors banded together and forced the company into receivership. A trust fund was eventually created that would repay the firm's debts over a four-year period. The system proved unwieldy, and new creditors were constantly appearing. Among these was the United States government, which, upon failing to prove that John Fraser and Company had been an extension of the

Confederate Treasury Department, brought suit for the Confederate property once held by the company's Liverpool office. Somehow, three of the proposed four payments were made, but finally, in late 1872, the plan ran into such difficulty that John Fraser and Company was forced to liquidate.[3]

The other blockade-running firms did not try to continue in business like John Fraser and Company, but closed when the conflict ended. In England, the Anglo-Confederate Trading Company sold off its vessels at a substantial loss, but this was more than covered by the firm's profits.

Other operations did not do as well. Alexander Collie's company lost heavily at the war's end. During the conflict Collie had overexpanded by placing a large amount of his returns in new steamers and North Carolina cotton bonds. It was also reported that at war's end the firm had some 16,000 bales of cotton in the South that were seized by the United States.

Collie worked hard to salvage something for his investors. The North Carolina bonds were worthless and the cotton gone. What remained were his steamers, which had fallen drastically in value. He first tried to sell his three-stackers to the British Navy for use against former blockade runners that were rumored going into the slave trade. This plan failed, as did a scheme to sell the vessels to the Brazilian government. Collie eventually sold his ships to private interests for a dismal loss of £18,000 apiece. For all their work Collie and Company closed their books with nothing to show for their efforts.[4]

Southern firms also ceased operations at war's end with varying degrees of success. Lamar's Importing and Exporting Company of Georgia was unable to show any profit. The firm had brought in large amounts of goods for Georgia's troops, but Lamar was unable to ship out enough cotton to cover his venture. At the end of the war, Lamar still controlled a large number of cotton bales, but they were confiscated by the Federals. He fought this seizure and, after gaining the support of Massachusetts Governor Benjamin Butler, received payment for the cotton from the United States government.[5]

The Charleston-based firms managed to do a little better. The highly successful Importing and Exporting Company of South Carolina concluded operations on January 20, 1865. By this time, William Bee had resigned as president and had been replaced by Theodore Jervey. Bee remained active in the firm and, on his recommendation, a dividend of

£50 and $2,000 in Confederate currency was paid to the shareholders. With this dividend the company had paid during the war a total of £120 and $9,000 per share. This return more than paid the stockholders for their investment even when adjusted to the high Confederate inflation. After the war, the company sold off its property in Europe and paid a final dividend of £70 before closing its books.

The Chicora and Charleston Importing and Exporting companies also repaid their investors, and gave them a profit. Like the South Carolina Importing and Exporting Company, the firms paid a closing dividend in January 1865. The Chicora Importing and Exporting Company managed to make one final payment of $100 in gold after the war when it sold off its English property and the vessel *Chicora* at Halifax.

Other Charleston businesses that produced earnings at least equal to the cost of their stock were the Steamship *Druid* Company and the Palmetto Importing and Exporting Company. One firm that did not repay its stockholders was the Consolidated Steamship Company. At war's end, its president Henry Hart fled to New York with the company's assets. When his backers tried to regain their investments, Hart refused to cooperate. He claimed that since the war was over he could not be held responsible for a business that was illegal under United States law.[6]

Along with the private companies, Governor Vance closed down North Carolina's blockade running shortly after Fort Fisher's capture. By February 28, 1865, he ordered all accounts settled and prepared for the eventual collapse of the Confederacy. North Carolina fared well with its blockade running, providing for both its citizens and military. Since the state ran in a large amount of unfinished material, an exact count of imports would be impossible, but enough dry goods came in to uniform at least 125,000 men and, by Vance's own estimate, the state made as many as 342,000 uniforms. North Carolina also imported some 36,000 to 50,000 blankets, 45,000 pairs of shoes as well as leather for shoes and harnesses. Vance claimed that the state made a profit of nearly $2,500,000, but other state officials placed it at about half that amount.

Whatever the exact returns of Vance's enterprise, it did more to assist the Confederate cause than to harm it. Even though the governor was unruly and on occasion insubordinate, Vance realized that the fate of his state was linked to a successful Confederate war effort. By employing blockade runners Vance added to the South's fighting ability. North Carolina provided more troops for the war than any other

Southern state and, by keeping them properly uniformed, Vance and his associates reduced the strain on the Confederate Quartermaster Bureau.[7]

Vance's accomplishments for North Carolina were remarkable, but the accomplishments of those men involved with the Confederacy's importation of military supplies were incredible. Without the work of such men as Huse, McRae, Bayne, Heyliger, Walker, Helm, Prioleau, Trenholm, and many others, the South would not have survived as long as it did. Home production never reached a level where it could supply even one-half of the military's needs. Imported supplies were vital to the Confederacy's existence.

In terms of basic military necessities, the South imported at least 400,000 rifles, or more than 60 percent of the nation's modern arms. About 3 million pounds of lead came through the blockade, which by Gorgas's estimate amounted to one-third of the Army's requirements. Besides these items, over 2,250,000 pounds of saltpeter, or two-thirds of this vital ingredient for powder, came from overseas. Without blockade running the nation's military would have been without proper supplies of arms, bullets, and powder.

Blockade running also supplied countless other essential items such as food, clothing, accouterments, chemicals, paper, and medicine. By the summer of 1862, the flow of supplies enabled the Confederate armies to stand up to the numerically superior Federals. Because of the work of the men involved in blockade running, a supply lifeline was maintained until the very last months of the war. The Confederate soldiers had the equipment and food needed to meet their adversaries. Defeat did not come from the lack of material; instead the Confederacy simply no longer had the manpower to resist, and the nation collapsed.[8]

# Appendix 1

**Value of Foreign Imports and Domestic Exports for Southern Ports, June 1858–June 1859[a]**

| City | Imports | Exports | Totals |
|------|---------|---------|--------|
| New Orleans | $20,606,316 | $107,559,594 | $120,195,910 |
| Mobile | 782,061 | 38,670,183 | 39,452,244 |
| Charleston | 1,569,570 | 21,179,350 | 22,748,920 |
| Savannah | 782,061 | 18,351,554 | 19,133,615 |
| Galveston | 533,153 | 5,772,588 | 6,305,741 |
| Norfolk | 201,460 | 479,885 | 681,345 |
| Total | $24,504,621 | $192,013,154 | $216,517,775 |

[a] "Commerce and Navigation," House Exec. Doc., 36th Congress, 2d Session, 1860, pp. 350, 552; "Report on the Internal Commerce of the United States by William P. Switzler, Chief of the Bureau of Statistics, Treasury Department," House Exec. Doc., No. 6, 50th Congress, 1st Session, 1887, pp. lXXXII–lXXXIII.

# Appendix 2

## Amounts Collected[a] by Custom Houses June 1858–June 1859.

| City | Profits |
| --- | --- |
| Southern Ports: | |
| New Orleans | $2,120,058.76 |
| Charleston | 299,339.43 |
| Mobile | 118,027.99 |
| Galveston | 92,417.72 |
| Savannah | 89,157.18 |
| Norfolk | 70,897.73 |
| Richmond | 47,763.63 |
| Wilmington | 33,104.67 |
| Pensacola | 3,577.60 |
| St. Marks | −161.24 |
| Key West | −7,687.32 |
| | |
| Northern Ports: | |
| New York | $35,155,452.75 |
| Boston | 5,133,414.55 |
| Philadelphia | 2,262,349.57 |

[a] Total revenue minus operating costs. "Statement Showing the Amount of Revenue Collected Annually in each Collection District from June 30, 1854, to June 30, 1859, Together with the Amount Expended and the Persons Employed in each District," Exec. Doc. No. 33, 36th Congress, 1st Session, 1860.

# Appendix 3

**Foreign Export of Cotton from U.S. Ports**
**September 1860–August 1861[a]**

| City | Bales |
| --- | ---: |
| New Orleans | 1,783,678 |
| Mobile | 456,421 |
| Savannah | 302,187 |
| New York | 248,049 |
| Charleston | 214,888 |
| Galveston | 68,202 |
| Florida ports | 28,073 |
| Boston | 23,225 |
| Philadelphia | 3,798 |
| Baltimore | 3,545 |
| Virginia ports | 810 |
| North Carolina ports | 195 |
| Total | 3,133,200 |

[a] *Hunt's*, XLV, (July–December 1861), p. 498.

# Appendix 4

## Southern Ocean and Coastal Steamers in 1861[a]

### Ocean Steamers

| | |
|---|---|
| *Isabel* | Sidewheeler; 1,115 tons; 220' × 33' × 21'; Spofford, Tileston Company, New York |
| *Jamestown* | Sidewheeler; 1,300 tons; 240' × 33' × 23'; New York and Virginia Steamship Company, New York |
| *Nashville* | Sidewheeler; 1,800 tons; 216' × 35' × 22'; Spofford, Tileston Company, New York |
| *North Carolina* | Screw; 618 tons; 165' × 32' × 13'; H. B. Cromwell, New York |
| *Star of the West* | Sidewheeler; 1,172 tons; 228' × 32' × 24'; captured off Texas coast and taken to New Orleans |
| *Tennessee* | Sidewheeler; 1,149 tons; 210' × 34' × 19'; Southern Steamship Company, New Orleans |
| *Yorktown* | Sidewheeler; 1,403 tons; 250' × 34' × 17'; New York and Virginia Steamship Company, New York |

### Older or Smaller Ocean Steamers

| | |
|---|---|
| *Governor Dudley* | Sidwheeler; 408 tons; 177' × 24' × 10'; Mordecai and Company, Charleston |
| *Habana* | Screw; 499 tons; 184' × 30' × 12'; New Orleans-Havana Packet Company, New Orleans |
| *Marquis de la Habana* | Screw; 600 tons; 176' × 29'6" × 14'; held by courts at New Orleans |

### Coasting Steamers

| | |
|---|---|
| *Alabama* | Sidewheeler; 510 tons; 226' × 32' × 7'4"; owned by the New Orleans-Mobile Steamship Company, Mobile |
| *Arizona* | Sidewheeler; 578 tons; 201' × 34' × 10'; Southern Steamship Company, New Orleans |
| *Atlantic* | Sidewheeler; 623 tons; 216' × 28' × 10'; Southern Steamship Company, New Orleans |

230

| | |
|---|---|
| *Austin* | Sidewheeler; 603 tons; 203' × 34' × 10'; Southern Steamship Company, New Orleans |
| *Calhoun* | Sidewheeler; 508 tons; 174' × 27' × 11'; Southern Steamship Company, New Orleans |
| *California* | Sidewheeler; 496 tons; 204' × 29' × 8'; New Orleans-Mobile Mail Company, Mobile |
| *Carolina* | Sidewheeler; 477 tons; 165' × 29'10" × 10'4"; Florida Steam Packet Company, Charleston |
| *Cecile* | Sidewheeler; 360 tons; 156' × 29' × 8'; Savannah Steam Packet Company, Charleston |
| *Charles Morgan* | Sidewheeler; 1,215 tons; 215' × 34' × 10'; Southern Steamship Company, New Orleans |
| *Cuba* | Sidewheeler; 604 tons; 250' × 33' × 9'; New Orleans-Mobile Mail Company, Mobile |
| *Florida* | Sidewheeler; 662 tons; 250' × 30'8" × 9'; New Orleans-Mobile Mail Company, Mobile |
| *Florida* | Screw; 429 tons; 180' × 31' × 9'; Apalachicola-New Orleans Company, New Orleans |
| *Galveston* | Sidewheeler; 945 tons; 236' × 37' × 12'; Southern Steamship Company, New Orleans |
| *General Miramon* | ?; 296 British tons; 133'6" × 24'6" × 9'8"; run by Joaquim Acebo between New Orleans and Havana |
| *General Rusk* | Sidewheeler; 417 tons; 200' × 31' × 12'; Southern Steamship Company, New Orleans |
| *Gordon* | Sidewheeler; 518 tons; 177' × 27'6" × 11'2"; Florida Steam Packet Company, Charleston |
| *Magnolia* | Sidewheeler; 843 tons; 246' × 37' × 10'; Southern Steamship Company, New Orleans |
| *Matagorda* | Sidewheeler; 616 tons; 220' × 30' × 10'; Southern Steamship Company, New Orleans |
| *Mexico* | Sidewheeler; 1,043 tons; 208' × 33' × 15'; Southern Steamship Company, New Orleans |
| *Oregon* | Sidewheeler; 532 tons; 217' × 26' × 9'; New Orleans-Mobile Mail Company, Mobile |
| *Suwanee* | Sidewheeler; 666 tons; 189'6" × 27'2" × 10'8"; Southern Steamship Company, New Orleans |

| | |
|---|---|
| *Texas* | Sidewheeler; 1,151 tons; 216′ × 34′6″ × 16′10″; Southern Steamship Company, New Orleans |
| *William G. Hewes* | Sidewheeler; 747 tons; 233′ × 33′ × 10′; Southern Steamship Company, New Orleans |
| *William H. Webb* | Sidewheeler; 670 tons; 190′ × 31′ × 12′; Southern Steamship Company, New Orleans |

[a] "Ship Registers and Enrollments," Record Group 41, Industrial and Social Branch, National Archives, Washington, D.C.

# Appendix 5

Appendixes 5 through 15 show the approximate arriving and clearing dates for steam blockade runners. Dates are given as accurately as possible. Data for the listings was compiled from the Pickett Papers, U.S. Consul Reports, Port Records, Newspaper accounts and all other primary sources that report entering and clearing dates. The roman numerals following ship names is used to distinguish between different ships having the same name. Since many vessels underwent name changes, the name in parenthesis refers to the vessel's name when it first ran the blockade. The appearance of an asterisk (*) after a date shows that the date is estimated.

## Steam Blockade Runners Arriving North Carolina Ports, December 1861–December 1864
### (All vessels ran to Wilmington unless otherwise noted)

| Name | Date | From |
|---|---|---|
| Theodora | Dec. 21, 1861* | Nassau |
| Nashville[a] | Feb. 28, 1862 | Beaufort from Bermuda |
| Thomas L. Wragg (Nashville) | Apr. 24, 1862 | Nassau |
| Kate | Aug. 6, 1862 | Nassau |
| Kate[b] | Nov. 18, 1862 | Nassau |
| Cornubia | Dec. 17, 1862* | Bermuda |
| Giraffe | Dec. 29, 1862 | Nassau |
| Mariner | January 1863 | Nassau |
| Annie Childs | Jan. 27, 1863* | Nassau |
| Cornubia | Jan. 30, 1863* | Bermuda |
| Robert E. Lee (Giraffe) | Feb. 11, 1863* | Bermuda |
| Eagle | Feb. 20, 1863 | Nassau |
| Emma (II) | Feb. 21, 1863 | Nassau |
| Douro | Feb. 22, 1863 | Nassau |

| Name | Date | From |
|------|------|------|
| *Granite City* | Feb. 25, 1863 | Nassau |
| *Cornubia* | Mar. 1, 1863 | Bermuda |
| *Britannia* | Mar. 15, 1863 | Nassau |
| *Robert E. Lee* (*Giraffe*) | Mar. 19, 1863 | Bermuda |
| *Emma* (*II*) | Mar. 29, 1863 | Nassau |
| *Cornubia* | Apr. 1, 1863 | Bermuda |
| *Flora* (*I*) | Apr. 13, 1863 | Nassau |
| *Merrimac* | Apr. 13, 1863 | Bermuda |
| *Pet* | Apr. 15, 1863* | Nassau |
| *Charleston* | Apr. 23, 1863 | Nassau |
| *Lizzie* | Apr. 23, 1863 | Nassau |
| *Margaret and Jessie* (*Douglas*) | Apr. 23, 1863 | Nassau |
| *Robert E. Lee* (*Giraffe*) | Apr. 30, 1863 | Bermuda |
| *Emma* (*II*) | May 10, 1863* | Nassau |
| *Pet* | May 12, 1863* | Nassau |
| *T. D. Wagner* (*Annie Childs*) | May 13, 1863* | Nassau |
| *Banshee* (*I*) | May 13, 1863 | Nassau |
| *Cornubia* | May 13, 1863* | Bermuda |
| *Robert E. Lee* (*Giraffe*) | May 18, 1863 | Bermuda |
| *Flora* (*I*) | May 22, 1863 | Nassau |
| *Eugenie* | May 22, 1863* | Bermuda |
| *Banshee* (*I*) | May 28, 1863 | Nassau |
| *Cornubia* | June 9, 1863* | Bermuda |
| *Robert E. Lee* (*Giraffe*) | June 10, 1863 | Bermuda |
| *Gladiator* | June 12, 1863 | Nassau |
| *Banshee* (*I*) | June 14, 1863 | Nassau |
| *Eugenie* | June 15, 1863 | Bermuda |
| *Arabian* | June 17, 1863 | Nassau |
| *Venus* | June 18, 1863 | Bermuda |
| *Flora* (*I*) | June 22, 1863 | Nassau |
| *Advance* | June 28, 1863* | Nassau |
| *Banshee* (*I*) | July 7, 1863 | Nassau |
| *Emma* (*II*) | July 10, 1863* | Bermuda |
| *Hebe* | July 10, 1863* | Nassau |
| *Arabian* | July 10, 1863 | Nassau |
| *Elizabeth* (*Atlantic*) | July 11, 1863* | Nassau |
| *Ella and Annie* (*William G. Hewes*) | July 11, 1863 | Nassau |

| Name | Date | From |
|------|------|------|
| Kate (II) | July 11, 1863* | Nassau |
| Pet | July 12, 1863* | Nassau |
| Cornubia | July 13, 1863* | Bermuda |
| Cronstadt | July 13, 1863* | Bermuda |
| Eugenie | July 13, 1863 | Bermuda |
| Phantom | July 15, 1863* | Bermuda |
| Flora (I) | July 25, 1863 | Nassau |
| General Beauregard (Havelock) | July 25, 1863* | Nassau |
| Robert E. Lee (Giraffe) | July 28, 1863 | Bermuda |
| Margaret and Jessie (Douglas) | Aug. 8, 1863* | Nassau |
| General Beauregard (Havelock) | Aug. 8, 1863* | Nassau |
| Hansa | Aug. 8, 1863* | Nassau |
| Arabian | Aug. 11, 1863* | Nassau |
| Banshee (I) | Aug. 12, 1863* | Bermuda |
| Venus | Aug. 16, 1863* | Bermuda |
| Eugenie | Aug. 17, 1863* | Bermuda |
| Mary Ann | Aug. 18, 1863* | Bermuda |
| Cornubia | Aug. 18, 1863* | Bermuda |
| Advance | Aug. 19, 1863* | Bermuda |
| Flora (II) | Aug. 22, 1863* | Bermuda |
| Gibraltar (Sumter) | Aug. 23, 1863* | Bermuda |
| Phantom | Aug. 23, 1863* | Bermuda |
| Elizabeth (Atlantic) | Aug. 26, 1863 | Bermuda |
| Don | August 1863 | Bermuda |
| Banshee (I) | Sept. 6, 1863* | Nassau |
| Pet | Sept. 7, 1863* | Nassau |
| Spunkie | Sept. 7, 1863* | Nassau |
| Robert E. Lee (Giraffe) | Sept. 7, 1863* | Nassau |
| Eugenie | Sept. 7, 1863 | Nassau |
| Alice | Sept. 12, 1863* | Nassau |
| Juno (II) | Sept. 14, 1863* | Bermuda |
| Fannie | Sept. 16, 1863* | Nassau |
| Hansa | Sept. 17, 1863* | Bermuda |
| Don | Sept. 18, 1863* | Nassau |
| General Beauregard (Havelock) | Sept. 19, 1863* | Nassau |
| Venus | Sept. 20, 1863* | Bermuda |
| Douro | Sept. 21, 1863* | Nassau |

| Name | Date | From |
|------|------|------|
| Cornubia | Sept. 22, 1863* | Bermuda |
| Margaret and Jessie (Douglas) | Sept. 22, 1863* | Nassau |
| Antonica (Herald) | Oct. 3, 1863* | Nassau |
| Dee | Oct. 7, 1863* | Bermuda |
| Flora (II) | Oct. 8, 1863 | Bermuda |
| Banshee (I) | Oct. 9, 1863* | Nassau |
| Advance | Oct. 10, 1863* | Bermuda |
| General Beauregard (Havelock) | Oct. 11, 1863* | Nassau |
| Spunkie | Oct. 14, 1863* | Nassau |
| Hansa | Oct. 14, 1863* | Nassau |
| Don | Oct. 19, 1863* | Nassau |
| Alice | Oct. 20, 1863* | Bermuda |
| Pet | Oct. 21, 1863* | Nassau |
| Fannie | Oct. 22, 1863* | Nassau |
| Antonica (Herald) | Oct. 31, 1863* | Nassau |
| Beatrice | Oct. 31, 1863 | Nassau |
| Hansa | Nov. 6, 1863* | Nassau |
| Dee | Nov. 6, 1863* | Bermuda |
| Syren | Nov. 9, 1863 | Nassau |
| Flora (II) | Nov. 9, 1863 | Bermuda |
| Despatch | Nov. 10, 1863* | Nassau |
| Spunkie | Nov. 10, 1863* | Nassau |
| Advance | Nov. 10, 1863* | Bermuda |
| Gem | Nov. 10, 1863* | Nassau |
| Alice | Nov. 11, 1863* | Nassau |
| General Beauregard (Havelock) | Nov. 11, 1863* | Nassau |
| Scotia (II) | Nov. 12, 1863 | Nassau |
| Fannie | Nov. 13, 1863* | Nassau |
| Bendigo | Nov. 17, 1863* | Bermuda |
| Pet | Nov. 18, 1863* | Nassau |
| Lucy | Nov. 21, 1863* | Nassau |
| Hansa | Nov. 21, 1863* | Nassau |
| Antonica (Herald) | Dec. 2, 1863* | Nassau |
| City of Petersburg | Dec. 2, 1863* | Nassau |
| Syren | Dec. 2, 1863* | Nassau |
| Dee | Dec. 6, 1863* | Bermuda |
| Flora (II) | Dec. 8, 1863 | Bermuda |

| Name | Date | From |
|------|------|------|
| Lucy | Dec. 9, 1863* | Nassau |
| Scotia (II) | Dec. 9, 1863* | Nassau |
| Fannie | Dec. 13, 1863* | Nassau |
| Spunkie | Dec. 15, 1863* | Nassau |
| Syren | Dec. 16, 1863 | Nassau |
| Heroine | Dec. 19, 1863 | Bermuda |
| Hansa | Dec. 19, 1863* | Nassau |
| Star | Dec. 20, 1863* | Nassau |
| City of Petersburg | Dec. 20, 1863* | Nassau |
| Pet | Dec. 28, 1863* | Nassau |
| Don | Jan. 3, 1864* | Nassau |
| Lucy | Jan. 3, 1864* | Nassau |
| Wild Dayrell | Jan. 5, 1864* | Nassau |
| Presto | Jan. 9, 1864* | Bermuda |
| Fannie | Jan. 15, 1864* | Nassau |
| Hansa | Jan. 16, 1864 | Nassau |
| Alice | Jan. 16, 1864 | Nassau |
| Wild Dayrell | Jan. 17, 1864* | Nassau |
| Mary Ann | Jan. 18, 1864* | Nassau |
| City of Petersburg | Jan. 18, 1864* | Bermuda |
| Heroine | Jan. 19, 1864* | Nassau |
| Advance | Jan. 20, 1864* | Bermuda |
| Rothesay Castle | Jan. 30, 1864* | Nassau |
| Pet | Jan. 30, 1864* | Nassau |
| Syren | Jan. 31, 1864* | Nassau |
| City of Petersburg | Feb. 2, 1864* | Nassau |
| Don | Feb. 2, 1864* | Nassau |
| Index | Feb. 6, 1864 | Bermuda |
| Alice | Feb. 7, 1864* | Nassau |
| Hansa | Feb. 8, 1864* | Nassau |
| Scotia (II) | Feb. 8, 1864* | Nassau |
| Mary Ann | Feb. 10, 1864 | Nassau |
| Caledonia | Feb. 12, 1864 | Bermuda |
| Fannie | Feb. 15, 1864* | Nassau |
| Syren | Feb. 18, 1864* | Nassau |
| Advance | Feb. 21, 1864* | Bermuda |
| Lucy | Feb. 27, 1864* | Nassau |

| Name | Date | From |
| --- | --- | --- |
| Alice | Mar. 1, 1864* | Nassau |
| Hansa | Mar. 2, 1864* | Bermuda |
| City of Petersburg | Mar. 3, 1864* | Bermuda |
| Annie | Mar. 3, 1864* | Nassau |
| Index | Mar. 5, 1864* | Bermuda |
| Coquette | Mar. 7, 1864 | Bermuda |
| Syren | Mar. 8, 1864* | Nassau |
| Thistle (II) | Mar. 9, 1864* | Bermuda |
| Lucy | Mar. 15, 1864* | Bermuda |
| Minnie | Mar. 30, 1864* | Bermuda |
| Annie | Mar. 30, 1864* | Nassau |
| Advance | Mar. 30, 1864* | Nassau |
| Index | Apr. 1, 1864* | Bermuda |
| Greyhound | Apr. 2, 1864* | Bermuda |
| North Heath | Apr. 2, 1864* | Bermuda |
| Edith | Apr. 12, 1864* | Bermuda |
| Will of the Wisp | Apr. 14, 1864 | Nassau |
| Lucy | Apr. 28, 1864* | Nassau |
| Minnie | Apr. 30, 1864* | Bermuda |
| Young Republic | Apr. 30, 1864 | Nassau |
| Helen | May 2, 1864 | Bermuda |
| Atalanta | May 3, 1864 | Bermuda |
| Annie | May 6, 1864* | Nassau |
| Will of the Wisp | May 9, 1864 | Nassau |
| Edith | May 9, 1864 | Nassau |
| Pevensey | May 10, 1864* | Bermuda |
| Tristram Shandy | May 10, 1864* | Nassau |
| Fannie | May 11, 1864* | Nassau |
| Index | May 12, 1864 | Bermuda |
| Alice | May 12, 1864* | Nassau |
| Coquette | May 12, 1864 | Bermuda |
| Syren | May 13, 1864 | Nassau |
| Lucy | May 14, 1864* | Nassau |
| City of Petersburg | May 15, 1864* | Bermuda |
| Mary Celestia | May 27, 1864* | Bermuda |
| Atalanta | May 27, 1864* | Bermuda |
| Lynx | May 28, 1864 | Bermuda |

| Name | Date | From |
| --- | --- | --- |
| Let Her Be | May 30, 1864* | Bermuda |
| Will of the Wisp | May 30, 1864 | Nassau |
| Helen | May 30, 1864* | Nassau |
| Badger (I) | May 31, 1864 | Nassau |
| Lucy | June 1, 1864 | Nassau |
| Lilian | June 5, 1864* | Bermuda |
| Florie | June 6, 1864 | Bermuda |
| Syren | June 7, 1864* | Nassau |
| Annie | June 7, 1864* | Nassau |
| Alice | June 9, 1864* | Nassau |
| Coquette | June 9, 1864 | Bermuda |
| Will of the Wisp | June 12, 1864 | Nassau |
| Helen | June 12, 1864* | Nassau |
| Edith | June 13, 1864* | Nassau |
| Mary Celestia | June 24, 1864* | Bermuda |
| Lynx | June 24, 1864* | Bermuda |
| Atalanta | June 24, 1864* | Bermuda |
| Edith | June 27, 1864* | Bermuda |
| City of Petersburg | June 29, 1864* | Bermuda |
| Old Dominion | June 28, 1864* | Bermuda |
| Chicora (Let Her Be) | June 30, 1864 | Bermuda |
| Let Her Rip | July 3, 1864* | Nassau |
| Lilian | July 6, 1864* | Bermuda |
| Florie | July 6, 1864 | Bermuda |
| Syren | July 6, 1864* | Nassau |
| Mary Celestia | July 10, 1864* | Bermuda |
| Falcon | July 10, 1864* | Bermuda |
| Lucy | July 11, 1864* | Nassau |
| Coquette | July 11, 1864 | Bermuda |
| Will of the Wisp | July 11, 1864* | Nassau |
| Atalanta | July 13, 1864* | Bermuda |
| Annie | July 17, 1864* | Nassau |
| Lynx | July 18, 1864* | Bermuda |
| Alice | July 29, 1864 | Bermuda |
| Advance | July 29, 1864* | Bermuda |
| Helen | July 29, 1864* | Bermuda |
| Lilian | July 30, 1864* | Bermuda |

| Name | Date | From |
|------|------|------|
| Little Hattie | July 30, 1864 | Bermuda |
| Mary Bowers | July 30, 1864* | Bermuda |
| Flamingo | Aug. 1, 1864* | Bermuda |
| Mary Celestia | Aug. 6, 1864* | Bermuda |
| Old Dominion | Aug. 10, 1864* | Bermuda |
| Elsie | Aug. 11, 1864* | Bermuda |
| Chicora (Let Her Be) | Aug. 12, 1864* | Bermuda |
| City of Petersburg | Aug. 13, 1864* | Bermuda |
| Ella (II) | Aug. 14, 1864* | Bermuda |
| Owl | Aug. 24, 1864* | Halifax |
| Tallahassee (Atalanta) | Aug. 26, 1864 | From Raid |
| Annie | Aug. 27, 1864 | Bermuda |
| Advance | Aug. 27, 1864* | Bermuda |
| Edith | Aug. 27, 1864* | Bermuda |
| Hope | Aug. 27, 1864* | Nassau |
| Lynx | Sept. 2, 1864* | Bermuda |
| Will of the Wisp | Sept. 5, 1864* | Nassau |
| Helen | Sept. 5, 1864* | Halifax |
| Florie | Sept. 6, 1864* | Bermuda |
| Falcon | Sept. 8, 1864* | Halifax |
| Ella (II) | Sept. 21, 1864* | Nassau |
| Wando (Let Her Rip) | Sept. 25, 1864* | Nassau |
| Wild Rover | Sept. 25, 1864* | Nassau |
| Agnes E. Fry | Sept. 26, 1864* | Nassau |
| Night Hawk | Sept. 29, 1864 | Bermuda |
| Annie | Sept. 30, 1864 | Halifax |
| Helen | Oct. 1, 1864* | Halifax |
| Talisman | Oct. 1, 1864* | Bermuda |
| Lady Sterling | Oct. 1, 1864* | Halifax |
| Night Hawk | Oct. 12, 1864 | Bermuda |
| Banshee (II) | Oct. 15, 1864 | Bermuda |
| Annie | Oct. 17, 1864* | Nassau |
| Armstrong | Oct. 21, 1864* | Nassau |
| Florie | Oct. 21, 1864 | Bermuda |
| Virginia | Oct. 21, 1864* | Nassau |
| Lucy | Oct. 24, 1864* | Nassau |
| North Heath | Oct. 29, 1864* | Halifax |

| Name | Date | From |
|---|---|---|
| Wild Rover | Oct. 30, 1864* | Bermuda |
| Beatrice | Oct. 31, 1864 | Nassau |
| Little Hattie | Nov. 1, 1864 | Bermuda |
| Agnes E. Fry | Nov. 5, 1864 | Bermuda |
| Blenheim | Nov. 5, 1864 | Nassau |
| Talisman | Nov. 6, 1864* | Bermuda |
| Armstrong | Nov. 6, 1864 | Bermuda |
| Olustee (Tallahassee)ᶜ | Nov. 7, 1864 | Sea |
| Caroline | Nov. 8, 1864* | Nassau |
| Banshee (II) | Nov. 8, 1864 | Nassau |
| Chickamauga (Edith)ᵈ | Nov. 19, 1864 | Sea |
| Old Dominion | Nov. 21, 1864* | Halifax |
| Emma Henry | Nov. 29, 1864 | Bermuda |
| Colonel Lamb | Nov. 29, 1864 | Halifax |
| Vulture | Nov. 29, 1864 | Nassau |
| Wild Rover | Dec. 1, 1864 | Nassau |
| Virginia | Dec. 1, 1864 | Nassau |
| Owl | Dec. 1, 1864 | Bermuda |
| Caroline | Dec. 2, 1864 | Nassau |
| Armstrong | Dec. 2, 1864* | Bermuda |
| Stag | Dec. 4, 1864 | Bermuda |
| Hansa | Dec. 4, 1864 | Bermuda |
| Blenheim | Dec. 4, 1864* | Nassau |
| Charlotte | Dec. 8, 1864 | Halifax |
| Talisman | Dec. 8, 1864* | Bermuda |
| Little Hattie | Dec. 23, 1864 | Nassau |
| Badger (II) | Dec. 23, 1864* | Nassau |
| Virginia | Dec. 27, 1864* | Nassau |
| Banshee (II) | Dec. 28, 1864 | Nassau |
| Wild Rover | Dec. 28, 1864* | Nassau |

ᵃ Entered as a warship

ᵇ Hit a snag after entering the Cape Fear River off Smithville. Her cargo was saved, but the vessel was a total loss.

ᶜ Entered as a warship. The *Olustee* was the third name given to the steamer *Atalanta*.

ᵈ Entered as a warship

\* Estimated time of arrival

# Appendix 6

**Steam Blockade Runners Clearing North Carolina Ports,
February 1861–January 1865
(All vessels ran from Wilmington unless otherwise noted)**

| Name | Date | Bound to |
| --- | --- | --- |
| *Annie Childs* | Feb. 5, 1862 | Liverpool |
| *Nashville*[a] | Mar. 17, 1862 | Beaufort for Georgetown |
| *Thomas L. Wragg* (*Nashville*) | Apr. 30, 1862 | Nassau |
| *Nassau* (*Theodora*) | May 1, 1862 | Nassau |
| *Kate*[b] | Aug. 26, 1862 | Nassau |
| *Mariner* | Oct. 4, 1862* | Nassau |
| *Cornubia* | Jan. 15, 1863* | Bermuda |
| *Robert E. Lee* (*Giraffe*) | Jan. 22, 1863* | Nassau |
| *Annie Childs* | Feb. 2, 1864* | Nassau |
| *Cornubia* | Feb. 15, 1863* | Bermuda |
| *Mariner* | February 1863 | Captured |
| *Robert E. Lee* (*Giraffe*) | Mar. 1, 1863* | Nassau |
| *Douro* | Mar. 9, 1863 | Nassau |
| *Emma* (*II*) | Mar. 12, 1863* | Nassau |
| *Granite City* | Mar. 12, 1863* | Nassau |
| *Eagle* | Mar. 14, 1863* | Nassau |
| *Cornubia* | Mar. 15, 1863* | Bermuda |
| *Emma* (*II*) | April 1863* | Nassau |
| *Robert E. Lee* (*Giraffe*) | Apr. 12, 1863* | Bermuda |
| *Britannia* | Apr. 16, 1863* | Nassau |
| *Cornubia* | Apr. 15, 1863* | Bermuda |
| *Pet* | Apr. 24, 1863* | Nassau |
| *Margaret & Jessie* (*Douglas*) | May 6, 1863 | Nassau |
| *Flora* (*I*) | May 9, 1863* | Nassau |
| *Robert E. Lee* (*Giraffe*) | May 18, 1863* | Bermuda |
| *Banshee* (*I*) | May 18, 1863 | Nassau |

| Name | Date | Bound to |
|------|------|----------|
| Pet | May 21, 1863* | Nassau |
| Cornubia | May 25, 1863* | Bermuda |
| Eugenie | May 25, 1863* | Bermuda |
| Banshee (I) | June 4, 1863* | Nassau |
| Flora (I) | June 6, 1863* | Nassau |
| Emma (II) | June 7, 1863* | Bermuda |
| Lizzie (I) | June 14, 1863* | Nassau |
| Charleston | June 14, 1863* | Nassau |
| Cornubia | June 16, 1863* | Bermuda |
| Eugenie | June 19, 1863* | Bermuda |
| Victory (Annie Childs) | June 21, 1863 | Captured |
| Banshee (I) | June 22, 1863* | Nassau |
| Robert E. Lee (Giraffe) | July 3, 1863* | Nassau |
| Flora (I) | July 7, 1863* | Nassau |
| Kate (II) | July 12, 1863* | Captured |
| Venus | July 14, 1863* | Bermuda |
| Gladiator | July 17, 1863* | Nassau |
| Arabian | July 17, 1863* | Nassau |
| Banshee (I) | July 22, 1863* | Bermuda |
| Cornubia | July 22, 1863* | Bermuda |
| Eugenie | July 23, 1863* | Bermuda |
| Merrimac | July 24, 1863 | Captured |
| Advance | July 24, 1863* | Bermuda |
| Emma (II) | July 26, 1863 | Captured |
| General Beauregard (Havelock) | July 27, 1863* | Nassau |
| Phantom | Aug. 6, 1863* | Bermuda |
| Pet | Aug. 6, 1863* | Nassau |
| Hebe | Aug. 6, 1863* | Nassau |
| Elizabeth (Atlantic) | Aug. 9, 1863* | Bermuda |
| Ella and Annie (William G. Hewes) | Aug. 10, 1863* | Bermuda |
| Robert E. Lee (Giraffe) | Aug. 15, 1863* | Bermuda |
| Cronstadt | Aug. 16, 1863 | Captured |
| Cornubia | Aug. 18, 1863 | Bermuda |
| Banshee (I) | Aug. 20, 1863* | Bermuda |
| Eugenie | Aug. 22, 1863 | Bermuda |
| Mary Anne | Sept. 3, 1863* | Nassau |
| Hansa | Sept. 3, 1863* | Bermuda |

| Name | Date | Bound to |
|---|---|---|
| *Cornubia* | Sept. 4, 1863* | Bermuda |
| *Venus* | Sept. 4, 1863* | Bermuda |
| *Don* | Sept. 5, 1863* | Nassau |
| *Margaret and Jessie (Douglas)* | Sept. 10, 1863* | Nassau |
| *Phantom* | Sept. 11, 1863* | Bermuda |
| *General Beauregard (Havelock)* | Sept. 12, 1863* | Nassau |
| *Flora (II)* | Sept. 12, 1863 | Bermuda |
| *Elizabeth (Atlantic)* | Sept. 13, 1863* | Nassau |
| *Arabian* | Sept. 15, 1863 | Destroyed |
| *Advance* | Sept. 23, 1863* | Bermuda |
| *Banshee (I)* | Sept. 26, 1863* | Nassau |
| *General Beauregard (Havelock)* | Sept. 30, 1863* | Nassau |
| *Spunkie* | Oct. 2, 1863* | Nassau |
| *Hansa* | Oct. 5, 1863* | Nassau |
| *Venus* | Oct. 6, 1863* | Nassau |
| *Don* | Oct. 7, 1863* | Nassau |
| *Alice* | Oct. 8, 1863* | Bermuda |
| *Fannie* | Oct. 10, 1863 | Nassau |
| *Pet* | Oct. 10, 1863* | Nassau |
| *Robert E. Lee (Giraffe)* | Oct. 10, 1863 | Halifax |
| *Douro* | Oct. 11, 1863 | Destroyed |
| *Cornubia* | Oct. 11, 1863* | Bermuda |
| *Flora (II)* | Oct. 11, 1863 | Bermuda |
| *Antonica (Herald)* | Oct. 12, 1863* | Nassau |
| *Dee* | Oct. 16, 1863* | Bermuda |
| *Hansa* | Oct. 19, 1863* | Nassau |
| *Margaret and Jessie (Douglas)* | Oct. 20, 1863* | Nassau |
| *Advance* | Oct. 24, 1863* | Bermuda |
| *Juno (II)* | Oct. 25, 1863 | Captured |
| *Spunkie* | Oct. 28, 1863* | Nassau |
| *Banshee (I)* | Oct. 28, 1863* | Nassau |
| *Pet* | Oct. 28, 1863* | Nassau |
| *Alice* | Oct. 31, 1863* | Bermuda |
| *General Beauregard (Havelock)* | Oct. 31, 1863* | Nassau |
| *Fannie* | Nov. 3, 1863* | Nassau |
| *Hansa* | Nov. 10, 1863* | Nassau |
| *Beatrice* | Nov. 11, 1863 | Nassau |

| Name | Date | Bound to |
| --- | --- | --- |
| Antonica (Herald) | Nov. 11, 1863* | Nassau |
| Gibraltar (Sumter) | Nov. 11, 1863* | Bermuda |
| Syren | Nov. 13, 1863* | Nassau |
| Flora (II) | Nov. 14, 1863 | Bermuda |
| Dee | Nov. 14, 1863* | Bermuda |
| Don | Nov. 14, 1863 | Nassau |
| Spunkie | Nov. 17, 1863* | Nassau |
| Scotia (II) | Nov. 17, 1863* | Nassau |
| Advance | Nov. 19, 1863* | Nassau |
| Lucy | Nov. 27, 1863* | Nassau |
| General Beauregard (Havelock) | Nov. 28, 1863* | Nassau |
| Fannie | Dec. 3, 1863* | Nassau |
| Syren | Dec. 4, 1863* | Nassau |
| Hansa | Dec. 6, 1863* | Nassau |
| Antonica (Herald) | Dec. 7, 1863* | Nassau |
| Pet | Dec. 10, 1863* | Nassau |
| Bendigo | Dec. 11, 1863* | Nassau |
| City of Petersburg | Dec. 12, 1863* | Nassau |
| Eugenie | Dec. 12, 1863* | Nassau |
| Gem | Dec. 14, 1863* | Nassau |
| Lucy | Dec. 17, 1863* | Nassau |
| Flora (II) | Dec. 20, 1863 | Bermuda |
| Syren | Dec. 31, 1863 | Nassau |
| Hansa | Jan. 2, 1864 | Nassau |
| Fannie | Jan. 2, 1864* | Nassau |
| Alice | Jan. 4, 1864* | Bermuda |
| Scotia (II) | Jan. 4, 1864 | Nassau |
| Spunkie | Jan. 4, 1864* | Nassau |
| Dee | Jan. 7, 1864* | Nassau |
| Wild Dayrell | Jan. 7, 1864* | Nassau |
| City of Petersburg | Jan. 8, 1864* | Bermuda |
| Heroine | Jan. 8, 1864* | Nassau |
| Pet | Jan. 9, 1864* | Nassau |
| Don | Jan. 10, 1864* | Bermuda |
| Presto | Jan. 14, 1864* | Nassau |
| Despatch | Jan. 15, 1864* | Nassau |
| Syren | Jan. 18, 1864 | Nassau |

| Name | Date | Bound to |
|------|------|----------|
| Star | Jan. 18, 1864* | Nassau |
| Lucy | Jan. 18, 1864* | Nassau |
| City of Petersburg | Jan. 19, 1864* | Bermuda |
| Wild Dayrell | Jan. 24, 1864* | Nassau |
| Fannie | Jan. 26, 1864* | Nassau |
| Alice | Jan. 27, 1864* | Nassau |
| Hansa | Jan. 28, 1864 | Nassau |
| Dee | Jan. 30, 1864 | Ran aground |
| Mary Ann | Jan. 30, 1864* | Nassau |
| Pet | Jan. 30, 1864 | Nassau |
| Advance | Feb. 6, 1864* | Bermuda |
| Syren | Feb. 8, 1864* | Nassau |
| Pet | Feb. 10, 1864* | Nassau |
| Heroine | Feb. 10, 1864* | Nassau |
| Alice | Feb. 11, 1864* | Nassau |
| Don | Feb. 12, 1864* | Nassau |
| Hansa | Feb. 12, 1864 | Bermuda |
| Index | Feb. 13, 1864* | Bermuda |
| City of Petersburg | Feb. 15, 1864* | Bermuda |
| Rothesay Castle | Feb. 18, 1864* | Nassau |
| Syren | Feb. 25, 1864* | Nassau |
| Fannie | Feb. 27, 1864* | Nassau |
| Scotia (II) | Feb. 28, 1864 | Captured |
| Caledonia | Mar. 1, 1864* | Bermuda |
| Lucy | Mar. 3, 1864 | Nassau |
| Mary Ann | Mar. 6, 1864 | Nassau |
| Alice | Mar. 10, 1864* | Nassau |
| City of Petersburg | Mar. 11, 1864* | Bermuda |
| Hansa | Mar. 12, 1864* | Nassau |
| Index | Mar. 13, 1864* | Bermuda |
| Annie | Mar. 14, 1864* | Nassau |
| Advance | Mar. 15, 1864* | Nassau |
| Syren | Mar. 31, 1864* | Nassau |
| Coquette | Apr. 1, 1864 | Nassau |
| Minnie | Apr. 11, 1864* | Bermuda |
| Advance | Apr. 12, 1864* | Nassau |
| Annie | Apr. 14, 1864* | Nassau |

| Name | Date | Bound to |
| --- | --- | --- |
| Lucy | Apr. 14, 1864* | Nassau |
| Will of the Wisp | Apr. 24, 1864 | Nassau |
| Edith | Apr. 26, 1864* | Nassau |
| Index | Apr. 28, 1864* | Bermuda |
| Lucy | Apr. 30, 1864* | Nassau |
| Young Republic | May 5, 1864 | Captured |
| Thistle (II) | May 6, 1864* | Bermuda |
| Atalanta | May 8, 1864* | Bermuda |
| Greyhound | May 8, 1864 | Captured |
| Minnie | May 9, 1864 | Captured |
| Helen | May 12, 1864* | Bermuda |
| Tristram Shandy | May 15, 1864 | Captured |
| Will of the Wisp | May 1864 | Nassau |
| Lucy | May 22, 1864* | Nassau |
| Alice | May 23, 1864* | Nassau |
| Fannie | May 25, 1864* | Nassau |
| Annie | May 25, 1864* | Nassau |
| Edith | May 26, 1864* | Nassau |
| Pevensey | May 26, 1864* | Bermuda |
| Syren | May 27, 1864* | Nassau |
| Coquette | May 29, 1864 | Bermuda |
| Lynx | May 31, 1864* | Bermuda |
| Will of the Wisp | June 1, 1864 | Nassau |
| Helen | June 2, 1864* | Nassau |
| Index | June 3, 1864* | Bermuda |
| Lucy | June 4, 1864* | Nassau |
| Atalanta | June 4, 1864* | Bermuda |
| Mary Celestia | June 5, 1864* | Bermuda |
| City of Petersburg | June 7, 1864* | Bermuda |
| Chicora (Let Her Be) | June 10, 1864* | Bermuda |
| Edith | June 16, 1864 | Bermuda |
| Lilian | June 22, 1864* | Bermuda |
| North Heath | June 23, 1864* | Bermuda |
| Syren | June 23, 1864* | Nassau |
| Florie | June 24, 1864* | Bermuda |
| Annie | June 25, 1864* | Nassau |
| Will of the Wisp | June 28, 1864 | Nassau |

| Name | Date | Bound to |
|------|------|----------|
| Mary Celestia | July 1, 1864* | Bermuda |
| Lynx | July 1, 1864* | Bermuda |
| Coquette | July 1, 1864 | Bermuda |
| Atalanta | July 2, 1864* | Bermuda |
| Alice | July 2, 1864* | Bermuda |
| Helen | July 2, 1864* | Bermuda |
| Edith | July 4, 1864 | Bermuda |
| Lilian | July 9, 1864 | Bermuda |
| Lucy | July 12, 1864 | Nassau |
| Old Dominion | July 15, 1864* | Bermuda |
| Syren | July 25, 1864 | Nassau |
| Mary Celestia | July 25, 1864 | Bermuda |
| Wando (Let Her Rip) | July 25, 1864 | Bermuda |
| Night Hawk | July 25, 1864 | Bermuda |
| Chicora (Let Her Be) | July 26, 1864* | Bermuda |
| Florie | July 31, 1864* | Bermuda |
| Lynx | July 31, 1864* | Bermuda |
| Alice | Aug. 1, 1864* | Bermuda |
| Annie | Aug. 6, 1864 | Nassau |
| Advance | Aug. 6, 1864* | Bermuda |
| Little Hattie | Aug. 6, 1864 | Halifax |
| Flamingo | Aug. 7, 1864* | Bermuda |
| Helen | Aug. 8, 1864* | Bermuda |
| Mary Bowers | Aug. 9, 1864* | Bermuda |
| Tallahassee (Atalanta)c | Aug. 9, 1864 | For a raid |
| City of Petersburg | Aug. 23, 1864* | Halifax |
| Will of the Wisp | Aug. 23, 1864 | Nassau |
| Old Dominion | Aug. 23, 1864 | Bermuda |
| Mary Celestia | Aug. 24, 1864* | Bermuda |
| Helen | Aug. 24, 1864 | Halifax |
| Falcon | Aug. 24, 1864 | Halifax |
| Lilian | Aug. 24, 1864 | Captured |
| Coquette | Aug. 30, 1864 | Nassau |
| Elsie | Sept. 5, 1864 | Captured |
| Old Dominion | Sept. 5, 1864* | Halifax |
| Chicora (Let Her Be) | Sept. 5, 1864 | Nassau |
| Annie | Sept. 6, 1864 | Halifax |

| Name | Date | Bound to |
|------|------|----------|
| Ella (II) | Sept. 8, 1864 | Nassau |
| Advance | Sept. 9, 1864 | Captured |
| Helen | Sept. 15, 1864* | Halifax |
| Will of the Wisp | Sept. 18, 1864 | Nassau |
| Lynx | Sept. 25, 1864 | Destroyed |
| Little Hattie | Sept. 28, 1864* | Halifax |
| Heroine | Sept. 29, 1864 | Nassau |
| Hope | Sept. 29, 1864* | Nassau |
| Owl | Sept. 31, 1864* | Bermuda |
| Wild Rover | Oct. 6, 1864 | Bermuda |
| Helen | Oct. 6, 1864* | Nassau |
| Florie | Oct. 6, 1864* | Nassau |
| Falcon | Oct. 6, 1864* | Nassau |
| Little Hattie | Oct. 7, 1864 | Nassau |
| Ella (II) | Oct. 8, 1864 | Nassau |
| Wando (Let Her Rip) | Oct. 14, 1864 | Captured |
| Agnes E. Fry | Oct. 15, 1864 | Bermuda |
| Talisman | Oct. 19, 1864 | Bermuda |
| Banshee (II) | Oct. 22, 1864 | Nassau |
| Virginia | Oct. 26, 1864* | Bermuda |
| Armstrong | Oct. 27, 1864* | Nassau |
| Chickamauga (Edith)d | Oct. 28, 1864 | On raid |
| Lady Sterling | Oct. 28, 1864* | Captured |
| Wild Rover | Oct. 28, 1864* | Nassau |
| Olustee (Tallahassee)e | Oct. 29, 1864 | On raid |
| Annie | Oct. 31, 1864 | Destroyed |
| Lucy | Nov. 1, 1864* | Captured |
| Little Hattie | Nov. 4, 1864 | Nassau |
| Beatrice | Nov. 3, 1864 | Nassau |
| Caroline | Nov. 7, 1864 | Nassau |
| Armstrong | Nov. 16, 1864* | Bermuda |
| Blenheim | Nov. 18, 1864* | Nassau |
| Talisman | Nov. 19, 1864* | Bermuda |
| Banshee (II) | Nov. 20, 1864 | Nassau |
| Agnes E. Fry | Dec. 1, 1864* | Nassau |
| Armstrong | Dec. 4, 1864 | Captured |
| Emma Henry | Dec. 7, 1864 | Captured |

| Name | Date | Bound to |
|---|---|---|
| Wild Rover | Dec. 7, 1864 | Nassau |
| Virginia | Dec. 11, 1864 | Nassau |
| Blenheim | Dec. 15, 1864* | Nassau |
| Old Dominion | Dec. 15, 1864* | Halifax |
| Caroline | Dec. 15, 1864 | Nassau |
| Vulture | Dec. 16, 1864* | Nassau |
| Talisman[f] | Dec. 18, 1864 | Returned |
| Charlotte | Dec. 19, 1864* | Bermuda |
| Colonel Lamb | Dec. 20, 1864* | Bermuda |
| Owl | Dec. 21, 1864 | Nassau |
| Chameleon (Olustee)[g] | Dec. 26, 1864 | Bermuda |
| Stag | Dec. 26, 1864* | Nassau |
| Talisman | Dec. 26, 1864 | Foundered |
| Little Hattie | Dec. 28, 1864 | Nassau |
| Banshee (II) | Dec. 28, 1864 | Nassau |
| Badger (II) | Dec. 28, 1864 | Nassau |
| Night Hawk | Dec. 31, 1864* | Nassau |
| Wild Rover | Jan. 3, 1865 | Nassau |
| Hansa | Jan. 3, 1865 | Nassau |

[a] Cleared as a warship

[b] Though information is lacking, the *Kate* seems to have run from Wilmington to Charleston before returning to Nassau.

[c] Cleared as a warship

[d] Cleared as a warship

[e] Cleared as a warship. The *Olustee* was the third name given to the *Atalanta*.

[f] Hit wreck of the Confederate ironclad *Raleigh* and returned to port.

[g] Vessel converted back to a blockade runner and run out of Wilmington by the Confederate Government. *Chameleon* was the fourth name given to the *Atalanta*.

* Estimated time of clearing

# Appendix 7

**Steam Blockade Runners Arriving South Carolina Ports,**
**November 1861–February 1865**
**(All vessels ran to Charleston unless otherwise noted)**

| Name | Date | From |
|---|---|---|
| Theodora | Nov. 4, 1861 | Havana |
| Ella Warley | Jan. 2, 1862 | Nassau |
| Nelly | Mar. 6, 1862 | Havana |
| Economist | Mar. 14, 1862 | Bermuda |
| Nashville[a] | Mar. 18, 1862 | Georgetown from Beaufort |
| Kate | Mar. 24, 1862 | Nassau |
| Cecile | Mar. 28, 1862 | Nassau |
| Nelly | Apr. 19, 1862 | Havana |
| Cecile | Apr. 28, 1862 | Nassau |
| Kate | May 20, 1862 | Nassau |
| Cecile | May 24, 1862 | Nassau |
| Minho | May 26, 1862 | Nassau |
| Memphis | June 23, 1862 | Nassau |
| Herald (I) | July 3, 1862 | Nassau |
| Lloyd | July 7, 1862* | Nassau |
| Hero | July 8, 1862* | Nassau |
| Scotia (I) | July 26, 1862* | Nassau |
| Anglia | July 30, 1862* | Nassau |
| Leopard | Aug. 3, 1862* | Nassau |
| Minho | Aug. 3, 1862* | Nassau |
| Herald (I) | Aug. 18, 1862* | Nassau |
| Kate[b] | Sept. 1, 1862* | Nassau |
| Leopard | Sept. 2, 1862* | Nassau |
| Kate | Oct. 1, 1862* | Nassau |
| Herald (I) | Nov. 1, 1862* | Bermuda |
| Aries | Nov. 15, 1862* | Nassau |

| Name | Date | From |
|------|------|------|
| *Antonica* (*Herald*) | Dec. 20, 1862 | Nassau |
| *Leopard* | Dec. 27, 1862 | Nassau |
| *Leopard* | Jan. 5, 1863 | Nassau |
| *Calypso* | Jan. 22, 1863 | Nassau |
| *Flora* (*I*) | Jan. 24, 1863* | Nassau |
| *Douglas* | Jan. 27, 1863* | Nassau |
| *Thistle* (*I*) | Jan. 29, 1863 | Nassau |
| *Annie Childs* | Feb. 11, 1863* | Nassau |
| *Ruby* (*I*) | Feb. 14, 1863 | Nassau |
| *Stonewall Jackson* (*Leopard*) | Feb. 14, 1863 | Nassau |
| *Havelock* | Feb. 24, 1863 | Nassau |
| *Margaret and Jessie* (*Douglas*) | Feb. 27, 1863* | Nassau |
| *Ruby* (*I*) | Mar. 1, 1863* | Nassau |
| *Flora* (*I*) | Mar. 15, 1863 | Nassau |
| *Gertrude* | Mar. 16, 1863 | Nassau |
| *Ruby* (*I*) | Mar. 17, 1863 | Nassau |
| *Calypso* | Mar. 18, 1863 | Nassau |
| *Antonica* (*Herald*) | Mar. 23, 1863 | Nassau |
| *Eagle* | Mar. 24, 1863 | Nassau |
| *Margaret and Jessie* (*Douglas*) | Mar. 24, 1863 | Nassau |
| *Ella and Annie* (*William G. Hewes*) | Apr. 10, 1863 | Nassau |
| *General Beauregard* (*Havelock*) | Apr. 12, 1863 | Bermuda |
| *Eagle* | Apr. 26, 1863 | Nassau |
| *Ella and Annie* (*William G. Hewes*) | Apr. 28, 1863 | Nassau |
| *Britannia* | May 11, 1863 | Nassau |
| *Norseman* | May 13, 1863 | Nassau |
| *Antonica* (*Herald*) | May 13, 1863 | Nassau |
| *Calypso* | May 15, 1863 | Nassau |
| *Ella and Annie* (*William G. Hewes*) | May 20, 1863 | Nassau |
| *Margaret and Jessie* (*Douglas*) | May 20, 1863 | Nassau |
| *Kate* (*II*) | May 20, 1863* | Nassau |
| *General Beauregard* (*Havelock*) | May 20, 1863* | Nassau |
| *Eagle* | May 22, 1863* | Nassau |
| *Fannie* | May 23, 1863 | Nassau |
| *Britannia* | May 25, 1863 | Nassau |
| *Alice* | May 25, 1863 | Nassau |
| *Elizabeth* (*Atlantic*) | May 26, 1863 | Nassau |

| Name | Date | From |
|------|------|------|
| Raccoon | June 11, 1863 | Nassau |
| Antonica (Herald) | June 11, 1863 | Nassau |
| Margaret and Jessie (Douglas) | June 16, 1863 | Nassau |
| Alice | June 27, 1863 | Nassau |
| Fannie | June 28, 1863 | Nassau |
| Juno (I) | July 8, 1863 | Nassau |
| Antonica (Herald) | July 10, 1863* | Nassau |
| Margaret and Jessie (Douglas) | July 20, 1863 | Nassau |
| Alice | July 22, 1863* | Nassau |
| Fannie | July 23, 1863 | Nassau |
| Spaulding | Aug. 16, 1863* | Nassau |
| Little Ada | Mar. 2, 1864* | Santee River from Nassau |
| Rothesay Castle | Apr. 10 1864* | Nassau |
| Mars | Apr. 13, 1864 | Nassau |
| General Whiting | May 14, 1864* | Nassau |
| Fox | June 8, 1864* | Nassau |
| Prince Albert | June 1864 | Nassau |
| Fox | June 26, 1864* | Nassau |
| Druid | July 1, 1864* | Nassau |
| Fox | Aug. 8, 1864* | Nassau |
| Syren | Aug. 11, 1864* | Nassau |
| Druid | Aug. 11, 1864* | Nassau |
| Fox | Aug. 31, 1864* | Nassau |
| Syren | Sept. 4, 1864* | Nassau |
| Druid | Sept. 6, 1864* | Nassau |
| Kate Gregg | September 1864 | Nassau |
| General Whiting | Sept. 21, 1864* | Nassau |
| Syren | Sept. 23, 1864 | Nassau |
| Fox | Sept. 28, 1864* | Nassau |
| Syren | Oct. 9, 1864* | Nassau |
| Chicora (Let Her Be) | Oct. 10, 1864* | Nassau |
| Coquette | October 1864 | Nassau |
| Fox | Nov. 4, 1864 | Nassau |
| Julia | Nov. 5, 1864 | Nassau |
| Chicora (Let Her Be) | Nov. 7, 1864* | Nassau |
| Syren | Nov. 21, 1864* | Nassau |

| Name | Date | From |
|------|------|------|
| *Druid* | Nov. 26, 1864* | Nassau |
| *Kate Gregg* | Dec. 1, 1864 | Nassau |
| *Laurel* | Dec. 1, 1864 | Nassau |
| *Julia* | December 1864 | Nassau |
| *Syren* | Dec. 20, 1864* | Nassau |
| *Chicora (Let Her Be)* | Dec. 25, 1864* | Nassau |
| *Fox* | Dec. 27, 1864* | Nassau |
| *G. T. Watson* | Dec. 27, 1864* | Nassau |
| *Caroline* | January 1865 | Georgetown from Nassau |
| *Little Hattie* | January 1865 | Nassau |
| *Fox* | Jan. 18, 1865* | Nassau |
| *Coquette* | January 1865 | Nassau |
| *Syren* | Jan. 23, 1865* | Nassau |
| *G. T. Watson* | Jan. 24, 1864* | Nassau |
| *Chicora (Let Her Be)* | Feb. 16, 1865* | Nassau |
| *Syren* | Feb. 16, 1865 | Nassau |

ᵃ Cleared as a warship

ᵇ Though information is lacking, the *Kate* seems to have run from Wilmington to Charleston before returning to Nassau.

* Estimated time of arrival

# Appendix 8

**Steam Blockade Runners Clearing South Carolina Ports, October 1861–February 1865**
**(All vessels ran from Charleston unless otherwise noted)**

| Name | Date | Bound to |
|------|------|----------|
| *Theodora* | Oct. 12, 1861 | Nassau |
| *Nashville*[a] | Oct. 29, 1861 | Liverpool |
| *Ella Warley* | Dec. 2, 1861* | Nassau |
| *Theodora* | Dec. 4, 1861 | Nassau |
| *Kate* | Jan. 12, 1862* | Nassau |
| *Cecile* | Feb. 20, 1862 | Nassau |
| *Ella Warley* | Feb. 27, 1862* | Nassau |
| *Thomas L. Wragg (Nashville)* | Mar. 23, 1862* | Nassau |
| *Nelly* | Mar. 25, 1862 | Havana |
| *Economist* | Apr. 1, 1862 | Nassau |
| *Cecile* | Apr. 5, 1862 | Nassau |
| *William Seabrook* | Apr. 15, 1862 | Nassau |
| *Kate* | Apr. 17, 1862 | Nassau |
| *Cecile* | May 3, 1862 | Nassau |
| *Nelly* | May 3, 1862 | Nassau |
| *Cecile* | May 30, 1862 | Nassau |
| *Kate* | June 2, 1862 | Nassau |
| *Minho* | June 4, 1862 | Nassau |
| *Herald (I)* | July 21, 1862 | Nassau |
| *Memphis* | July 26, 1862 | Captured |
| *Lloyd* | Aug. 14, 1862* | Liverpool |
| *Leopard* | Aug. 28, 1862* | Nassau |
| *Minho* | Aug. 28, 1862* | Bermuda |
| *Kate*[b] | Sept. 1, 1862* | Nassau |
| *Anglia* | Sept. 21, 1862* | Nassau |

| Name | Date | Bound to |
| --- | --- | --- |
| Scotia (I) | Sept. 26, 1862 | Nassau |
| Leopard | Sept. 30, 1862 | Nassau |
| Herald (I) | Oct. 12, 1862 | Bermuda |
| Kate | Oct. 29, 1862* | Nassau |
| Leopard | Nov. 10, 1862* | Nassau |
| Herald (I) | Nov. 17, 1862* | Nassau |
| Aries | Dec. 20, 1862 | Havana |
| Nina | Dec. 27, 1862 | Georgetown for Nassau |
| Antonica (Herald) | Dec. 27, 1862 | Nassau |
| Leopard | Jan. 14, 1863* | Nassau |
| Tropic (Huntress) | Jan. 18, 1863 | Destroyed |
| Calypso | Feb. 5, 1863* | Nassau |
| Flora (I) | Feb. 11, 1863 | Nassau |
| Thistle (I) | Feb. 13, 1863 | Ran aground, salvaged |
| Margaret and Jessie (Douglas) | Feb. 13, 1863* | Nassau |
| Ruby (I) | Feb. 18, 1863 | Nassau |
| Hero | Feb. 19, 1863* | Nassau |
| Stonewall Jackson (Leopard) | Feb. 21, 1863 | Nassau |
| T. D. Wagner (Annie Childs) | Mar. 3, 1863 | Nassau |
| Ruby (I) | Mar. 7, 1863 | Nassau |
| Margaret and Jessie (Douglas) | Mar. 10, 1863 | Nassau |
| Ruby (I) | Mar. 19, 1863 | Nassau |
| General Beauregard (Havelock) | Mar. 19, 1863* | Nassau |
| Flora (I) | Mar. 19, 1863 | Nassau |
| Gertrude | Mar. 23, 1863* | Nassau |
| Eagle | Apr. 1, 1863* | Nassau |
| Margaret and Jessie (Douglas) | Apr. 6, 1863* | Nassau |
| Ella and Annie (William G. Hewes) | Apr. 18, 1863* | Nassau |
| Calypso | Apr. 20, 1863* | Nassau |
| Antonica (Herald) | Apr. 20, 1863* | Nassau |
| Ella and Annie (William G. Hewes) | May 5, 1863* | Nassau |
| General Beauregard (Havelock) | May 7, 1863 | Nassau |
| Cherokee (Thistle I) | May 8, 1863 | Captured |

| Name | Date | Bound to |
|------|------|----------|
| Eagle | May 9, 1863* | Nassau |
| Britannia | May 15, 1863* | Nassau |
| Norseman | May 19, 1863* | Destroyed |
| Calypso | May 21, 1863* | Nassau |
| Antonica (Herald) | May 21, 1863* | Nassau |
| Margaret and Jessie (Douglas) | May 27, 1863 | Nassau |
| Stono (Isaac Smith) | June 5, 1863 | Destroyed |
| Fannie | June 14, 1863* | Nassau |
| Raccoon | June 18, 1863 | Destroyed |
| Alice | June 18, 1863* | Nassau |
| Kate (II) | June 19, 1863* | Nassau |
| Ella and Annie (William G. Hewes) | June 21, 1863* | Nassau |
| Antonica (Herald) | June 21, 1863* | Nassau |
| Elizabeth (Atlantic) | June 21, 1863* | Nassau |
| Britannia | June 22, 1863* | Captured |
| General Beauregard (Havelock) | June 23, 1863* | Nassau |
| Margaret and Jessie (Douglas) | July 7, 1863* | Nassau |
| Alice | July 7, 1863 | Nassau |
| Fannie | July 8, 1863 | Nassau |
| Margaret and Jessie (Douglas) | July 8, 1863* | Nassau |
| Margaret and Jessie (Douglas) | Aug. 1, 1863* | Nassau |
| Antonica (Herald) | Aug. 3, 1863* | Nassau |
| Alice | Aug. 15, 1863* | Nassau |
| Fannie | Aug. 22, 1863 | Nassau |
| Spaulding | Sept. 18, 1863* | Nassau |
| General Moultrie | Mar. 4, 1864* | Nassau |
| Helen (Juno I) | Mar. 8, 1864* | Foundered |
| Rothesay Castle | May 1864 | Nassau |
| Mars | May 26, 1864* | Nassau |
| Fox | June 10, 1864* | Nassau |
| Little Ada | June 10, 1864* | Santee River for Nassau |
| Fox | July 22, 1864 | Nassau |
| Druid | July 26, 1864 | Nassau |
| Prince Albert | July 26, 1864 | Nassau |
| Fox | Aug. 22, 1864 | Nassau |

| Name | Date | Bound to |
|------|------|----------|
| Syren | Aug. 23, 1864 | Nassau |
| Druid | Aug. 24, 1864 | Nassau |
| General Whiting | Sept. 1, 1864* | Nassau |
| Fox | Sept. 9, 1864 | Nassau |
| Syren | Sept. 9, 1864 | Nassau |
| Syren | Sept. 27, 1864 | Nassau |
| Kate Gregg | September 1864 | Nassau |
| Fox | Oct. 3, 1864 | Nassau |
| Coquette | Oct. 23, 1864* | Nassau |
| Chicora (Let Her Be) | Oct. 27, 1864 | Nassau |
| Syren | Oct. 27, 1864* | Nassau |
| Kate Gregg | Nov. 1, 1864 | Nassau |
| General Clinch | Nov. 3, 1864 | Nassau |
| Druid | Nov. 3, 1864* | Nassau |
| Julia | Nov. 18, 1864 | Nassau |
| Syren | Dec. 1, 1864* | Nassau |
| Chicora (Let Her Be) | Dec. 14, 1864* | Nassau |
| Fox | Dec. 15, 1864* | Nassau |
| Kate Gregg | Dec. 1864 | Nassau |
| Julia | Dec. 20, 1864 | Captured |
| General Whiting | Dec. 23, 1864* | Nassau |
| Laurel | Dec. 28, 1864 | Nassau |
| Syren | Dec. 1864 | Nassau |
| G. T. Watson | Jan. 2, 1865* | Nassau |
| Fox | Jan. 2, 1865* | Nassau |
| Chicora (Let Her Be) | January 1865 | Nassau |
| Caroline | January 1865 | Georgetown for Nassau |
| Syren | Jan. 26, 1865* | Nassau |
| Fox | Feb. 2, 1865* | Nassau |
| Coquette | February 1865 | Nassau |
| Druid | Feb. 4, 1865* | Nassau |
| Little Hattie | Feb. 7, 1865 | Nassau |
| Chicora (Let Her Be) | Feb. 13, 1865* | Nassau |
| Celt | February 1865 | Destroyed |

| Name | Date | Bound to |
|------|------|----------|
| G. T. Watson | Feb. 18, 1865 | Nassau |

ª Cleared as a warship

ᵇ Though information is lacking, the *Kate* seems to have run from Wilmington to Charleston before returning to Nassau.

* Estimated time of clearing

# Appendix 9

**Steam Blockade Runners Arriving Georgia and East Florida Ports,
September 1861–December 1865**

| Name | Date | Arrived |
|---|---|---|
| *Bermuda* | Sept. 18, 1861 | Savannah from West Hartlepool |
| *Fingal* | Nov. 14, 1861 | Savannah from Bermuda |
| *Kate* | Jan. 31, 1862 | New Smyrna from Nassau |
| *Kate* | Feb. 28, 1862 | New Smyrna from Nassau |
| *Cecile* | Mar. 2, 1862 | New Smyrna from Nassau |
| *Kate* | June 30, 1862 | Savannah from Nassau |
| *Thomas L. Wragg* (*Nashville*) | July 6, 1862 | Ogeechee River from Nassau |
| *Antonica* (*Herald*) | Jan. 13, 1863* | Savannah from Nassau |

* Estimated time of arrival

# Appendix 10

## Steam Blockade Runners Clearing Georgia and East Florida Ports, October 1861–December 1865

| Name | Date | From |
| --- | --- | --- |
| Bermuda | Oct. 29, 1861 | Savannah for Liverpool |
| Kate | Feb. 15, 1862 | New Smyrna for Nassau |
| Cecile | Mar. 7, 1862 | New Smyrna for Nassau |
| Kate | Mar. 10, 1862 | New Smyrna for Nassau |
| Reliance | July 19, 1862 | Savannah, captured |
| Kate | July 22, 1862* | Savannah for Nassau |
| Emma (I) | Aug. 30, 1862 | Savannah, captured |
| Antonica (Herald) | Jan. 28, 1863* | Savannah for Nassau |
| St. Johns | Feb. 13, 1863* | Savannah for Nassau |
| Charleston | Mar. 25, 1863* | Savannah for Nassau |
| Oconee (Savannah) | Aug. 18, 1863 | Savannah, foundered |
| Herald (II) | Sept. 25, 1863 | Savannah, captured |
| Chatham | Dec. 15, 1863 | Savannah, captured |
| Ida | July 8, 1864 | Savannah, captured |

* Estimated time of clearing

# Appendix 11

**Steam Blockade Runners Arriving West Florida Ports, March 1862–February 1864**
**(All vessels ran to St. Marks unless otherwise noted)**

| Name | Date | From |
| --- | --- | --- |
| *Florida*[a] | March 1862 | St. Andrews Bay from Havana |
| *Havana* | May 1, 1862 | Havana |
| *Havana* | May 30, 1862 | Havana |
| *Cuba* | May 30, 1862 | Havana |
| *Cuba* | December 1862 | Havana |
| *Cuba*[b] | January 1863 | Suwannee River from Mobile |
| *Little Lilly* | June 22, 1863* | Havana |
| *Isabel* | June 1863 | Havana |
| *Little Lilly* | August 1863 | Havana |
| *Mail* | September 1863 | Bayport from Havana |
| *Laura* | October 1863 | Havana |
| *Scottish Chief* | October 1863 | Tampa from Havana |
| *Mary Ann* | October 1863 | Havana |
| *Rosita* | October 19, 1863* | Havana |
| *Little Lilly* | October 1863 | Havana |
| *Little Lilly* | November 1863 | Havana |
| *Laura* | Dec. 19, 1863 | Havana |
| *Little Lilly* | December 1863 | Havana |
| *Mayflower* | December 1863 | Coast |

| Name | Date | From |
|------|------|------|
| *Powerful* | December 1863 | Suwannee River from Havana |
| *Rosita* | Dec. 31, 1863 | Havana |
| *Little Lilly* | Feb. 2, 1864 | Havana |

a Captured April 6, 1862, before she could escape from St. Andrews bay.

b Operated along Alabama and Florida coast. The *Cuba* was involved in establishing a naval depot in the Suwannee River, which was later abandoned. Exact information is lacking on her movements during this period.

* Estimated time of arrival.

# Appendix 12

**Steam Blockade Runners Clearing West Florida Ports,
May 1862–February 1984
(All vessels ran from St. Marks unless otherwise noted)**

| Name | Date | From |
|---|---|---|
| *Havana* | May 7, 1862* | Havana |
| *Havana* | June 5, 1862 | Destroyed |
| *Cuba*ᵃ | January 1863 | Suwannee River for Mobile |
| *Cuba* | February 1863 | Havana |
| *Isabel* | July 12, 1863* | Havana |
| *Little Lilly* | July 24, 1863 | Havana |
| *Little Lilly* | September 1863 | Havana |
| *Mail* | Oct. 15, 1863 | Bayport, Captured |
| *Little Lilly* | October 1863 | Havana |
| *Scottish Chief* | Oct. 16, 1863 | Tampa, Destroyed |
| *Mary Ann* | October 1863 | Havana |
| *Little Lilly* | Nov. 18, 1863* | Havana |
| *Rosita* | Nov. 20, 1863* | Havana |
| *Laura* | Nov. 23, 1863 | Havana |
| *Powerful* | Dec. 20, 1863 | Suwannee River, Destroyed |
| *Laura* | Dec. 28, 1863* | Havana |
| *Little Lilly* | Dec. 29, 1863* | Havana |
| *Rosita* | Jan. 9, 1864* | Havana |
| *Mayflower* | Jan. 14, 1864 | Captured |
| *Little Lilly* | Feb. 24, 1864 | Destroyed |

ᵃ *Cuba* operated along the Alabama and Florida coasts. The vessel was used to establish and later evacuate a naval depot in the Suwannee River. Exact information on her movements during this period is lacking.

* Estimated date of clearing

# Appendix 13

## Steam Blockade Runners Arriving Mobile, July 1862–August 1864

| Name | Date | From |
|------|------|------|
| *Alice (Matagorda)* | July 22, 1862 | Havana |
| *Cuba* | July 25, 1862 | Havana |
| *Florida*[a] | Sept. 4, 1862 | Havana |
| *Cuba*[b] | January 1863 | Suwannee River |
| *Alice (Matagorda)* | April 1863 | Havana |
| *Fox*[c] | Apr. 15, 1863 | Sea |
| *Neptune* | Apr. 15, 1863 | Havana |
| *General Buckner (Eugenie)* | April 1863 | Havana |
| *Neptune* | May 16, 1863* | Havana |
| *Ruby* | May 16, 1863* | Havana |
| *Nita (Crescent)* | May 20, 1863* | Havana |
| *Alice (Matagorda)* | May 23, 1863* | Havana |
| *Soler* | May 27, 1863 | Havana |
| *Boston*[c] | June 11, 1863 | Sea |
| *Alabama* | June 15, 1863 | Havana |
| *Alice (Matagorda)* | June 23, 1863* | Havana |
| *Alice Vivian* | July 15, 1863* | Havana |
| *Fanny (Fox)* | July 28, 1863* | Havana |
| *Alabama* | Aug. 16, 1863* | Havana |
| *Isabel* | Sept. 16, 1863* | Havana |
| *Donegal (Austin)* | Jan. 8, 1864 | Havana |
| *Denbigh* | Jan. 10, 1864 | Havana |
| *Donegal (Austin)* | February 1864 | Havana |
| *Denbigh* | Mar. 14, 1864 | Havana |
| *Denbigh* | Apr. 14, 1864 | Havana |
| *Alice (Matagorda)* | April 1864 | Havana |
| *Donegal (Austin)* | April 1864 | Havana |
| *Denbigh* | Apr. 30, 1864 | Havana |

| Name | Date | From |
|------|------|------|
| *Mary* | March 1864 | Havana |
| *Denbigh* | May 18, 1864 | Havana |
| *Alice (Matagorda)* | May 23, 1864 | Havana |
| *Mary* | May 2, 1864 | Havana |
| *Mary* | June 1, 1864 | Havana |
| *Heroine* | June 6, 1864 | Havana |
| *Denbigh* | June 7, 1864 | Havana |
| *Alice (Matagorda)* | June 23, 1864 | Havana |
| *Mary* | July 1864 | Havana |
| *Virgin* | July 10, 1864 | Havana |
| *Denbigh* | July 1864 | Havana |
| *Red Gauntlet* | Aug. 4, 1864 | Havana |

ᵃ Entered as a warship.

ᵇ Operated along coast between Mobile and Florida Dec.–March 1863. The *Cuba* was involved in establishing a Naval depot in the Suwannee River. Exact information on her movements is lacking.

ᶜ Captured as a prize in the Mississippi River and brought to Mobile.

* Estimated time of arrival.

# Appendix 14

## Steam Blockade Runners Clearing Mobile, November 1861–December 1862

| Name | Date | Port Bound to |
| --- | --- | --- |
| Cuba | May 7, 1862 | Havana |
| Swan | May 24, 1862 | Captured |
| Yorktown | Aug. 26, 1862 | foundered |
| Cuba | Sept. 19, 1862 | Havana |
| Alice (Matagorda) | Sept. 29, 1862* | Havana |
| Florida[a] | Jan. 16, 1863 | On raid |
| Cuba[b] | January 1863 | Suwannee River |
| General Buckner (Eugenie) | Apr. 20, 1863* | Havana |
| Nita (Crescent) | Apr. 16, 1863* | Havana |
| Alice (Matagorda) | Apr. 16, 1863* | Havana |
| Cuba | April 1863 | Havana |
| Neptune | April 1863 | Havana |
| Alice (Matagorda) | May 1863 | Havana |
| Neptune | May 22, 1863* | Havana |
| Ruby | May 22, 1863* | Havana |
| Soler | June 1863 | Havana |
| Nita (Crescent) | June 1863 | Havana |
| Planter | June 11, 1863* | Captured |
| Alice Vivian | June 12, 1863* | Havana |
| Fanny (Fox) | June 13, 1863* | Havana |
| Alice (Matagorda) | July 7, 1863 | Havana |
| Alice Vivian | July 8, 1863 | Captured |
| Alabama | July 10, 1863* | Havana |
| Fanny (Fox) | July 13, 1863* | Havana |
| Kate Dale | July 14, 1863 | Captured |
| James Battle | July 16, 1863 | Captured |
| William Bagley | July 17, 1863 | Captured |

| Name | Date | Port Bound to |
|------|------|---------------|
| *Lizzie Davis* | July 18, 1863* | Havana |
| *Warrior* | Aug. 17, 1863 | Captured |
| *Fanny (Fox)* | Aug. 18, 1863 | Havana |
| *Alabama* | Aug. 20, 1863 | Havana |
| *Grey Jacket* | Dec. 31, 1863 | Captured |
| *Isabel* | Jan. 11, 1864* | Havana |
| *Denbigh* | January 1864 | Havana |
| *Donegal (Austin)* | Feb. 6, 1864 | Havana |
| *Donegal (Austin)* | March 1864 | Havana |
| *Denbigh* | Mar. 16, 1864 | Havana |
| *Mary* | Apr. 14, 1864* | Havana |
| *Donegal (Austin)* | April 1864 | Havana |
| *Denbigh* | Apr. 16, 1864 | Havana |
| *Alice (Matagorda)* | Apr. 16, 1864 | Havana |
| *Denbigh* | May 7, 1864 | Havana |
| *Mary* | May 7, 1864 | Havana |
| *Denbigh* | May 26, 1864 | Havana |
| *Alice (Matagorda)* | June 1864 | Havana |
| *Mary* | June 4, 1864 | Havana |
| *Denbigh* | June 14, 1864 | Havana |
| *Alice (Matagorda)* | July 7, 1864 | Havana |
| *Denbigh* | July 26, 1864 | Havana |

[a] Cleared as a warship

[b] Operated along the Alabama and Florida coast between Mobile and the Suwannee River.

* Estimated time of clearing

# Appendix 15

**Steam Blockade Runners Arriving Louisiana Ports,
December 1861–April 1862
(All vessels ran from Havana)**

| Name | Date | Port |
|------|------|------|
| *Elizabeth (General Miramon)* | Feb. 16, 1862 | Grand Caillou |
| *Victoria* | Feb. 20, 1862 | Barataria Bay |
| *Fox (A. J. Whitmore)* | March 11, 1862 | Brashear City |

# Appendix 16

**Steam Blockade Runners Clearing Louisiana Ports,[a]**
**November 1861–April 1862**
**(All vessels ran to Havana)**

| Name | Date | From |
|------|------|------|
| C. Vanderbilt | Nov. 28, 1861* | Mississippi River |
| Pizarro[b] | Dec. 11, 1861* | Mississippi River |
| General Miramon | December 1861 | Lakes |
| Calhoun | Jan. 2, 1862* | Mississippi River |
| Victoria | Jan. 15, 1862* | Mississippi River |
| James L. Day | Jan. 22, 1862 | Mississippi River captured |
| Magnolia | Feb. 19, 1862 | Mississippi River captured |
| Florida | Feb. 19, 1862 | Mississippi River |
| Tennessee | Feb. 19, 1862 | Mississippi River unable to escape |
| A. J. Whitmore | Feb. 23, 1862* | Brashear City |
| William H. Webb | Feb. 24, 1862 | Mississippi River unable to escape |
| Enterprise[c] | Feb. 26, 1862* | Brashear City |
| Elizabeth (General Miramon) | late March 1862 | Grand Caillou |
| Austin | Mar. 28, 1862 | Brashear City |
| Fox (A. J. Whitmore) | Apr. 2, 1862 | Brashear City |
| Arizona | Apr. 4, 1862 | Brashear City |
| William G. Hewes | Apr. 13, 1862* | Brashear City |
| Atlantic[d] | Apr. 15, 1862* | Brashear City |
| Victoria | Apr. 19, 1862* | Barataria Bay |

| Name | Date | From |
|------|------|------|
| California | Apr. 23, 1862* | Lakes |
| Granite City | Jan. 20, 1865 | Calcasieu Pass Destroyed |
| Wave[e] | January 1865 | Calcasieu Pass for Mexico |

[a] Dates given as accurately as possible. Dates given refer to probable time of running the blockade, not when vessel cleared the custom house. New Orleans Custom House handled all Louisiana ports.

[b] No evidence was found of the *Pizarro* reaching a Cuban port. She may have run to Mexico.

[c] There is very little information on the *Enterprise*. There is evidence that she was the towboat *America*, which was reported sinking in the same storm that claimed the *C. Vanderbilt* on March 15, 1862.

[d] The *Atlantic* cleared the custom house on Feb. 18, 1862, did not run the blockade until mid-April.

[e] No hard information on the *Wave*. She may have escaped to Mexico.

* Estimated time of clearing.

# Appendix 17

**Steam Blockade Runners Arriving Texas Ports,**
**December 1861–June 1865**
**(All vessels ran to Galveston unless otherwise noted)**

| Name | Date | From |
|------|------|------|
| C. Vanderbilt | Dec. 29, 1861 | Sabine Pass from Havana |
| Union | August 1862 | Havana |
| Victoria | September 1862 | Sabine Pass from Havana |
| Blanche (General Rusk) | August 1862 | Indianola from Havana |
| Alice (Matagorda) | April 1863 | Havana |
| Alice (Matagorda) | February 1864 | Brazos River from Havana |
| Isabel | Mar. 18, 1864 | Havana |
| Alice (Matagorda) | April 1864 | Havana |
| Donegal (Austin) | April 1864 | Brazos River |
| Susanna | Apr. 12, 1864* | Havana |
| Alice (Matagorda) | May 1864 | Havana |
| Susanna | June 2, 1864* | Havana |
| Carolina | June 9, 1864 | Havana |
| Alice (Matagorda) | June 1864 | Havana |
| Susanna | July 1864 | Havana |
| Alice (Matagorda) | August 1864 | Havana |
| Susanna | Aug. 24, 1864* | Havana |
| Denbigh | Aug. 25, 1864 | Havana |
| Zephine | Sept. 10, 1864* | Havana |
| Denbigh | September 1864 | Havana |
| Susanna | Sept. 28, 1864* | Havana |
| Zephine | November 1864 | Havana |
| Susanna | November 1864 | Havana |
| Denbigh | Nov. 12, 1864 | Havana |
| Triton | December 1864 | Havana |
| Luna | Dec. 8, 1864 | Havana |

| Name | Date | From |
|------|------|------|
| Maria | December 1864 | Havana |
| Ptarmigan | January 1865 | Havana |
| Jeanette | January 1865 | Havana |
| Lark | Jan. 20, 1865* | Havana |
| Denbigh | Jan. 21, 1865* | Havana |
| Wren | Feb. 7, 1865 | Havana |
| Luna | February 1865 | Havana |
| Lark | Feb. 20, 1865* | Havana |
| Denbigh | Feb. 22, 1865* | Havana |
| Flamingo | Feb. 22, 1865* | Havana |
| Evelyn | Feb. 27, 1865* | Havana |
| Zephine | March 1865 | Havana |
| Evelyn | Mar. 9, 1865* | Havana |
| Banshee (II) | March 1865 | Havana |
| Wren | Mar. 30, 1865* | Havana |
| Pelican | Mar. 30, 1865* | Havana |
| Fox | Apr. 1, 1865 | Havana |
| Badger (II) | Apr. 3, 1865* | Havana |
| Denbigh | Apr. 5, 1865* | Havana |
| Lark | Apr. 5, 1865* | Havana |
| Imogene | Apr. 16, 1865 | Havana |
| Wren | May 5, 1865* | Havana |
| Lark | May 24, 1865 | Havana |

* Estimated date of arrival

# Appendix 18

**Steam Blockade Runners Clearing Texas Ports,
February 1862–June 1865
(All vessels ran from Galveston unless otherwise noted)**

| Name | Date | Bound To |
| --- | --- | --- |
| *C. Vanderbilt* | Feb. 15, 1862 | Sabine City for Havana |
| *Matagorda* | Apr. 15, 1862* | Sabine City for Havana |
| *General Rusk* | June 5, 1862* | Havana |
| *Texas Ranger* | June 19, 1862* | Havana |
| *Union* | Aug. 28, 1862 | Captured |
| *Victoria* | Sept. 17, 1862* | Sabine City |
| *Blanche (General Rusk)* | Sept. 29, 1862* | Indianola for Havana, captured |
| *Alice (Matagorda)* | Apr. 30, 1863 | Havana |
| *Alice (Matagorda)* | Apr. 30, 1863 | Havana |
| *Clifton*[a] | Mar. 21, 1864 | Sabine Pass, destroyed |
| *Alice (Matagorda)*[b] | April 1864 | Brazos River for Galveston |
| *Lavinia (Harriet Lane)* | Apr. 30, 1864 | Havana |
| *Alice (Matagorda)* | Apr. 30, 1864 | Havana |
| *Isabel* | Apr. 30, 1864 | Havana |
| *Susanna* | May 1864 | Havana |
| *Donegal (Austin)* | Apr. 28, 1864* | Havana |
| *Alice (Matagorda)* | May 31, 1864 | Havana |
| *Susanna* | June 1864 | Havana |
| *Alice (Matagorda)* | July 1864 | Havana |
| *Carolina* | July 7, 1864 | Destroyed |
| *Susanna* | July 14, 1864 | Havana |
| *Denbigh* | September 1864 | Havana |
| *Alice (Matagorda)* | Sept. 10, 1864 | Captured |
| *Susanna* | Sept. 10, 1864 | Havana |
| *Denbigh* | October 1864 | Havana |
| *Susanna* | Oct. 9, 1864 | Havana |

| Name | Date | Bound To |
|------|------|----------|
| Zephine | Oct. 14, 1864 | Havana |
| Susanna | Nov. 27, 1864 | Captured |
| Denbigh | Dec. 10, 1864* | Havana |
| Triton | December 1864 | Vera Cruz |
| Maria | Jan. 1, 1865* | Havana |
| Luna | Jan. 1, 1865* | Havana |
| Zephine | Jan. 10, 1865 | Havana |
| Flamingo | January 1865 | Havana |
| Jeanette | January 1865 | Havana |
| Ptarmigan | Jan. 26, 1865* | Havana |
| Lark | Jan. 30, 1865* | Havana |
| Denbigh | Jan. 30, 1865* | Havana |
| Evelyn | February 1865 | Havana |
| Evelyn | Mar. 4, 1865* | Havana |
| Wren | Mar. 5, 1865* | Havana |
| Denbigh | Mar. 18, 1865* | Havana |
| Zephine | March 1865 | Havana |
| Lark | March 1865 | Havana |
| Banshee (II) | March 1865 | Havana |
| Imogene | Apr. 3, 1865 | Havana |
| Luna | Apr. 11, 1865* | Havana |
| Evelyn | Apr. 16, 1865* | Havana |
| Wren | Apr. 17, 1865* | Havana |
| Badger (II) | Apr. 17, 1865* | Havana |
| Fox | Apr. 18, 1865 | Havana |
| Pelican | Apr. 27, 1865* | Havana |
| Denbigh | Apr. 28, 1865 | Havana |
| Lark | Apr. 30, 1865* | Havana |
| Wren | May 13, 1865 | Havana |
| Lark | May 24, 1865 | Havana |

* Estimated time of clearing

# Appendix 19

**Steam Blockade Runners Unable to Reach Southeastern Ports, April 1862–February 1865**

|  | From Nassau |
| --- | --- |
| *Ella and Warley (Isabel)* | Captured by the *Santiago de Cuba* Apr. 24, 1862, while heading for Charleston |
| *Stettin* | Captured by the *Bienville* May 24, 1862, while heading for Charleston |
| *Nelly (Governor Dudley)* | Wrecked May 25, 1862, while trying to enter Charleston |
| *Cambria* | Captured by the *Huron* May 26, 1862, while heading for Charleston |
| *Elizabeth (General Miramon)* | Captured by the *Keystone State* May 29, 1862, while heading for Charleston |
| *Nassau (Theodora, Gordon)* | Captured by the *State of Georgia* and *Victoria* May 28, 1862, while heading for Wilmington |
| *Patras* | Captured by the *Bienville* May 28, 1862, while heading for Charleston |
| *Emilie (William Seabrook)* | Captured by the *Flag* and *Restless* July 7, 1862, while heading for Charleston |
| *Tubal Cain* | Captured by the *Octorora* July 24, 1862, while heading for Charleston |
| *Columbia* | Captured by the *Santiago de Cuba* Aug. 3, 1862, while heading for Charleston |
| *Lodona* | Captured by the *Unadilla* Aug. 4, 1862, while heading for Savannah |
| *Ouachita* | Captured by the *Memphis* Oct. 14, 1862, while heading for Charleston |

| | |
|---|---|
| *Scotia (I)* | Captured by the *Restless* Oct. 24, 1862, while heading for Charleston |
| *Anglia* | Captured by the *Flag* Oct. 27, 1862, while heading for Charleston |
| *Pearl* | Captured by the *Tioga* Jan. 20, 1863, at sea heading for Charleston |
| *Nina* | Foundered Jan. 25, 1863, heading for Charleston |
| *Wave Queen* | Destroyed by the *Conemaugh* Feb. 25, 1863, in North Santee River, S.C. |
| *Georgiana* | Destroyed Mar. 18, 1863, while entering Charleston Harbor |
| *Nicholas I* | Captured by the *Victoria* and *William Bacon* Mar. 21, 1863, off New River Inlet, N.C. |
| *Mariner* | Captured Mar. 1863, at sea heading for Wilmington |
| *Granite City* | Captured by the *Tioga* Mar. 22, 1863, off Eleuthera Island, Bahamas |
| *Dolphin* | Captured by the *Wachusett* Mar. 25, 1863, at sea |
| *Stonewall Jackson* | Destroyed by the *Flag* and *Huron* Apr. 12, 1863, while entering Charleston Harbor |
| *Gertrude* | Captured by the *Vanderbilt* Apr. 16, 1863, off the Bahamas |
| *St. Johns* | Captured by the *Stettin* Apr. 18, 1863, off Cape Romain, S.C. |
| *Calypso* | Captured by the *Florida* June 11, 1863, off Old Inlet, N.C. |
| *Ruby (I)* | Destroyed June 11, 1863, off Charleston |
| *Charleston* | Captured by the *Seminole* July 11, 1863, at sea |
| *Lizzie (I)* | Captured by the *Santiago de Cuba* July 15, 1863, off the Florida coast |
| *Raccoon* | Destroyed July 19, 1863, off Charleston |
| *Hebe* | Destroyed by the *Shokokon* Aug. 18, 1863, off New Inlet, N.C. |

| | |
|---|---|
| *Jupiter* (*I*) | Captured by the *Cimarron* Sept. 13, 1863 in Wassaw Inlet, Georgia |
| *Diamond* | Captured by the *Stettin* Sept. 23, 1863, off Georgia coast |
| *Elizabeth* | Destroyed Sept. 26, 1863, off Cape Fear, N.C. |
| *Spaulding* | Captured by the *Union* Oct. 11, 1863, near St. Andrews Bay, Georgia |
| *Venus* | Destroyed by the *Nansemond* Oct. 21, 1863, off New Inlet, N.C. |
| *Ella and Annie* | Captured by the *Niphon* Nov. 5, 1863, while trying to reach New Inlet, N.C. |
| *Margaret and Jessie* | Captured by the *Nansemond* and the *Fulton* Nov. 5, 1863, while heading for Wilmington |
| *Banshee* (*I*) | Captured by the *Montgomery* Nov. 21, 1863, heading for Wilmington |
| *Minna* | Captured by the *Circassian* Dec. 9, 1863, off Cape Romain, S.C. |
| *General Beauregard* | Destroyed by the *Howquah* Dec. 11, 1863, off New Inlet, N.C. |
| *Antonica* | Destroyed by the *Governor Buckingham* Dec. 19, 1863, while trying to enter Old Inlet, N.C. |
| *Bendigo* | Destroyed Jan. 2, 1864, off Lockwood Folly, N.C. |
| *Wild Dayrell* | Destroyed by the *Sassacus* Feb. 1, 1864, off Topsail Inlet, N.C. |
| *Spunkie* | Destroyed Feb. 9, 1864, off Old Inlet, N.C. |
| *Fanny and Jenny* | Destroyed by the *Florida* Feb. 9, 1864, off Masonboro Inlet, N.C. |
| *Pet* | Captured by the *Montgomery* Feb. 16, 1864, off Lockwood Folly Inlet, N.C. |
| *Don* | Captured by the *Pequot* Mar. 4, 1864, off Beaufort, N.C. |
| *Alliance* | Captured by the *South Carolina* Apr. 12, 1864, near Daufuskie Island, S.C. |

| | |
|---|---|
| *Georgiana McCaw* | Destroyed by the *Victoria* June 2, 1864, off Old Inlet, N.C. |
| *Rose* | Destroyed by the *Wamsutta* June 2, 1864, off Georgetown, S.C. |
| *Jupiter (II)* | Captured by the *Cimarron* June 27, 1864, near the Bahamas Islands |
| *Prince Albert* | Destroyed Aug. 9, 1864, off Fort Moultrie, while trying to enter Charleston Harbor |
| *Hope* | Captured by the *Eolus* Oct. 22, 1864, heading for Wilmington |
| *Flora (II)* | Destroyed Oct. 22, 1864, off Fort Moultrie while trying to enter Charleston Harbor |
| *Beatrice* | Destroyed Nov. 27, 1864, while trying to enter Charleston Harbor |
| *Stormy Petrel* | Destroyed Dec. 7, 1864, off New Inlet, N.C. |
| *Agnes E. Fry* | Destroyed Dec. 27, 1864, off Old Inlet, N.C. |
| *Blenheim* | Captured by the *Tristram Shandy* Jan. 25, 1865, in Cape Fear River |
| *Rattlesnake* | Destroyed Feb. 1865, while trying to enter Charleston Harbor |
| *Deer* | Captured by the *Canonicus, Catskill,* and *Monadnock* Feb. 18, 1865, while trying to enter Charleston Harbor |

### From Bermuda

| | |
|---|---|
| *Bermuda* | Captured by the *Mercedita* Apr. 27, 1862, while heading for Nassau |
| *Adela* | Captured by the *Quaker City* and *Huntsville* July 27, 1862, while heading for Nassau |
| *Minho* | Driven ashore and destroyed by the *Flambeau* Oct. 20, 1862, while trying to enter Charleston harbor |
| *Princess Royal* | Captured by the *Unadilla* Jan. 29, 1863, while trying to enter Charleston harbor |

| | |
|---|---|
| *Phantom* | Ran aground and destroyed by the *Connecticut* Sept. 23, 1863, off Topsail Inlet, N.C. |
| *Cornubia* | Captured by the *Niphon* and the *James Adger* Nov. 8, 1863, at sea heading for Wilmington |
| *Robert E. Lee* | Captured by the *James Adger* Nov. 9, 1863, at sea heading for Wilmington |
| *Ella* | Captured by the *Howquah* Nov. 10, 1863, off New Inlet, N.C. |
| *Ceres* | Captured by the *Violet* Dec. 6, 1863, off Old Inlet, N.C., after having run aground and being abandoned by her crew |
| *The Dare* | Destroyed by the *Aries* and the *Montgomery* Jan. 7, 1864, off Lockwood Folly Inlet, N.C. |
| *Vesta* | Destroyed by the *Nansemond* Jan. 11, 1864, near Little River Inlet, N.C. |
| *Ranger* | Destroyed by the *Minnesota, Governor Buckingham, Daylight,* and *Aries* Jan. 11, 1864, off Old Inlet, N.C. |
| *Presto* | Destroyed Feb. 4, 1864, off Fort Moultrie, Charleston Harbor |
| *Nutfield* | Destroyed by the *Sassacus* Feb. 4, 1864, off New River Inlet, N.C. |
| *Dee* | Destroyed by the *Cambridge* Feb. 5, 1864, off Masonboro Inlet, N.C. |
| *Emily (I)* | Destroyed Feb. 9, 1864, off Masonboro Inlet, N.C. |
| *Caledonia* | Captured by the *Keystone State* and the *Massachusetts* May 30, 1864, at sea while heading for Wilmington |
| *Thistle (II)* | Captured by the *Fort Jackson* June 4, 1864, at sea while heading for Wilmington |
| *Siren* | Captured by the *Keystone State* June 5, 1864, at sea heading for Wilmington |

| | |
|---|---|
| *Pevensey* | Destroyed by the *New Berne* June 9, 1864, off Beaufort, N.C. |
| *Rouen* | Captured by the *Keystone State* July 2, 1864, at sea while heading for Wilmington |
| *Boston* | Captured by the *Fort Jackson* July 8, 1864, at sea while heading for Wilmington |
| *Mary Bowers* | Destroyed Aug. 31, 1864, off Long Island, S.C. |
| *Florie* | Destroyed Oct. 1864, inside bar of Cape Fear River |
| *Ella (II)* | Destroyed by the *Emma* Dec. 1, 1864, off Old Inlet, N.C. |
| *Vixen* | Captured by the *Rhode Island* Dec. 1, 1864, while heading for Wilmington |
| *Charlotte* | Captured by the *Malvern* Jan. 20, 1865, in the Cape Fear River |
| *Stag* | Captured by the *Malvern* Jan. 20, 1865, in the Cape Fear River |

**From Halifax**

| | |
|---|---|
| *Condor* | Destroyed Oct. 1, 1864, off New Inlet, N.C. |
| *Constance* | Destroyed Oct. 6, 1864, while trying to enter Charleston harbor |

# Appendix 20

**Steam Blockade Runners Unable to Reach Gulf Ports, January 1862–June 1865**

### (All Cleared from Havana)

| | |
|---|---|
| *Calhoun* | Captured by the *Rachel Seaman* Jan. 22, 1862, at the mouth of the Mississippi River |
| *Black Joker (C. Vanderbilt)* | Foundered Mar. 15, 1862, in Gulf of Mexico |
| *Fox (A. J. Whitmore)* | Captured early May, 1862, at Berwick Bay |
| *Ann* | Captured by the *Kanawha* and the *Susquehanna* July 3, 1862, off Mobile Point |
| *Arizona* | Captured by the *Montgomery* Oct. 28, 1862, in the Gulf of Mexico |
| *Victoria* | Reportedly destroyed in mid-November in Atchafalaya Bay, Louisiana |
| *Virginia* | Captured by the *Wachusett* Jan. 18, 1863, off coast of Yucatan, Mexico |
| *Eugenie* | Captured by the *R. R. Cuyler* May 6, 1863, heading for Mobile |
| *Union* | Captured by the *Huntsville* May 19, 1863, at sea |
| *Cuba* | Destroyed May 19, 1863, while heading for Mobile to prevent capture |
| *Soler* | Foundered June 1863 |
| *Neptune* | Captured by the *Lackawanna* June 14, 1863, heading for Mobile |
| *Warrior* | Captured by the *Gertrude* Aug. 6, 1863, heading for Mobile |
| *Nita (Crescent)* | Captured by the *DeSoto* Aug. 17, 1863, heading for Mobile |

| | |
|---|---|
| *Alabama* | Captured by the *Eugenie* Sept. 12, 1863, heading for Mobile |
| *Fanny (Fox)* | Destroyed by the *Genessee, Jackson,* and *Calhoun* Sept. 12, 1863, at sea |
| *Montgomery* | Captured by the *DeSoto* Sept. 13, 1863, at sea |
| *Lizzie Davis* | Captured by the *San Jacinto* Sept. 16, 1863, heading for Mobile |
| *Rosita* | Captured by the *Western Metropolis* Jan. 28, 1864, off Key West |
| *Cumberland* | Captured by the *DeSoto* Feb. 5, 1864, at sea |
| *Ruby (II)* | Captured by the *Proteus* Feb. 27, 1864, at sea |
| *Isabel* | Captured by the *Admiral* May 28, 1864, heading for Galveston |
| *Donegal (Austin)* | Captured by the *Metacomet* June 6, 1864, off Mobile |
| *Ivanhoe* | Destroyed by the *Glasgow* June 30, 1864, off Mobile |
| *Acadia* | Ran aground Feb. 2, 1865, off Velasco, Texas |
| *Will of the Wisp* | Ran aground Feb. 9, 1865, off Galveston |
| *Denbigh* | Ran aground May 23, 1865, while entering Galveston Harbor |

# Appendix 21

**Steam Blockade Runners Captured or Destroyed at Wilmington and Charleston, January and February 1865**

|  | **Wilmington** |
|---|---|
| *North Heath* | Sunk as an obstruction in the Cape Fear River off Fort Strong, Jan. 1865 |
| *Chickamaugua* | Destroyed Feb. 25, 1865, in Cape Fear River near Indian Wells |
| *Cape Fear (Flora I)* | Destroyed on evacuation of defenses of Cape Fear River off Fort Caswell |
|  | **Charleston** |
| *Syren* | Captured Feb. 18, 1865, on evacuation of Charleston |

# Appendix 22

## Steam Blockade Runners and Their Consorts

The following appendix lists as completely as possible all the steamers involved in blockade running. The information given has come from a compilation of data taken from the various sources used in researching this book. The list gives vessels that actually ran the blockade and vessels that supported the trade, were considered as blockade runners, or were finished too late to enter the trade. Captures were made by United States Naval vessels unless otherwise noted. Only the vessel's Civil War period names are cross referenced in this appendix. Complete name listings can be found in the index.

Listings for each ship will consist of the following format: Name; attempts/successful runs through the blockade; area of operation; builder; dimensions; tonnage; construction material/propulsion; owner; cost; notes. Abbreviations used: bt = burden tons; gt = gross tons; rt = registered tons; dt = displacement tons; w = wooden hull; i = iron hull; s = steel hull; sc = single screw; ts = twin screw; sw = sidewheel.

*A. J. Whitmore*: 4/3; Gulf, 2/62–5/62; Thomas Collyer, New York, New York, 1857; 180′ × 28′ × 8′11″; 432 bt; w/sw; renamed *Fox* at Havana in February 1862. Captured in Berwick Bay, May 1862, served as a USN despatch boat and later as a private towboat. Recaptured Apr. 12, 1863, by Confederate raiders in Pass a l'Outre and taken to Mobile, where she was converted to the blockade runner *Fanny* (q.v.).

*Abigail*: William C. Miller and Sons, Liverpool, England, 1865; 250′ × 30′ × 13′; 644 gt; 1100 bt; s/sw; William C. Miller for Fraser, Trenholm and Company; finished too late to run the blockade.

*Acadia*: 1/0; Gulf, 12/64–2/65; Sorel, Quebec, Canada, 1864; 211′11″ × 31′1″ × 12′6″; 738 bt; ?/sw; Jacques Felix Lincennes and William McNaughton, ran aground Feb. 6, 1865, near Velasco, Texas.

*Acorn*: See *Havana*.

*Adela*: 1/0; Atlantic, 6/62–7/62, J. & G. Thomson, Govan, Scotland, 1859; 211' × 23.5' × 12'; 585 bt; 175 rt; i/sw; Malcolmson, Henderson and Montgomerie, Earle of Eglinton; vessel captained by James Walker, onetime commander of the *Great Eastern*. Captured July 7, 1862, by the *Quaker City* and *Huntsville* near the Bahamas Islands. Purchased from prize court and taken into USN. Sold to private interests Nov. 30, 1865, at New York.

*Adelaide*: i/sc; Fraser, Trenholm and Company; used to carry supplies out of England. Sister to the *Victoria*.

*Adler*: Built at Newcastle, England, 1857; 176.4' × 25.6' × 15.5'; 523 gt; 355 rt; i/sc; registered owner William Grazebrook.

*Advance*: 18/17; Atlantic, 6/63–9/64; Caird and Company, Greenock, Scotland, 1862; 236' × 26' × 10'; 902 bt; 431 rt; i/sw; North Carolina until December 1863, when one-half interest sold to Power, Low and Company; £35,000; purchased as the *Lord Clyde*, sometimes referred to as the *A. D. Vance* and *Ad-Vance*, but name on register and port records is *Advance*. Captured by the *Santiago de Cuba* coming out of Wilmington Sept. 10, 1864. Purchased from prize court and taken into the USN as the *Frolic*, she served until Oct. 1, 1877, when sold to private interests.

*Adventure*: Denny and Company, Dumbarton, Scotland, 1865; 250' × 30' × 16'; 776 gt; 830 bt; 459 rt; 1600 dt; i/ts; contracted by James Bulloch for the Confederacy for use as a CSN gunboat; £38,000; reportedly sold to private interests Mar. 1, 1865. Also referred to as the *Tientsin* and *Amazon*.

*Agnes E. Fry*: 6/4; Atlantic, 8/64–12/64; Caird and Company, Greenock, Scotland, 1864; 236.6' × 25.2' × 13.5'; 559 gt; i/sw; Crenshaw and Company; sources vary as to her name while on the stocks, it may have been *Roe* (*II*) or *Fox* (*II*), the former seems more likely. She was renamed for the wife of Lt. Joseph Fry who commanded the vessel. Ran aground off Old Inlet, N.C., near Fort Campbell, Dec. 27, 1864.

*Agnes Louisa*: built in 1864; 243.8' × 25' × 12.5'; 578 gt; 434 rt; i/sw; registered owner Alfred Wilson; also referred to as the *Grapeshot*. Ran aground clearing Nassau on Sept. 4, 1864, and destroyed.

*Ajax*: William Denny and Brothers, Dumbarton, Scotland, 1865; 176' × 25' × 12.5'; 341 gt; 515 bt; 202 rt; 600 dt; i/ts; £17,500; contracted for by James D. Bulloch for the CSA. Built as a tug and a gunboat for use on the Cape Fear River. Left England in March 1865, but was unable to reach the South and returned to Liverpool on June 9, 1865. May have been renamed *Olustee* if she had been taken in to the Confederate Navy.

*Alabama* (*I*): 4/3; Gulf, 6/63–9/63; Samuel Sneden, Brooklyn, N.Y., 1859; 226' × 32' × 7.3'; 510 bt; i/sw; Robert Geddes owner in 1861, later sold; converted to a blockade runner in 1863, she was captured by the *Eugenie* heading to Mobile on

Sept. 12, 1863 near the Chandeleur Islands in the Mississippi Sound. Sold to private interests from prize court. Abandoned in 1892.

*Alabama (II)*: Built at Newcastle, England, 1860; 1690 gt; 1434 rt; originally named *Rangoon*. Carried supplies to the West Indies from England.

*Albatross*: Laird and Sons, Birkenhead, England, 1865; 240' × 30' × 13.2'; 659 gt; 1063 bt; s/sw; Built by Fraser, Trenholm and Company for the Confederacy; Fraser, Trenholm and Company to operate vessel until paid in cotton from the Confederacy when vessel would be turned over to the CSA. Unfinished at war's end.

*Alert*: Built at Hull, England, 1855; 176' × 21.4' × 10.8'; 329 gt; operated out of Nassau, but no record of her running the blockade.

*Alexandra*: William C. Miller and Sons, Liverpool, England, 1862; 145' × 20' × 10.6'; 124 rt; w/sc; Henry Lafone for Fraser, Trenholm and Company; built as a gunboat, she was to be a gift to the Confederacy from Fraser, Trenholm and Company, but was stopped from sailing by the British government. After lengthy litigation, she was allowed to clear but only after being converted to a merchantman. Renamed *Mary*, she sailed in July 1864. She arrived in Halifax in need of repairs and did not reach Nassau until Nov. 26, 1864, when she was again involved in court proceedings that kept her from ever sailing for the Confederacy. She eventually left Nassau and returned to England on May 30, 1865.

*Alice*: See *Matagorda*.

*Alice*: 24/24; Atlantic, 5/63–3/65; Caird and Company, Greenock, Scotland, 1857; 231.6' × 26.2' × 13.4'; 803 bt; i/sw; Importing and Exporting Company of South Carolina; purchased for $244,403.69 Confederate; built as the *Sirius*, she returned to Glasgow for repairs in the fall of 1864. Survived the war, sold to private interests. Scrapped in 1898.

*Alice Vivian*: 3/2; Gulf, 6/63–8/63; New Albany, Indiana, 1856; 175' × 32' × 6'; 376 bt; w/sw; Alabama river packet, she was captured by the *DeSoto* Aug. 16, 1863, coming out of Mobile. Sold by prize court to private interests. Abandoned in 1867.

*Alliance*: 1/0; Atlantic, 10/63–4/64; Tod and McGregor, Glasgow, Scotland, 1856; 140' × 30' × 7'; 324 bt; i/sw; William J. Grazebrook; originally built with a double hull and central paddlewheel. On being sold to Grazebrook she was given a new engine and sidewheels. Ran aground near Daufuskie Island, S.C., and captured by boats from the *South Carolina*. Purchased from prize court and taken into the USQD, sold Feb. 20, 1866, to private interests. Converted to a barge in 1890.

*Amelia*: ?/?; Gulf, 1864; ?/sc; James Brown; reported to be operating on the west coast of Florida in March 1864.

*America*: See *Enterprise*.

*Anglia*: 4/3; Atlantic, 7/62–10/62; Ditchburn and Mare, West Ham, England, 1847; 195′ × 28′ × 12.5′; 473 gt; 201 rt; 210 bt; i/sw; Edward Bates; purchased for £5,750 in 1862; captured Oct. 27, 1862, in Bull's Bay, S.C., by the *Flag*. Sold by prize court to private interests. Renamed *Admiral Du Pont* Jan. 28, 1863. Lost in a collision June 8, 1865. Sometimes referred to as the *Anglica*.

*Ann*: 1/0; Gulf, 6/62; Richardson, Duck and Company, Stockton-on-Tees, England, 1860; 175′ × 28.5′ × 17.5′; 687 gt; 467 rt; i/sc; Z. C. Pearson and Company; captured by the *Susquehanna* and *Kanawha* attempting to enter Mobile June 29, 1862.

*Annie*: 14/13; Atlantic, 2/64–11/64; John and William Dudgeon, London, England, 1863; 170′ × 23′1″ × 13′4″; 428 gt; 263 rt; i/ts; Probably named *Pallas* when launched. Alexander Collie and Company; used by Collie for his North Carolina contract. Ran aground coming out of New Inlet, N.C., Nov. 1, 1864. Purchased by the USN from prize court and taken into USN as the *Preston*. Sold to private interests Nov. 30, 1865 and renamed *Rover*. Foundered in 1868.

*Annie Childs*: 7/6; Atlantic, 2/62–6/63; Novelty Iron Works, New York, New York, 1860; 169.5′ × 29.5′ × 13.24′; 630 bt; i/sc; John Fraser and Company; vessel built as the *North Carolina*, renamed *Annie Childs*, 2/62–4/62; *Julie Usher*, 4/62–11/62; *Annie Childs*, 11/62–3/63; *T. D. Wagner*, 3/63–5/63. Sold by John Fraser and Company and renamed *Victory*, 5/63–6/63. Captured by the *Santiago de Cuba* coming out of Wilmington June 21, 1863, near the Bahamas Islands. Purchased from prize court and taken into the USN as the *Queen*. Sold to private interests and renamed *Gulf Stream*, Sept. 29, 1865. Stranded Jan. 30, 1903, at Hartford Inlet, N.J.

*Antona*: 1/0; Gulf, 1/63; Neilson and Company, Whiteinch, Glasgow, Scotland, 1859; 166.9′ × 23.1′ × 13.7′; 549 bt; 352 rt; i/sc; Navigation Company; captured by the *Pocahontas* Jan. 6, 1863, off Cape San Blas, Florida. Purchased from prize court and taken into USN. Sold to private interests at New York, Nov. 30, 1865.

*Antonica*: See *Herald*.

*Arabian*: 4/3; Atlantic, 6/63–9/63; Niagara Harbor Company, Niagara, Ontario, Canada, 1851; 174′ × 24′ × 18.3′; 263 rt; w/sw; Robert Henry Sawyer and Ramos A. Menendez. Ran aground out of New Inlet, N.C., Sept. 15, 1863.

*Aries*: 3/2; Atlantic, Spring, 1863; James Laing, Deptford, Sunderland, England, 1862; 202.3′ × 27.6′ × 15.6′; 749 gt; 479 rt; i/sc; V. Malga, Captured by the *Stettin* March 28, 1863, in Bull's Bay, S.C. Purchased from prize court and taken into USN, sold to private interests Aug. 12, 1865. Abandoned in 1908.

*Arizona*: 2/1; Gulf, 4/62–10/62; Harlan and Hollingsworth, Wilmington, Del., 1859; 201′ × 34′ × 10′; 1100 gt; 632 bt; i/sw; J. L. Maculey; renamed *Caroline* 10/62; captured Oct. 28, 1862, by the *Montgomery* while heading for Mobile.

Taken into the USN as the *Arizona*. Accidentally burned Feb. 27, 1865, at New Orleans.

*Armstrong*: 6/5; Atlantic, 9/64–12/64; Wingate and Company, Whiteinch, Glasgow, Scotland, 1864; 230′ × 26.5′ × 10.5′; i/sw; Crenshaw and Company; captured by the *R. R. Cuyler, Gettysburg, Mackinaw*, and *Montgomery*, coming out of Wilmington Dec. 4, 1864.

*Atalanta*: 10/8 as a blockade runner, 4/4 as a warship; Atlantic, 4/64–4/65; John and William Dudgeon, London, England, 1863; 220′ × 24′ × 14′; 253 rt; i/ts; Stringer, Pembroke and Company, sold to CSN in July 1864, and commissioned as CSS *Tallahassee*. Renamed *Olustee* in October 1864 for second raid. In December 1864, converted back to a blockade runner and named *Chameleon*. Returned to Liverpool in April 1865. Handed over to US by court order Apr. 26, 1866. Renamed *Amelia*. Sold and renamed *Haya Maru*. Sunk in 1869.

*Atlantic*: 8/7; Gulf and Atlantic, 4/62–9/63; Thomas Collyer, New York, New York, 1852; 216′ × 28′ × 10′; 660 bt; ?/sw; A. L. Davis, February 1862, sold to John Fraser and Company in October 1862, and renamed *Elizabeth*. Ran aground off Cape Fear, N.C., Sept. 26, 1863.

*Austin*: 10/9; Gulf, 3/62–6/64; Harlan and Hollingsworth, Wilmington, Del., 1860; 203′ × 34′ × 10′; 1150 gt; 643 bt; i/sw; renamed *Donegal* in Havana in October 1862; captured by the *Metacomet* trying to reach Mobile June 6, 1864. Purchased from prize court and taken into USN. Sold to private interests Nov. 11, 1865, and renamed *Austin*. Lost June 6, 1876, below New Orleans in the Mississippi River.

*Austrian*: 2/2; Gulf, 4/64; Very little information on this vessel. U.S. Havana consul reports that she made a round trip to Mobile in April 1864, but there is no other evidence to verify this.

*Badger (I)*: 2/1; Atlantic, 5/64–9/64; Jones, Quiggin and Company, Liverpool, England, 1864; 218′ × 24.3′ × 11.6′; 375 gt; 233 rt; 623 bt; i&s/sw; John B. Lafitte for Fraser, Trenholm and Company; ran aground in the Cape Fear River, Sept. 10, 1864.

*Badger (II)*: 4/4; Atlantic, 12/64–6/65; 218′ × 24′ × 11′; 405 gt; 253 rt; i/sw; Henry Lafone; sometimes confused with the *Badger (I)*, survived the war, returned to Liverpool.

*Bahama*: Pearse, Stockton-on-Tees, 1862; 215′ × 29.2′ × 20′; 897 gt; 716 rt; 1530 dt; i/sc; Edwin Haigh for Fraser, Trenholm and Company. Sister to the *Bermuda*, she carried supplies from England to the West Indies.

*Banshee (I)*: 15/14; Atlantic, 4/63–11/63; Jones, Quiggin and Company, Liverpool, England, 1863; 214′ × 20′ × 8′; 325 gt; 217 rt; 533 bt; i&s/sw, steel hull on an iron frame; John T. Lawrence for the Anglo-Confederate Trading Company; first steel-hulled vessel to cross the Atlantic. Captured by the *James Adger* Nov. 21,

1863, trying to enter Wilmington. Purchased from prize court and taken into USN, sold to private interests Nov. 30, 1865.

*Banshee (II)*: 8/8; Atlantic and Gulf, 9/64–5/65; Aitken and Mansel, Glasgow, Scotland, 1864; 252′ × 31′ × 11′; 627 gt; 439 rt; s/sw; John Lawrence for the Anglo-Confederate Trading Company; survived the war, returned to Liverpool, April 1865.

*Bat*: 1/0; Atlantic, 9/64–10/64; Jones, Quiggin and Company, Liverpool, England, 1864; 230′ × 26′ × 9.5′; 466 gt; 770 bt; s/sw; William Quiggin for Fraser, Trenholm and Company; owned and operated by Fraser, Trenholm and Company; vessel to be turned over to Confederacy upon payment in cotton. Captured by the *Montgomery* Oct. 8, 1864, trying to reach Old Inlet. Purchased from prize court and taken into the USN. Sold to private interests and renamed *Teazer* Nov. 6, 1865. Purchased by the Quebec Steamship Company and named *Miramichi* in 1872. Sold to the Richelieu and Ontario Navigation Company in June 1897.

*Beatrice*: 3/2; Atlantic, 9/64–11/64; McNab, Greenock, Scotland, 1863; 167.5′ × 24.1′ × 12′; 342 gt; 274 rt; i/sc; Edward J. Lomnitz of Manchester, England; ran aground and destroyed off Charleston Nov. 29, 1864.

*Bendigo*: 3/2; Atlantic, 8/63–1/64; 162.1′ × 20.1′ × 10.9′; 178 rt; i/sw; M. I. Wilson for Fraser, Trenholm and Company; original name may have been *Milly*, renamed *Bendigo* in 1863. Sunk off Lockwood's Folly Inlet while trying to reach Wilmington, Jan. 2, 1864.

*Bermuda*: 2/2; Atlantic, 8/61–4/62; Pearse and Lockwood, Stockton-on-Tees, England, 1861; 211′ × 21′4″ × 21′2″; 897 gt; 716 rt; 1238 bt; i/sc; Edward Haigh for Fraser, Trenholm and Company; built as the *Czar*, renamed on purchase by Fraser, Trenholm and Company. Captured by the *Mercedita* between Bermuda and Nassau Apr. 27, 1862. Taken into USN. Sold to private interests and renamed *General Meade* Oct. 7, 1865, renamed *Bahamas* in 1878. Foundered in 1878 southwest of New York. She was the first steam blockade runner to run the blockade.

*Bijou*: See *Mary Celestia*.

*Black Joker*: See *C. Vanderbilt*.

*Blanche*: See *General Rusk*.

*Blenheim*: 5/4; Atlantic, 10/64–1/65; Glasgow, Scotland, 1848; 210′ × 30.6′ × 16′; 948 bt; ?/sw; Richard Eustace; originally operated by the Belfast Steamship Company, sold to Eustace in 1864. Captured by the *Tristram Shandy* in New Inlet after the fall of Fort Fisher on Jan. 25, 1865. Sold to private interests and renamed *Richmond*. Burned Nov. 12, 1866, at Baltimore, Maryland.

*Boston (I)*: 1/0; Atlantic, 7/64; Quebec, Canada, 1852; 170′ × 22′ × 10.5′; 355 gt; 224 rt; 430 bt; ?/sw; Francis William James Gurst; sometimes confused with a steamer used in Charleston harbor during the war. Captured by the *Fort Jackson* July 8, 1864, off Wilmington. Sold to private interests by prize court and renamed *Nashua*, lost in 1866.

*Boston (II)*: 1/1; Gulf, 6/63; Sold at a CSA prize court for $89,000 in Mobile. While serving as a towboat she was captured by a party of Confederate sailors under Master James Duke at Pass á l'Outre June 8, 1863. She was taken to Mobile, where she was sold by a prize court to private interests who planned to convert her into a privateer. There is conflicting evidence that either she escaped to Havana or was still at Mobile at the time of Farragut's attack. The latter seems more plausible, as there is no evidence to show her arriving at Havana. It was also reported that the vessel was being lengthened some 25' at Mobile, but caught on fire and was damaged. Vessel was probably used as a blockship or a floating battery and was destroyed at the evacuation of Mobile. Reported to have been a screw tug.

*Britannia*: 6/5; Atlantic, 2/63–6/63; Barclay, Curle and Company, Glasgow, Scotland, 1862; 189' × 26' × 11'; 371 gt; 275 rt; 495 bt; i/sw; Robert Barclay for Leech, Harrison and Forwood. Captured by the *Santiago de Cuba* June 23, 1863, off Eleuthera Island, Bahamas, after clearing Charleston. Purchased from prize court and taken into USN. Sold to private interests Sept. 8, 1865. Sold to foreign interests in 1866.

*British Queen*: 2/2; Gulf, 3/62; 566 gt; vessel operated between New York-Nassau-Havana from June 1862 to July 1862. Reportedly made one round trip to Mobile in July 1862.

*C. Vanderbilt*: 4/3; Gulf, 11/61–3/62; Bishop Simonson, New York, New York, 1837; 170.6' × 23.3' × 9'; 346 bt; w/sw; Robert D. Smith; Renamed *Black Joker* 12/61. Foundered in the Gulf on the way to Havana, Mar. 15, 1862.

*Caledonia*: 4/2; Atlantic, 1/64–5/64; Tod and McGregor, Glasgow, Scotland, 1856; 115 rt; 450 bt; i/sw; Captured by the *Keystone State* and the *Massachusetts* May 30, 1864, trying to enter Wilmington.

*Calhoun*: 2/1; Gulf, 12/61–1/62; Lawrence Sneden, New York, New York, 1851; 174.3' × 27.5' × 11'; 508 bt; w/sw; George McGregor June 6, 1861; James B. McConnell Jan. 2, 1862; from June to August 1861, she served as a privateer, from August through December she was used as a Confederate gunboat. Released and converted to a blockade runner in early December. Captured by the *Rachel Seaman* Jan. 23, 1862, while trying to enter the Mississippi River. Purchased from prize court and taken into the USN. Transferred to the USQD as the *General Sedgwick* June 1864. Sold to private interests Mar. 19, 1866. Abandoned in 1883.

*California*: 3/3; Gulf, 3/62–5/62; built New York, New York, 1847; 204'6" × 29'7" × 8'6"; w/sw; vessel operated in the Mississippi Sound during the summer of 1861. Escaped to Havana from Lake Pontchartrain on the fall of New Orleans and made one round trip to Mobile in May 1862. It was later reported that she then operated to Matamoras for the rest of the war.

*Calypso*: 7/6; Atlantic, 1/63–6/63; Denny and Brothers, Dumbarton, Scotland, 1855; 190.3′ × 27.1′ × 13.7′; 535 gt; i/sc; John Fraser and Company 12/62–4/63, Steamship *Calypso* Company 4/63–6/63; sold to the Steamship *Calypso* Company for $555,555.55 Confederate. Captured by the *Florida* June 11, 1863 while trying to enter Old Inlet, N.C. Purchased from prize court and taken into the USN. Sold to private interests and renamed *Winchester* Jan. 23, 1866. Abandoned in 1886.

*Cambria*: 1/0; Atlantic, 4/62–/5/62; Thomas Toward, Newcastle, England, 1854; 157′ × 21.9′ × 22.8′; i/sc; Fraser, Trenholm and Company; captured by the *Huron* May 26, 1862, while trying to enter Charleston.

*Carolina*: 2/1; Gulf, 6/64–7/64; built at Philadelphia, 1861; 128′ × 23′11″ × 8′6″; 115 gt; 52 rt; 238 bt; ?/sw; the *Carolina* the third name given to the tug *Union* (q.v.). After being captured for a second time as the *Rosita* (q.v.), she was condemned at a prize court and sold to private interests who renamed her the *Carolina*. Ran aground on July 7, 1864, while trying to clear Galveston.

*Caroline*: See *Arizona*.

*Caroline* : 7/6; Atlantic, 10/64–3/65; William Denny and Brothers, Dumbarton, Scotland, 1864; 225′ × 28′ × 13′; 634 gt; 403 rt; 1165 dt; i/sw; Importing and Exporting Company of South Carolina; vessel went to Havana in February 1865, but there is no record of her running to Galveston. Survived the war. Returned to England in March 1865.

*Catawba*: See *Nelly*.

*Cecile*: 10/9; Atlantic, 2/62–6/62; Harlan and Hollingsworth, Wilmington, Del., 1857; 156.5′ × 29′ × 8.5′; 460 gt; 360 bt; i/sw; owned by the Florida Steam Packet Company until January 1862, when sold to John Fraser and Company, which operated the vessel from 1/62 to 3/62, when sold to the Importing and Exporting Company of South Carolina. Ran aground on Abaco reef in the Bahamas, June 17, 1862.

*Celt*: 1/0; Atlantic, 2/65; w/sw; Steamer *Celt* Company of Charleston; vessel built in Charleston in 1863. Used by Quartermaster Bureau in Charleston harbor. Cotton bond taken out for the vessel in August 1864, but no record of her ever clearing Charleston until February 1865. Sometimes confused with the much larger English steamer *Celt* which operated to Nassau and Matamoras, but never ran the blockade. The Charleston *Celt* ran aground in Charleston harbor off Fort Moultrie while trying to clear on Feb. 14, 1865.

*Ceres*: 1/0; Atlantic, 11/63–12/63; John and William Dudgeon, London, England, 1863; 173′ × 22′10″ × 12′5″; 271 rt; 479 bt; i/ts; Crenshaw and Collie; ran aground off Old Inlet, N.C., Dec. 6, 1863. Set on fire by her crew, floated free and was captured by the *Violet*. Sold by prize court to private interests and burned Oct. 1, 1869.

*Chameleon*: See *Atalanta*.

*Charles Morgan*: Jacob A. Westervelt, New York, New York, 1854; 220.2' × 34' × 15.6'; 1250 bt; w/sw; a Southern Steamship Company vessel, she was converted into the gunboat *Governor Moore*. Destroyed Apr. 24, 1862, at the Battle of New Orleans.

*Charleston*: 4/3; Atlantic, 3/63–7/63; built 1836; 124' × 22.5' × 8.5'; 203 bt; w/sw; Steamer *Charleston* Company; captured by the *Seminole* trying to enter the Cape Fear River July 11, 1863. Sold by prize court to private interests and abandoned in 1876.

*Charlotte*: 3/2; Atlantic, 11/64–1/65; Archibald Denny and Brothers, Dumbarton, Scotland, 1864; 226.3' × 28.2' × 13'; 632 gt; 403 rt; 1165 dt; i/sw; Edward Stringer and Edward Pembroke; £12,000; sister of the *Caroline* and *Ella*. Captured by the *Malvern* inside Old Inlet bar after fall of Fort Fisher Jan. 20, 1865. Sold by prize court to private interests as the *Agnes Mary* May 4, 1865. Lost in 1870.

*Chatham*: 1/0; Atlantic 12/63; Laird, Birkenhead, England, 1838; 115' × 24' × 7.5'; 198 bt; i/sw; the *Chatham* was brought to the United States in sections and assembled for use on the Savannah River by Gazaway B. Lamar. The vessel was used as a transport by the Confederacy in the summer of 1863. Captured by the *Huron* Dec. 16, 1863, in Doboy Sound, Georgia, trying to escape from Savannah.

*Cherokee*: See *Thistle (I)*.

*Chickamauga*: See *Edith*.

*Chicora*: 14/14; Atlantic, 5/64–3/65; William C. Miller and Sons, Liverpool, England, 1864; 221' × 26' × 10'; 365 gt; 930 bt; s/sw; Chicora Importing and Exporting Company; originally named *Let Her Be*, she was renamed *Chicora* on her arrival in the Confederacy. Referred to mistakenly as the *Letter B*, and *Let Her B*. Survived the war, sold at Halifax and later taken to Montreal. There she was cut in half to pass the locks and reassembled at Buffalo, New York. She served on the Great Lakes as an excursion boat until 1919. The hull survived as a barge until 1938.

*Circassian*: 1/0; Gulf, 4/62–5/62; Robert Hickock and Company, Belfast, Ireland, 1856; 242' × 29' × 23.5'; 1387 rt; 1750 bt; i/sc; Z. C. Pearson of Pearson and Company; captured by the *Somerset* in the Gulf May 4, 1862. Purchased from prize court and taken into the USN. Sold to private interests July 20, 1865, converted to sail May 1873.

*City of Petersburg*: 16/16; Atlantic, 11/63–2/65; Caird and Company, Greenock, Scotland, 1863; 223' × 25' × 13.5'; 426 rt; i/sw; Virginia Importing and Exporting Company; built as *Roe (I)*, name changed in England. Survived the war.

*City of Richmond*: John and William Dudgeon, London, England, 1864; 230′ ×
27′ × 14.6′; 829 gt; i/sw; Crenshaw and Company; carried supplies to the West
Indies and was hired to oufit the CSS *Stonewall* in January 1865.

*Clarinda*: See *Sachem*.

*Clifton*: 1/0; Gulf, 3/64; Jeremiah Simonson, Brooklyn, New York, 1861; 210′ ×
40′ × 13.5′; 892 bt; w/s; USN gunboat, captured at Sabine Pass, Sept. 8, 1863, sold
to private interests by the Confederacy and converted to a blockade runner. Ran
aground and destroyed by her crew Mar. 20, 1864, while coming out of Sabine
Pass.

*Colonel Lamb*: 2/2; Atlantic and Gulf, 9/64–1/65; Jones, Quiggin and Company,
Liverpool, England, 1864; 279′ × 36′ × 15.5′; 1132 gt; 800 rt; 1788 bt; s/sw;
William Quiggin for Fraser, Trenholm and Company; cost £50,000 to build; went
to Gulf in January 1865, but was unsuccessful in running to Galveston. Returned
to England in April 1865. Survived the war.

*Columbia*: See *Cornubia*.

*Columbia*: 1/0; Atlantic, 7/62–8/62; Archibald Denny, Dumbarton, Scotland;
168′ × 24′ × 14′; 503 bt; i/sc; Thomas Sterling Begbie; captured by the *Santiago de
Cuba* off the Florida coast Aug. 3, 1862. Purchased from prize court and taken into
the USN. Wrecked Jan. 14, 1863, off Masonboro Inlet, N.C.

*Condor*: 1/0; Atlantic, 9/64–10/64; Randolph, Elder and Company, Govan,
Scotland, 1864; 270′ × 24′ × 12′; 283 rt; i/sw; Donald McGregor for Alexander
Collie and Company; on her maiden voyage carried Rose O'Neal Greenhow.
After the vessel ran aground on Oct. 1, 1864, off Fort Fisher, Mrs. Greenhow was
sent ashore, but the small boat she was in capsized and she was drowned. The
*Condor* eventually became a total loss.

*Confederate States*: See *Laurel*.

*Constance*: 1/0; Atlantic, 4/64–10/64; John Scott and Sons, Greenock, Scotland,
1864; 201.4′ × 20.15′ × 9.4′; 254 gt; 163 rt; 345 bt; w/sw; Duncan McGregor for
Alexander Collie and Company; built as the *Constance Decima*. Ran aground off
Long Island, S.C., while trying to enter Charleston harbor Oct. 6, 1864.

*Coquette*: 14/13; Atlantic, 11/63–2/65; Hoby and Son, Renfrew, Scotland; 228′ ×
25′ × 12′2″; 390 rt; i/ts; contracted to Henderson and Coulborn who built the
engines and subcontracted the hull to Hoby and Son; purchased by the Confederate Navy in September 1863. Sold July 1864, to J. R. Anderson and Company,
who operated the vessel until December 1865 when vessel was seized by her
captain at Havana and taken to Baltimore. Sold to private interests and renamed
*Maryland*, Feb. 25, 1868. Sold to foreign interests in 1873.

*Cornubia*: 19/18; Atlantic, 12/62–11/63; Harvey and Son, Hayle, England, 1858;
190′ × 24.5′ × 12.5′; 411 gt, 259 rt; 588 bt; i/sw; James Seddon for the Confederate

States of America; purchased and registered as the *Columbia*, also referred to as the *Lady Davis*. Captured by the *James Adger* and the *Niphon* Nov. 8, 1863, while trying to enter Wilmington. Purchased from prize court and taken into USN. Sold to private interests Apr. 23, 1866 and renamed *New England*. Engines removed Mar. 18, 1871.

*Crescent*: 5/2; Gulf, 4/63–8/63; 146′ × 22.3′ × 7′; 171 bt; w/sw; renamed *Nita* for blockade running. Vessel leased by the Confederate Quartermaster Bureau to Julius Buttner, who operated the vessel as a blockade runner to carry in Confederate supplies. Captured by the *DeSoto* near Apalachicola Bay Aug. 17, 1863. Purchased from prize court and taken into USN. Sold to private interests May 25, 1865.

*Cronstadt*: 2/1; Atlantic, 6/63–8/63; Martin Samuelson and Company, Kingston, Ontario, Canada, 1859; 149.4′ × 21.6′ × 12.5′; 232 rt; ?/sw; owned by Thomas J. Dodson; captured by the *Rhode Island* after clearing Wilmington Aug. 16, 1863, near the Bahamas Islands.

*Cuba*: 8/7; Gulf, 1/62–5/63; Samuel Sneden, Greenpoint, New York, 1854; 250′ × 32.6′ × 9′; 604 bt; w/sw; burned to prevent capture May 19, 1863, while heading toward Mobile.

*Cumberland*: 1/0; Gulf, 9/63–2/64; 232.5′ × 31′ × 14.3′; 677 bt; ?/sw; captured by the *DeSoto* while heading for Mobile Feb. 5, 1864. Sold by prize court to private interests Jan. 20, 1865. Abandoned in 1871.

*Curlew*: Jones, Quiggin and Company, Liverpool, England 1865; 225′ × 24′ × 11′; 410 gt; 645 bt; s/sw; Richard Phillips for J. K. Gilliat and Company, who built the vessel under contract for the Confederacy. Unfinished at war's end.

*Dare*: See *The Dare*.

*Dee*: 7/6; Atlantic, 9/63–2/64; John and William Dudgeon, London, England, 1863; 165′ × 23′ × 13′; 215 rt; i/ts; F. Muir for the Crenshaw and Collie and Company; probably built as the *Aurora*. Chased ashore and destroyed by the *Cambridge* near Masonboro Inlet on Feb. 5, 1864, while trying to reach Wilmington.

*Deer*: 2/0; Atlantic, 1/65–2/65; W. H. Potter and Company, Liverpool, England, 1864; 230′ × 26′2″ × 11′; 465 gt; 330 rt; 857 bt; s/sw; Richard Philips for Fraser, Trenholm and Company, who operated the vessel until paid for in cotton by the Confederacy. Vessel contracted with Jones, Quiggin and Company who subcontracted construction to W. H. Potter and Company. Captured Feb. 18, 1865, while trying to enter Charleston harbor. Vessel grounded off Fort Moultrie and was taken by boat parties of the monitors *Canonicus*, *Catskill* and *Monadnock*. Sold at prize court to private interests and renamed *Palmyra*, Aug. 26, 1865. Sold to foreign interests in 1870.

*Denbigh*: 27/26; Gulf, 12/63–5/65; Laird and Sons, Birkenhead, England, 1860; 182' × 22' × 8.7'; 250 gt; 162 rt; i/sw; Fenton Magnall of Manchester, England, for the European Trading Company; cost to build £10,512; ran aground on Bird Key, Galveston Bay, May 23, 1865, while trying to enter the harbor. Burned by Union blockaders the following morning.

*Despatch (I)*: Vessel sent out by the Anglo-Confederate Trading Company in the Summer of 1862 under Thomas Taylor but was not fit for blockade running and eventually returned to Liverpool. Very little hard information on this vessel.

*Despatch (II)*: 2/2; Atlantic, 12/63–6/64; 294 rt; sometimes referred to as a rebuilt version of the *Despatch (I)* which had been brought out of England in 1862 by Thomas Taylor, but this seems doubtful. Vessel made one round trip to Wilmington. Survived the war.

*Diamond*: 1/0; Atlantic, 9/63; James Henderson, Renfrew, Scotland, 1853; 250 bt; i/sw; captured by the *Stettin* Sept. 23, 1863, off the coast of Georgia. Taken into USQD. Sold to private interests Oct. 16, 1866. Abandoned in 1872.

*Dolphin*: 1/0; Atlantic, 3/63; Robert Napier, Glasgow, Scotland, 1844; 170.2' × 21.2' × 10.5'; 129 bt; i/sw; William Grazebrook; captured Mar. 25, 1863, between Puerto Rico and St. Thomas by the *Wachusett*. Sold by prize court to private interests and renamed *Annie*, Sept. 29, 1863. Lost in 1866.

*Don*: 12/10; Atlantic, 8/63–3/64; John and William Dudgeon, London, England, 1863; 162' × 23' × 12'3"; 244 rt; 390 bt; 425 dt; i/ts; Collie and Company; probably built as the *Diana*. Captured by the *Pequot* off Beaufort, N.C., Mar. 4, 1864. Purchased from prize court and taken into USN. Sold to private interests Dec. 17, 1868. Sold to foreign interests in 1871.

*Douro (I)*: 2/1; Atlantic, 1/63–3/63; 185 bt; i/sc; Otto Theodore Fallenstein; captured Mar. 9, 1863, by the *Quaker City*. Vessel condemned at a prize court, sold to private interests who returned her to blockade running in September 1863, under the same name.

*Douro (II)*: 2/1; Atlantic, 9/63–10/63; 185 bt; i/sc; same vessel as *Douro (I)*: driven ashore off Wrightsville Beach by the *Nansemond* while trying to escape Wilmington on Oct. 11, 1863.

*Dream*: W. H. Potter and Company, Liverpool, England, 1864; 231' × 26' × 11.2'; 466 gt; 800 bt; 296 rt; s/sw; built for Fraser, Trenholm and Company, later sold to Beech, Root and Company. Vessel contracted with Jones, Quiggin and Company who subcontracted construction to W. H. Potter and Company. Arrived Nassau in January 1865, but never ran the blockade.

*Druid*: 8/8; Atlantic, 3/64–2/65; Barclay, Curle and Company, Glasgow, Scotland, 1857; 160.1' × 20.6' × 9.7'; i/sw; Herbert Charles Dunkwater of Manchester, England for the Steamship Druid Company of Charleston, S.C. Survived war.

*Eagle*: 7/6; Atlantic, 2/63–5/63; Denny, Dumbarton, Scotland, 1852; 169.9' × 16.5' × 8.3'; 147 gt; 76 rt; i/sc; George Wigg for the Navigation Company; Purchased for £8,000; Captured by the *Octorora* May 18, 1863, coming out of Charleston. She was later sold to private interests that readied her to run the blockade under the name *Jeanette* (q.v.).

*Economist*: 2/2; Atlantic, 2/62–4/62; Archibald Denny, Dumbarton, Scotland, 1860; 191' × 26' × 17.6'; 572 gt, 389 rt, 819 bt; i/sc; Melchir Klingender for Fraser, Trenholm and Company; after service as a blockade runner the vessel was used to transport supplies to the islands. Renamed *Bonita*, August 1862. Survived the war.

*Edith*: 10/9 as a blockade runner, 2/2 as a warship; Atlantic, 4/64–2/65; John and William Dudgeon, London, England, 1864; 175' × 25' × 15'; 370 gt, 239 rt, 501 dt; i/te; Collie and Company until September 1864, when sold to the CSN; Commissioned *Chickamauga*, September 1864. Destroyed Feb. 25, 1865, at Indian Wells, North Carolina, in an attempt to block the Cape Fear River after the fall of Wilmington.

*Elizabeth*: See *Atlantic*.

*Elizabeth*: See *General Miramon*.

*Ella (I)*: 1/0; Atlantic, 7/63–11/63; built at Brooklyn, New York, 1863; 150' × 23' × 8.5'; 368 gt; 124 rt; 311 bt; w/sw; George Bushby; vessel to be purchased by the Confederacy upon her arrival at Wilmington. Captured by the *Howquah* off New Inlet, N.C., while heading for Wilmington Nov. 10, 1863. Purchased from prize court and taken into USN as the *Philippi*. Destroyed by gunfire off Mobile Bay Aug. 5, 1864.

*Ella (II)*: 6/4; 8/64–12/64; William Denny, Dumbarton, Scotland, 1864; 225' × 28' × 13'; 634 gt; 404 rt; 1165 dt; i/sw; Importing and Exporting Company of South Carolina; chased ashore and destroyed Dec. 1, 1864, while trying to enter Old Inlet by the *Emma*.

*Ella and Annie*: See *William G. Hewes*.

*Ella Warley*: 4/3; Atlantic, 11/61–4/62; S. H. Duncan, Baltimore, Maryland, 1848; 220' × 33' × 21'; 1115 bt; w/sw; Edwin Adderly for John Fraser and Company; built as the *Isabel*, renamed November 1861. Captured by the *Santiago de Cuba* at sea heading from Havana to Charleston Apr. 24, 1862. Sold by prize court to private interests. Lost in a collision Feb. 9, 1863, off the New Jersey coast.

*Elsie*: 2/1; Atlantic, 8/64–9/64; John Scott and Sons, Greenock, Scotland, 1864; 201.4' × 20.15' × 9.5'; 262 gt; 169 rt; 354 bt; i/sw; Duncan McGregor for Alexander Collie and Company; built for £13,500; captured by the *Keystone State* and the *Quaker City* Sept. 5, 1864, southeast of Cape Fear while coming out of Wilmington.

*Emilie*: See *William Seabrook*.

*Emily (I)*: 1/0; Atlantic, 1/64–2/64; William Simons and Company, Renfrew, Scotland, 1863; 181′ × 22.4′ × 12.1′; 355 gt; 253 rt; i/sc; Thomas Sterling Begbie; sank heading for Wilmington off Wrightsville Beach, Feb. 9, 1864.

*Emily (II)*: William Denny, Dumbarton, Scotland, 1864; 255′ × 34′ × 16.5′; 1100 gt; 865 bt; 1690 dt; i/sw; built for the Importing and Exporting Company of South Carolina; cost to build £35,000; cleared Glasgow Nov. 23, 1864, arrived in Bermuda with two engines for the CSN, but never ran the blockade.

*Emily*: See *Tartar*.

*Emma (I)*: 1/0; Atlantic, 8/62; built at Charleston, 1861; 150′ × 30′ × 9′9″; 460 bt; w/sw; burned by crew to prevent capture after running aground while trying to escape from from the Savannah River Aug. 30, 1862.

*Emma (II)*: 8/7; Atlantic, 2/63–7/63; Barclay, Curle and Company, Glasgow, Scotland, 1862; 164.5′ × 21.2′ × 11.1′; 279 gt; 192 rt; i/sc; Thomas Sterling Begbie; captured by the *Arago* coming out of Cape Fear River July 26, 1863. Purchased from prize court and taken into the USN. Sold to private interests Nov. 1, 1865. In May 1867 purchased by the Quebec Steamship Company and renamed *Gaspe*. Wrecked June 14, 1872 at Langlois, Canada.

*Emma (III)*: Denny and Company, Dumbarton, Scotland, 1865; built for the Importing and Exporting Company of South Carolina. Unfinished at the war's end.

*Emma Henry*: 2/1; Atlantic, 11/64–12/64; J. & G. Thomson, Govan, Scotland, 1864; 211′ × 25.2′ × 9.9′; 242 rt; i/sw; Henry Lafone for the Importing and Exporting Company of Georgia; purchased from builder for £27,250.12.3; captured by the *Cherokee* Dec. 7, 1864, coming out of the Cape Fear River.

*Enterprise (I)*: 1/0; Gulf, 3/62; Built Brownsville, Pa., 1852; 172′2″ × 26′6″ × 8′6″; 372 bt; w/sw; Stephen K. Fowler; a towboat used at New Orleans, reportedly sank in a storm about Mar. 15, 1862.

*Enterprise (II)*: Denny and Company, Dumbarton, Scotland, 1865; 250′ × 30′ × 16′; 776 gt; 830 bt; 1600 dt; i/ts; contracted by James Bulloch for the Confederacy for use as a CSN gunboat; Unfinished at war's end. Also referred to as the *Yangtze* and *Brasil*.

*Eugenie*: See *General Buckner*.

*Eugenie*: 10/10; Atlantic, 5/63–1/64; Martin Samuelson and Company, Hull, England, 1862; 235′ × 24.2′ × 11.9′; 428 gt; 239 rt; i/sw; Confederate States of America; badly damaged while running into Wilmington Sept. 7, 1863. She was repaired and sent to Nassau in December 1863. From there the vessel returned to Liverpool, where she was sold at the end of the war.

*Evelyn*: 5/4; Atlantic and Gulf, 11/64–4/65; Randolph, Elder and Company, Govan, Scotland, 1864; 270′ × 24′ × 12′; 284 rt; i/sw; Duncan McGregor for Alexander Collie and Company; survived the war.

*Fairy*: J. & G. Thomson, Govan, Scotland, 1861; 149′4″ × 21′ × 6′9″; 151 qt; 200 bt; i/sw; operated between Havana and Matamoras.

*Falcon*: 5/4; Atlantic, 7/64–4/65; Randolph, Elder and Company; Govan, Scotland, 1864; 270′ × 24′ × 12′; 285 rt; i/sw; Duncan McGregor for Alexander Collie and Company; survived the war.

*Fannie*: 20/2; Atlantic, 5/63–4/65; Caird and Company, Greenock, Scotland, 1859; 231.5′ × 26.2′ × 13.3′; 654 gt; 803 bt; i/sw; Arthur B. Forwood for the Importing and Exporting Company of South Carolina; purchased for $245,471.85 Confederate; built as the *Orion*, name changed on arrival in the South. Survived the war. Sold to British interests. Broken up in 1890.

*Fanny*: 5/4; Gulf, 4/63–9/63; Thomas Collyer, New York, 1857; 180′ × 28′ × 8′ 11″; 432 bt; w/sw; J. L. Harris; built as the *A. J. Whitmore* (q.v.), taken by the Union Navy at the fall of New Orleans and renamed *Fox*. Captured by Confederate raiders as the *Fox* April 12, 1863, at the mouth of the Mississippi River. She was taken to Mobile where she was sold to private parties and turned into a blockade runner. Renamed *Fanny*, she was eventually burned to prevent capture while trying to reach Mobile on Sept. 12, 1863, off Pascagoula, Mississippi, while being pursued by the *Genessee*, *Jackson*, and *Calhoun*.

*Fanny and Jenny*: 1/0; Atlantic, 8/63–2/64; Wigram and Company, Blackwell, England, 1847; 202′2″ × 28′4″ × 13′7″; 479 gt; 727 bt; i/sw; former blockade runner *Scotia* (q.v.), she was sold at a prize court and returned to the trade under the name *Fanny and Jenny*. Chased aground and destroyed while trying to enter New Inlet near Masonboro Inlet, N.C., while heading for Wilmington by the *Florida*, Feb. 9, 1864.

*Fergus*: see *Presto*.

*Fingal*: 2/1; Atlantic, 10/61–11/61; J. & G. Thomson, Govan, Scotland, 1861; 178′ × 25′ × 18′; i/sc; Confederate States of America; trapped at Savannah, she was eventually converted into the ironclad *Atlanta*.

*Flamingo*: 2/2; Atlantic, 7/64–4/65; Randolph, Elder and Company, Govan, Scotland, 1864; 270′ × 24′ × 12′; 283 rt; i/sw; Alexander Collie and Company; survived the war.

*Flora* (*I*): 11/11; Atlantic, 1/63–1/65; John and William Dudgeon, London, England, 1862; 161.3′ × 22.5′ × 12.4′; 434 bt; i/ts; Alexander Collie and Company 12/62-9/63; sold to Henry Hart of the Consolidated Steamship Company 9/63, sold to the Confederate States of America for $500,000 in cotton in 10/63. On her sale to Hart, the vessel was renamed *Virginia*, and then a month later Confederate authorities renamed her the *Cape Fear*. Operating under this name she served out the war as a transport on the Cape Fear River. After transporting troops from Fort Holmes to Smithville on the evacuation of the Confederate defenses, the ship was scuttled by her crew off Smithville on the night of Jan. 16, 1865.

*Flora (II)*: 10/9; Atlantic, 8/63–1/64; John Scott and Sons, Glasgow, Scotland, 1858; 215' × 25.7' × 13.5'; 571 gt, 359 rt; i/sw; W. S. Lindsay and Company; purchases for £35,000; foundered at sea about Jan. 11, 1864 while sailing to Halifax from Bermuda for repairs.

*Flora (III)*: 1/0; Atlantic, 10/64; i/sw; Henry Lafone for the Importing and Exporting Company of Georgia; ran aground Oct. 22, 1864, off Fort Moultrie, Charleston, S.C., and destroyed by Union shore batteries on Morris Island.

*Flora (IV)*: Millwood, London, England, 1853; 178.5' × 20.1' × 9'; 283 gt; 165 rt; Former *Rouen* (q.v.), which had been captured July 2, 1864 by the *Keystone State* while heading for Wilmington. Condemned at a prize court and sold to private interests. Went to the Gulf in October 1864 under the name *Flora*, but no evidence that she was being returned to blockade running.

*Florence*: Aitken and Mansel, Whiteinch, Glasgow, Scotland, 1864; 252' × 25' × 11'; i/sw; Arrived in Bermuda in January 1865, but never ran the blockade.

*Florida (I)*: 3/2; Gulf, 2/62–4/62; E. S. Whitlock, Greenpoint, New York, 1859; 180' × 31' × 9'; 460 bt; w/sc; R. B. Summer of Nashville; vessel operated before the war by the Apalachicola and New Orleans Steam Navigation Company, sold February 1862 to R. B. Summer. Captured in St. Andrew's Bay, Florida, April 6, 1862, by a small boat expedition. Purchased from prize court and taken into the USN as the *Hendrick Hudson*. Sold to private interests November 10, 1865. Stranded November 13, 1867.

*Florida (II)*: 2/2; Gulf, 8/62–1/63; William C. Miller and Sons, Liverpool, England, 1862; 191' × 27' × 14'; 410 gt; w/sc; Confederate States of America; built as the *Oreto*, commissioned as the *Florida* Aug. 4, 1863. Also referred to as the *Manassas*. Ran into Mobile Sept. 4, 1862. She cleared Jan. 16, 1863, to begin her career as a privateer. Captured at Bahia, Brazil, by the *Wachusett*. While at Hampton Roads awaiting disposition, she was rammed and sunk by the transport *Alliance* on Nov. 19, 1864.

*Florie*: 8/6; Atlantic, 2/64–10/64; Wingate and Company, Whiteinch, Glasgow, Scotland, 1863; 222.4' × 23.5' × 9.6'; 349 gt; 215 rt; i/sw; Henry Lafone for the Importing and Exporting Company of Georgia; impressed by the Confederate Navy for use in the Point Lookout Expedition in August, 1864 Reported to have run aground inside the Cape Fear River in October 1864.

*Flushing*: See *Little Lilly*.

*Fox*: 18/18; Atlantic and Gulf, 5/64–5/65; Jones, Quiggin and Company, Liverpool, England, 1864; 219′ × 22′ × 10.2′; 325 gt, 230 rt; s/sw; Josiah Jones for Fraser, Trenholm and Company; survived war.

*Frances*: See *Zephine*.

*Frances Marion*: See *Zephine*.

*G. T. Watson*: 4/4; Atlantic, 12/64–2/65; John and William Dudgeon, London, England, 1863; 165′ × 22.5′ × 13.5′; 344 rt;. i/ts; after being captured as the *Kate (II)* (q.v.), the vessel was condemned and sold. She was sent to Havana where she was eventually purchased by blockade-running interests. She was the last blockade runner to clear Charleston. Survived the war.

*Galveston*: Jeremiah Simonson, Brooklyn, New York, 1857; 236′ × 37′ × 12′3″; 945 bt; i/sw; became the Confederate gunboat *General Quitman*. Destroyed at the Battle of New Orleans, Apr. 24, 1862.

*Gem*: 2/2; Atlantic, 8/63–3/65; James Henderson, Renfrew, Scotland, 1854; 161′ × 15.9′ × 7.5′; 84 rt; i/sw; Otto Henry Kaselack, chartered to Cobia Company of Charleston, later sold to Henry Rowland Saunders of Nassau; survived the war.

*General Beauregard*: See *Havelock*.

*General Buckner*: 3/2; Gulf, 4/63–5/63; Keyport, New Jersey, 1862; 119.2′ × 22.1′ × 7.8′, 168 rt; 252 bt; ?/sw; John Scott of Mobile for a stock company formed in Mobile; registered as the *General Buckner* at Nassau in April 1863. On arriving in Mobile she took on a Confederate register and was named the *Eugenie*. Captured by the *R. R. Cuyler* while steaming from Havana to Mobile May 6, 1863. Purchased from prize court and taken into the USN as *Eugenie*. Name changed to *Glasgow* Jan. 21, 1864. Sold to private interests June 4, 1869.

*General Clinch*: 1/1; Atlantic, 11/64; James Poyas, Charleston, S.C., 1839; 131′ × 24′ × 8.6′; 256 bt; w/sw; H. L. P. McCormick for the Palmetto Importing and Exporting Company; escaped to Nassau Nov. 3, 1864, where she remained for the rest of the war. Survived the war.

*General Miramon*: 6/4; Gulf and Atlantic, 5/61–5/62; built in Glasgow, 1859; 133.5′ × 24.5′ × 9.6′; 296 rt; Joaquim Acelso (?) purchased her in the spring of 1862 at New Orleans, later sold to John Fraser and Company, who operated the vessel from April to May 1863; built as the *Pagnes Coneo*, she was used as a gunboat by General Miguel de Miramon during his blockade of Vera Cruz, where it was captured by the U.S. warship *Saratoga* on March 6, 1860. The vessel was brought to New Orleans, where she was condemned and sold. Her new owners ran her as a packet between New Orleans and Havana under her Mexican name. She was sold to blockade-running interests in the spring of 1861. In April 1862 she was sold to John Fraser and Company and renamed *Elizabeth*. Captured by the *Keystone State* May 29, 1862, on her way to Charleston.

*General Moultrie*: 1/1; Atlantic, 2/64; William Collyer, New York, New York, 1856; 150′ × 26′8″ × 10′3″; 365 bt; w/sc; Palmetto Importing and Exporting Company; Charleston dredge boat, escaped to Nassau early March 1864. She was sold to private interests in Nassau in May 1864. Survived the war.

*General Rusk*: 3/2; Gulf, 6/62–10/62; Harlan and Hollingsworth, Wilmington, Del., 1857; 200′ × 31′ × 12′; 750 gt, 417 bt; i/sw; owned by the Confederacy, operated by private parties in the summer of 1862, when she was used as a blockade runner; built as *General Rusk*, renamed *Blanche* in the summer of 1862. Chased ashore and burned in Cuban waters by the *Montgomery*. Her destruction in Cuban waters caused an international incident, forcing the United States to pay reparations to Spain.

*General Whiting*: 4/4; Atlantic and Gulf, 4/64–1/65; 199.5′ × 30′ × 19.1′; 816 gt; 425 rt; Consolidated Steamship Company; possibly named *Rafael* before becoming a blockade runner. Survived the war.

*Georgia*: Denny and Company, Dumbarton, Scotland, 1862, built as the *Japan*; 219′ × 27.25′ × 14.75′; 648 gt; 427 rt; w/sc; vessel had a wooden hull on an iron frame; purchased by the CSA in March 1863 for use as a commerce raider; sold in the summer of 1864 to E. Bates, who converted her to a merchantman. Sometimes referred while building as the *Virginian*. Captured off coast of Portugal by the *Niagara*. Condemned at a prize court, sold to the Quebec Steamship Company in Aug. 1865. Wrecked on Triangle Ledge, Maine, Jan. 14, 1875.

*Georgia Belle*: Jones, Quiggin and Company, Liverpool, England, 1864; 250′ × 28′ × 10′9″; 972 bt; 452 rt; s/sw; cleared Liverpool in December 1864, but never ran the blockade.

*Georgiana*: 1/0; Atlantic, 1/63–3/63; J. G. Lawrie and Company, Whiteinch, Glasgow, Scotland, 1862; 205.6′ × 25.2′ × 14.9′; 519 gt, 407 rt; i/sc; N. Matheson for the Navigation Company. Chased ashore and destroyed by the *Wissahickon* Mar. 18, 1863, off Long Island, S.C., while trying to enter Charleston harbor.

*Georgiana McCaw*: 1/0; Atlantic, 5/64–6/64; 373 rt; i/sw; M. G. Klingender; vessel reported to have been named *Dundalk* before running the blockade. Destroyed by the *Victoria* off Old Inlet, N.C., while trying to enter the river on June 2, 1864.

*Gertrude*: 3/2; Atlantic, 2/63–4/64; Barclay, Curle and Company, Greenock, Scotland, 1863; 156′ × 21′ × 11′×; 249 bt; i/sc; Thomas S. Begbie; captured by the *Vanderbilt* Apr. 16, 1863, near the Bahamas Islands while heading for the southern coast. Purchased from prize court and taken into the USN. Sold to private interests Jan. 27, 1866. Abandoned in 1878.

*Gibraltar*: 1/1 as a warship, 2/2 as a blockade runner; Gulf and Atlantic, 5/61–11/63; Reaney Neaffie, Philadelphia, 1859; 170.9′ × 28.1′ × 18′; 387 rt; w/sc; built as the steam packet *Habana*, purchased by the Confederate Navy in

May 1861, and renamed *Sumter*. Sold to Fraser, Trenholm and Company during the summer of 1863 and renamed *Gibraltar*. Returned to the Confederate government to run in the Blakely cannons. Survived the war.

*Giraffe*: See *Robert E. Lee*.

*Gladiator*: 2/2; Atlantic, 6/63–7/63; Pearse, Stockton-on-Tees, England, 1860; 195′ × 27.5′ × 16′; 591 gt, 467 rt; i/sc; Fraser, Trenholm and Company. Survived the war.

*Gordon*: See *Theodora*

*Governor Dudley*: See *Nelly*

*Granite City*: 4/2; Atlantic, 2/63–3/63; Archibald Denny, Dumbarton, Scotland, 1862; 160′ × 23′ × 9′2″; 400 bt; i/sw; reportedly named *City of Dundee* before being used as a blockade runner. She was initially owned by Alexander Collie and Company until captured Mar. 22, 1863, off Eleuthera Island, Bahamas, by the *Tioga* after having escaped from Wilmington. Purchased from prize court and taken into the USN. She was captured by the Confederates at Calcasieu Pass, Louisiana, Apr. 24, 1864. She was then sold to Thomas W. House of Galveston for $36,000 Confederate. Ran aground and destroyed by the *Penguin* off Velasco, Texas, Jan. 20, 1865, after escaping from Calcasieu Pass.

*Greyhound*: 2/1; Atlantic, 3/64–5/64; Kirkpatrick McIntyre and Company, Greenock, Scotland, 1863; 201.4′ × 22.7′ × 13′; 372 gt; 290 rt; i/sc; captured off Wilmington by the *Connecticut*. Belle Boyd was on board when vessel captured. This vessel is often confused with the steamer *Greyhound*, which served as General Benjamin Butler's flagship. They were two different vessels.

*Grey Jacket*: 1/0; Gulf, 12/63; Thomas Meaher, Mobile, Alabama, 1863; 165.5′ × 24′ × 10′; 371 bt; w/sc; Timothy Meaher; Captured Dec. 31, 1863, by the *Kennebec*.

*Habanero*: 1/0; Gulf, 9/63; renamed *Montgomery* on running the blockade. Reported to have been an old Spanish vessel. Captured Sept. 13, 1863, in the Gulf by the *DeSoto*.

*Hansa*: 21/20; Atlantic, 7/63–3/65; built at Glasgow, Scotland, 1858, 177′ × 22.2′ × ??; 257 rt; ?/sw; F. Muir for Alexander Collie and Company; survived the war.

*Harriet Lane*: See *Lavinia*.

*Harriet Pinckney*: Richardson's, Middlesborough, England, 1862; 191.3′ × 28.9′ × 17.6′; 714 gt; 571 rt; w/sc; vessel had a wooden hull on an iron frame; owned by the Confederate States of America; carried supplies from England to the West Indies. Sold by the CSA in August 1864, and renamed *Leda*.

*Hattie*: Caird and Company, Greenock, Scotland, 1864; 219.4′ × 20.2′ × 8.4′; 284 gt; 203 rt; i/sw; owner listed as J. L. Martin; cleared Glasgow in November 1864, lost at sea May 8, 1865.

*Havana*: 3/2; Gulf, 5/62–6/62; Allison Builders, Hoboken, New Jersey, 1855; 115.3′ × 22.5′ × 7′; 169 bt; ?/sc; built as the *Acorn*. Burned by the *Isilda* in Dead Man's Bay, Florida, June 5, 1862.

*Havelock*: 17/16; Atlantic, 2/63–12/63; J. & G. Thompson, Govan, Scotland, 1858; 223′2″ × 26′2″ × 14′3″; 629 gt; 339 rt; i/sw; J. Archibald Wilson for the Chicora Importing and Exporting Company of Charleston; renamed *General Beauregard* on her arrival in Charleston. Chased ashore and destroyed by the *Howquah* north of Fort Fisher Dec. 11, 1863.

*Hawk*: Henderson and Coulborn, Renfrew, Scotland, 1864; 254′ × 28′ × 12.5′; 530 rt; w/sc; purchased by the Virginia Volunteer Navy for use as a privateer; reached Bermuda in June 1864; but the company ran out of funds and the vessel never operated as a privateer or as a blockade runner.

*Hebe*: 3/2; Atlantic, 6/63–8/63; John and William Dudgeon, London, England, 1863; 165′ × 23′ × 13.5′; i/ts; Collie, Crenshaw and Company; chased ashore and destroyed by the *Shokokon* while trying to enter New Inlet Aug. 18, 1863.

*Helen*: See *Juno* (*I*).

*Helen*: 10/10; Atlantic, 4/64–10/64; 1864; 230.2′ × 25.9′ × 13.5′; 539 gt; 343 rt; i/sw; William Boyle or Thomas Begbie for the Universal Trading Company; survived the war.

*Helen Denny*: A. J. Inglis, Glasgow, Scotland, 1864; 212.8′ × 25.2′ × 12′; 483 gt; 295 rt; i/sw; J. R. Young for the Importing and Exporting Company of South Carolina; arrived in Havana in November 1865 but reportedly drew too much water to run to Galveston and returned to England.

*Herald* (*I*) 25/24; Atlantic, 3/62–12/63; John Reid and Company, England; 222′ × 22′ × 14.5′; 283 rt, 450 bt; i/sw; Charles Taylor for Fraser, Trenholm and Company who purchased the vessel in late 1861 and in November 1862 sold her to the Chicora Importing and Exporting Company of Charleston: Renamed *Antonica* September 1862 when sold to Chicora; ran aground while trying to enter Old Inlet Dec. 19, 1863, destroyed by the *Governor Buckingham* and others.

*Herald* (*II*): 1/0; Atlantic, 9/63; built in Baltimore, 1839; 115′ × 24′ × 7′; 221 bt; w/sw; captured by the *Tioga* near the Bahamas Sept. 26, 1863, after escaping from Savannah. Sold by prize court to private interests and renamed *Exchange* Apr. 21, 1864. Abandoned in 1867.

*Hercules*: Denny and Company, Dumbarton, Scotland, 1865; 176′ × 25′ × 12.5′; 341 gt; 515 bt; 202 rt; 600 dt; i/ts; f17,500; contracted for the Confederacy by James Bulloch for use as a CSN tug and warship on the Cape Fear River; unfinished at war's end. She was to be renamed *Vicksburg* for Confederate service.

*Hero*: 2/2; Atlantic, 7/62–2/63; C. and W. Earle, Hull, England, 1861; 224.3′ × 29.2′ × 15.7′; 899 gt; i/sc; William Whitworth; remained in Charleston from July

1862 until February 1863. There were attempts to sell the ship in Charleston. On her return to Liverpool sold to James Baines of that city. Sold 1863 to Australian interests. Lost Jan. 22, 1901 in a hurricane at Kaouaouva, New Caledonia. Survived the war.

*Heroine*: 5/5; Atlantic and Gulf, 11/63–7/64; Glasgow, Scotland, 1862; 179′ × 19.2′ × 7′; 214 bt, 108 rt; i/sw; John Fraser and Company; trapped at Mobile in August 1864, used by the CSA as a transport and captured on the evacuation of Mobile. Sold to private interests Dec. 15, 1866. Abandoned in 1907.

*Hope*: 3/2; Atlantic, 8/64–10/64; Jones, Quiggin and Company, Liverpool, England, 1864; 281′ × 35′ × 15′; 1698 gt; s/sw; John Lafitte for Fraser, Trenholm and Company; cost to build £38,000; Captured Oct. 22, 1864, heading for Wilmington by the *Eolus*. Sold by prize court to private interests and renamed *Savannah* on Jan. 11, 1865. Sold to the Spanish government in 1866 for $76,000. She became the gunboat *Churruca*. Sold from service in 1885.

*Hornet*: Jones, Quiggin and Company, Liverpool, England, 1865; 250′ × 28′ × 10.9′; 573 gt; 770 bt; 290 rt; s/sw; Charles K. Prioleau for Fraser, Trenholm and and Company; unfinished at war's end.

*Huntress*: see *Tropic*.

*Ida*: 1/0; Atlantic, 7/64; 70′ × 17′ × 7′; 45 bt; w/sw; Captured by the *Sonoma* July 8, 1864 while trying to escape Savannah near Sapolo Inlet, Ga. Sold by Prize court to private interests and named the *Admiral Thatcher*.

*Imogene*: 2/2; Atlantic and Gulf, 3/65–6/65; William Denny and Brothers, Dumbarton, Scotland, 1865; 225′ × 28′ × 13.5′; 633 gt; i/sw; James Carlin for the Importing and Exporting Company of South Carolina; survived the war.

*Index*: 8/8; Atlantic, 1/64–6/64; Deptford, England, 1863; 208.8′ × 25.7′ × 11.5′; 363 rt; Edgar Pinchback Stringer for Alexander Collie and Company; too slow for service and returned to London in July 1864.

*Iona (I)*: J. & G. Thomson, Govan, Scotland; 225.2′ × 20.4′ × 9′; 325 gt; 174 rt; i/sw; George Wigg for the Navigation Company; purchased for £20,000; collided with the *Chanticleer* and sank in the Clyde River, Oct. 2, 1862.

*Iona (II)*: J. & G. Thomson, Govan, Scotland, 1863; 249.2′ × 25′ × 9.1′; 368 gt; 173 rt; i/sw; purchased by C. Hopkins Bostier of Richmond for £20,000; foundered Feb. 2, 1864 in the Bristol Channel off Lundy Island while enroute to Nassau.

*Isabel*: See *Ella Warley*.

*Isabel*: 7/6; Gulf; Jimenez and Sabino of Havana; sometimes referred to as the *Isabella*, the vessel operated under a British register. Captured by the *Admiral* while heading for Galveston, May 28, 1864. The *Isabel* was damaged by gunfire and sank near the quarantine station in the Mississippi River before she could reach New Orleans on June 1, 1864.

*Isaac Smith*: see *Stono*.

*Ivanhoe*: 1/0 Gulf, 5/64–6/64; John Scott and Sons, Glasgow, Scotland, 1864, 201.4′ × 20.15′ × 9.5′; 266 gt; 173 rt; 308 bt; i/sw; Thomas S. Begbie for the Albion Trading Company; chased ashore by the *Glasgow* near Fort Morgan while trying to enter Mobile Bay on June 30, 1864.

*James Battle*: 1/0; Gulf, 7/63; New Albany, Indiana, 1860; 209′ × 34′6″ × 6′3″; 407 bt; w/sw; captured by the *Ossipee* and *Kennebec* while trying to escape from Mobile Bay, July 18, 1863. Purchased from prize court and taken into the USQD. Sold to private interests Oct. 18, 1865. Abandoned in 1870.

*James L. Day*: 1/0; Gulf, 1/62; New York, 1843; 187′ × 25.5′ × 9′; 414 bt; w/sw; used as a gunboat from May 1861 to January 1862, she was returned to her owners and converted to a blockade runner. Reported to have been captured in February 1862, though exact information is lacking.

*Jamestown*: Jacob Westervelt, New York, New York, 1852; 240′ × 33′ × 23′; 1300 bt; w/sw; seized at Richmond and taken into the Virginia Navy. In July 1861 turned over to the CSN and renamed *Thomas Jefferson*. Sunk as an obstruction in the James River May 15, 1862.

*Jeanette*: 2/2; Gulf, late 1864 to early 1865; Denny, Dumbarton, Scotland, 1852; 169.9′ × 16.5′ × 8.3′; 147 gt; 76 rt; i/sw; former *Eagle* (q.v.), purchased from a prize court and returned to blockade running in the Gulf. Name sometimes spelled *Jeannette*. Reportedly made one round trip to Galveston late in the war.

*Julia*: 2/1; Atlantic, 10/64–12/64; William Simons and Company, Renfrew, Scotland, 1863; 210′ × 23.2′ × 9.8′; 735 bt; 117 rt; i/sw; Donald McGregor; reported to have run into the Santee River, S.C., sometime in December 1864. Caught in a gale while escaping from Charleston, she was forced into Bull's Bay, where she ran aground. There she was discovered and captured by small boats from the *Acadia*. Sold by prize court to private interests Dec. 27, 1865. Abandoned in 1867.

*Juno* (*I*): 2/1; Atlantic, 6/63–3/64; Tod and McGregor, Glasgow, Scotland, 1860; 185 rt; purchased by the Confederacy in Dec., 1863 and renamed *Helen*. The purchase price was £21,000. She was used as a gunboat in Charleston Harbor until March 1864, when she was sent out as a blockade runner. She was lost in a gale after escaping from Charleston about Mar. 10, 1864.

*Juno* (*II*): 2/1; Atlantic, 8/63–9/63, G. K. Stuthart and Company, Bristol, England, 1853; 163.2′ × 19.7′ × 11.4′; 298 gt, 155 rt; i/sw; William Shaw Lindsay for Merchantile Trading Company; captured by the *Connecticut* Sept. 22, 1863, while coming out of New Inlet.

*Jupiter* (*I*): 1/0; Atlantic, 8/63–9/63; Tod and McGregor, Glasgow, Scotland, 1856; 184.9′ × 18.2′ × 8.3′; 280 rt; i/sw; J. Reid and D. A. McKeller; captured by the *Cimarron* Sept. 13, 1863, in Wassaw Sound, Georgia. Sold by prize court to private interests Oct. 13, 1865. Abandoned in 1877.

*Jupiter* (*II*): 1/0; Atlantic, 6/64; Miller, Ravenill and Company, Blackwall, England, 1849; 163.5′ × 17′ × 8′; 172 gt; 91 rt; i/sw; Matthew Isaac Wilson or Curtis Smuthwaite; captured by the *Proteus* June 27,1864 near the Bahamas. Sold by prize court to private interests and renamed *Comet* Sept. 16, 1864. Abandoned in 1865.

*Kate* (*I*): 20/20; Atlantic, 1/62–11/62; Samuel Sneden, Greenpoint, New York; 165′ × 29′10″ × 10′4″; 477 bt; w/sw; John Fraser and Company; built as the *Carolina*, name changed to *Kate* on her purchase by John Fraser and Company in December 1861. Hit snag inside the Cape Fear River bar Nov. 18, 1862. Cargo saved but vessel was a total loss.

*Kate* (*II*): 4/3; Atlantic, 5/63–7/63; John and William Dudgeon, London, England, 1863; 165′ × 22.6′ × 13.5′; 344 rt; i/ts; E. James for Beech and Root and Company; ran aground coming out of Wilmington July 12, 1863, by the *Penobscot*. Floated free by the Confederates, she was seized by the *Mount Vernon*, *James Adger, Iroquois* and *Niphon* on Aug. 1, 1863. She was condemned at a prize court and sold to private interests who returned her to the blockade running trade as the *G. T. Watson* (q.v.).

*Kate Dale*: 1/0; Gulf, 7/63; built in New Albany, Indiana, 1855; 193′9″ × 37′ × 8′4″; 428 bt; w/sw; Charles Linn of Montgomery, Alabama; an Alabama River packet, captured July 14, 1863, by the *R. R. Cuyler* near the Tortugas after escaping from Mobile Bay. Sold by the prize court to private interests Sept. 26, 1863. Taken into USQD Jan. 6, 1864. Burned at Mobile Bay May 25, 1865.

*Kate Gregg*: 4/4; Atlantic, 8/64–1/65; Denny, Dumbarton, Scotland, 1854; 213.5′ × 23.6′ × 13.3′; 498 gt; 314 rt; David McNutt of Glasgow, on arrival at Charleston sold to the Atlantic Steam Packet Company of Charleston; she was built as the *Stag* and ran the blockade as the *Stag*, then renamed *Kate Gregg* at Charleston September 1864; survived the war.

*Kelpie*: Tod & McGregor, Glasgow, 1857; 191′ × 18′ × 10′; ?/sw; sank while entering Nassau harbor December 1862.

*Kenilworth*: 1/0; Atlantic, 10/64–3/65; John Scott and Sons, Greenock, Scotland, 1864; 201.4′ × 20.15′ × 9.5′; 266 gt; 173 rt; 359 bt; i/sw; John Ross Young for the Albion Trading Company; forced back to Nassau by bad weather in her only attempt to run the blockade. Survived the war.

*Lady Davis*: See *Cornubia*.

*Lady Sterling*: 2/1; Atlantic, 9/64–10/64; Scott Russell, Blackwall, England, 1864; 241′ × 26′ × 13.4′; 416 rt; 835 bt; i/sw; Thomas Sterling Begbie for the Albion Trading Company; captured by the *Calypso* and *Eolus* coming out of Wilmington on Oct. 28, 1864. Purchased from prize court and taken into the USN as the

*Hornet*. Sold to private interests Aug. 11, 1869. Became a gun runner to Cuba. Seized by U.S. authorities Oct. 4, 1869. Sold to foreign interests in 1872.

*Lark*: 8/8; Gulf, 1/65–5/65; Laird and Sons, Birkenhead, England, 1864; 210' × 23' × 10.4'; 388 gt; 267 rt; 800 bt; s/sw; John Laird for Fraser, Trenholm and Company until paid for when ownership of the vessel would be transferred to the Confederacy; designed to operate the Gulf of Mexico, she was the last steam blockade runner to clear a Confederate port, she survived the war and returned to Liverpool. Broken up in 1890.

*Laura*: 5/4; Gulf, 9/63–1/64; 121' × 22.7' × 7.6'; 136 bt; w/sw; captured by the *Stars and Stripes* Jan. 18, 1864, at the mouth of the Ochlockonee River, Florida. Purchased from prize court and taken into USQD. Sold to civilian interests Dec. 16, 1865. Abandoned 1879.

*Laurel*: 2/2; Atlantic, 11/64–1/65; A. & J. Inglis, Glasgow, Scotland; 207' × 27' × 10'; 296 rt; i/sc; Henry Lafone for the Confederate States of America; purchased as the *Laurel* by the CSN. After arriving in Charleston she was transferred to the Treasury Department and renamed *Confederate States*, used as a supply ship for the *Shenandoah*. Survived the war.

*Lavinia*: 1/1; Gulf, 4/64–1/65; William H. Webb, New York, New York, 1857; 180' × 30' × 12.5'; 674 bt; w/sw; T. W. House of Galveston for King and Company; Built and operated as a revenue cutter, tranferred to USN Sept. 17, 1861. Captured at Galveston as the *Harriet Lane* Jan. 1, 1863. Sold by the Confederacy to T. W. House and renamed *Lavinia* in early 1864. Burned at Havana Jan. 18, 1865. She was later raised and converted to a sailing ship. Sold to U.S. interests and renamed *Elliott Richie*. Abandoned off Pernambuco, Brazil May 13, 1884.

*Lelia*: William C. Miller and Sons, Liverpool, England, 1865; 252' × 30' × 12.6'; 640 gt; 1100 bt; 430 rt; s/sw; Crenshaw and Company; foundered Jan. 14, 1865, at the mouth of the Mersey River.

*Leopard*: 9/8; Atlantic, 6/62–4/63; William Denny and Brothers, Dumbarton, Scotland, 1857; 222' × 27' × 14.6'; 691 gt; 435 rt; 824 bt; 1230 dt; i/sw; purchased by Fraser, Trenholm and Company May 1862 for £24,000; Renamed *Stonewall Jackson* in February 1863. Ran aground and burned by the *Flag* and *Huron* off Sullivan's Island while trying to enter Charleston harbor April 12, 1863.

*Let Her Be*: See *Chicora*.

*Let Her Rip*: See *Wando*.

*Let Her Run*: ?/sw; lost while crossing the Atlantic, October 1864.

*Leviathan*: Raney and Son, Chester, Pa., 1863; 120' × 30' × 12'; 356 bt; ?/sc; captured by Confederate raiders, Sept. 22, 1863, at the mouth of the Mississippi River. She was recaptured the same day by the *DeSoto*.

*Lilian*: 6/5; Atlantic, 5/64–8/64; J. & G. Thomson, Govan, Scotland, 1864; 225′ × 26′ × 11′; 246 rt; 630 bt; i/sw; Henry Lafone for the Importing and Exporting Company of Georgia; built for £14,896,9.2; sometimes referred to as the *Lillian*, all official documents list the vessel as the *Lilian*. Captured by the *Keystone State* and the *Gettysburg* coming out of Wilmington Aug. 24, 1864. Purchased from prize court and taken into the USN. Sold to private interests Feb. 23, 1866. Sold to the Spanish government in 1870 and became the gunboat *Victoria de las Tunas*. Lost November 1870.

*Little Ada*: 3/2; Atlantic, 2/64–7/64; 112′ × 18.5′ × 10′; 94 rt, 208 bt; i/sc; Henry Lafone for the Importing and Exporting Company of Georgia; ran into the Santee River in March 1864. While there she was seized and held briefly by a Union expedition. Captured at sea off Cape Romain, S.C., July 9, 1864, by the *Gettysburg*. Sold to civilian interests at Georgetown, S.C., in 1865.

*Little Hattie*: 12/10; 6/64–2/65; J. & G. Thomson, Govan, Scotland, 1864; 226′ × 26′ × 10.6′; 439 gt; 247 rt; i/sw; Henry Lafone for the Importing and Exporting Company of Georgia; £9877.2.0; went to Havana in February 1865, but there is no record that she ever ran to Galveston. Survived the war. Sold at Rio de Janeiro, Mar. 7, 1866.

*Little Lilly*: 12/11; Gulf, 6/63–2/64; built at Brooklyn, New York, 1860; 156′4″ × 27′2″ × 8′4″; 147 rt., 303 bt; i/sw; built as the *Flushing*, when sold became the *Nan Nan*. Purchased by blockade running interests in the spring of 1863, renamed the *Little Lilly*, other variations include *Little Lily* and *Little Lilia*. Destroyed by the *Nita* Feb. 24, 1864, near the east pass of the Suwannee River.

*Lizzie* (*I*): 3/2; Atlantic, 3/63–7/63; 89′ × 20.2′ × 7.6′; 72 rt; captured at sea off the eastern coast of Florida July 15, 1863, by the *Santiago de Cuba*. Purchased from prize court and taken into the USQD. Sold to private interests July 17, 1866, sold to foreign interests in 1866.

*Lizzie* (*II*): Henderson, Coulborn and Company, Renfrew, Scotland, 1864; 230′ × 22′ × 9′; i/sw; Arrived in Havana in October, 1864, but there is no evidence that she ever ran the blockade.

*Lizzie Davis*: 2/1; Gulf, 7/63–9/63; built in Mobile 1862; 115′ × 25′ × 6′; 178 bt; w/sw; captured Sept. 16, 1863, while heading from Havana to Mobile by the *San Jacinto*. Purchased from prize court and taken into the USQD. Sold to private interests and renamed *Orleans* Jan. 22, 1866. Lost in 1875.

*Lloyd*: 2/2; Atlantic, 6/62–8/62; J. Pile and Company, West Hartlepool, England, 1862; 938 gt, 741 rt, 1025 bt; i/sc; John Fleming for Leech, Harrison and Company. Sold to James Spence, April 1863; renamed *Sea Queen* April 1863 when sold to new owners. Operated between Havana and Matamoras late in the war as the *Sea Queen*. Survived the war.

*Lodona*: 1/0; Atlantic, 6/62–8/62; built in 1862; 204.2′ × 28.4′ × 16.5′; 688 gt, 573 rt; i/sc; Z. C. Pearson and Company. Captured by the *Unadilla* as she tried to reach Savannah at Hell's Gate. Purchased from prize court by USN. Sold to private interests July 19, 1865. Lost May 31, 1879.

*Louisa Ann Fanny*: John and William Dudgeon, London, England, 1865; 250′ × 15.5′ × 10′; 972 gt; i/ts; she and her sister, the *Mary Augusta* (q.v.) were contracted by James D. Bulloch for use as blockade runners/commerce raiders. The *Louisa Ann Fanny*, under the command of Lieutenant William F. Carter, CSN, delivered despatches and personnel to the *Stonewall* at Lisbon. The *Louisa Ann Fanny* arrived at Bermuda in late Jan. 1865, and then went on to Havana, but never ran the blockade. She probably would have been renamed the *Waccamaw* on being commissioned into the CSN.

*Lucy*: 23/21; Atlantic, 11/63–11/64; Jones Quiggin and Company, Liverpool, England, 1863; 215′ × 20′ × 10′9″; s/sw; E. J. Lomnitz for Fraser, Trenholm and Company; captured by the *Santiago de Cuba* Nov. 3, 1864 after escaping from Wilmington. Sold by prize court to private interests Jan. 14, 1865. Sold to foreign interests in 1866.

*Luna*: 4/4; Gulf, 12/64–6/65; ?/sw; sometimes referred to as the *Witch*. Survived the war, returned to Liverpool in June 1865.

*Lynx*: 10/9; Atlantic, 5/64–9/64; Jones, Quiggin and Company, Liverpool, England, 1864; 220′ × 24′ × 11.5′; 372 gt; 233 rt; s/sw; Richard Wright for Fraser, Trenholm and Company; chased ashore and destroyed by the *Howquah*, *Niphon*, and *Governor Buckingham* while trying to escape from Wilmington Sept. 25, 1864, near New Inlet.

*McRae*: 176′ × 29.5′ × 14′; 600 bt; w/sc; vessel was the Mexican *Marquis de la Habana*, which had been captured off Vera Cruz by the *Saratoga* in March 1860. Taken to New Orleans as a prize, she was converted to a Confederate warship in March 1861. She was often suggested for use as commerce raider, but never ran the blockade and was badly damaged at the Battle of New Orleans on Apr. 24, 1862. She sank three days later after carrying wounded to New Orleans.

*Magnolia*: 1/0; Gulf, 2/62; Jeremiah Simonson, Greenpoint, N.Y., 1857; 246′ × 37′ × 10′9″; 843 bt; i/sw; R. B. Summer of Nashville; captured by the *Brooklyn* and the *South Carolina* Feb. 18, 1862, coming out of Pass a l'Outre. Purchased from prize court and taken into the USN. Sold to private interests Aug. 23, 1865. Abandoned in 1866.

*Mail*: 2/1; Gulf, 8/63–10/63; Tod and McGregor, Glasgow, Scotland, 1860; 179′ × 18′ × 7′; 198 rt; i/sw; after her capture she was condemned and sold. Returned to blockade running in early 1864 under the name *Susanna* (q.v.). Also referred to as the *Susanna Mail*. Captured Oct. 15, 1863, by the *Honduras* near Bayport, Florida.

*Margaret and Jessie*: 20/18, Atlantic, 12/62–11/63; Robert Napier, Glasgow, Scotland, 1858; 205' × 26' × 14'; 950 bt; w/sw; Melchir G. Klingender purchased vessel in England for Fraser, Trenholm and Company November 1862. Sold June 1863 to Importing and Exporting Company of South Carolina; £24,000 by Fraser; built and purchased as the *Douglas*, renamed February 1863 at Charleston. Captured by the *Nansemond* and the Quartermaster Department vessel *Fulton* while trying to enter New Inlet Nov. 5, 1863. Purchased from prize court and taken into the USN as the *Gettysburg*. Sold to foreign interests May 8, 1879 at Genoa, Italy.

*Maria*: 3/2; Gulf, 9;64–2/65; ?/sw; survived the war.

*Mariner*: 2/2 as privateer, 3/2 as a blockade runner; Atlantic 10/62–3/63; built Philadelphia, 1854; 92' × 20' × 8'; 135 bt; ?/sc; privateer from July 1861 to August 1861. Captured March 1863 while trying to return to Wilmington.

*Marian*: See *Zephine*.

*Marmion*: 1/0; 11/64–8/65; John Scott and Sons, Greenock, Scotland, 1864; 201.4' × 20.15' × 9.5'; 266 gt; 173 rt; 358 bt; i/sw; John Ross Young for the Albion Trading Company; tried to reach Wilmington in early December 1864, but forced back due to bad weather. Survived the war.

*Mars*: 2/2; Atlantic, 1/64–6/64; built 1849; 180' × 19' × 9.5'; 144 rt; i/sw; survived the war.

*Mary* (*I*) 7/7; Gulf, 1/64–7/64; Laird and Sons, Birkenhead, England, 1863; 198.6' × 30.3' × 9.6'; 389 gt; 279 rt; i/sw; Arthur B. Forwood for Leech, Harrison and Forwood; built as the *Prince Albert*, renamed when she entered blockade running. Also referred to as the *Mary Virginia*. Trapped at Mobile on the capture of the forts. Taken over for use by the CSA army, taken to Gainsville on the evacuation of Mobile. Captured at Gainsville, Ala., Apr. 12, 1865. Redocumented Jan. 8, 1867. Abandoned in 1875.

*Mary* (*II*): John and William Dudgeon, London, England, 1865; 230' × 27' × 14.6'; i/ts; 829 gt; unfinished at war's end.

*Mary Anne*: 6/5; Atlantic and Gulf, 7/63–3/64; Charles Connell and Company, Glasgow, Scotland, 1863; 203.4' × 20.6' × 12.3'; 235 gt, 426 bt; i/sw; sometimes referred to as the *Mary Ann*. Captured by the *Grand Gulf* Mar. 6, 1864, after escaping from Wilmington, 50 miles south of Cape Fear. Sold by prize court to private interests July 25, 1864, and renamed *Russia*. Abandoned in 1865.

*Mary and Ella*: Caird and Sons, Greenock, Scotland, 1864; 221.3' × 22.1' × 10.4'; 352 gt; 242 rt; i/sw; owner listed as David McNutt; arrived in Nassau in December 1864, but never ran the blockade. Returned to England Jan. 1865.

*Mary Augusta*: John and William Dudgeon, London, England, 1865; 250' × 15.5' × 10'; 829 gt; i/ts; She and her sister the *Louisa Ann Fanny* (q.v.), were contracted for by James D. Bulloch for use as a gunboat/commerce raider. She was unfinished at war's end. If she had been commissioned into the CSN, she would have probably been named the *Black Warrior*.

*Mary Bowers*: 3/2; Atlantic, 7/64–8/64; William Simons and Company, Renfrew, Scotland; 226' × 25' × 10.5'; 220 rt, 750 bt; i/sw; Henry Lafone for the Importing and Exporting Company of Georgia; £22,686,16.3; ran into the wreck of the *Georgiana* while trying to enter Charleston harbor, Aug. 31, 1864, was a total loss.

*Mary Celestia*: 8/8; Atlantic, 5/64–9/64; William C. Miller and Sons, Liverpool, England, 1864; 221' × 22.1' × 10.4'; 314 gt; 207 rt; i/sw; James Cameron for Crenshaw and Company; Built as the *Bijou*, renamed before joining the blockade running trade. Struck a rock and sank while clearing St. George harbor, Sept. 26, 1864.

*Matagorda*: 19/18; Gulf, 4/62–9/64; Harlan and Hollingsworth, Wilmington, Del, 1858; 220' × 30' × 10.5'; 1250 gt, 616 bt; i/sw; E. B. Shannon; renamed *Alice* August 1862. Captured by the *Magnolia* Sept. 10, 1864, after clearing from Galveston. Sold by prize court to private interests Nov. 12, 1864. Abandoned in 1871.

*Matilda*: Hoby and Son, Renfrew, Scotland; 228' × 25' × 12'; 390 rt; i/ts; owned by the Confederate States of America; contract given to Henderson and Coulborn who built the engines and subcontracted the hull to Hoby and Son; hit a rock and destroyed in the Clyde River, Apr. 4, 1864.

*Maude Campbell*: Archibald Denny, Dumbarton, Scotland, 1864; 226.3' × 28.2' × 13'; 631 gt; 403 rt; i/sw; Importing and Exporting Company of South Carolina; built for £12,000; arrived Bermuda Nov. 24, 1864, but never ran the blockade.

*Mayflower*: 2/1; Gulf, 1/64; a very small vessel, captured Jan. 14, 1864, near Tampa Bay by the *Union*.

*Memphis*: 2/1; Atlantic, 5/62–7/62; William Denny and Brothers, Dumbarton, Scotland, 1861; 230' × 30× 19.5'; 1010 gt; 1780 dt; i/sc; Thomas S. Begbie and William Denny; captured by the *Magnolia* after escaping from Charleston July 31, 1862. Purchased from prize court and taken into the USN. Sold to private interests and renamed *Mississippi* Oct. 9, 1869. Burned at Seattle, Washington, May 13, 1883.

*Merrimac*: 2/1; Atlantic, 9/62–7/63; 230' × 30' × 11'; 634 gt; 536 rt; i/sw; Z. C. Pearson and Company until December 1862, sold to CSA in December 1862, and after her successful run to Wilmington sold to Richard Bradley, who represented the interests of Joseph Anderson, owner of the Tredegar Iron Works; bought for £7000 by CSA; built as the *Nangis*. Captured by the *Magnolia* July 24, 1863, while trying to escape from New Inlet. Purchased from prize court and taken into the USN. Foundered at sea Feb. 15, 1865.

*Mexico*: Westervelt and McKay, New York, New York, 1851; 208′ × 32.8′ × 15′; 1043 bt; w/sw; owned by the Southern Steamship Company, taken by CSA and converted to a gunboat in January 1862, and renamed *General Bragg*. Captured at the Battle of Memphis June 6, 1862, and transferred to the USN. Sold Sept. 2, 1865 to private interests. Foundered in 1870.

*Minho*: 5/4, Atlantic, 4/62–10/62; Blackwood and Gordon, Paisley, Scotland, 1854; 175.3′ × 22′ × 13.5′; 400 gt; 253 rt; w/sc; vessel had a wooden hull on an iron frame; Fraser, Trenholm and Company April–September 1862; Navigation Company September-October 1862; ran aground and destroyed while trying to enter Charleston, Oct. 2, 1862, after being struck by a shell from the *Flambeau*.

*Minna*: 1/0; Atlantic, 4/62–12/63; built at Newcastle, England, 1858; 214.1′ × 26.4′ × 18.6′; 615 gt; 727 bt; i/sc; Melchir G. Klingender for Fraser, Trenholm and Company; purchased for £9000; served as a transport between Nassau and Liverpool for most of her career. Captured off Cape Romain, S.C., Dec. 9, 1863, by the *Circassian*. Sold by prize court to private interests. Lost in 1876.

*Minnie*: 4/3; Atlantic, 1/64–5/64; Barclay Curle and Company, Glasgow, Scotland, 1863; 181.1′ × 22.4′ × 12.1′; 355 gt; 253 rt; i/sc; William Boyle for Albion Trading Company; captured by the *Connecticut* May 9, 1864 coming out of Wilmington.

*Modern Greece*: 1/0; Atlantic, 5/62–6/62; Richardson, Stockton-on-Tees, England, 1859; 210′ × 29′ × 17′; i/sc; Z. C. Pearson and Company; chased ashore and destroyed by the *Cambridge* while trying to reach Wilmington June 27, 1862, off Cape Fear.

*Montgomery*: See *Habanero*.

*Nan Nan*: See *Little Lilly*.

*Nashville*: 3/3 as a warship, 5/4 as a blockade runner; Atlantic, 11/61–2/63; Thomas Collyer, New York, New York, 1853; 216′ × 34′9″ × 22′; 1800 bt; w/sw; taken by the CSN at the start of the war, sold to John Fraser and Company March 1862, in November 1862 sold to a private stock company for use as a privateer. Built as the *Nashville*, renamed *Thomas L. Wragg* March 1862, renamed *Rattlesnake* November 1862. Destroyed by the monitor *Montauk* in the Ogeechee River off Fort McAllister, Georgia, Feb. 28, 1863.

*Nassau*: See *Gordon*.

*Nelly*: 6/5; Atlantic, 2/62–5/62; built at Wilmington, Del. 1838; 177′ × 24′ × 10′; 408 bt; w/sw; J. A. Enslow; built as the *Governor Dudley*, renamed *Catawba* May 8, 1857; when sold to Enslow, renamed *Nelly*, June 1861; ran aground and destroyed while trying to enter Charleston harbor May 25, 1862. Her hull and engines were saved and sold to Robert Hunter for $1,700.

*Neptune*: 5/4; Gulf, 4/63–6/63; Robert Napier, Glasgow, Scotland, 1861; 166.6′ × 27.4′ × 9.5′; 260 bt; i/sw; J. H. Wilson for Fraser, Trenholm and Company;

captured by the *Lackawanna* June 14, 1863 in Gulf while heading for Mobile. Purchased from prize court and taken into the USN and renamed *Clyde* on August 11, 1863. Sold to private interests Nov. 16, 1865 and renamed *Indian River*. Lost in 1867.

*Neva*: 1/0; Gulf, 12/64–1/65; sailed from New York and arrived in Havana in December 1864, with munitions. Cleared for St. Marks in early January 1865, but returned to port without completing her voyage. Survived the war.

*Nicolas I*: 1/0; Atlantic, 2/63–3/63; London, 1839; 182.4′ × 28′ × 17.3′; 536 rt; ?/sw; William Grazebrook; said to have been a British prize from the Crimean War, she was sometimes referred to as the *Nicholas III*. Captured by the *Victoria* and the *William Bacon* March 21,1863, near Little River Inlet, N.C. Sold by the prize court to private interests and renamed *Hudson*. Possibly used by the USQD.

*Night Hawk*: 2/2; Atlantic, 9/64–4/65; McAndrew, Preston, Liverpool, England, 1864; 220′ × 21.5′ × 11′; i/sw; M. J. Wilson for the Anglo-Confederate Trading Company; badly damaged coming into Wilmington Sept. 29, 1864. Repaired at Wilmington, she escaped to Nassau, arriving there Jan. 7,1865. Survived the war.

*Nina*: 2/1; Atlantic, 12/62–1/63; Thomas McDowell, Washington, N.J., 1848; 145′ × 26′ × 9.5′; 205 rt; 338 bt; w/sw; Gazaway B. Lamar for the Importing and Exporting Company of Georgia; purchased for $40,000 Confederate; foundered in late January 1863, while trying to reach Charleston from Nassau.

*Nita*: See *Crescent*.

*Nola*: Caird and Company, Greenock, Scotland, 1863; 228.4′ × 25.2′ × 13.5′; 607 gt; 432 rt; i/sw; registered owner D. McNutt; hit reef on clearing Bermuda about Jan. 1, 1864.

*Norseman*: 2/1; Atlantic, 5/63–6/63; ran aground and destroyed coming out of Charleston about May 19, 1863.

*North Heath*: 5/5; Atlantic, 3/63–1/65; 229.9′ × 25′ × 13.4′; 541 gt; 343 rt; i/sw; Thomas S. Begbie for the Universal Trading Company. Vessel damaged on entering Wilmington in October 1864. Sunk as an obstruction in the Cape Fear River off Fort Strong, Jan. 15, 1864.

*Nutfield*: 1/0; Atlantic, 1/64–2/64; James Ash and Company, Cubitt Town, London, England, 1863; 224.2′ × 26.6′ × 12.6′; 531 gt; 402 rt; i/sw; E. P. Stringer; Chased ashore and destroyed by the *Sassacus* off New Inlet, N.C., Feb. 4, 1864.

*Oconee*: See *Savannah*.

*Old Dominion*: 6/6; Atlantic, 6/64–2/65; Caird and Company, Greenock, Scotland, 1864; 227.8′ × 26.2′ × 14.2′; 703 gt; 518 rt; i/sw; Virginia Importing and Exporting Company; survived the war. Possibly built as the *Alfred*.

*Olustee*: See *Atalanta*.

*Oregon*: built at New York, New York, 1846; 216'10" × 26'6" × 9'6"; 532 bt; w/sw; owned by Robert Geddes of the New Orleans and Mobile Mail Company; vessel served under a charter to the State of Louisiana in 1861, until purchased by the Confederacy and converted into a gunboat in July 1861; vessel purchased by CSA from Geddes for $30,000; destroyed on Lake Pontchartrain in late April 1862.

*Oreto*: See *Florida (II)*.

*Orion*: See *Fanny*.

*Orizaba*: Jeremiah Simonson, New York, New York, 1858; 210' × 30' × 10.5'; 630 bt; w/sw; owned by the Southern Steamship Company; seized by the CSA and converted to the gunboat *Resolute* in January 1862. Destroyed at the Battle of New Orleans April 24, 1862.

*Ouachita*: 1/0; Atlantic, 9/62–10/62; England, 1858; 116' × 16' × 6.5'; 286 bt; i/sw; Thomas Begbie; captured Oct. 14, 1862, off Cape Romain, S.C., by the *Memphis*. Sold by prize court to private interests and renamed *Sonora*.

*Owl*: 7/4; Atlantic, 8/64–7/65; Jones, Quiggin and Company, Liverpool, England, 1864; 230' × 26' × 10.9'; 466 gt; 330 rt; s/sw; William Quiggin for Fraser, Trenholm and Company, turned over to the Confederacy in December 1864 after payment in cotton to Fraser, Trenholm and Company. Vessel went to the Gulf in March 1865, but there is no evidence that she ever ran to Galveston. Survived the war.

*Pacific*: London, England, 1854; 255' × 32.1' × 18'; 1469 gt; 985 rt; i/sw; carried supplies between the West Indies and England.

*Pagnes Coneo*: See *General Miramon*.

*Patras*: 1/0; Atlantic, 5/62; Richardson, Stockton-on-Tees, England, 1859; 150' × 20' × 12.5'; 263 gt; 192 rt; i/sc; Zachariah C. Pearson for Z. C. Pearson and Company; captured May 27, 1862, off Bull's Bay, S.C., by the *Bienville*. Sold by prize court to private interests and renamed *Mexico*, March 14, 1864.

*Pearl*: 1/0; Atlantic, 1/63; James Henderson, Renfrew, Scotland, 1859; 182.2' × 19.5' × 7.6'; 168 gt; 72 rt; w/sw; vessel had a wooden hull on an iron frame. George Wigg for the Navigation Company; captured Jan. 20, 1863, off the Bahamas Islands by the *Tioga*.

*Pelican*: 2/2; Gulf, 1/65–5/65; Hull, England, 1863; 187'5" × 24' × 12'8"; 445 bt; i/sc; Thomas W. House for King and Company. Survived the war. Sold to U.S. interests in 1868 and sold foreign in 1878.

*Penguin*: Laird and Sons, Birkenhead, England, 1865; 240' × 30' × 13.2'; 659 gt; 1063 bt; s/sw; built by Fraser, Trenholm and Company for the Confederacy; Fraser, Trenholm and Company to operate vessel until payment in cotton from the Confederacy when the vessel would be turned over to the CSA. Unfinished at war's end.

*Pet*: 17/16; Atlantic, 3/63–2/64; Blackhouse, Middlesborough, England, 1862; 141′ × 20.6′ × 11.4′; 244 gt; 171 rt; i/sc; Isaac Rich for the Steamship *Pet* Company; captured by the *Montgomery* Feb. 16, 1864 off Lockwood Folly Inlet, N.C., while heading for Wilmington. Sold to private interests May 7, 1864. Sold foreign in 1864.

*Peterhoff*: 210′ × 28′ × 15′; i/sw; owned by Z. C. Pearson and Company at the start of the war, obtained by James Spence for Pile, Spence and Company. Captured by the *Vanderbilt* Feb. 25, 1863 off St. Thomas while bound for Matamoras. Prize court declared her to be a blockade runner and condemned the vessel. Though the verdict was appealed by her owners, the vessel was purchased by the USN. Sunk off Wilmington after a collision with the *Monticello* on Mar. 6, 1864.

*Petrel*: See *Stormy Petrel*.

*Pevensey*: 3/2; Atlantic, 4/64–6/64; 485 rt; i/sw; reportedly operated by Stringer, Pembroke and Company, chased ashore and destroyed by the *New Berne* near Beaufort, N.C., while trying to reach Wilmington.

*Phantom*: 5/4; Atlantic, 7/63–9/63; William C. Miller and Sons, Liverpool, England, 1863; 192.9′ × 22′ × 12.4′; 322 gt; 266 rt; s/sc; William Mann for Fraser, Trenholm and Company; sold to CSA July 1863 at Wilmington. Ran aground and destroyed by the *Connecticut* near Topsail Inlet, N.C., while trying to enter New Inlet.

*Phoebe*: Dumbarton, 1851; 172.8′ × 25.5′ × 15.6′; i/sc; 585 gt; 397 rt; owned by Z. C. Pearson and Company; arrived Bermuda July 28, 1862, but firm declared bankruptcy and she never ran the blockade. Sold to the Australian Steamship Company.

*Pizarro*: 1/1; Gulf, 12/61; 190′ × 25.3′ × 9′; 419 bt; Andrea T. Alexander of New Orleans; cleared from New Orleans custom house Dec. 11, 1861. No record of her arrival at Cuba. Possibly sunk in same storm that claimed the *C. Vanderbilt* or ran to Mexico.

*Planter*: 1/0; Gulf, 6/63; Wheeling (West) Virginia, 1860; 156′ × 35′ × 6′5″; 313 bt; w/sw; captured by the *Lackawanna* June 15, 1863 after escaping from Mobile. Purchased from prize court and taken into the USQD. Sold to private interests March 24, 1866.

*Plover*: Jones, Quiggin and Company, Liverpool, England, 1865; 224′ × 24′ × 11.4′; 409 gt; 645 bt; s/sw; J. K. Gilliat and Company contracted to build the vessel for the Confederacy. J. K. Gilliat and Company were to operate the vessel until they received payment from the Confederacy. Unfinished at the war's end.

*Powerful*: 1/0; Gulf, 12/63; Lewis, Quebec, Canada, 1862; 126′ × 23′ × ??; 119 rt; 189 bt; w/sw; destroyed at the mouth of the Suwannee River, Florida, Dec. 20, 1863, by the *Fox*.

*Presto*: 3/2; Atlantic, 12/63–2/64; Alexander Stephen and Sons, Glasgow, Scotland, 1863; 210′ × 23′ × 9.5′; 552 gt; 164 rt; i/sw; built as the *Fergus*; ran aground off Fort Moultrie while trying to enter Charleston Harbor, Feb. 2, 1864, and destroyed by gunfire from Union batteries on Morris Island.

*Prince Albert*: 3/2; Atlantic, 5/64–8/64; William Denny and Brothers; Dumbarton, Scotland, 1849; 138.1′ × 16.7′ × 7′; 132 gt; 94 rt; ?/sw; ran onto wreck of *Minho* while trying to enter Charleston Harbor, Aug. 9, 1864. Destroyed by gunfire from Union shore batteries.

*Princess Royal*: 1/0; Atlantic, 1/63; Tod and McGregor, Glasgow, Scotland, 1861; 196′9″ × 27′3″ × 16′; 494 rt; 828 bt; i/sc; Fraser, Trenholm and Company; captured by the *Unadilla* Jan. 29, 1863, while trying to enter Charleston Harbor. Purchased from prize court and taken into the USN. Sold to civilian interests Sept. 23, 1865, and renamed *Sherman*. Lost Jan. 10, 1874 off Cape Fear Light, N.C.

*Ptarmigan*: 3/2; Atlantic and Gulf, 8/64–2/65; Randolph, Elder and Company, Govan, Scotland, 1864; 270′ × 24′ × 12′; 283 rt; i/sw; Donald McGregor for Alexander Collie and Company; survived the war.

*Raccoon*: 3/2; Atlantic, 12/63–7/63; 201.2′ × 21.4′ × 9′; 159 rt; ?/sw; Fraser, Trenholm and Company; ran aground off Sullivan's Island while trying to enter Charleston Harbor, July 19, 1863, and burned by her crew.

*Ranger*: 2/0; Atlantic, 12/63–1/64; i/sw; driven ashore and destroyed by the *Minnesota*, *Governor Buckingham*, *Daylight* and *Aries* Jan. 11, 1864, off Old Inlet, N.C., while trying to reach Wilmington.

*Rattlesnake*: See *Nashville*.

*Rattlesnake*: 2/0; Atlantic, 1/65; John and William Dudgeon, London, England, 1864; 201.8′ × 24.4′ × 12.5′; 529 gt; 259 rt; i/ts; E. L. Coulburn for Collie and Company; ran aground while trying to enter Charleston Harbor in late January or early February 1865.

*Ray*: William Miller and Sons, Liverpool, England, 1865; 252′ × 29′ × 12.5′; 644 gt; 430 rt; 1100 bt; s/sw; Fraser, Trenholm and Company; unfinished at the war's end.

*Red Gauntlet*: 1/1; Gulf, 7/64–8/64; John Scott and Sons, Greenock, Scotland, 1864; 201.4′ × 21.1′ × 9.5′; 265 gt; 173 rt; 357 bt; i/sw; William Boyle; vessel purchased by the Confederacy, Mar. 1, 1865. Trapped at Mobile at the fall of the harbor forts, she was used as a transport before fleeing to Gainesville on the evacuation of Mobile. Captured at Gainesville, Ala., Apr. 12, 1865.

*Reliance*: 1/0; Atlantic, 7/62; 134' × 26.9' × 11'; 352 bt; w/sw; built as the *Hollyhock*, taken into the Confederate service and renamed *Reliance*. Captured by the *Huntsville* Sept. 19, 1862, while trying to escape from Savannah.

*Robert E. Lee*: 15/14; Atlantic, 12/62–11/63; J. & G. Thomson, Govan, Scotland, 1860; 268' × 26' × 12'; 900 bt; 360 rt; i/sw; Confederate States of America; purchased for £32,000; built and purchased as the *Giraffe*, renamed *Robert E. Lee* on arrival in the Confederacy in late December 1862. Captured by the *James Adger* Nov. 9, 1863, southwest of Beaufort, N.C., while heading for Wilmington. Purchased from prize court and taken into the USN as the *Fort Donelson*. Sold to private interests and renamed *Isabella*, Dec. 16, 1865. Sold to foreign interests in 1869.

*Rose*: 1/0; Atlantic, 4/64–6/64; 125.3' × 18.7' × 12'; 67 rt; Donald McGregor; ran aground off Georgetown, S.C., June 2, 1864 and destroyed by the *Wamsutta*.

*Rosine*: Jones, Quiggin and Company, Liverpool, England, 1865; 270' × 33' × 15'; 900 gt; 500 rt; 1391 bt; s/sw; J. K. Gilliat and Company contracted to build the vessel for the Confederacy. J. K. Gilliat and Company to operate the vessel until they received payment in cotton from the Confederacy. Unfinished at the war's end. Sold to the Turkish Navy and converted to a gunboat.

*Rosita*: 5/4; Gulf, 9/63–1/64; built in Philadelphia, 1861; 128' × 23'11" × 8'6"; 115 gt; 52 rt; 238 bt; ?/sw; formerly *Union* (q.v.), captured, condemned and sold to new owners who returned her to the blockade running trade as the *Rosita*. Captured by the *Western Metropolis* Jan. 28, 1864, in the Gulf while heading for St. Marks. Sold at a prize court to private interests who again returned her to blockade running under the name *Carolina* (q.v.).

*Rothesay Castle*: 5/4; Atlantic; 12/63–6/65; William Simons and Company, Renfrew, Scotland, 1861; 191' × 28'9" × 8'4"; i/sw; David McNutt; survived the war and in June 1865 sailed from Nassau to Halifax. Sold at Halifax on Oct. 3, 1865, to Canadian interests. Scrapped in 1888 or 1889.

*Rouen*: 1/0; Atlantic, 5/64–7/64; Millwood, London, England, 1853; 178.5' × 20.1' × 9'; 283 gt; 165 rt, i/sw; W. Patrick Campbell of St. George, Bermuda; captured by the *Keystone State* July 2, 1864, while heading toward Wilmington. Condemned at a prize court and sold to private interests who returned her to blockade running as the *Flora (IV)* (q.v.).

*Ruby (I)*: 10/8; Atlantic and Gulf, 2/63–6/63; Henderson and Company, Renfrew, Scotland, 1854; 177.4' × 17.1' × 8.3'; i/sw; George Wigg for Alexander Collie and Company; chased ashore and destroyed while trying to reach Charleston June 11, 1863, off Lighthouse Inlet, S.C.

*Ruby (II)*: 1/0; Gulf, 12/64–2/65; Henderson, Coulborn and Company, Renfrew, Scotland, 1857; 187' × 16.8' × 9'; 182 rt; ?/sw; captured by the *Proteus* Feb. 27,

1864, while heading toward St. Marks. Sold by prize court to private interests June 26, 1865. Abandoned in 1874.

*Ruby (III)*: Jones, Quiggin and Company, Liverpool, England, 1865; 261.1' × 33' × 15.6'; 900 gt; 500 rt; 1391 bt; s/sw; J. K. Gilliat and Company contracted to build the vessel for the Confederacy. J. K. Gilliat and Company to operate the vessel until they received payment in cotton from the Confederacy. Unfinished at the war's end, sold to Turkish Navy and converted to a gunboat.

*Run Her*: John and William Dudgeon, London, England, 1865; 230' × 27' × 14.6'; 829 gt; i/ts; lost at Terceira Island, Azores, on voyage out.

·*Sachem*: Gulf; built in New York, New York, 1844; 121' × 23.5' × 7.5'; 197 bt; w/ sc; T. W. House for King and Company; Union gunboat captured by Confederates Sept. 8, 1864, at Sabine Pass, Texas. Later sold by Confederacy to T. W. House. Reportedly renamed *Clarinda* by King and Company. There is no evidence that she ever ran the blockade, though she may have escaped to Mexico.

*Saint Johns*: 2/1; Atlantic, 2/63–4/63; W. F. Willink, New York, New York, 1853; rebuilt in Savannah in 1857; 150' × 26' × 8.3'; 355 bt; w/sw; William McLean, possibly for the Importing and Exporting Company of Georgia; captured Apr. 18, 1863 off Cape Romain, S.C. heading toward Charleston by the *Stettin*. Sold by prize court to private interests, she was returned to blockade running under the name *Spaulding* (q.v.).

*Saint Mary*: Harlan and Hollingsworth, Wilmington, Delaware, 1856; 160' × 28' × 8'; 450 bt; 337 gt; i/sw; vessel sunk in the St. John's River in May 1862, on the evacuation of Jacksonville. She was purchased while still under water by the Importing and Exporting Company of Georgia. The vessel was raised and renamed *Nick King* but increased Union pressure forced her to be scuttled a second time on Feb. 7, 1864. Raised by Federal forces she was used as a Union transport in the Quartermaster Department from 1864 to 1868, under the name *Genesee*. Sold to private interests in 1868, she was renamed *Nick King*. Lost off Darien, Georgia June 30, 1874.

*Salvor*: 1/0; Gulf, 10/61; Van Syke, Motter and Company, Buffalo, New York, 1856; 183' × 26.6' × 19'; w/sc; John McKay; built as the *M. S. Perry*, later renamed *Salvor*. Captured by the *Keystone State* in Gulf, Oct. 31, 1861, while trying to reach Tampa Bay. Sold at prize court to private interests March 1, 1862. Abandoned in 1877.

*Savannah*: 1/0; Atlantic, 8/63; built at New York, New York, 1856; 169.5' × 30' × 8.5'; 406 bt; w/sw; built as the *Everglade*, she was taken over by the state of Georgia at the start of the war and renamed *Savannah*. She was transferred to the CSN as the *Savannah*, but on April 28, 1863, she was renamed *Oconee*. In the summer of 1863, she was declared unfit for naval service and sold to private interests who returned her to the name *Savannah*. Foundered while trying to run out of Savannah via St. Catherine's Sound, Aug. 18, 1863.

*Scotia (I)*: 3/2; Atlantic, 7/62–10/62; Wigram and Company, Blackwall, England, 1847; 202'2" × 28'4" × 13'7"; 479 gt; i/sw; W. Forwood and A. Forwood for Leech, Harrison and Forwood and Company; purchased for £6750 in December 1861; captured by the *Restless* Oct. 24, 1862, while trying to reach Charleston in Bull's Bay, S.C. Sold by prize court to private interests who returned her to blockade running as the *Fanny and Jenny* (q.v.).

*Scotia (II)*: 6/5; Atlantic, 10/63–3/64; Tod and McGregor, Glasgow, Scotland, 1845; 141.3' × 17.5' × 8.7'; 165 gt; 82 rt; i/sw; owner Otto Henry Kaselack; captured by the *Connecticut* March 1, 1864, coming out of Wilmington.

*Scottish Chief*: 1/0; Gulf, 10/63; built at Wilmington, N.C., 1855; 123'9" × 18' × 4'9"; 102 bt; w/sw; destroyed Oct. 16, 1863, in Hillsboro River, Florida, by a Union small boat expedition.

*Sea King*: Alexander Stephen and Sons, Glasgow, Scotland, 1863; 230' × 32' × 20.5'; w/sc; 790 gt; purchased by the Confederacy in 1864, sailed from Liverpool in October 1864, and was outfitted at sea by the *Laurel*. Renamed *Shenandoah*, she served as a commerce raider until Nov. 6, 1865, when she was turned over to English authorities at Liverpool. Eventually sold to private owners, she was lost in the Indian Ocean in 1879.

*Sea Queen*: See *Lloyd*.

*Secret*: Bowdler, Chaffer and Company, Seacomb, England, 1864; 231' × 26' × 11'; 467 gt; 800 bt; s/sw; owned by John Newton Beech; Contracted to Jones, Quiggin and Company who subcontracted construction to Bowdler, Chaffer and Company. Vessel arrived at Nassau Jan. 19, 1865, but never ran the blockade. She then went to Halifax where she was eventually sold to the Quebec Steamship Company March 1, 1867. Sold to foreign interests in 1888.

*Selma*: New York, New York, 1856; 250' × 30.6' × 9'; 672 bt; ?/sw; built as the *Florida* for the New Orleans and Mobile Mail Company, converted to a CSA gunboat, renamed *Selma* July 1862; captured Aug. 5, 1864, at the Battle of Mobile Bay. Sold to private interests July 12, 1865. Foundered in 1868 off the coast of Texas.

*Siren*: 2/0; Atlantic, 4/64–6/64; 110' × 17' × 7'; 87 rt; ?/sc; named *Lady of Lyon* before being sold to blockade running interests. Captured by the *Keystone State* June 5, 1864, off Beaufort, N.C.

*Sirius*: See *Alice*.

*Snipe*: Jones, Quiggin and Company, Liverpool, England, 1865; 224' × 24' × 11.4'; 409 gt; 645 bt; s/sw; J. K. Gilliat contracted to build the vessel for the

Confederacy. She was to be turned over to the Confederacy upon payment in cotton to J. K. Gilliat. Unfinished at the war's end.

*Soler*: 4/2; Gulf, 5/63–6/63; built in New York, New York, 1841; 249′ × 28.5′ × 10′; 605 bt; built as the *Worcester*, sold to Spanish interests in April 1863, and renamed *Soler*; lost at sea while heading for Mobile in mid-June, 1863.

*Southerner*: Stockton-on-Tees, England, 1863; 294′9″ × 38′2″ × 24′; 1953 gt; w/sc; vessel had a wooden hull on an iron frame; John Archibald Kerr Wilson for Fraser, Trenholm and Company; used to carry goods to and from England to the West Indies. She was the largest vessel built at Stockton-on-Tees up to this time.

*Southwick*: Sunderland, England, 1861: 210′ × 28′ × 17.7′; 591 gt; 467 rt; ?/sc; Edward Lawrence and Company; used to carry goods to and from England to the West Indies

*Spaulding*: 3/2; Atlantic, 7/63–10/63; W. F. Willink, New York, New York, 1853, rebuilt in Savannah in 1857; 150′ × 26′ × 8.3′; 355 bt; w/sw; formerly *St. Johns* (q.v.), she was sold at a prize court to private interests who renamed her *Spaulding* and returned her to blockade running. Captured by the *Union* Oct. 11, 1863, east of St. Andrews Bay, Georgia, while heading for Charleston.

*Spunkie*: 9/8; Atlantic, 8/63–2/64; Tod and McGregor, Glasgow, (Partick) Scotland, 1857; 191.3′ × 18.2′ × 7.6′; 166 gt; 81 rt; i/sw; owner listed as E. L. Lomnitz; sank while trying to enter Old Inlet off Fort Caswell, N.C., Feb. 9, 1864.

*Stag*: 3/2; Atlantic, 11/64–1/65; Bowdler, Chaffer and Company, Seacomb, England, 1864; 230′ × 26′ × 12′; 465 gt; 299 rt; s/sw; J. Jones for Fraser, Trenholm and Company; vessel to be transferred to the Confederacy upon receipt of payment in cotton; Contracted to Jones, Quiggin and Company who subcontracted construction to Bowdler, Chaffer and Company. Captured by the *Malvern* Jan. 19, 1865, in the Cape Fear River after the fall of Fort Fisher. Sold by prize court to private interests and renamed *Zenobia* Mar. 24, 1865. Sold to foreign interests in 1870.

*Star*: 2/2; Atlantic, 12/63–12/64; Tod and McGregor, Glasgow (Partick), Scotland, 1849; 156′ × 17.9′ × 8.4′; i/sw; burst a boiler in Nassau December 1864. Removed from blockade running in the spring of 1864, though continued to operate between the islands for the rest of the war. Survived the war.

*Star of the West*: Jeremiah Simonson, Greenpoint, New York, 1852; 228′ × 32′ × 24′; 1172 bt; w/sw; built as the *San Juan*, but renamed *Star of the West* before launching. Chartered to carry relief forces to Fort Sumter and later chartered to pick up Federal forces in Texas. Captured by the *General Rusk* Apr. 17, 1861, and taken to New Orleans. Taken into CSN in May 1861, and renamed *St. Philip*. Sunk as an obstruction in the Yazoo River in March 1863.

*Stettin*: 1/0; Atlantic, 4/62–5/62; Pile, Sunderland, England, 1861; 171′ × 27′ × 15.5′; 480 rt; i/sc; Zachariah C. Pearson for Z. C. Pearson and Company; captured by the *Bienville* May 4, 1862, off Charleston. Taken into the USN. Sold to private interests July 2, 1865, renamed *Sheridan*. Lost in 1866.

*Stonewall Jackson*: See *Leopard*.

*Stono*: 1/0; Atlantic, 6/63; Lawrence and Foulks; Nyack, New Jersey, 1851; 171'6" × 31'4" × 9'; 453 bt; w/sc; CSN; The *Stono* had been the USN gunboat *Isaac Smith*, which was captured Jan. 30, 1863, in the Stono River near Charleston, S.C. Taken over by the CSN she was eventually outfitted as a blockade runner. Ran aground and burned by her crew on June 5, 1863, off Fort Moultrie while trying to escape from Charleston harbor.

*Stormy Petrel*: 1/0; 10/64–12/64; William Simons and Company, Renfrew, Scotland, 1864; 225' × 25' × 11.5'; 220 rt; i/sw; John Lawrence for the Anglo-Confederate Trading Company; Sometimes referred to as the *Petrel*. Ran aground and destroyed in a gale while trying to enter New Inlet, N.C., Dec. 7–15, 1864.

*Sunbeam*: 1/0; Atlantic, 9/62; built in England, 1857; 132' × 25.6' × 9'; 283 bt; i/sw; Henry Lafone for Leech, Harrison and Forwood; captured by the *State of Georgia* and the *Mystic* near New Inlet, N.C., Sept. 28, 1862. Sold by prize court to private interests and renamed *Moonlight*.

*Susan Beirne*: 1/0; Atlantic, 12/64; Aitken and Mansel, Whiteinch, Scotland, 1864; 252.2' × 31' × 11.5'; 637 gt; 495 rt; s/sw; Henry Lafone for the Importing and Exporting Company of Georgia; cost to build £12,345.3.6; attempted to run into Wilmington in late December 1864, but returned to Bermuda in a leaking condition. Survived the war.

*Susanna*: 12/11; Gulf, 4/64–11/64; Tod and McGregor, Glasgow, Scotland, 1860; 179' × 18' × 7'; 198 rt; i/sw; originally built and operated as the *Mail* (q.v.), the vessel was captured in October 1863, condemned, and sold to private interests who returned her to blockade running under the name *Susanna*. Sometimes referred to as the *Susanna Mail*. Captured by the *Metacomet* Nov. 27, 1864, coming out of Galveston.

*Suwanee*: Baltimore, 1850; 189.6' × 27.2' × 10.6'; 666 bt; w/sw; built as the *Pampero*, rebuilt and lengthened, and renamed *Suwanee* March 1856. Hired by USQD to bring troops out of Texas and later seized by the USQD to keep her from returning to a Southern port. Foundered Dec. 4, 1866, off Cape Romano, Florida.

*Swan (I)*: 1/0; Gulf, 5/62; 188' × 36'6" × 7'7"; 487 bt; w/sw; a river steamboat, captured by the *Amanda* and the *Bainbridge*. Sold by prize court to private interests Jan. 9, 1863. Lost Feb. 19, 1863.

*Swan (II)*: Bowdler, Chaffer and Company, Seacomb, England, 1865; 216' × 26' × 10.9'; 470 gt; 296 rt; s/sw; Contracted to Jones, Quiggin and Company who subcontracted construction to Bowdler, Chaffer and Company. Unfinished at the war's end.

*Syren*: 33/33; Atlantic, 10/63–2/65; built at Greenwich, Kent, England, 1863; 169.5' × 24' × 15.5'; 169 rt; 475 bt; ?/sw; Charleston Importing and Exporting Company; captured Feb. 18, 1865, at Charleston after the city was evacuated. Sold to private interests and renamed *Reindeer* July 7, 1865. Lost in 1870. The most successful of the blockade runners.

*Talisman*: 6/5; Atlantic, 9/64–12/64; John Scott and Sons, Greenock, Scotland, 1864; 201.3' × 21.15' × 9.5'; 266 gt; 173 rt; 359 bt; i/sw; William Boyle for the Albion Trading Company; often confused with a large screw steamer also built by John Scott and Sons and named *Talisman*, which carried supplies to the islands and Matamoras. Hit wreck of *Raleigh* while trying to escape out of New Inlet Dec. 18, 1864. She returned to Wilmington for repairs, but was caught in a gale after escaping from Wilmington and was sunk on Dec. 29, 1864.

*Tulluhussee*: See *Alalanta*.

*Tartar*: Henderson, Coulborn and Company, Renfrew, Scotland, 1864; 230' × 25' × 11.5'; i/sw; contracted to carry two pairs of CSN torpedo boat engines to the Confederacy. Left Glasgow in November 1864, but damaged in a storm and put into Cardiff, she never ran the blockade. Also referred to as the *Emily*.

*Tennessee*: 1/0; Gulf, 2/62; John R. Robb, Baltimore, Maryland, 1853; 210' × 33'11" × 16'11"; 1149 bt; w/sw; vessel had a wooden hull on an iron frame. R. B. Summer listed as owner on a CSA register dated Feb. 6, 1862; captured at New Orleans on the evacuation of the city and commissioned as the USS *Tennessee* May 2, 1862. Renamed *Mobile* Sept. 1, 1864. Sold to private interests and renamed *Republic* May 12, 1865. Foundered Oct. 25, 1865, off Savannah, Georgia.

*Texas*: Thomas Collyer, New York, New York, 1852; 216' × 34'6" × 16'10"; 1223 bt; w/sw; probably converted to a gunboat at New Orleans and destroyed at the Battle of New Orleans, though exact disposition is unclear.

*Texas Ranger*: 1/1; Gulf, 7/62; built in New Albany, Indiana, 1851; 137' × 27.5' × 6.5'; 159 bt; w/sw; survived the war.

*The Dare*: 1/0; Atlantic, 12/63-1/64; Alexander Stephen and Sons, Glasgow, Scotland; 211.7' × 23.1' × 9.4'; 311 gt; 179 rt; i/sw; David McNutt for the Richmond Importing and Exporting Company; vessel seems to have been under charter to the above company. Chased ashore and destroyed by the *Aries* and *Montgomery* Jan. 7, 1864, off Lockwood Folly, N.C. while trying to reach Wilmington.

*Theodora*: 7/6; Atlantic, 7/61–6/62; Lawrence Sneden, Greenpoint, New York, 1851; 177' × 27.5' × 11'2"; 518 bt; w/sw; vessel built as the *Carolina* but name changed to *Gordon* before her launching. She was owned by a stock company that used her as a privateer. In August 1861 she was purchased by John Fraser and Company and renamed *Theodora*. In early 1862 she was sold to the Confederate Navy and renamed *Nassau*. Captured by the *State of Georgia* and the

*Victoria* off Old Inlet, N.C., May 28, 1862 while trying to reach Wilmington. She was also referred to as the *Black Witch*.

*Thistle (I)*: 2/1; Atlantic, 1/62–5/63; Lawrence Hill and Company, Port Glasgow, Scotland, 1859; 184.5′ × 25.2′ × 12.5′; 386 gt; 206 rt; 606 bt; w/sc; vessel had a wooden hull on an iron frame; George Wigg for the Navigation Company until March 1862, when sold to John Ferguson; ran aground Mar. 8, 1862, off Battery Beauregard while trying to escape from Charleston. Salvaged and sold to John Ferguson for $80,000 Confederate. Renamed *Cherokee*, she was captured by the *Canandaigua* and *Flag* May 8, 1862, while trying to leave Charleston. Purchased from prize court and taken into the USN. Sold to private interests Aug. 1, 1865. Sold to foreign interests in 1868.

*Thistle (II)*: 3/2; Atlantic, 2/64–6/64; Lawrence Hill and Company, Port Glasgow, Scotland, 1864; 201.5′ × 25.9′ × 12.3′; 305 rt; 636 bt; i/sw; James Archibald Kerr Wilson for Fraser, Trenholm and Company; cost to build £22,000; captured by the *Fort Jackson* June 4, 1864, while heading for Wilmington. Purchased from prize court and taken into the USN as the *Dumbarton*. Sold to the Quebec Steamship Company in 1867, and renamed *City of Quebec*. Wrecked April 28, 1870 off Green Island, Canada.

*Thomas L. Wragg*: See *Nashville*.

*Tristram Shandy*: 3/1; 4/63–5/63; Aitken, Mansel, Whiteinch, Glasgow, Scotland; 225.5′ × 23.5′ × 9.6′; 344 gt; 211 rt; i/sw; Matthew Isaac Wilson for the Anglo-Confederate Trading Company; captured by the *Kansas* May 15, 1864, coming out of Wilmington. Purchased from prize court and taken into the USN. Name changed to *Boxer* June 15, 1865. Sold to private interests Sept. 1, 1868 and renamed *Firefly*. Ran aground and lost in 1874.

*Triton*: 2/2; Gulf, 8/63–1/65; ?/sc; J. H. Wilson; very little information on this vessel.

*Tropic*: 1/0; Atlantic, 1/63; built at New York, New York, 1838; 225′ × 24.5′ × ??; 500 bt; 333 rt; w/sw; built as the *Huntress*, she was purchased by the State of Georgia in March 1861 for use as a gunboat. Turned over to the CSN at Charleston in April 1861 and served as a transport until October 1862, when she was sold to A. J. White and Son for use as a blockade runner for $133,650 Confederate. Renamed *Tropic*, ran aground and was burned by her crew while trying to escape from Charleston Harbor Jan. 18, 1863.

*Tubal Cain*: 1/0; Atlantic, 6/62–7/62; Blackwood and Gordon, Paisley, Scotland, 1853; 151.7′ × 22′ × 12.4′; 286 gt; 194 rt; i/sc; G. S. Sanderson; captured by the *Octorora* July 24, 1862, trying to reach Charleston.

*Union (I)*: 1/0; Gulf, 5/63; built at Philadelphia, 1861; 128′ × 23′11″ × 8′6″; 115 gt; 52 rt; 238 bt; ?/sw; M. Avendano of Havana; seems to have left Galveston before the blockade was established. Sold to M. Avendano, who may have converted her to a blockade runner, or, as by testimony at the prize court hearing, had sent her to Matamoras for use as a tug when captured by the *Huntsville* on May 19, 1863. She was condemned as a blockade runner at the prize court and sold to private interests who named her *Rosita* (q.v.), who operated her as a blockade runner. She was again captured, sold at a prize court and again operated as a blockade runner under the name *Carolina* (q.v.).

*Union (II)*: 2/1; Gulf, 8/62; William H. Webb, New York, New York, 1850; 215' × 34' × 22'; 1200 bt; w/sw; a Cuban owned vessel; captured by the *J. S. Chambers* coming out of Galveston, Aug. 28, 1862.

*Venus*: 7/6; Atlantic, 6/63–10/63; J. & G. Thomson, Govan, Scotland, 1862; 159.2' × 17.1' × 8.7'; i/sw; Crenshaw, Collie and Company; chased ashore and destroyed by the *Nansemond* near New Inlet, N.C., while trying to enter the Cape Fear River, Oct. 21, 1863.

*Vesta*: 1/0; Atlantic, 12/63–1/64; John and William Dudgeon, London, England, 1863; 165' × 23' × 13'; 262 rt; i/ts; Crenshaw, Collie and Company; ran aground and destroyed while trying to reach Wilmington near Little River Inlet, N.C., Jan. 11, 1864.

*Victoria (I)*: 6/5; Gulf, 1/62–11/62; George Greenman, Mystic, Conn., 1859; 180' × 29.5' × 9.6'; 487 bt; w/sw; John D. Champlin of New Orleans; there are contradictory reports that the vessel survived the war or that she was destroyed in November 1862, in Atchafalaya Bay, Louisiana. The latter seems more likely.

*Victoria (II)*: Hull, England, 1856; 173' × 26' × 14'; 441 gt; 300 rt; ?/sc; Fraser, Trenholm and Company; used to carry supplies to and from the West Indies.

*Virgin*: 1/1; Gulf, 6/64–8/64; Aitken and Mansel, Whiteinch, Glasgow, Scotland, 1864; 216' × 24.5' × 10.9'; 442 bt; 291 rt; i/sw; European Trading Company; taken over at Mobile by the CSA after the fall of the harbor forts. Escaped to Gainesville, Ala., on evacuation of Mobile, and was captured there on April 12, 1865. Sold to private interests by prize court Mar. 12, 1866. Sold to the federal government May 15, 1867. Sold to private interests Sept. 26, 1870, and renamed *Virginius*. Employed as a gun-runner to Cuba under the former blockade-running captain Joseph Fry, she was captured by Spanish authorities in 1873. The resulting execution of Fry and the majority of his crew caused an international incident between the United States and Spain. She was returned to her owners and later lost off Cape Fear, N.C., Dec. 26, 1873.

*Virginia (I)*: 7/6; Atlantic, 9/64–4/65; John and William Dudgeon, London, England, 1864; 829 gt; 456 rt; i/sw; survived the war.

*Virginia (II)*: 1/0; Gulf, 12/62–1/63; 170' × 26'2" × 14'8"; 800 bt; i/sc; H. O. Brewer and Company; former slaver *Noe-Daquy*, renamed *Virginia* in December 1862, when converted to a blockade runner. Captured by the *Sonoma* and the *Wachusett* off the coast of Mexico, Jan. 18, 1863. Purchased from prize court and taken into the USN. Sold to private interests Nov. 30, 1865. Converted to a barge March 24, 1885.

*Vixen*: 1/0; Atlantic, 10/64–12/64; London, England, 1864; 224' × 26.3' × 9'; 462 bt; i/sw; captured by the *Rhode Island* Dec. 1, 1864, heading to Wilmington. Sold by prize court to private interests May 1, 1865. Sold foreign in 1869.

*Vulture*: 2/2; Atlantic, 11/64–4/65; Aitken and Mansel, Kelvinhaugh, Scotland, 1864; 242' × 25.7' × 10.6'; 482 gt; 355 rt; i/sw; survived the war.

*Wando*: 4/3; Atlantic, 6/64–10/64; Kirkpatrick and McIntyre, Glasgow, Scotland, 1864; 225.3' × 26.1' × 11.3'; 650 bt; i/sw; Henry Lafone for the Chicora Importing Exporting Company; came out of England as the *Let Her Rip*, renamed *Wando* on her arrival at Wilmington. Captured by the *Fort Jackson* Oct. 21, 1864 off Cape Romain, S.C., after clearing Wilmington.

*Warrior*: 1/0; Gulf, 8/63; built in Mobile, Ala., 1857; 129'9" × 33' × 6'5"; 378 bt; w/sw; an Alabama River packet. Captured by the *Gertrude* Aug. 17, 1863, coming out of Mobile. Returned to private interests after the war. Abandoned in 1872.

*Wasp*: Jones, Quiggin and Company, Liverpool, England, 1864; 250' × 28' × 10'9"; 800 bt; 280 rt; s/sw; unfinished at war's end.

*Wave*: 1/1; Gulf, 6/64–1/65; built in Mongohela, Pa., 1863; 154' × 31' × 5'2"; 229 bt; w/sw; Thomas W. House for King and Company; built as the *Argosy* 2, renamed *Wave* when she was purchased by the USN for use as a gunboat. Captured by the Confederacy May 6, 1864, in Calcasieu Pass, sold to Thomas W. House for use as a blockade runner. Little information on the vessel, may have escaped to Mexico.

*Wave Queen*: 1/0; Atlantic, 2/63; Alexander Stephen and Sons, Kelvinghaugh, Glasgow, Scotland, 1861; 180' × 30' × 12.5'; 775 bt; ?/sc; destroyed by the *Conemaugh* Feb. 25, 1863, in the North Santee River, S.C.

*Whisper*: 2/2; Atlantic, 12/64–2/65; Pile, Spence and Company, West Hartlepool, England, 1864; 260' × 27' × 13'; i/sw; survived the war.

*Widgeon*: Jones, Quiggin and Company, Liverpool, England, 1865; 224' × 24' × 11.4'; 409 gt; 645 bt; s/sw; J. K. Gilliat and Company contracted to build the vessel for the Confederacy. Vessel to be turned over to the Confederacy once she had been paid for in cotton. Unfinished at war's end.

*Wild Dayrell*: 5/4; Atlantic, 12/63–2/64; Jones, Quiggin and Company, Liverpool, England, 1863; 215' × 20' × 10.9'; 320 gt; i/sw; Edward Lawrence for Anglo-Confederate Trading Company; chased aground and destroyed by the *Sassacus* Feb. 1, 1864, near Topsail Inlet, N.C.

*Wild Rover*: 9/8; Atlantic, 9/64–1/65; J. & G. Thomson, Govan, Scotland; ?/sw; Anglo-Confederate Trading Company; survived the war.

*William Bagley*: 1/0; Gulf, 7/63; built in Belle Vernon, Pa., 1854; 173′ × 32′9″ × 7′6″; 396 bt; w/sw; an Alabama River packet, captured by the *DeSoto, Kennebec* and *Ossipee* July 18, 1863, coming out of Mobile. Purchased from prize court and taken into USQD.

*William G. Hewes*: 12/9; Gulf and Atlantic, 5/62–11/63; Harlan and Hollingsworth, Wilmington, Del., 1860; 239.4′ × 33′ × 10′; 747 gt; 1477 bt; i/sw; owned by R. D. Smith in April 1861, sold in Havana, April 1863, to the Importing and Exporting Company of South Carolina; renamed *Ella and Annie*, April 1863. Chartered by the Confederacy to run supplies to Texas in the summer of 1863, she was badly damaged in a storm and was unable to make the voyage. Captured by the *Niphon* Nov. 9, 1863, while trying to reach Wilmington. Purchased from prize court and taken into the USN as the *Malvern*. Sold to private interests Jan. 4, 1866, and renamed *William G. Hewes*. Lost Feb. 20, 1895, off Cuba.

*William H. Webb*: 1/0 as a blockade runner, 1/0 as a warship; William H. Webb, New York, New York, 1856; 190′ × 31′ × 12′; 655 bt; w/sw; taken over by the CSN after the fall of New Orleans; sometimes referred to as the *Webb*. Reported to be one of the fastest vessels in the nation. Attempted to run to the Gulf from the mouth of the Red River, but was stopped by the *Richmond* on April 24, 1865, below New Orleans. The vessel was run aground and destroyed by her crew to prevent capture.

*William Seabrook*: 2/1; Atlantic, 4/62–7/62; built at New York, New York, 1831; 136′ × 24′ × 9′2″; 227 bt; w/sw; registered owner George Alexander Stuart of St. Vincent; renamed *Emilie*, June 3, 1862, captured by the *Flag* and *Restless* in Bull's Bay, S.C., while trying to reach Charleston.

*Will of the Wisp*: 15/12; Atlantic and Gulf, 11/63–2/65; William Simons and Company, Renfrew, Scotland, 1863; 210′ × 23′ × 10′; 117 rt; 511 bt; i/sw; H. Lawrence for the Anglo-Confederate Trading Company 11/63–10/64, then sold to Power, Low and Company in Oct. 1864; ran aground and destroyed Feb. 9, 1865, while trying to reach Galveston.

*Wren*: 7/6; Gulf, 1/65–4/65; Laird and Sons, Birkenhead, England, 1864; 211.1′ × 23.2′ × 10.4′; 389 gt; 296 rt; 800 bt; s/sw; John Laird for Fraser, Trenholm and Company until paid for in cotton by the Confederacy; seized by her crew, who refused to return to Liverpool in June 1865. She was taken to Key West, where she was condemned and sold as a prize of war. In a following court case the *Wren* was eventually returned to her owners, 1868.

*Yorktown* (*I*): 1/0; Gulf, 8/62; built in Cincinnati, Ohio, 1848; 173′ × 28′3″ × 6′6″; 298 bt; w/sw; John Johnson and Charles A. Deshon of Mobile; foundered after clearing Mobile about Aug. 26, 1862.

*Yorktown* (*II*): William H. Webb, New York, New York, 1859; 250′ × 34′ × 17.5′; 1403 bt; w/sw; seized at Richmond April 1861, later turned over to the CSN and renamed *Patrick Henry*. In October 1863 she became the home of the Confederate Naval Academy. Burned April 3, 1865, on the evacuation of Richmond.

*Young Republic*: 2/1; Atlantic, 4/64–5/64; built in Brooklyn, New York, 1864; 205′ × 29′10″ × 9′6″; 755 bt; ?/sw; captured by the *Grand Gulf* after escaping from Wilmington May 6, 1864.

*Zephine*: 7/6; Gulf, 8/64–3/65; Harlan and Hollingsworth, Wilmington, Del., 1864; 225′ × 32′ × 10′; 850 bt; i/sw; reportedly sold to blockade running interests for £20,000; built as the *Frances*, sold to blockade running interests in Havana and renamed *Marian*. She is later listed as being named the *Zephine*. Sometimes mistakenly referred to as the *Frances Marion*. Survived the war and returned to U.S. trade. Abandoned in 1899.

# Notes

## Chapter One. We Have No Commercial Marine

1. Memorandum Book Relating to Agents and Supplies. Record Group 109, National Archives, Washington, D.C., hereafter listed as Quartermaster Memorandum Book; Josiah Gorgas, "Ordnance of the Confederacy," *Army Ordnance*, Vol. XVI (1936), pp. 212–214; Josiah Gorgas, "Notes on the Ordnance Department of the Confederate Government," *Southern Historical Society Papers*, Vol. XII (January–February 1884), pp. 68–75.

2. *Charleston News and Courier*, May 20–Apr. 12, 1861.

3. William Howard Russell, *My Diary North and South*, 2 Vols. (London: Bradbury and Evans, 1863), Vol. I, pp. 142, 170–171, 258.

4. *Hunt's Merchant Magazine and Commercial Review*, XLI (July–December 1859), p. 129; XLII (January–June, 1860), pp. 167–168; XLIII (July–December 1860), p. 456; XLIV (January–June 1861), p. 354; XLV (July–December 1861), pp. 1–3; hereinafter listed as *Hunt's*. "Statistics of Foreign and Domestic Commerce of the United States." Sen. Exec. Doc. No. 55, 38th Congress, 1st Session, 1864, p. 61; Robert Royal Russel, *Economic Aspects of Southern Sectionalism, 1840–1861* (Urbana: University of Illinois, 1924), pp. 199–204, 207–210; Frank L. Owsley, *King Cotton Diplomacy; Foreign Relations of the Confederate States of America* (Chicago: University of Chicago Press, 1935), pp. 3–15.

5. Russell, *My Diary*, Vol. I, p. 142; Russel, *Economic Aspects*, pp. 40–41, 46–49, 190, 290.

6. "Statistics of Foreign and Domestic Commerce," p. 61; "Record of Entrances and Clearances of Charleston, New Orleans, Mobile, 1858–1860," and "Mobile and New Orleans Manifests, 1858–1860," Record Group 36; "Outward and Inward Manifests for Charleston, South Carolina, December 1858–December 1864," Record Group 365, Treasury Department Records, National Archives, Washington, D.C.; John H. Morrison, *History of American Steam Navigation* (New York: Argosy-Antiquarian, 1967), pp. 434–469.

7. John B. Hefferman, "The Blockade of the Southern Confederacy; 1861–1865," *Smithsonian Journal of History* II (Winter 1967–1968), p. 25; Gerald S. Graham, "The Ascendary of the Sailing Ship 1850–1885," *Economic History Review* IX (1956–1957), pp. 74–77; Charleston, Mobile and New Orleans Entrances and Clearances."

8. *War of the Rebellion: Official Records of the Union and Confederate Navies* (Washington: Government Printing Office, 1921), Series I, Vol. IV, pp. 156, 340, hereinafter listed as *O.R.N.*; all citations will be Series I unless otherwise noted. Owsley, *King Cotton Diplomacy*, p. 229.

9. Russell, *My Diary*, Vol. I, p. 258; Owsley, *King Cotton Diplomacy*, pp. 222–226.

10. John D. Hays, editor, *Samuel Francis Du Pont: A Selection from His Civil War Letters*, 3 Vols. (Ithaca: Cornell University Press, 1969), Vol. I, pp. 71, 75, 85, 86; "Papers of the Blockade Board," Record Group 45, Old Military Records, National Archives, Washington, D.C.

11. Hefferman, "Blockade of the Southern Confederacy," pp. 25–26; Russel, *Economic Aspects*, pp. 111–113, 118.

12. "Permanent Fortifications and Sea Coast Defences." House of Representatives, Report No. 36, 37th Congress, 2d Sess., Apr. 23, 1862, p. 41.

13. Morrison, *American Steam Navigation*, pp. 462–464; *Hunts* XLV, p. 17; "Permanent Fortifications," pp. 39, 188.

14. *O.R.N.*, Vol. XII, pp. 198–200; *Hunt's* XLV, p. 17.

15. *Hunt's* XLV, pp. 17–18; *O.R.N.*, Vol. XII, pp. 187–195; "Report of the Superintendent of the Coast Survey Showing the Progress of the Survey during the Year 1863," Exec. Doc. No. 11, 38th Congress, 1st Session (Washington: Government Printing Office, 1864), Map 11.

16. Russell, *My Diary*, p. 138; *Hunt's* LV, p. 17; *O.R.N.*, Vol. XII, pp. 196–201.

17. Chris Fonvielle, "Fall of Fort Fisher," Manuscript, Blockade Runner Museum, Carolina Beach, North Carolina; James R. Soley, *The Blockade and the Cruisers* (New York: Scribner, 1883), pp. 91, 158; Richard E. Wood, "Port Town at War; Wilmington North Carolina 1860–1865," (Ph.D. dissertation, Florida State University, 1976), pp. 8–11; *Wilmington Daily Journal*, June 4, 1861; *O.R.N.*, Vol. VI, pp. 177–178, Vol. XII, pp. 198–201; Morrison, *American Steam Navigation*, pp. 442–443.

18. *Hunt's* XLV, p. 18.

19. Edward King, *The Great South*, 2 Vols. (New York: Burr Franklin, 1875), Vol. II, pp. 440–441; *Hunt's* XLV, p. 18; Soley, *The Blockade*, pp. 107–108; "Statement of Revenue Collected Annually 1854–1859;" Francis B. C. Bradlee, *Blockade Running during the Civil War and the Effect of Land and Water Transportation on the Confederacy* (Salem: Essex Institute, 1925), pp. 209–210; John C. Schwab, *A Financial and Industrial History of the South during the Civil War* (New York: C. Scribner, 1901), p. 274; Russel, *Economic Aspects*, pp. 113, 118, 256; Gregory Allen Greb, "Charleston, South Carolina Merchants, 1815–1860; Urban Leadership in the Antebellum South," (Ph.D. dissertation, University of California, San Diego, 1975), pp. 24–26, 148–213; *Report on the Harbor of Charleston, S.C.* (Charleston: Walker, Evans, and Company, 1858); Schwab, *A Financial History*, p. 272–275; Ethel Trenholm Seabrook Nepveux, *George Alfred Trenholm* (Charleston: Comprint, 1973), pp. 21–23; *Charleston Mercury*, June 7, 1861; "Report on the Harbor of Charleston"; "Particulars of the Steam Dredger General Moultrie," *Journal of the Franklin Institute* LXII (December 1956), p. 407.

20. *Hunt's* XLV, p. 19; *War of the Rebellion: The Official Records of the Union and Confederate Armies* (Washington: Government Printing Office, 1889–1901), Series I, Vol. XLV, pp. 47–73, hereinafter listed as *O.R.A.*; all citations will be Series I unless otherwise noted. John Edwin Johns, "Florida in the Confederacy," (Ph.D. dissertation, University of North Carolina, 1959), p. 123; Marcus W. Price, "Ships that Tested the Blockade of Georgian and East Florida Ports, 1861–1865," *American Neptune* XV (January 1962), pp. 241–260.

21. Russell, *My Diary*, Vol. I, p. 217; *Hunt's* XLV, p. 19.

22. Russell, *My Diary*, p. 217; *Hunt's* XLV, pp. 19, 497–498; James D. Griffin, "Savannah Georgia during the Civil War," (Ph.D. dissertation, University of Georgia, 1963), pp. 23–25; Price, "Ships of the Georgian and East Florida Ports," p. 99; Bradlee, *Blockade Running during the Civil War*, p. 134.

23. *Hunt's* XLV, p. 19–20; Griffin, "Savannah during the Civil War," p. 35; Soley, *The Blockade*, p. 109; *O.R.N.*, Vol. XII, p. 198–201.

24. *Hunt's* XLV, pp. 19–20; *O.R.N.*, Vol. XII, pp. 196–198; J. P. Staudenras, editor, "A War Correspondent's View of St. Augustine and Fernandina," *Florida Historical Quarterly* XLI (July 1962), pp. 60–65.

25. *Hunt's* XLV, pp. 20–21; Staudenras, "War Correspondent," pp. 60–65; "Permanent Fortifications," p. 195; "Papers of the Blockade Board."

26. Ibid.

27. *Hunt's* XLV, pp. 20–22; "Permanent Fortifications," p. 39.

28. Ibid.

29. *Hunt's* XLV, p. 21, 497–498; "Permanent Fortifications," p. 39.

30. *Hunt's* XLV, p. 21; William Watson Davis, "Civil War and Reconstruction in Florida," (Ph.D. dissertation, Columbia University, 1913), p. 138; Edwin B. Coddington. "The Civil War Blockade Reconsidered," in *Essays in History and International Relations in Honor of George Hubbard Blakeslee*, editors Dwight E. Lee and George McReynolds (Worchester: Clark University Press, 1949), p. 287; Alfred Thayer Mahan, *Gulf and Inland Waters* (New York: Jack Brussel, n.d.), p. 3; J. Thomas Scharf, *History of the Confederate Navy*, 2 Vols. (New York: Rogers and Sherwood, 1887), Vol. II, pp. 599–601; Permanent Fortifications," pp. 45–46.

31. Ibid.

32. *Hunt's* XLV, pp. 22, 497; *O.R.N.*, Vol. XVI, pp. 618–630.

33. *Hunt's* XLV, p. 22; Mahan, *Gulf and Inland Waters*, p. 219; "Report of the Superintendent of the Coast Survey Showing the Progress of the Survey During the Year 1860," Exec. Doc. No. 14, 36th Congress, 2d Session (Washington: Government Printing Office, 1861), Map 29.

34. Russell, *My Diary*, Vol. I, pp. 272, 280; *Hunt's* XLV, p. 22; *O.R.N.*, Vol. XVI, pp. 618–630.

35. *O.R.N.*, Vol. XVI, pp. 618–630; *Hunt's* XLV, p. 22; "Mobile and New Orleans Entrances and Clearances," Scharf, *Confederate Navy*, p. 535; Russell, *My Diary*, Vol. I, pp. 330–331.

36. Ibid.

37. Russell, *My Diary*, Vol. I, pp. 331–340; King, *The Great South*, Vol. I, pp. 50–52; *Hunt's* XLIII, p. 456; "Statement Showing the Amount of Revenue Collected Annually in Each District From June 30, 1854 to June 30, 1859, together with the Amount Expended and the persons Employed in each District." Exec. Doc. No. 33, 36th Congress, 1st Session, 1860; Robert Neal Sheridan, "The Confederate Naval Effort at New Orleans," (Masters thesis, University of South Carolina, 1954), pp. 1–4.

38. *Hunt's* XLV, pp. 22–23; 497–498; *O.R.N.*, Vol. XVI, pp. 618–630; Rollin G. Osterweis, *Romanticism and Nationalism in the Old South* (Baton Rouge; Louisiana State University Press, 1949), p. 158.

39. Osterweis, *Romanticism and Nationalism*, p. 158; Charles L. Dufour, *The Night the War Was Lost* (Garden City: Doubleday, 1960), pp. 25–27.

40. *O.R.N.*, Vol. XVI, pp. 618–630; *Hunt's* XLV, pp. 22–23.

41. *O.R.N.*, Vol. XVI, pp. 618–630; *Hunt's* XLV, pp. 22–23; *New Orleans Daily Picayune*, May 5, 1861; Robert Warren Glover, "The West Gulf Blockade, 1861–1865; An Evaluation." (Ph.D. dissertation, North Texas State University, 1974), pp. 153–155.

42. *O.R.N.*, Vol. XVI, pp. 618–630; Charles R. Haberlein, "Former Blockade Runners in the United States Navy," (Unpublished B.A. paper, Kalamazoo College, 1965), p. 5.

43. *O.R.N.*, Vol. XVI, pp. 618–630.

44. James P. Baughman, *Charles Morgan and the Development of Southern Transportation* (Nashville: Vanderbilt University Press, 1968), pp. 96–124; Morrison, *American Steam Navigation*, pp.455–457; *New Orleans Daily Picayune*, May 2, 3, 14, 26, 1861; *O.R.N.*, Vol. XVI, pp. 618–630.

45. Baughman, *Charles Morgan*, pp. 48, 96–104, 126–128; Morrison, *American Steam Navigation*, pp. 466–469.

46. Ruby Garner, "Galveston during the Civil War," (Master's thesis, University of Texas, 1927), pp. 21–22; *Galveston Weekly News*, Feb. 9, 1861; Glover, "West Gulf Blockade," pp. 177–179; George B. Davis, editor, *The Official Atlas of the Civil War* (New York: Arno Press, 1978), Plate XXXVIII, No. 1; Robert Lee Kerby, *Kirby Smith's Confederacy; The Trans-Mississippi South, 1863–1865*, p. 123; King, *The Great South*, Vol. I, pp. 101–103; *Hunt's* XLV, pp. 23–25.

47. King, *The Great South*, Vol. I, pp. 101–103; *Hunt's* XLV, pp. 23–24, 497; "New Orleans Manifests."

48. Soley, *The Blockade*, pp. 26–33; Robert Irwin Johnson, "Investment by Sea: The Civil War Blockade," *American Neptune*, XXXII (January 1972), pp. 46–47; John Niven, *Gideon Welles* (New York: Oxford University Press, 1973), pp. 355–360; For the original French text of the Declaration of Paris, see Clive Parry, ed., *The Consolidate Treaty Series*, 220 Vols. (Dobbs Ferry: Oceans Publications, 1969), Vol. CXV, pp. 1–3; For English translation, see Francis Deak and Philip C. Jesup, editors, *A Collection of Neutrality Laws, Regulations and Treaties of Various Countries*, 2 Vols. (Washington: Carnegie Endowment for International Peace, 1939), Vol. II, pp. 1473–1474.

49. Johnson, "Investment by Sea," p. 51; Soley, *The Blockade*, pp. 15–16, 27, 32–33; Charles Cowley, *Leaves from a Lawyer's Life Afloat* (Boston: Lee and Shepard, 1879), p. 11.

50. Soley, *The Blockade*, pp. 15–18; Niven, *Gideon Welles*, pp. 355–360; Hayes, *Du Pont Papers*, Vol. II, p. 446; Johnson, "Investment by Sea," p. 5.

51. Soley, *The Blockade*, pp. 14–18; Scharf, *Confederate Navy*, p. 400; Samuel B. Thompson, *Confederate Operations Abroad* (Chapel Hill: University of North Carolina Press, 1935), p. 21; Henry D. Capers, *The Life and Times of C. G. Memminger* (Richmond: Everett Waddey and Company, 1893), pp. 348–357; "Cotton Export Bonds for New Orleans, Savannah and Charleston," Record Group 365, Treasury Department Records, National Archives, Washington, D.C.

52. Johnson, "Investment by Sea," pp. 46–47; Glover, "West Gulf Blockade," p. 162; Dufour, *The Night the War was Lost*, p. 41; Marcus W. Price, "Ships that Tested the Blockade of the Gulf Ports, 1861–1865," *American Neptune* XI (October 1951), pp. 264–266; *Wilmington Daily Journal*, July 23, 1861; Soley, *The Blockade*, pp. 35, 82–91; *O.R.N.*, Vol. XVI, pp. 528–529.

53. Glover, "West Gulf Blockade," pp. 152–155; Soley, *The Blockade*, pp. 42–45; *British and Foreign Papers*, 170 Vols. (London: William Ridgeway, 1870), Vol. LV, p. 675; Price, "Ships of the Gulf Ports," pp. 264–266; Vessel Entrances and Clearances for Georgetown, Wilmington, Charleston, Mobile, New Orleans, Savannah and Beaufort," Pickett Papers, Library of Congress, Washington, D.C.; "Charleston, Mobile and New Orleans Entrances and Clearances, hereinafter referred to as Pickett Papers, Vessel Entrances and Clearances.

54. The *Nashville* was part of a steamship line organized by Spofford, Tileston, and Company of New York and James Adger of Charleston. The line was originaly made up of the steamers *Nashville, Southerner, Northerner, Marion*, and *James Adger*. On Adger's death complete control went to his New York partners. John Guthrie, *A History of Marine Engineering*, London: Hutchinson, 1971), pp. 139–142; James D. Bulloch, *The Secret Service of the Confederate States in Europe*, 2 Vols. (New York: G. P. Putnam and Sons, 1884), Vol. I, p. 104–105, 124; *Wilmington Daily Journal*, June 14, Aug. 1, 1861; Bradlee, *Blockade Running during the Civil War*, pp. 134–136; Morrison, *American Steam Navigation*, pp. 442, 463; *Charleston Mercury*, June 7, 1861; Eric Heyl, *Early American Steamers*, 6 Vols. (Buffalo: Eric Heyl, 1953–1969). Vol. I, pp. 197–198, 277–278, Vol. II, pp. 115–116; Russel, *Economic Aspects*, pp. 255–256; Creb, "Merchants," pp. 178–179; *O.R.N.*, Vol. I, p. 124, Vol. V, p. 828.

55. Lewis C. Hunter, *Steamboats on the Western Waters* (New York: Octagon Books, 1969), pp. 65–66; C. Bradford Mitchell, editor, *Merchant Steam Vessels of the United States, 1790–1868*, (Staten Island: Steamship Historical Society of America, 1975); Morrison, *American Steam Navigation*, pp. 434–472; Johns, "Florida in the Confederacy," p. 123; Price, "Ships of the Georgian and East Florida Ports," pp. 99–100; *Charleston Mercury*, July 2, 1860, and June 2, 1861; Edward A. Mueller, East Florida Steamboating, 1831–1861," *Florida Historical Quarterly* XL (January 1962), pp. 241–260.

56. Mitchell, *Merchant Steam Vessels*; Mobile Entrances and Clearances;" Scharf, *History of the Confederate Navy*, Vol. II, p. 535; Papers Pertaining to Vessels of or Involved with the Confederate States of America: Vessel Papers," Reel 29, Southern Steamship Company, Record Group 109, National Archives, Washington, D.C., hereinafter listed as Vessel Papers; Baughman, *Charles Morgan*, pp. 111–124; Haberlein, "Former Blockade Runners," p. 5; *New Orleans Daily Picayune*, May 2, 19, June 6, July 28, 1861; Morrison, *American Steam Navigation*, pp. 455–457; Mobile Inward Manifest, and Mobile Coastal Entrances, Record Group 36, Treasury Department Records, National Archives, Washington, D.C.; Mobile Entrances and Clearances, Price, "Ships of the Gulf Ports," pp. 267–268; *New Orleans Daily Picayune*, June 6, July 28, 1861; "In answer to a resolution of the Senate of the 21st instant, a report of the Secretary of the Navy, accompanied by copies of instructions given to the United States Naval forces on the coasts of Mexico, to protect the persons and property of the citizens of the United States, and copies of the official reports of Captain Jarvis and Commander Turner of the two Mexican war steamers, and the causes that led to said capture," Exec. Doc. No. 29, 36th Congress, 1st session, March 30, 1860; *O.R.N.*, Vol. IV, pp. 196–198, Vol. V, pp. 634–635; Vol. XVI, pp. 813–814; Charleston and Mobile Inward Manifests, Charleston and Mobile Coastal Vessel Entrances and Clearances, 1861, and New Orleans Clearances 1861, Record Group 36, National Archives, Washington, D.C.; Pickett Papers, Vessel Entrances and Clearances; Mobile Entrances and Clearances; *Charleston Mercury*, July 2, 1860, Aug. 22, 1860, June 3, 7, 10, 12, 1861, Nov. 11, 1861; Marcus W. Price, "Ships that Tested the Blockade of the Carolina Ports, 1861–1865," *American Neptune* VIII (April 1948), p. 99; *O.R.N.*, Vol. V, pp. 634–635; *Charleston Mercury*, July 2, 1860, Aug. 22, 1860, June 12, Nov. 11, 1861; Bradlee, *Blockade Running during the Civil War*, pp. 134–136; Charleston and Mobile Inward Manifests; Charleston and Mobile Entrances and Clearances; Soley, *The Blockade*, p. 153; Price, "Ships of the Gulf Ports," pp. 267–268; Price, "Ships of the Georgian and East Florida Ports," p.99.

57. Pickett Papers, Vessel Entrances and Clearances; Dufour, *Night the War Was Lost*, p. 64; Isaac McNeel Papers, Aug. 4, 1861, West Virginia Library, University of West

Virginia, Morgantown, West Virginia; Wood, *Port Town at War*, p. 162; Kathryn A. Hanna, "Incidents of the Confederate Blockade," *Journal of Southern History* XI (May 1945), pp. 219–221.

58. Pickett Papers, Vessel Entrances and Clearances, New Orleans, Charleston, and Mobile Cargo Manifests, 1861; Charleston Inward and Outward Manifests, 1861.

59. *O.R.N.*, Vol. I, pp. 820, 827–828; *New Orleans Daily Picayune*, July 20, 1861; Schwab, *A Financial History*, pp. 233–234.

60. *British and Foreign State Papers*, Vol. XVI, pp. 855–857; *Charleston Mercury*, Aug. 15, 1861; *New Orleans Daily Picayune*, July 23, 1861; Hugh McRae Papers, C. Memminger to McRae and Company, Oct. 16, 1861 and Dix to D. McRae, Aug. 11, 1861; Perkins Library, Duke University, Durham, North Carolina; Coddington, "The Civil War Blockade Reconsidered," pp. 291–293; John D. Winters, *The Civil War in Louisiana* (Baton Rouge: Louisiana State University Press, 1963), p. 45; Owsley, *King Cotton Diplomacy*, pp. 16–44; Richard Cecil Todd, *Confederate Finance* (Athens: University of Georgia Press, 1954), pp. 127–129; Schwab, *A Financial History*, pp. 250–251; "Charleston, Savannah, Mobile, New Orleans Cotton Bonds."

61. Russell, *My Diary*, Vol. I, pp. 142, 170, 258.

62. *O.R.N.*, Series II, Vol. III, p. 97; Raphael Semmes, *Service Afloat* (Baltimore: Baltimore Publishing Company, 1887), pp. 93–119; Joseph T. Durkin, *Stephen R. Mallory* (Chapel Hill; University of North Carolina Press, 1954), pp. 157–160; W. Adolphe Roberts, *Semmes of the Alabama* (Indianapolis: Bobbs-Merrill, 1938), pp. 43–46, 50–42.

63. Heyl, *American Steamers*, Vol. I, pp. 277–278; *O.R.N.*, Ser. II, Vol. II, p. 261: *Civil War Naval Chronology*, 6 Vols. (Washington: Naval History Division, 1971), Vol. VI, pp. 274–275.

64 *O.R.N.*, Vol. I, pp. 1–25, 124, Ser. II, Vol. I, pp. 329–429; Roberts, *Semmes*, pp. 48–50; Winters, *Louisiana*, p. 46; Pickett Papers, Vessel Entrances and Clearances.

## Chapter Two.   The First Blockade Runners

1. Nepveux, *Trenholm*, pp. 6–7; Henry Schulz Holmes, "The Trenholm Family," *South Carolina Geneological Magazine* XVI (October 1915), pp. 151–163.

2. Profits of the Charleston and Liverpool companies were divided as follows: For John Fraser and Company, John Fraser 10%, G. A. Trenholm 35%, Theodore A. Wagner 22.5%, E. L. Trenholm 22.5%, James Welsman 5%, Charles K. Prioleau. For Fraser, Trenholm, and Company, John Fraser 10%, G. A. Trenholm, E. L. Trenholm 20%, Theodore A. Wagner 20%, J. T. Welsman 10%, Charles K. Prioleau 5%. Losses were divided up G. A. Trenholm 40%, T. A. Wagner 22%, E. L. Trenholm 22%, J. Welsman 11%, and C. K. Prioleau 5%. George Alfred Trenholm Papers, Library of Congress, Washington, D. C.; Waddell Papers, North Carolina State Archives, Raleigh, North Carolina.

3. Nepveux, *Trenholm*, p. 21: A. Toomer Porter, *Led On!* (New York: G. P. Putnam and Sons, 1898), pp. 112–113.

4. Nepveux, *Trenholm*, p. 23.

5. Bradlee, *Blockade Running during the Civil War*, p. 25; Nepveux, *Trenholm*, p. 33; *O.R.N.*, Vol. VI, pp. 164–165.

6. Correspondence of the Confederate Treasury Department, 2 Reels, Treasury Department Records, National Archives, Washington, D.C., Reel 2, pp. 62, 83–84, 467, 478–479.

Notes to Pages 47–51                                                    335

7. Correspondence of the Confederate Treasury Department, Reel 2, p. 62; Frank J. Merli, *Great Britain and the Confederate Navy* (Bloomington: Indiana University Press, 1970), p. 62.

8. Frank E. Vandiver, *Ploughshares into Swords: Josiah Gorgas and Confederate Ordnance* (Austin: University of Texas Press, 1952), pp. 54–57; George W. Cullum, *Biographical Registrar of the Officers and Graduates of West Point*, 3 vols. (Boston: Houghton, Mifflin and Company, 1891), Vol. II, p. 8.

9. Carl L. Davis, *Arming the Union* (Port Washington: Kennekat Press, 1973), pp. 40–41; Charles B. Dew, *Ironmaker to the Confederacy: Joseph R. Anderson and the Tredegar Iron Works* (New Haven: Yale University Press, 1966), pp. 13, 5–67; William B. Edwards, *Civil War Guns* (Harrisburg: Stackpole Company, 1962), p. 378; Larry J. Daniel and Riley W. Gunter, *Confederate Cannon Foundries* (Union City: Pioneer Press, 1977), pp. 3–24; D. H. Hill, "The Confederate Ordnance Department," *Proceedings of the Twentieth and Twenty-first Annual Sessions of the State Library and Historical Associations of North Carolina* (Raleigh, 1922), pp. 82–84; Gorgas, "Ordnance of the Confederacy," pp. 212–214; Gorgas, "Notes" 68–75; "Forts and Arsenals," House Report No. 85, 36th Congress, 2d Session, 1861, pp. 1–32; O.R.A., Vol. I, pp. 349, 495, 688, Vol. II, pp. 792, 940, Vol. V, pp. 806–808; Ser. IV, Vol. I, pp. 292, 555.

10. O.R.A., Ser. IV, p. 220, 555; Frank E. Vandiver, ed. *Confederate Blockade Running through Bermuda, 1861–1865; Letter and Cargo Manifests* (Austin: University of Texas Press, 1947), p. xi; Gorgas, "Ordnance of the Confederacy," p. 283.

11. Thompson, *Confederate Purchasing Operations*, pp. 21–25; O.R.A., Ser. IV, Vol. I, p. 220; Bradlee, *Blockade Running during the Civil War*, pp. 11–12; Caleb Huse, *The Supplies for the Confederate Army* (Boston: T. R. Martin and Son, 1904), pp. 9–12; Cullum, *West Point*, Vol. II, p. 282.

12. O.R.A., Ser. IV, Vol. I, p. 343; Huse, *Confederate Purchasing*, pp. 10–24; Thompson, *Confederate Purchasing Operations*, pp. 14–15; Edwards, *Civil War Guns*, pp. 86–87.

13. O.R.N., Ser. II, Vol. II, pp. 80–83; Thompson, *Confederate Purchasing Operations*, p. 31.

14. Bulloch, *Secret Service*, Vol. I, pp. 48–50.

15. O.R.A., Ser. IV, vol. I, pp. 332–333; Correspondence of the Confederate Treasury Department, Reel 2, p. 85; Stanley W. Hoole, editor, *Confederate Foreign Agent: The European Diary of Major Edward C. Anderson* (University, Alabama: Confederate Publishing Company, 1976), pp. 2, 17; Edward Clifford Anderson papers, Southern Historical Collection, University of North Carolina, Chapel Hill, North Carolina.

16. Hoole, *Confederate Foreign Agent*, pp. 22–23; Edward C. Anderson Papers; James Heyward North Papers, Southern Historical Collection, University of North Carolina, Chapel Hill, North Carolina.

17. Edward C. Anderson Papers; O.R.A., Ser. IV, Vol. I, p. 538; Regis A. Courtmanche, *No Need of Glory: The British Navy in American Waters, 1860–1864* (Annapolis: Naval Institute Press, 1977), pp. 94–95.

18. Hoole, *Confederate Foreign Agent*, pp. 27–29; Edward C. Anderson Papers.

19. Fletcher Pratt, "Starvation Blockade, "*American Mercury* XXXVI (November 1935), p. 337; O.R.N., Vol. VI, pp. 6, 34, 164–165; Consular Despatches from Liverpool, State Department Records, National Archives, Reel 19, May 12, 1861; Charles Francis Adams Letterbooks, Adams Papers, Massachusetts Historical Society, Boston, Massachusetts,

Aug. 16, 1861, p. 196 and Aug. 23, 1861, pp. 207–210; Liverpool Consul, Reel 19, July 5, Aug. 17, 1861; Heyl, *Early American Steamers*, Vol. I, pp. 163–164; Arthur Wardle, "Blockade Runners Built and Registered at the Port of Liverpool during the American Civil War, 1861–1865." Liverpool Public Library, Liverpool England, p. 78; Bradlee, *Blockade Running during the Civil War*, pp. 21–24; Edward C. Anderson Papers.

20. *O.R.N.*, Vol. VI, pp. 100–101; Liverpool Consul, Reel 19, Aug. 13 and 19, 1861; Alexander Lawrence, *A Present for Mr. Lincoln* (Macon: Ardivan Press, 1861), p. 82; Vessel Papers, Reel 4, *Bermuda*.

21. Waddell Papers; *O.R.A.*, Ser. IV, Vol. I, pp. 614–618, 623, 635–639, 688; Bulloch, *Secret Service*, Vol. I, pp. 70–71.

22. *O.R.A.*, Ser. IV, Vol. I, pp. 623, 633, 688; Waddell Papers.

23. *Charleston Daily Courier*, Aug. 22, 1861; Pickett Papers, Entrances and Clearances of Savannah; Liverpool Consul, Reel 19, December 6, 1861.

24. Ibid.

25. Edward C. Anderson Papers.

26. *O.R.A.*, Ser. IV, Vol. I, pp. 493–496, 594–597, 822; *O.R.N.*, Ser. II, Vol. II, pp. 80–82; Hill, "Confederate Ordnance Department," p. 82.

27. There is some confusion over the exact makeup of the *Fingal's* cargo. The figures given are a compilation from the following sources. There is also confusion over the two smaller cannons carried by the vessel. Long after the war Bulloch refers to them as two 2.5" breech-loading guns while another source reports them to be one Clay breech-loading gun and a Blakely 12-pounder. Thomas R. Neblett, "Edward C. Anderson and the Fingal," *Georgia Historical Quarterly* LII (June 1968), pp. 132–158; Edward C. Anderson Papers; Hoole, *Confederate Foreign Agent*, pp. 53–77; Bulloch, *Secret Service*, Vol. I, pp. 109–118; Virgil C. Jones, "Slipping through the Blockade," *Civil War Times Illustrated* II October 1960), p. 6; Liverpool Consul, Reel 20, Oct. 26, 1861; William Stanley Poole, *Four Years in the Confederate Navy* (Athens: University of Georgia Press, 1964), pp. 1–5; Vessel Papers, Reel 11, *Fingal*; *O.R.N.*, Vol. XII, pp. 331, 380; Consular Despatches from Bermuda, State Department Records, National Archives, Washington, D.C., Reel 5, Nov. 3, 1861; Virgil C. Jones, "Mr. Lincoln's Blockade," *Civil War Times Illustrated* X (December, 1971), p. 18; Vandiver, *Confederate Blockade Running*, p. xiv; David L. Horner, *The Blockade Runners; True Tales of Running the Blockade of the Confederate Coast* (New York: Dodd and Mead, 1968), p. 14; Glasgow Consul, Reel 6, Oct. 11, 1861.

28. Anderson met with George W. Randolph, who at that time was the designated secretary of war. Judah P. Benjamin was currently the provisional secretary of war and was succeeded by Randolph in March 1862. Edward C. Anderson Papers; Bulloch, *Secret Service*, Vol. I, pp. 130–135.

29. Edward C. Anderson Papers.

30. Ibid.

31. Bulloch returned to England on the *Annie Childs*, a John Fraser and Company vessel. Bulloch, *Secret Service*, Vol. I, pp. 105–107, 114–115; Correspondence of the Confederate Treasury Department, Reel 2, p. 232.

32. *O.R.N.*, Ser. II, Vol. III, pp. 275–283.

33. *O.R.N.*, Ser. II, Vol. III, pp. 281–283; *O.R.A.*, Vol. I, pp. 835–836; Pickett Papers, Charter Document of the Gordon.

34. *O.R.N.*, Ser. II, Vol. III, pp. 281–283; *O.R.A.*, Ser. IV, Vol. I, pp. 835–836; Liverpool Consul, Reel 20, Feb. 12, 1862.

35. *O.R.N.*, Ser. II, Vol. II, pp. 275, 284, 291; Inward Manifests for Charleston; Vessel Papers, Reel 29, *Theodora*.

36. "Blockade Running," *City of Charleston Yearbook, 1883* (Charleston: News and Courier Book Press, 1883), p. 557; Heyl, *Early American Steamers*, Vol. II, pp. 115–116; *Charleston Mercury*, Nov. 8, 1861.

37. The *Theodora* was still under charter to the Confederacy and commanded by Thomas Lockwood. Charleston Cotton Bonds; Charleston Clearances; *O.R.A.*, Vol. I, Series IV, Vol. I, pp. 781, 798–799, 801–802, 806–807, 815–819; Correspondence of the Confederate Treasury Department, Reel 2, p. 449–453, 499; *Nassau Guardian*, Apr. 12, 1862; Heyl, *Early American Steamers*, Vol. II, pp. 115–116; Bahamas Consul, Reel 10, Dec. 9, 1861; *O.R.A.*, Vol. I, pp. 815–817; *O.R.N.*, Vol. VI, pp. 257, 453–455; Pickett Papers, Entrances and Clearances of Nassau, *Charleston Courier*, Dec. 27, 1861.

38. *O.R.A.*, Ser. IV, Vol. I, pp. 819, 830–831, 835–836.

39. *O.R.A*, Ser. IV, Vol. I, pp. 835–836; "Vessel Papers, Reel 18, *Kate*.

40. *O.R.A*, Ser. IV, Vol. I, pp. 828–829, 830–831.

41. *O.R.A.*, Ser. IV, Vol. I, pp. 828–829; Emma Martin Maffitt, *The Life and Services of John Newland Maffitt* (New York: Neale Publishing Company, 1906), pp. 64–106; John Newland Maffitt Papers, Southern Historical Collection, University of North Carolina, Chapel Hill, North Carolina.

42. *O.R.A.*, Ser. IV, Vol I, pp. 895–896; Bahamas Consul, Reel 10, January 19, 1862; *Nassau Guardian*, Apr. 12, 1862.

43. Davis, "Civil War and Reconstruction in Florida," p. 198; Hayes, *Du Pont*, Vol. I, pp. 376–382; *O.R.N.*, Vol. XII, p. 627; *Nassau Guardian*, Apr. 12, 1862.

44. The *Cecile* was under the command of Ferdinand Peck. Maffitt was on board the vessel, but did not command her. Hayes, *Du Pont*, Vol I, pp. 376–382; *O.R.N.*, Vol. XII, p. 627, 646–647; *Nassau Guardian*, Apr. 12, 1862; Charleston Cotton Bonds; Charleston Clearances; Maffitt Papers.

45. Bradlee, *Blockade Running During the Civil War*, p. 12; Bulloch, *Secret Service*, Vol. I, p. 53.

46. The cotton from the *Fingal* was shipped on the *Economist*, a John Fraser and Company vessel that sailed from Charleston. Correspondence of the Confederate Treasury Department, Reel 2, pp. 232, 506–510; *O.R.A.*, Ser. IV, Vol. I, pp. 985–986, 1017; Vessel Papers, Reel 10, *Economist*, Reel 12, *Gladiator*; *O.R.N.*, Ser. II, Vol. II, pp. 105–107, 113–115, 118–120.

47. Heyl, *Early American Steamers*, Vol. I, pp. 277–278; *O.R.N.*, Vol. VII, p. 264, Ser. II, pp. 112, 118; Jane Stubbs, Virginians Run the Sea Blockade," *Virginia Cavalcade* (April 1960), pp. 21–22.

48. *O.R.A.*, Ser. IV, Vol. I, pp. 831–832, 1055–1057; Vessel Papers, Reel 12, *Gordon*, Reel 29, *Theodora*; Hinsdale Family Papers, letter of Florie Maffitt, July 4, 1862, Perkins Library, Duke University, Durham, North Carolina; Maffitt Papers.

49. *O.R.N.*, Vol. I, pp. 753–760.

50. Courtemanche, *No Need for Glory*, pp. 101–107; Peters, "Running the Blockade in the Bahamas," pp. 20–21.

51. Joseph T. Durkin, *Stephen R. Mallory* (Chapel Hill: University of North Carolina Press, 1938), pp. 155–156.

52. *O.R.A.*, Ser. IV, Vol. I, pp. 1017–1018; Correspondence of the Secretary of the Treasury, Reel 2, p. 340.

53. Liverpool Consul, Reel 20, Feb. 7, 12, 14, 1862, Apr. 10, 1862; *O.R.A.*, Ser. IV, Vol. I, pp. 1003–1005; Vessel Papers, Reel 20, *Minho*.

54. Bahamas Consul, Reel 10, June 29, 1862; Thomas E. Taylor, *Running the Blockade* (London: J. Murray, 1897), pp. 24–25.

55. Michael Craton, *A History of the Bahamas* (London: Collins, 1962), p. 228; Courtemanche, *No Need of Glory*, pp. 40–41.

56. Waddell Papers; Soley, *The Blockade*, pp. 36–37; Bahamas Consul, Reel 10, June 29, 1862; Courtemanche, *No Need of Glory*, p. 87; Thelma Peters, "Running the Blockade During the Civil War," *Tequesta: Journal of the Historical Association of Southern Florida* V (1945), pp. 17–20; John Wilkinson, *The Narrative of a Blockade Runner* (New York: Sheldon, 1877), pp. 140–141.

57. Bahamas Consul, Reel 10, Sept. 30, 1861, Dec. 10, 1861.

58. John Lafitte Papers, South Caroliniana Library, University of South Carolina, Columbia, South Carolina; Letter from John Howells to the author, Feb. 15, 1981; Taylor, *Running the Blockade*, p. 26; *Charleston Mercury*, July 2, 1860, Jan. 1, 1861.

59. *O.R.A.*, Ser. IV, Vol. I, pp. 1003–1005, 1056–1057; *O.R.N.*, Vol. VII, pp. 216, 217–218, 432–433, 463–464, 628–629, 683, Ser. II, Vol. II, pp. 177–180; Thompson, *Confederate Purchasing Operations*, pp. 18–20; Liverpool Consul, Reels 20–23, Jan. 11, 24, 1862; May 7, 1862; August 13, 29, 1862; Sept. 2, 6, 1862.

60. Ibid.

61. *O.R.N*, Vol. XII, p. 797; Bermuda Consul, Reel 6, Feb. 20, 1862, Mar. 20, 1862.

62. *O.R.N.*, Vol. XII, p. 797, Vol. XVII, pp. 220–221.

63. *Cases Argued and Decided in the Supreme Court of the United States in the December Term, 1865*, (Rochester: Lawyer Co-operative Publishing Company, 1901), Vol. LXX, pp. 200–207; Alfred M. Low, *Blockade and Contraband* (Washington: Columbian Printing, 1916), pp. 7–9.

64. Bermuda Customs Manifests, Bermuda Archives, Hamilton. Bermuda; Liverpool Consul, Reel 20, Feb. 7, 12, 14, 15, 1862; Correspondence of the Confederate Treasury Department, Reel 2, p. 31.

65. Ibid.

66. *O.R.A.*, Series IV, Vol. I p. 1056; *Nassau Guardian*, Apr. 12, 1862; "Charleston Entrances and Clearances;" *Civil War Naval Chronology*, Vol. II, pp. 56, 67.

67. *O.R.A.*, Series IV, Vol. I, pp. 1075, 1175; *O.R.N.*, Vol. VII, pp. 264–276, Vol. XIII, pp. 136–137; Bahamas Consul, Reel 10, Apr. 22, 1862; Vessel Papers, Reel 22, *Nashville*; Hayes, *Du Pont*, Vol. II, pp. 138–139; Heyl, *Early American Steamers*, Vol. I, pp. 277–278.

68. The *Herald* had come out of England under the command of a Captain Tate, who, with the majority of the crew, refused to go on to the Confederacy. As Captain, Tate held power of attorney over the vessel and refused to give up the *Herald* until he and the crew received payment for the contracted twelve-month voyage. These difficulties cost Coxetter nearly three months before he could take command of the *Herald*. Bermuda Consul, Reel 6, Apr. 1, June 4, 14, 1862; *O.R.N.*, Ser. IV, Vol. I, pp. 1174–1175; Vandiver, *Bermuda*, pp. 12–15, 21.

69. Hayes, *Du Pont*, Vol. II, pp. 287–288; Liverpool Consul, Reel 20, Feb. 12, 1862; Bermuda Consul, Reel 6, Apr. 1, June 4, 14, 1862; *O.R.A.*, Ser. IV, Vol. I, pp. 1174–1175; Vandiver, *Bermuda*, pp. 12–15, 21.

70. *O.R.N.*, Vol. VII, p. 433; *O.R.A.*, Ser. IV, Vol. II, p. 19, 52; Hugh McRae Papers, Letter of Aug. 29, 1862; Vessel Papers, Reel 18, *Kate*; Bahamas Consul, Reel 10, Apr. 30, 1862; Owsley, *King Cotton*, pp. 243–244; Charleston Clearances and Entrances.

71. Correspondence of the Confederate Treasury Department, Reel 2, pp. 366–367; Vessel Papers, Reel 18, *Kate*; Bahamas Consul, Reel 10, July 3, 1862.

72. *Charleston Mercury*, Dec. 5, 1862; Catherine Buie Papers, Perkins Library, Duke University, Durham, North Carolina; Correspondence of the Confederate Treasury Department, Reel 2, pp. 608–609.

73. Other stockholders included Benjamin Mordecai, E. L. Kerrison, and William Ravenel. Papers of the Importing and Exporting Company of South Carolina, Captured and Abandoned Property Records, Treasury Department Records, Record Group 56, National Archives, Washington D.C.; Lynda Worley Skelton, "The Importing and Exporting Company of South Carolina," *South Carolina Historical Magazine* LXXV (Spring 1974), pp. 26–27; Marcus W. Price, "Blockade Running as a Business in South Carolina during the War between the States, 1861–1865," *American Neptune* IX (January 1949), pp. 35–40.

74. Papers of the Importing and Exporting Company of South Carolina; Horner, *The Blockade Runners*, p. 130; Skelton, "The Importing and Exporting Company of South Carolina," pp. 26–27; Vessel Papers, Reel 7, *Cecile*.

75. Skelton, "The Importing and Exporting Company of South Carolina," p. 26: *O.R.A.*, Ser. IV, Vol. I, p. 1175.

76. Ibid.

77. Anonymous, Account of the Capture of the *Emilie*, formerly *William Seabrook*, South Caroliniana Library, University of South Carolina, Columbia, South Carolina; *O.R.N.*, Vol. VII, p. 90, Vol. XIII, pp. 181–184; *Charleston Mercury*, Sept. 2, 1862; Edwin B. Coddington, "The Civil War Blockade Reconsidered," In *Essays in History and International Relations in Honor of George Hubbard Blakeslee*, Dwight E. Lee and George McReynolds, eds. (Worchester: Clark University Press, 1949), pp. 25–26.

78. Liverpool Consul, Reel 22, Aug. 1, 1862; *Liverpool Daily Post*, July 29, 1863; *O.R.N.*, Vol. VIII, p. 88; Leslie S. Bright, *The Blockade Runner Modern Greece and Her Cargo* (Raleigh: Division of Archives and History, 1977), p. 4; *Circassian*, Key West Admiralty Records, U.S. District Court, North, Middle and South District of Florida, Judicial Records, Record Group 21, Atlanta Federal Archives and Records Center, East Point, Georgia.

79. David John Lyon, Compiler, *The Denny List*, 4 Vols. (London: National Maritime Museum, 1975), Vol. I, No. 82; Peter Payne and Frank J. Merli, "A Blockade Running Chapter, Spring 1862," *American Neptune* XXVI (April 1966), p. 135; Vessel Papers, Reel 21, *Memphis*.

80. The English merchants who chartered the *Memphis* were listed as Zollinger and Andreas of Manchester, England. Ibid.

81. Vessel Papers, Reel 21, *Memphis*; *O.R.N.*, Vol. XVII, pp. 299–300.

82. Ibid.

83. *O.R.N.*, Vol. XVII, p. 299–300; Charleston Cotton Bonds; Vessel Papers, Reel 21, *Memphis*; Charleston Inward Manifests.

84. See tables 5, 6, 7.

85. *O.R.A.*, Ser. IV, Vol. II, pp. 51–52; Liverpool Consul, Reel 26, Apr. 12, 1864; *O.R.N.*, Vol. VII, pp. 217–218, 432–433, 554–556.

## Chapter Three.  New Orleans: Lost Opportunity

1. New Orleans, Mobile, Galveston Entrances and Clearances; *O.R.N.*, Ser. II, Vol. III, pp. 411–413.

2. *O.R.N.*, Vol. XVI, p. 827; Vessel Papers, Reel 23, *Oregon*, Reel 11, *Florida*.

3. Vessel Papers, Reel 29, Southern Steamship Company; *O.R.N.*, Vol. IV, pp. 165–166, 184; Vol. XVI, pp. 827–828; Haberlein, "Former Blockade Runners," pp. 5–6.

4. Ibid.

5. *O.R.A.*, Ser. IV, Vol. I, pp. 275–277, 356, 498–503; Pickett Papers, C. J. Helm to R. Hunter, Oct. 22, 1861. Hoole, *Confederate Foreign Agent*, pp. 60–61, 66–67.

6. Pickett Papers, C. J. Helm to R. Hunter, Nov. 9, 15, 1861; Taylor, *Running the Blockade*, p. 146: Soley, *The Blockade*, pp. 36–37; Mary Caldwalader Jones, "Chapters from Unwritten Autobiographies," *Bookman* LIX (April 1924), p. 161: U.S. Congress, House, *Report on Commercial Relations of the United States for the Year Ending Sept. 30, 1861*, Ex. Doc. No. 6, 36th Cong., 2d Sess., 1861.

7. Ibid.

8. Since the Custom House at New Orleans served ships arriving and departing from the city, Lake Pontchartrain, Barataria Bay, Brashear City, and all other points within the Louisiana coast, it is difficult to determine the exact port from which ships operated. *O.R.N.*, Ser. II, Vol. I, pp. 672–673, 678–680, 684–686, Vol. II, pp. 657–658, Vol. III, pp. 396–397; New Orleans Entrances and Clearances; *Wilmington Daily Journal*, Mar. 6, 1862; Ship Registers and Enrollments, *C. Vanderbilt*, Record Group 41, Industrial and Social Branch, National Archives, Washington, D.C.; Letters sent by Confederate Secretary of War J. Benjamin to M. Lovell, Feb. 19, 23, 1862, Record Group 109, Old Military Records Branch, National Archives, Washington, D.C.; Maurice K. Melton, "Major Military Industries of the Confederate Government," (Ph.D. dissertation, Emory University, 1978), pp. 36–43, 87; Winters, *Civil War in Louisiana*, pp. 60–62.

9. *Magnolia*, Key West Admiralty Records; Haberlein, "Former Blockade Runners," pp. 6–7; New Orleans Entrances and Clearances; *O.R.N.*, Vol. XVIII, p. 121.

10. *Charleston Mercury*, Apr. 1, 1862; Glover, "West Gulf Blockade," p. 159; *O.R.N.*, Vol. XVIII, p. 91; New Orleans Vessel Entrances and Clearances.

11. *O.R.N.*, Ser. II, Vol. I, pp. 670–671.

12. *O.R.N.*, Vol. XVIII, pp. 64–69.

13. Particulars of the Steamer *William H. Webb*, "*Journal of the Franklin Institute* LXIII (January 1857), p. 48; *Civil War Naval Chronology*, Vol. VI, p. 323; *O.R.N.*, Vol. XVIII, pp. 69–70; New Orleans Vessel Entrances and Clearances.

14. New Orleans Entrances and Clearances.

15. *O.R.N.*, Vol. XVII, pp. 201–210, 217–218, Ser. II, Vol. II, pp. 689–690.

16. New Orleans Entrances and Clearances.

17. Ibid.

18. New Orleans Entrances and Clearances; Havana Consul, Reel 45, May 17, 1862; *Havana Mercantile Weekly*, May 17, 1862.

19. *New Orleans Daily Picayune,* Nov. 20, 29, Dec. 3, 7, 1861; *Florida* Logbook, Southern Historical Collection, University of North Carolina, Chapel Hill, North Carolina; Vessel Papers, Reel 15, *Havana.*

20. *Mobile Register,* Jan. 18, 1862; New Orleans and Mobile Entrances and Clearances. *Swan,* Key West Admiralty Records; *O.R.N.,* Vol. XVIII, p. 852. Mobile. Entrances and Clearances. George A. Tuthill Account Book, City of Mobile Museum, Mobile, Alabama.

21. *O.R.N.,* Vol. XVIII, p. 653–661.

22. Edward Harleston Edwards Papers, South Caroliniana Library, University of South Carolina, Columbia, South Carolina; West, "The Blockading Service," p. 233; *O.R.N.,* Vol. I, pp. 431–432, 765–770.

23. Vessel Papers, Reel 15, *Havana;* Mobile Entrances and Clearances.

24. *O.R.N.,* Vol. XVI, p. 859; Vandiver, *Ploughshares into Swords,* p. 140; Brother August Raymond Ogden, "A Blockaded Seaport" (M.A. thesis, St. Mary's University, 1939), p. 50.

25. Albert Gleaves, "The Affair of the Blanche," *United States Naval Institute Proceedings* XLVIII (October 1922), pp. 1662–1670; *O.R.N.,* Ser. II, Vol. III, pp. 725–728, 781, 855–857; Pickett Papers, J. Benjamin to C. Helm, April 15, 1863; Thompson, *Confederate Purchasing Operations,* pp. 78–81; James Murry Mason Papers, Manuscript Division, Library of Congress, Washington, D.C.; Stuart L. Bernath, *Squall Across the Atlantic* (Berkeley: University of California Press, 1970), pp. 100–103.

26. Ibid.

27. *Union,* Key West Admiralty; Heyl, *Early American Steamers,* Vol. VI pp. 325–326; Galveston Cotton Bonds, *O.R.N.,* Vol. XIX, pp. 224–229, 257–260.

28. Ronnie Curtis Tyler, "The Age of Cotton; Santiago Vidaurri and the Confederacy," (Ph.D. dissertation, Texas Christian University, 1968), pp. 53–56; Owsley, *King Cotton Diplomacy,* pp. 118–119.

29. Pickett Papers, Despatches of J. Quintero for Aug. 22 and Nov. 10, 1861; Tyler, "The Age of Cotton," pp. 65–70.

30. Pickett Papers, Despatches of J. Quintero for March 22, 1862; *O.R.A.,* Ser. IV, Vol. I, p. 774, Vol. III, pp. 565–566.

31. Pickett Papers, Despatches of J. Quintero for Mar. 22, 1862.

32. Bernath, *Squall Across the Atlantic,* pp. 117–118; Low, *Blockade and Contraband,* pp. 12–13.

33. Bernath, *Squall Across the Atlantic,* pp. 37–62; Glover, "West Gulf Blockade," pp. 35–37; *O.R.N.,* Vol. XVIII, pp. 50–51, 77–86, 122.

34. Tyler, "The Age of Cotton," pp. 78–90, 112–113; Pickett Papers, J. Quintero to S. Vidaurri, Apr. 4, 1862, Despatch of J. Quintero for Apr. 17, 1862.

35. L. Tuffly Ellis, "Maritime Commerce on the Far Western Gulf, 1861–1865," *Southwestern Historical Quarterly* CXXVII (October 1973), pp. 206–211; Glover, "West Gulf Blockade," pp. 114–115; William T. Windham, "The Problem of Supply in the Trans-Mississippi Confederacy," *Journal of Southern History* XXVII (May 1961), pp. 150–151.

36. *O.R.N.,* Vol. XIX, pp. 321–326, 379–380, 386; Gleaves, "The Blanche Affair," pp. 1666–1667.

## Chapter Four.   King Cotton: A Tottering Throne

1. Richard D. Goff. *Confederate Supply* (Durham: Duke University Press, 1969), pp. 128–219, 250–251; Gorgas, "Ordnance of the Confederacy," p. 215.

2. Edwards, *Civil War Guns*, pp. 376–378; Goff, *Confederate Supply*, pp. 128–129; Gorgas, "Ordnance of the Confederacy," p. 214; Melton, "Major Military Industries," p. 126; Gorgas, "Notes," pp. 82–84; *O.R.A.*, Ser. IV, Vol. I, pp. 618–622, Vol. II, pp. 955–957.

3. Gorgas, "Ordnance of the Confederacy," p. 214; Gorgas, "Notes," pp. 82–84; Frank E. Vandiver, "A Sketch of Efforts to Equip the Confederate Army at Macon," *Georgia Historical Quarterly* XXVIII (March 1944), pp. 34–40.

4. Dew, *Ironmaker*, p. 125; Melton, "Major Military Industries," p. 126, 375, 492; Vandiver, *Bermuda*, p. xxv.

5. Goff, *Confederate Supply*, p. 68; Richard I. Lester, *Confederate Finance and Purchasing in Great Britain* (Charlottesville: University Press of Virginia, 1975), pp. 161–162; Norman H. Franke, *Pharmaceutical Conditions and Drug Supply in the Confederacy* (Madison: American Institute of Pharmacy, 1955); Ordnance Records, Old Military Records Branch, National Archives, Washington, D.C.; Frank E. Vandiver, "Texas and the Confederate Army's Meat Problem," *Southwestern Historical Quarterly* XLVII January 1944), p. 225; *O.R.A.*, Ser. IV, Vol. II, pp. 157–159.

6. Ibid.

7. Goff, *Confederate Supply*, p. 43; *O.R.A.*, Ser. IV, Vol. II, pp. 30–31, 335–336, 233; Pickett Papers, L. Heyliger to J. Benjamin, Oct. 13, 1862, and Jan. 10, 1863.

8. *O.R.A.*, Ser. IV, Vol. II, pp. 335–336, 382–385; *O.R.N.*, Ser. II, Vol. III, p. 625–627; Pickett Papers, L. Heyliger to J. Benjamin, Oct. 30 and Nov. 12, 1862, E. DeLeon to J. Benjamin, Nov. 1, 1862.

9. Edith Fenner Gentry, "A Confederate Success in Europe: The Erlanger Loan," *Journal of Southern History* XXXVI (May 1970), p. 157; Judith Ann Fenner "Confederate Finances Abroad" (Ph.D. dissertation, Rice University, 1969), pp. 26–37.

10. Owsley, *King Cotton Diplomacy*," pp. 49–50; Norman B. Ferris, *Desperate Diplomacy* (Knoxville: University of Tennessee Press, 1976), p. 93: Lynn Case and Warren Spencer, *The United States and France: Civil War Diplomacy* (Philadelphia: University of Pennsylvania Press, 1970), p. 315; Pickett Papers, E. DeLeon to J. Benjamin, Nov. 1 and 13, 1862.

11. Liverpool Consul, Reel 20, July 25, 1862.

12. Richard Cecil Todd, *Confederate Finance* (Athens: University of Georgia Press, 1954), pp. 35–45; Schwab, *A Financial History*, pp. 10–26; Lester, *Confederate Finance*, pp. 14–18.

13. Thompson, *Confederate Purchasing Operations*, pp. 66–69, 51–52; Lester, *Confederate Finance*, pp. 18–20; Schwab, *A Financial History*, pp. 29–32; Charles S. Davis, *Colin J. McRae, Confederate Financial Agent* (Tuscaloosa: Confederate Centennial Studies, 1961), pp. 35–37; *O.R.N.*, Ser. II, Vol. II, pp. 309–318.

14. Todd, *Confederate Finance*, pp. 179–183; Mason Papers, Letter of Caleb Huse, Oct. 16, 1862; C. Memminger to J. Mason, Oct. 21, 1862; Liverpool Consul, Reel 22, Dec. 8, 1862; Virginia Mason, *The Public Life and Diplomatic Correspondence of James M. Mason, with Some Personal History* (Roanoke: n.p., 1903), p. 351; *O.R.N.*, Ser. II, Vol. II, pp. 440–446; Gentry, "A Confederate Success," pp. 159–166; Lester, *Confederate Finance*, pp. 34–45, Davis, *Colin J. McRae*, pp. 37–40; Thompson, *Confederate Purchasing Operations*, pp. 55–58.

15. Liverpool Consul, Reel 22, Dec. 6, 8, 1862 and March 27, 1863.

16. Walter B. Heyward, *Bermuda Past and Present* (New York: Dodd, Mead and Company, 1911), p. 83; Vandiver, *Bermuda*, pp. xxi–xxii, xxxii; Gorgas, "Notes," p. 79;

Vandiver, *Ploughshares*, pp. 94–95; Thompson, *Confederate Purchasing Operations*, p. 24; *O.R.A.*, Ser. IV, Vol. II, p. 227.

17. Hayward, *Bermuda Past and Present*, pp. 72–83; Eugene P. Jervey Papers, South Caroliniana Library, University of South Carolina, Columbia, South Carolina.

18. Vandiver, *Bermuda*, pp. ix, 10, 19–21; *Charleston Mercury*, May 16, 1863.

19. Vandiver, *Bermuda*, p. xxxii; Vandiver, *Ploughshares*, 90–100; Gorgas, "Notes," p. 80; *O.R.A.*, Ser. IV, Vol. II, pp. 826, 955–959.

20. Ibid.

21. Gorgas, "Notes," p. 79; *Cornubia*, Boston Admiralty Records, U.S. District Court of Boston, Judicial Records, Record Group 21, Boston Federal Archives and Records Center, Waltham, Massachusetts; Bermuda Custom Manifests.

22. Bermuda Customs Manifest; Haberlein, "Former Blockade Runners," pp. 14–15; Liverpool Consul, Reel 23, Jan. 11, 1863; Frank Vandiver, ed., *The Civil War Diary of Josiah Gorgas* University: University of Alabama Press, 1947), p. 34; Bermuda Consul, Reel 6, Feb. 3, 1863; *O.R.N.*, Vol. IX, pp. 131–133, Vessel Papers, Reel 22, *Merrimac*.

23. On the Confederate ship registers for the Ordnance Bureau vessels, Secretary of War James Seddon was listed as the owner. Bermuda Customs Manifests; Gorgas, "Notes," p. 79; Vessel Papers.

24. *O.R.N.*, Vol. IX, pp. 280–283; Bermuda Customs Manifests; Bermuda Consul, Reel 6, June 22, 1864.

25. Bermuda Manifests; Bermuda Consul, Reel 6, June 22, 1863; Peter Evans Smith Papers, Southern Historical Collection, University of North Carolina, Chapel Hill, North Carolina.

26. Bermuda Customs Manifests; Bermuda Consul, Reel 6, June 22, 1864; Vandiver, *Ploughshares*, p. 102; Thompson, *Confederate Purchasing Operations*, p. 24.

27. "Correspondence of the Confederate Treasury Department," Reel 2, pp. 305, 419–420, 468, 483, 487, 544, 555; Bermuda Customs Manifests; Vessel Papers, Reel 12, *Giraffe*; Liverpool Consul, Reel 22, Dec. 31, 1862; Heyl, *Early American Steamers*, Vol. I, pp. 361–362, Vol. IV, 267–268; Wilkinson, *Narrative of a Blockade Runner*, pp. 104–134.

28. Liverpool Consul, Reel 22, Dec. 31, 1863; Wilkinson, *Narrative of a Blockade Runner*, pp. 104–134; "Correspondence of the Confederate Treasury Department," Reel 2, pp. 419–420.

29. *O.R.A.*, Series IV, Vol. II, pp. 244–245; *O.R.N.*, Ser. II, p. 368; Thompson, *Confederate Purchasing Operations*, p. 22; "Correspondence of the Confederate Treasury Department," Reel 2, p. 375.

30. Mason Papers, A. Collie to J. Mason, January 22, 30, 1863; J. Seddon to W. Crenshaw, Mar. 20, 1863; *O.R.A.*, Ser. IV, Vol. II, pp. 449, 478–482; *London Times*, Mar. 28, Apr. 28, 1863.

31. *O.R.A.*, Ser. IV, Vol. II, pp. 487–498, 525–527, 660.

32. *O.R.A.*, Ser. II, Vol. IV, pp. 478–479, 482, 535–546, 554–555, 565–567, 588–589, 623–631, 644–647, 826–827, 886–894; Mason Papers, C. Huse to H. Bosher, April 13, 1863, W. Crenshaw to J. Mason, Apr. 27, 1863.

33. *O.R.N.*, Vol. XIV, pp. 252, 492–494, Ser. II, Vol. II, pp. 529–536; *Civil War Naval Chronology*, Vol. VI, p. 306, 298; *Charleston Mercury*, June 8, 1863.

34. Liverpool Consul, Reel 25, Nov. 20, 1863, and Oct. 23, 1863; *O.R.N.*, Ser. II, pp. 476–478, 502–503, 511–513, 523–524; Bulloch, *Secret Service*, Vol. II, pp. 234–235.

35. Copies of Letters and Telegrams Received and Sent by Governor Zebulon B. Vance of North Carolina, 1862–1865," Confederate Records, War Department, Record Group 109, National Archives, Washington, D.C., p. 299; Frontis Johnson, ed., *The Papers of Zebulon Baird Vance* (Raleigh: State Department of Archives and History, 1963), Vol. I, pp. 288–290, 361–363.

36. Vance Papers, Vol. I, pp. 288–290, 361–363; Liverpool Consul, Reel 23, May 13, 1863; Walter Clark, "The Raising, Organization and Equipment of North Carolina Troops during the Civil War," *North Carolina Booklet* XIX (July–October 1919), pp. 60–65; A. G. Dickinson, "Blockade Running from Wilmington," *Confederate Veteran* III (January–December 1895), p. 361.

37. There has been wide discussion over the exact name of the steamer purchased by the state of North Carolina. From existing port records and official correspondence the name of the vessel was the *Advance*. William K. Boyd, "Fiscal and Economic Conditions in North Carolina during the Civil War," *North Carolina Booklet* XIV (April 1915), p. 206; "Vance Letters," p. 299; Vance, *Papers*, Vol. I, pp. 288–290, 360–363; Bradlee, *Blockade Running during the Civil War*, pp. 113, 137–139; Clark, "Raising, Organization and Equipment," pp. 60–63; Bermuda Custom Manifest; Heyl, *Early American Steamers*, Vol. III, pp. 153–155.

## Chapter Five.   Time for Champagne Cocktails

1. Taylor, *Running the Blockade*, p. 10; Glasgow Consul, Reel 7, Jan. 27, 1863; Erik Heyl, "The Blockade Runner *Sciota*," Steamboat *Bill of Facts* XII (December 1955), pp. 79–81; Price, "Blockade Running as a Business," pp. 31–62.

2. Haberlein, "Former Blockade Runners," pp. 13, 18; *O.R.N.*, Vol. VIII, p. 266; Liverpool Consul, Reel 22, Nov. 8, 1862; W. R. C. Simpson, "Britain and the Blockade," *Journal of the Confederate Historical Society* VI (Spring 1981), pp. 17–19; Augustus C. Hobart Hampden, *Never Caught . . .* (London: John Camden Holton, 1867), p. 4.

3. Charles R. Anderson and Aubrey H. Starke, editors, *The Centennial Edition of the Works of Sidney Lanier*, 10 Vols. (Baltimore: Johns Hopkins University Press, 1945), Vol. VII, pp. 225–228; Price, "Masters and Pilots," pp. 81–106; James Sprunt, *Chronicles of the Cape Fear River* (Raleigh: Edwards and Broughton, 1916), pp. 400–404; W. F. Clayton, *A Narrative of the Confederate Navy* (Weldon: Harrell's Printing House, 1910), p. 68; William O. Dundas, "Blockade Running in the Civil War," *United Daughters of the Confederacy Magazine* XV (November 1952), p. 5; *O.R.A.*, Series IV, Vol. II, p. 664; A. Sellew Roberts, "High Prices and the Blockade in the Confederacy," *South Atlantic Quarterly* XXIV (April 1925), pp. 159–160; *O.R.N.*, Vol. X, p. 61.

4. Price, "Masters and Pilots," pp. 81–106.

5. Soley, *The Blockade*, p. 165; Horner, *The Blockade Runners*, p. 15; DeRossett Family Papers, Southern Historical Collection, Chapel Hill, North Carolina, letter of L. DeRossett for Oct. 23, 1864; Bermuda Customs Manifest, Vessel Entrances and Clearances.

6. Horner, *The Blockade Runners*, p. 9; Wilkinson, *Narrative of a Blockade Runner*, pp. 132–133; James Macdonald Oxley, *Baffling the Blockade* (London: Nelson, 1896), p. 255; A. G. Dickinson, "Running the Blockade," *ERA* XIII (April 1904), pp. 251–253; Soley, *The Blockade*, pp. 93–94.

7. Horatio L. Wait, "The Blockade of the Confederacy," *Century Illustrated Magazine* XXXIV (October 1898), p. 918; Soley, *The Blockade*, pp. 166–167; Bradlee, *Blockade Running during the Civil War*, p. 143.

8. Glasgow Consul, Reel 6, Sept. 20, 1862; Liverpool Consul, Reel 22, Aug. 1, 1862; *O.R.A.*, Series IV, Vol. II, p. 234; Simpson, "Britain and the Blockade," p. 19; Glasgow Consul, Reel 6, Sept. 29, 1862; *Pearl*, Key West Prize Court Records; Frank Brutt, *Cross Channel and Coastal Paddle Steamers* (London: Richard Tilling, 1934), p. 317; *O.R.N.*, Vol. II, p. 208.

9. Liverpool Consul, Reel 23, Jan. 6, 9, 17, 20, 23, Apr. 8, 1863, Reel 30, Feb. 3, 1865; *London Times*, Feb. 2, 1865; Nassau Consul, Reel 11, Feb. 28, Mar. 2, 20, 27, 1863; *Charleston Mercury*, Mar. 20, 25, 1863; *Nassau Guardian*, Mar. 25, 1863; *O.R.N.*, Vol. XIII, pp. 769–775; Vessel Papers, Reel 12, *Georgiana*.

10. Dundas, "Blockade Running in the Civil War," pp. 5, 8–9, 12; William O. Dundas, "Blockade Running in the Civil War," *Bellman* XXVI (Mar 31, 1919), pp. 606–608; Liverpool Consul, Reel 22, Dec 31, 1862, Pickett Papers, Nassau Entrances and Clearances; Nassau Guardian, Ship Entrances and Clearances; Charleston Entrances and Clearances; Mobile Entrances and Clearances; Vessel Papers, Reel 11, *Flora*; *London Times*, Mar. 2, 1863.

11. Edward Lawrence was elected mayor of Liverpool in 1864; Taylor, *Running the Blockade*, pp. 14–17; *Liverpool Chronicle*, June 1, 1909.

12. Taylor, *Running the Blockade*, pp. 22–26, 70–101; Bradlee, *Blockade Runners during the Civil War*, p. 119; Haberlein, "Former Blockade Runners," pp. 16–17; Liverpool Consul, Reel 22; Sept. 2, 5, Nov. 28, 1862, Reel 23, Jan. 10, 1863.

13. Taylor, *Running the Blockade*, pp. 44–54.

14. Ibid., *Running the Blockade*, pp. 64–93.

15. *Acts of the General Assembly of South Carolina for December 1862 and February and April 1863*, pp. 162–163; Cotton and Captured Property, Depositions of Theodore D. Jervey, Benjamin Mordecai and William C. Bee.

16. Haberlein, "Former Blockade Runners," pp. 9–10; Cotton and Captured Property, Depositions of Theodore Jervey, Benjamin Mordecai, and William C. Bee; Liverpool Consul, Reel 23, Apr. 18, 1863; Vessel Papers, Reel 10, *Ella and Annie*.

17. Cotton and Captured Property, Depositions of Richard Dowie, F. Richards, A. S. Johnson and G. W. Williams; Theodore D. Wagner Papers, South Carolina Historical Society, Charleston, South Carolina; Price, "Blockade Running as a Business," pp. 44–45; *Acts of the General Assembly of South Carolina for September and December, 1863* pp. 214–215; Vessel Papers, Reel 1 *Antonica*, Reel 12, *General Beauregard*.

18. Haberlein, "Former Blockade Runners," pp. 9–10; Cotton and Captured Property, Depositions of Theodora Jervey, Benjamin Mordecai, W. C. Bee, Richard B. Dowie, A. S. Johnson, George W. Williams; Theodore Wagner Papers, South Carolina Historical Society, Charleston, South Carolina; Liverpool Consul, Reel 23, Apr. 18, 1863; Vessel Papers, Reel 1, *Antonica*, Reel 10, *Ella and Annie* and Reel 12, *General Beauregard*.

19. *O.R.N.*, Vol. II, pp. 361–362; Vol. IV, p. 126, Vol. XIII, pp. 282–283; Liverpool Consul, Reel 22, Dec. 12, 20, Waddell Papers, Thomas Haines Dudley Papers, Henry Huntington Library, San Marino, California; Charleston Entrances and Clearances; *Charleston Mercury*, Apr. 13, 1863; Samuel Welles Leland Diary, South Caroliniana Library, Columbia, South Carolina; Trenholm Papers, Library of Congress, Chamberlain, Miller and Company to John Fraser and Company, Apr. 16, 1863; *The Burkmyer Letters* (Columbia:

The State Company, 1926); Account Book of Captain John M. Payne, Museum of the Confederacy, Richmond, Virginia; hereafter referred to as Ordnance Account Book: Chew Papers.

20. Heyl, Early *American Steamers*, Vol. VI, pp. 101–104; Charleston Entrances and Clearances: "Running the Blockade," *Southern Historical Society Papers* XXIV (1896), p. 225.

21. Forrest Family Papers, Southern Historical Collection, University of North Carolina, Chapel Hill, North Carolina; *O.R.N.*, Vol. II, pp. 235–250, Series II, Vol. III, p. 826; *Nassau Guardian*, June 3, 1863; Pickett Papers, L. Heyliger to J. Benjamin, June 12, 1863.

22. Cotton and Captured Property, Deposition of Henry Cobia; Price, "Blockade Running as a Business," 45–46; Heyl, *Early American Steamers*, Vol. VI, pp. 101–104; *Burckmyer Letters*, p. 214.

23. Vessel Papers, Reel 10, *Elizabeth*; Ordnance Account Book: Charles K. Prioleau Papers, Merseyside Archives, Merseyside, England.

24. Bermuda Consul, Reel 6, Jan. 24, 1863; *Wilmington Daily News*, Mar. 12, 1863; *O.R.N.*, Vol. XIII, pp. 551–556; Heyl, *Early Steamers*, Vol. I, pp. 351–352.

25. Liverpool Consul, Reel 22, Nov. 28, Dec. 31, 1862; Dudley Papers: Ripley, *Artillery and Ammunition of the Civil War*, pp. 157–158.

26. Heyl, *Early American Steamers*, Vol. I, pp. 201–202; Liverpool Consul, Reel 22, Dec. 31, 1862, Reel 23, May 30, June 3, 10, 1863, Reel 25, July 1, 8, 1863; "Running the Blockade," pp. 226–227; Prioleau Papers.

27. *O.R.A.*,Vol. XXVIII, Pt. II, pp. 291, 296, 300, 3013, 329–330, 337, 343, 387–388; Pierre G. T. Beauregard, "Torpedo Service and Water Defenses of Charleston," Southern Historical Society Papers V (April 1878), pp. 158-160.

### Chapter Six.   Charleston and Wilmington: Gateways to the South

1. *O.R.N.*, Ser. II, Vol. III, pp. 883–889; *O.R.A.*, Ser. IV, Vol. II, pp. 562–563; *Charleston Mercury*, Mar. 19, 31, June 9, Nov. 2–5, 1863; Liverpool Consul, Reel 23, Jan. 6, 1863; Charleston Entrances and Clearances; Charleston Cotton Bonds; Hutson Lee Papers, South Carolina Historical Society, Charleston, South Carolina.

2. Charleston Entrances and Clearances; Pickett Papers, Nassau Entrances and Clearances; West, "The Blockade Service," p. 243; W. F. G. Peck, "Four Years under Fire," *Harper's New Monthly Magazine* XXXI August 1865), pp. 358–366; Theodore D. Jervey, "Charleston during the Civil War," *Annual Report of the American Historical Association for the Year 1913* I (1915), pp. 167–177; Stephen R. Wise, "The Campaign for Morris Island," (Master's Thesis, Bowling Green State University, 1978).

3. Leora H. McEachern and Isabel. M. Williams, "The Prevailing Epidemic—1862," *Lower Cape Fear Historical Society Bulletin* XI (November 1967), pp. 1–20; *O.R.N.*, Vol. VIII, p. 89; Wood, "Port Town at War," p. 76; Vandiver, *Gorgas Diary*, p. 16; Wilmington Daily Journal, Nov. 17, 1862; John Johns, "Wilmington During the Blockade," *Harper's New Monthly Magazine* XXXIII (September 1866), pp. 497–499.

4. Ordnance Account Book.

5. James Ryder Randall Papers, Southern Historical Collection, University of North Carolina, Chapel Hill, North Carolina, J. Randall to K. Hammond, Oct. 6 and 17, 1863;

Johns, "Wilmington during the Blockade," pp. 497–499; Wood, "Port Town at War," p. 76; *O.R.N.*, Vol. VIII, p. 89.

6. Johns, "Wilmington during the Blockade," p. 497; Gragg, "Fort Fisher," p. 43.
7. Ibid.
8. William Lamb, *Colonel Lamb's Story of Fort Fisher* (Wilmington Printing Company, 1966); Robert Carse, *Blockade* (New York: Rhinehart, 1958; Gragg, "Fort Fisher," pp. 22–28; Hobart-Hampden, *Never Caught*, pp. 9–16, 70–72.
9. Wilmington Daily Journal, Sept. 1, Oct. 24, 26, 1863; William Conway Whittle Diary, Norfolk Public Library, Norfolk, Virginia.
10. Wood, "Port Town at War," pp. 176–178.
11. Pickett Papers, Nassau and Bermuda Entrances and Clearances; Bermuda Manifests; *Nassau Guardian*, Vessels Entrances and Clearances; *Bermuda Gazette*, Vessel Entrances and Clearances; Pickett Papers, L. Heyliger to J. Benjamin, Apr. 7, 1863; *O.R.A.*, Ser. IV, Vol. II, pp. 633–634; Bahamas Consul, Reel 6, June 1, 27, 1863.
12. After the war the United States Supreme Court ruled that the seizure of the *Springbok* was illegal. The court decided that the carrying of contraband to Nassau did not "infect the ship." The cargo was liable for seizure but not the vessel, which was eventually returned to her owners. Bernath, *Squall across the Atlantic*, p. 85; *United States Supreme Court Cases*, Book 15, pp. 480–486; Vandiver, *Bermuda*, p. xvi; Hayward, *Bermuda Past and Present*, pp. 76–77; *Blockade and Contraband*, p. 7–9.
13. Pickett Papers, L. Heyliger to J. Benjamin, Apr. 7, 1863.
14. *O.R.A.*, Ser. IV, Vol. II, pp. 633–634, 658–659.
15. Vandiver, *Bermuda*, pp. 81–82, 93–94; Ordnance Account Book.
16. Vessel Papers, Reel 10, *Ella*.
17. Vandiver, *Bermuda*, pp. 84–85, 96; *O.R.N.*, Vol. IX, pp. 282–284; Heyl, *Early American Steamers*, Vol. I, pp. 237–238.
18. James R. Randall Papers, J. Randall to K. Hammond, Oct. 21, 1863.
19. J. Randall Papers, J. Randall to K. Hammond, Oct. 21, 1863; *O.R.N.*, Vol. IX, pp. 168–174, 248–251; Mason Papers, A. Collie to J. Mason, Dec. 10, 1863.
20. J. Randall Papers, J. Randall to K. Hammond, Jan. 16, 1864; *O.R.N.*, Vol. IX, pp. 336–339, 402–404.
21. *O.R.N.*, Vol. VIII, pp. 80, 303, 332, 502, 595–596, 699–700, 801, Vol. IX, pp. 350–358; *Nassau Guardian*, Vessel Entrances and Clearances; Bermuda Gazette, Vessel Entrances and Clearances; Bermuda Manifests.
22. *O.R.N.*, Vol. IX, p. 248.
23. Ibid., p. 216.
24. Ibid., pp. 386, 409.
25. Ibid., pp. 264–268, Ser. II, Vol. I, p. 133.
26. *Nassau Guardian*, Vessel Entrances and Clearances; *Bermuda Gazette*, Vessel Entrances and Clearances; Bermuda Manifests.
27. Wilkinson, *Narrative of a Blockade Runner*, pp. 168–188.
28. *O.R.N.*, Vol. IX, pp. 273–286.
29. Ibid., pp. 287–291.
30. Ibid., pp. 291–296.
31. *O.R.N.*, Ser. II, Vol. I, pp. 85, 95, 66–67.
32. *O.R.N.*, Vol. IX, pp. 297–298, Ser. II, Vol. I, p. 177.

33. Ibid., p. 42; Taylor, *Running the Blockade*, pp. 84–85.

34. *O.R.N.*, Vol. IX, pp. 354–355.

35. Ibid., pp. 354–356.

36. Vessel Papers, Reel 4, *Banshee*; Pickett Papers, E. DeLeon to J. Benjamin, Aug. 8, 1863; *O.R.A.*, Ser. IV, Vol. II, pp. 714–715.

37. *O.R.A.*, Ser. IV, Vol. II, pp. 885, 895–896, 908–909, 1068–1069; Davis, *Colin J. McRae*, p. 41.

38. *O.R.N.*, Ser. II, Vol. IV, pp. 982–985; Thompson, *Confederate Purchasing Operations*, p. 84; Davis, *Colin J. McRae*, pp. 49–55. *O.R.N.*, Ser. II, Vol. II, pp. 496–498; *O.R.A.*, Ser. IV, Vol. II, pp. 824–827, 1013–1016.

39. *O.R.A.*, Ser. IV, Vol. II, p. 918.

## Chapter Seven.    The Confederacy Takes Control

1. Hugh McRae Papers, W. McRae to D. McRae, Jan. 22, 1864; *O.R.A.*, Ser. IV, Vol. II, pp. 736.

2. Gorgas, "Notes," pp. 215–216; Hill, "The Confederate Ordnance Department," pp. 89–90.

3. Goff, *Confederate Supply*, p. 177; *O.R.N.*, Vol. IX, pp. 392–393; *O.R.A.*, Ser. IV, Vol. II, pp. 852, Vol. III, p. 154.

4. Dudley Papers; Liverpool Consul, Reel 25, Sept. 8, 18, Nov. 27, Dec. 2, 1863, Reel 26 Apr. 18, 1864; *O.R.N.*, Ser. II, Vol. III, p. 1107; Hobart-Hampden, *Never Caught*, pp. 3–4, 75, 90; Haberlein, "Former Blockade Runners," pp. 20–21.

5. It was later discovered that a number of the articles that were prohibited from being imported were necessary for the Confederate war effort, and the law had to be altered. Among the items removed from the list were brushes, which were needed by the Ordnance Bureau, and meat packaged in tins, as a number of the foods shipped in by the Commissary Bureau were so packaged. Pickett Papers, J. Benjamin to H. Holtz, Feb. 24, 1864; *O.R.A.*, Ser. IV, Vol. III, pp. 80–82; Goff, *Confederate Supply*, pp. 178–180.

6. *O.R.A.*, Ser. IV, Vol. III, pp. 187–189.

7. James Randall Papers, J. Randall to K. Hammond, Mar. 10, 1864; Thompson, Confederate Purchasing Operations, pp. 95–98.

8. *Nassau Guardian*, Vessel Entrances and Clearances; *Bermuda Gazette*, Vessel Entrances and Clearances; Bermuda Manifests.

9. Charleston, St. Marks and Mobile Cotton Bonds; Vandiver *Ploughshares*, pp. 99–103; Todd, *Confederate Finances*, pp. 189–194.

10. Vessel Papers, Reel 4, *Banshee*; Todd, *Confederate Finance*, pp. 189–194; Fenner, "Confederate Finances Abroad," p. 194.

11. Bermuda Manifests; *O.R.A.*, Ser. IV, Vol. III, pp. 155–157, 210, 288–289, 295–297.

12. Liverpool Consul, Reel 32, July 28, 1865; Correspondence of the Confederate Treasury Department, pp. 610–611; *O.R.A.*, Ser. IV, Vol. III, pp. 525–529; *Civil War Naval Chronology*, Vol. VI, pp. 188–189; Records Relating to the Erlanger Loan, Record Group 365, Treasury Department Records, National Archives, Washington, D.C.

13. Ibid.

14. *O.R.A.*, Ser. IV, Vol. III, pp. 525–529.

15. Ibid., pp. 527–530; Pickett Papers, L. Heyliger to J. Benjamin, Apr. 9, 1864; Edward Stuart Wortley-Mackenzie, First Earl of Wharncliffe Papers, Sheffield City Libraries, Sheffield, England.

16. *O.R.A.*, Ser. IV, Vol. III, pp. 301–302; Miscellaneous Contract Book, Mar. 23, 1864–Mar. 8, 1865, Record Group 109, Old Army Records, National Archives, Washington, D.C.

17. *O.R.A.*, Ser. IV, Vol. III, pp. 258, 364–365, 423–424, 486; Correspondence of the Confederate Treasury Department, pp. 662, 658, 700, 725, 727–728, 734; Ordnance Account Book; Memorandum Book Relating to Agents and Supplies, Record Group 109, Old Army Records, National Archives, Washington, D.C.

18. *O.R.A.*, Ser. IV, Vol. III, pp. 525–529.

19. Capers, *Memminger*, p. 369; Schwab, *A Financial History*, p. 69; Fenner, "Confederate Finances Abroad," pp. 199–200; *O.R.A.*, Ser. IV, Vol. III, pp. 587–589; Memorandum Book; George Alfred Trenholm Papers, Library of Congress, Washington, D.C.

20. George Alfred Trenholm Papers, South Caroliniana Library, University of South Carolina, Columbia, South Carolina, G. Trenholm to C. Wallace, Aug. 18, 1864.

21. In his despatches, Bulloch refers to one engine being sent on the *Coquette*, with another being finished in December; however there is no mention in later despatches on how it was delivered. After the war Bulloch wrote that both engines came in on the *Coquette*. It is probable that the engines came out on separate vessels. The final deposition of the engines is unknown. *O.R.N.*, Ser. II, Vol. II, pp. 332–334, 483–485, 574, 608–609, 611–612, 627–628; 682; Bulloch, *Secret Service*, II, pp. 229–233; Letters from Robert Holcombe, Curator, Confederate Naval Museum, Mar. 12, May 1, July 5, Oct. 16, 1981, in possession of the author.

22. The *Petrel* had run out of Charleston one day after the *Helen*. *O.R.N.*, Ser. II, Vol. II, pp. 564–565, 575–578; Marcus W. Price, "Four from Bristol," *American Neptune* XVII (October 1957), p 253; *Charleston Mercury*, Apr. 14, 1864.

23. *O.R.N.*, Ser. II, Vol. II, pp. 511–513, 565–566, 574, 687; Liverpool Consul, Reel 25, Oct. 23, 1863; Bulloch, *Secret Service*, Vol. II, pp. 234–235; Logbook of the *Coquette*, Record Group 56, Treasury Department Records, National Archives, Washington, D.C.; Dudley Papers.

24. Wilkinson, *Narrative of a Blockade Runner*, pp. 192–197; Edward Crenshaw, "Diary of Captain Edward Crenshaw," *Alabama Historical Quarterly* Vol. I (Winter 1930), pp. 448–452; *O.R.N.*, Vol. X, pp. 187, 281, 289, 292, 295, 303, 713, 714, 721–722; *O.R.A.*, Vol. XL, Pt. III, pp. 757, 759, 761.

25. *Civil War Naval Chronology*, Vol. VI, pp. 309–310; *O.R.N.*, Ser. II, Vol. II, pp. 633–634, 689.

26. *Wilmington Daily Journal*, Feb. 19, June 2, 1864; Sprunt, *Chronicles of the Cape Fear River*, pp. 400–401; West, "Blockading Service," p. 226; *O.R.A.*, Ser. IV, Vol. III, p. 351; Anderson, *Works of Sidney Lanier*, Vol. VII, pp. 157, 166, 168, 178; Hobart-Hampden, *Never Caught*, pp. 102–104; Clifford A. Lanier Papers, Johns Hopkins Library, Johns Hopkins University, Baltimore, Maryland; *London Index*, June 3, 1864; *Nassau Guardian*, Vessel Entrances and Clearances.

27. There is some confusion as to if Lynch was leaving or coming on board the *North Carolina* when he was challenged, though Randall's account, which is cited, is the more contemporary. William F. Clayton, *A Narrative of the Confederate Navy* (Weldon: Harrell's

Printing House, 1910), pp. 68–70; J. R. Randall Papers, March 10, 16, June 3, 1864; Johns, "Wilmington during the Blockade," p. 500; *O.R.A.*, Vol. XXXIII, pp. 1218–1227.

28. In his book, Wilkinson writes that he returned to the Confederacy in the Spring of 1864 on the *Whisper*, but the *Whisper* had not yet been built. Wilkinson, *Narrative of a Blockade Runner*, pp. 189–193; *O.R.N.*, Vol. IX, pp. 804–805.

29. Johnston, *Vance Papers*, p. 364; Zebulon B. Vance Papers, North Carolina State Archives, Raleigh, North Carolina; Julius Guthrie Papers, North Carolina State Archives, Raleigh, North Carolina; Bermuda Manifests; Vessel Papers, Reel I, *Advance*.

30. "Vance Letters," pp. 426–427, 453–454, 466, 491–492, 503, 508–509; Vance Papers, J. Seddon to Z. Vance, Jan. 6, 1864; *O.R.A.*, Ser. IV, Vol. III, pp. 10–11, 28–29, 42, 113–114, 151, 154; Guthrie Papers.

31. Edwin B. Coddington, "Activities and Attitudes of a Confederate Businessman: Gazaway B. Lamar," *Journal of Southern History* IX (February 1943), pp. 26–32; Records of Gazaway B. Lamar, Record Group 366, Treasury Department Records, National Archives, Washington, D.C.

32. Records of Lamar; Vessel Papers, Reel 20, *Little Ada*; *O.R.N.*, Vol. XV, pp. 375–380; *O.R.A.*, Ser. IV, Vol. III, pp. 439–442.

33. *O.R.N.*, Vol. X, pp. 388–395; Bermuda Manifests; James Sprunt, *Tales of the Cape Fear Blockade; Being a Turn of the Century Account of Blockade Running*, (Raleigh: Capital Printing, 1902), pp. 118–125.

34. Taylor, *Running the Blockade*, pp. 110–113; Bermuda Consul, Reel 6, Jan. 18, 1864; *O.R.N.*, Vol. IX, pp. 437–439.

35. Taylor, *Running the Blockade*, pp. 101–110; Bermuda Manifests, *Bermuda Gazette*, Vessel Entrances and Clearances.

36. Taylor, *Running the Blockade*, pp. 95–97; *O.R.N.*, Vol. IX, pp. 60–61; *Bermuda Gazette*, Vessel Entrances and Clearances; Bermuda Manifests; Ordnance Account Book.

37. Vessel Papers, Reel 21, *General Moultrie; Charleston Mercury*, May 3, 1864; Charleston Cotton Bonds.

38. Price, "Blockade Running as a Business," pp. 45–46; Charleston Cotton Bonds; *Burckmyer Letters*, pp. 214, 308; Deposition of Henry S. Cobia, Cotton and Captured Property Records; Charleston *Mercury*, Feb. 18, 1864.

39. Depositions of Robert B. Dowie and G. W. Williams, Cotton and Captured Property Records; Charleston *Mercury*, Feb. 27, 1864, Nov. 18, 1864; Price, "Blockade Running as a Business," pp. 214–215; Vessel Papers, Reel 20, *Let Her Be*.

40. William C. Bee Company Papers, South Carolina Historical Society, Charleston, South Carolina; Wagner Papers; Lyon, *The Denny List*, No. 105–107; Depositions of W. Bee, T. D. Jervey, B. Mordecai, Cotton and Captured Property Records; Glasgow Consul, Reel 7, July 8 and Nov. 18, 1864; Bermuda Manifests; *Bermuda Gazette*, Vessel Entrances and Clearances.

41. Correspondence of the Confederate Treasury Department, p. 623; Vessel Papers, Reel 19, *Lucy; Bermuda Gazette*, Vessel Entrances and Clearances; *Nassau Guardian*, Vessel Entrances and Clearances.

42. Ordnance Account Book; Quartermaster Memorandum Book, Goff, *Confederate Supply*, pp. 211–227; *O.R.A.*, Ser. IV, Vol. III, pp. 379–380; 733–734; 987–988.

## Chapter Eight.   Failures in the Gulf

1. Mobile Entrances and Clearances; Havana Consul, Reel 46, Feb. 13, 1863; Mobile Manifests; Bradlee, *Blockade Running During the Civil War*, pp. 122–123.

2. *O.R.N.*, Vol. XIX, pp. 437–477.

3. *O.R.N.*, Vol. II, pp. 27–34, 673–674, Vol. XIX, pp. 410, 422, 479, 528–536, 533–573.

4. *O.R.N.*, Vol. XIX, pp. 506–509.

5. Mobile Entrances and Clearances, Mobile Manifests; Vessel Papers, Reel 6, *Cuba*.

6. Davis, *McRae*, pp. 151–152; *O.R.N.*, Vol. XVII, p. 405; Alfred Thayer Mahan, *The Gulf and Inland Waters* (New York: Jack Brussel, n.d.), pp. 218–221; Robert Holcombe, *Notes on the Classification of Confederate Ironclads* (Savannah: Corps of Engineers, 1980), pp. 20–23; Vessel Papers, Reel 6, *Cuba*; Mobile Entrances and Clearances, Mobile Manifests.

7. *O.R.A.*, Ser. IV, Vol. II, pp. 461–463; 472–473; *O.R.N.*, Vol. XVII, pp. 537–538; Havana Consul, Reel 46, Sept. 10, 1863.

8. Vessel Papers, Reel 1, *Alabama*.

9. Vessel Papers, Reel 1, *Alabama*, Reel 6, *Crescent*; *O.R.N.*, Vol. XVII, pp. 294–297, 397–399, 442–443; 463–465, 505–506, 511–512, Havana Consul, Reel 46, July 31, 1863; Ship Registers and Enrollments, *Lizzie Davis*; Mobile Entrances and Clearances, Mobile Manifests; *Warrior*, New Orleans Prize Court Records.

10. *O.R.N.*, Vol. XVII, pp. 556–568, Vol. XX, pp. 141, 155, 809, 818; Vessel Papers, Reel 11, *Fanny*; *Charleston Mercury*, May 22, 1863; *Leviathan*, New Orleans Prize Court Records, U.S. District Court of New Orleans, Admiralty Records, Fort Worth Federal Archives and Records Center, Fort Worth, Texas.

11. Vessel Papers, Reel I, *Alabama*; *O.R.N.*, Vol. XX, pp. 582–587.

12. Mobile Entrances and Clearances, Mobile Manifests. Ship Registers and Enrollments, *Grey Jacket*; Vessel Papers, Reel 13, *Grey Jacket*.

13. Havana Consul, Reel 46, June 10, Sept. 10, Nov. 2, Dec. 1, 1863, Jan. 2, 3, 13, 15, 1864; *O.R.N.*, Vol. II, p. 265, Vol. XVII, pp. 568, 602, 608; St. Marks Entrances and Clearances; Dudley Papers.

14. Havana Consul, Reel 46, May 9, 1863, June 22, 1864; *Union* and *Rosita*, Key West Prize Court Records.

15. St. Marks Entrances and Clearances; Havana Consul, Reel 46, Dec. 1, 1864; Correspondence of the Confederate Treasury Department, p. 617.

16. Bradlee, *Blockade Running during the Civil War*, p. 142.

17. Vessel Papers, Reel 8, *Denbigh*, Reel 9, *Donegal*; Richard Lucian Page Logs, Southern Historical Collection, University of North Carolina, Chapel Hill, North Carolina.

18. Bradlee, *Blockade Running during the Civil War*, p. 142; Liverpool Consul, Reel 26, Apr. 1, 1864.

19. Mobile Entrances and Clearances, Mobile Manifests; Vessel Papers, Reel 15, *Isabel*, Reel 9, *Donegal*, Reel 21, *Mary*; Pickett Papers, C. Helm to J. Benjamin, Aug. 17, 1864; Page Logs.

20. Havana Consul, Reel 46, July 9, 1864; Sallie Lightfoot Tarleton Papers, East Carolina State University Manuscripts, Greenville, North Carolina, Robert Tarleton to Sallie Lightfoot, Mar. 18, 1864.

21. Page Logs.

22. *O.R.N.*, Vol. XXI, pp. 321–323, 344–345; Page Logs.

23. Ibid.

24. Tarleton Papers, Robert Tarleton to Sallie Lightfoot, July 5, 7, 10, 12, 21, 1864; *O.R.N.*, Vol. XXI, pp. 353–357, 642, 904–907, 936; Havana Consul, Reel 46, July 1, 1864; Page Logs; *Civil War Naval Chronology*, Vol. VI, pp. 72–74.

25. *O.R.N.*, Vol. XXI, pp. 35–39.

26. Ibid., pp. 263–264; Vessel Papers, Reel 14, *Heroine*, Reel 25, *Red Gauntlet*.

27. *Civil War Naval Chronology*, Vol. IV, pp. 94–98, 108, Vol. VI, pp. 92–96.

28. Vessel Papers, Reel 14, *Heroine*.

29. Fry would later take command of the gunboat *Morgan*. After the war he became involved in running arms to Cuban revolutionaries. While in command of the *Virginius* (the former blockade runner *Virgin*), he was captured while attempting to land arms in Cuba. Fry and several of his crew were executed, sparking an international incident that nearly led to war between the United States and Spain. Jennie M. Walker, *Life of Captain Fry* (Hartford: J. B. Burr, 1875), p. 175; *O.R.N.*, Vol. XXI, pp. 263–264; Vessel Papers, Reel 25, *Red Gauntlet*.

30. Charleston, Mobile and Wilmington Entrances and Clearances, Glover, "West Gulf Blockade," pp. 235, 248–249.

31. Goff, *Confederate Supply*, p. 153; Glover, West Gulf Blockade, pp. 61–65; Thomas L. Connelly, "Vicksburg: Strategic Point or Propaganda Device?" *Military Affairs* XXXIV (April 1970), pp. 49–53.

32. Garner, "Galveston during the Civil War," p. 92; Galveston Cotton Bonds.

33. Thomas L. Connelly, *Army of the Heartland* (Baton Rouge: Louisiana State University Press, 1967), pp. 63, 66, 174; Connelly, "Vicksburg," pp. 49–53; *O.R.A.*, Vol. LIII, pp. 854, 925, Ser. IV, Vol. II, p. 1019.

34. Connelly, "Vicksburg," pp. 49–51; Allan Ashcraft, "Texas: 1860–1866. The Lone Star State in the Civil War," (Ph.D. dissertation, Columbia University, 1960), p. 199; Michael F. Wright, "Vicksburg and the Trans-Mississippi Supply Line (1861–1863)," *Journal of Mississippi History* LIII, (August 1981), pp. 210–225; Windham, "The Problem of Supply," p. 157.

35. Kerby, *Kirby Smith's Confederacy*, p. 170; Annie Cowling, "The Civil War Trade of the Lower Rio Grande Valley," (M.A. thesis, University of Texas, 1926), pp. 33–36; *O.R.A.*, Vol. LIII, p. 873, Vol XLIII, p. 986.

36. Glover, "West Gulf Blockade," pp. 64–67; Kerby, *Kirby Smith's Confederacy*, pp. 156–158; Ogden, "Blockaded Seaport," p. 116.

37. Kerby, *Kirby Smith's Confederacy*, pp. 84–85, 168–179, 198–206; Cowling, "Trade of the Lower Rio Grande," pp. 37–43; Windham, "The Problem of Supply," p. 167; Goff, *Confederate Supply*, pp. 135–136; Glover, "West Gulf Blockade," p. 206; *O.R.A.*, Ser. IV., Vol. III, pp. 567–568, 572–574; Pickett Papers, J. Quintero to J. Benjamin, June 10, 1863; Ronnie C. Tyler, *Santiago Vidaurri and the Southern Confederacy* (Austin: Texas State Historical Association, 1973), p. 108.

38. *O.R.N.*, Ser. II, Vol. III, pp. 732, 749, 751, 761, 804, 895; Herbert W. Biggs, *The Doctrine of Continuous Voyage* (Baltimore: Johns Hopkins Press, 1926), pp. 55–56; Bernath, *Squall across the Atlantic*, pp. 63–84; *Cases Argued and Decided in the Supreme Court of the United States*, Vol. 71, pp. 564–572; Carlton Savage, *Policy of the United States towards Maritime Commerce in War*, 2 Vols. (New York: Kraus Reprint Company, 1969), Vol. I, pp. 466–467.

39. Goff, *Confederate Supply*, pp. 135–136; Connelly, "Vicksburg," p. 50; William Diamond, "Imports of the Confederate Government from Europe and Mexico," *Journal of Southern History* VI (November 1940), pp. 497–500; Glover, "West Gulf Blockade," p. 136; Tyler, "The Age of Cotton," p. 108.

40. *Civil War Naval Chronology*, Vol. IV, pp. 50–51, Vol. VI, pp. 248–249; *O.R.N.*, Vol. XXI, pp. 159, 161, 170, 176–178, 194, 204.

41. There is very little information on the *Sachem* to substantiate her escape. *O.R.N.*, Vol. XXI, pp. 158–163.

42. Ibid., pp. 162, 176–177; Galveston Cotton Bonds.

43. Ibid., pp. 226–229; New Orleans Admiralty Records, *Isabel*.

44. *O.R.N.*, Vol. XXI, pp. 247–263.

45. Ibid., pp. 305–310.

46. Ogden, *Blockaded Seaport*, pp. 122–126; Key West Admiralty Records, *Mail, Union, Rosita*; Vessel Papers, Reel 7, *Carolina*.

47. Galveston Cotton Bonds.

## Chapter Nine.　The Lifeline Is Cut

1. Dudley Papers; Liverpool Consul, Reel 28, Sept. 18, 1864.

2. Liverpool Consul, Reel 28, Sept. 30, 1864.

3. Liverpool Consul, Reel 28, Sept. 17, 1864; *O.R.N.*, Vol. III, pp. 320–321; Bermuda Consul, Reel 6, Aug. 5, 1864; Middleton Family Papers, South Carolina Historical Society, Charleston, South Carolina, C. F. Middleton to his wife, Aug. 9, 21, 1864; Richard Paddington Papers, East Carolina State University, Greenville North Carolina.

4. Maffitt Papers, Mallory to Maffitt, Sept. 14, 1864; *O.R.N.*, Vol. III, pp. 320–321; Vol. X, pp. 468, 741–742; Diamond, "Imports of the Confederate Government," pp. 494–495; Ella Lonn, *Salt as a Factor in the Confederacy* (University: University of Alabama Press, 1965), pp. 167–169; Halifax Consul, Reel 46, Mar. 29, May 7, 12, 21, Aug. 17, 18, 19, 22, 23, 26, 30, 31, Sept. 5, 8, 12, 13, 17, Oct. 5, 6, 7, 11, 17, 24, 24, 25, Nov. 14, Dec. 21, 1864.

5. Nassau Consul, Reel 12, Oct. 20, 1864; Diamond, "Imports of the Confederate Government," pp. 494–495; Lonn, *Salt as a Factor in the Confederacy*, pp. 167–169.

6. Taylor, *Running the Blockade*, pp. 98–99, 100–101, 114–116.

7. Taylor, *Running the Blockade*, pp. 116–127; *O.R.N.*, Vol. X, pp. 492–501, 800.

8. M. P. Usina, "Blockade Running in Confederate Times," *Addresses Delivered before the Confederate Veterans Association of Savannah, Georgia* (George N. Nicols Press, 1895), pp. 2–39.

9. *O.R.A.*, Ser. IV, Vol. III, pp. 781–785, 930–932, 941; Taylor, *Running the Blockade*, pp. 138–140; Liverpool Consul Reel 25, Dec. 24, 1864; Nassau Consul, Reel 12, Oct. 31, 1864; *O.R.A.*, Ser. IV, Vol. III, pp. 733–734; Ordnance Account Books; Gorgas, "Notes," pp. 67–94; Gorgas, "Ordnance," p. 1036; Melton, "Major Military Industries," pp. 438–439.

10. *O.R.A.*, Ser. IV, Vol. III, pp. 733–734; Ordnance Account Book; Gorgas, "Notes," pp. 67–94; Gorgas, "Ordnance," p. 1036; Melton, "Major Military Industries," pp. 438–439.

11. Miscellaneous Contract Book; James Sprunt, "Running the Blockade," *Southern Historical Society Papers* XXIV (January–December 1896), p. 158; Diamond, "Imports of the Confederate Government," pp. 489–491; *O.R.A.*, Ser. IV, Vol. III, pp. 673–675, 677–680, 683–684.

12. Miscellaneous Contract Book; Wharncliffe Papers; *O.R.A.*, Ser. IV, Vol. III, pp. 527–530; Pickett Papers, L. Heyliger to J. Benjamin, Apr. 6, 1864.

13. There has been confusion in recent writing on blockade running concerning William Nathan Wrighte Hewett (1834–1886), and Augustus Charles Hobart-Hampden (1822–1886), as both operated under aliases and captained steamers owned by Collie and Company. *O.R.N.*, Vol. X, pp. 531–533, 552, 476, 484; *Dictionary of National Biography*, 27 Vols. (New York: Macmillan Company, 1908), Vol. X, pp. 756–757, 930–931; Taylor, *Running the Blockade*, pp. 128–130; Sprunt, *Chronicles of the Cape Fear*, p. 98.

14. Correspondence of the Confederate Treasury Department, Reel 2, pp. 531; Maffitt Papers; *O.R.N.*, Ser. II, Vol. II, pp. 720, 765–767; Press Copies of letters sent by the Treasury Department, Sept. 17–Nov. 28, 1864, Confederate Museum, Richmond, Virginia; Records Relating to the Erlanger Loan.

15. *O.R.N.*, Vol. X, pp. 547–551.

16. *O.R.N.*, Vol. III, pp. 298, 343, 372, 749, 785, Ser. II, pp. 778–781; Bulloch, *Secret Service*, Vol. II, pp. 124–143, 187–189; Liverpool Consul, Reel 30, Oct. 7, 1864.

17. Vessel Papers, Reel 10, *Edith*; *O.R.N.*, Vol. XI, pp. 7, 31–32.

18. Vance Papers, E. Murray to Z. Vance, Sept. 5, 1864; *O.R.N.*, Vol. X, pp. 435–456, 503, 783, 794.

19. *O.R.N.*, Vol. X, pp. 750–751, 744–775, 782–783, 793–794, 801–802; *O.R.A.*, Vol. LI, Pt. II, pp. 1042, 1044–1046; *Nassau Guardian*, Vessel Entrances and Clearances; *Bermuda Gazette*, Vessel Entrances and Clearances.

20. *O.R.A.*, Vol. LI, Pt. II, pp. 1043–1044, Ser. IV, Vol. III, 1055–1057; Vance Papers, J. Seddon to Z. Vance, Nov. 20, 1864; Nassau Consul, Reel 12, Nov. 1, 1864; Bermuda Consul, Reel 7, Jan. 13, 1865.

21. *O.R.A.*, Vol. LXI, Pt. II, pp. 1044–1045; *O.R.N.*, Vol. X, pp. 478–482, 578; Wilkinson, *Narrative of a Blockade Runner*, pp. 212–213; Scharf, *Confederate Navy*, Vol. II, pp. 808–809.

22. Scharf, *Confederate Navy*, Vol. II, pp. 806–808.

23. Ibid., pp. 808–809; Wilkinson, *Narrative of a Blockade Runner*, pp. 219–224.

24. Liverpool Consul, Reel 28, July 16, 26, Aug. 10, 1864; *Liverpool Journal of Commerce*, July 23, 1864; *O.R.N.*, Vol. IX, p. 393; Sprunt, *Chronicles of the Cape Fear River*, pp. 426–427, 432.

25. Bradlee writes that the Anglo-Confederate Trading Company issued two dividends in the fall of 1864, one $1,000 and the other $1,500 per $100 share. Bradlee, *Blockade Running during the Civil War*, pp. 45, 61–62; *O.R.A.*, Ser. IV, Vol. III, pp. 738–739; Liverpool Consul, Reel 29, Nov. 16, 1864.

26. Wharncliffe Papers, A. Collie to Lord Wharncliffe, Jan. 3, 7, 1865, J. Spence to Lord Wharncliffe, July 22, 1865, J. Spence to E. Stringer, Apr. 13, 1865.

27. Records of Gazaway B. Lamar.

28. Liverpool Consul, Reel 27, June 1, 15, 1864, Reel 28, July 6, 1864, Sept. 7, 14, 21, 24, Reel 29, Oct. 22, 28, 1864; *O.R.N.*, Vol. X, pp. 592–594, Vol. XI, 126–134; Prioleau Papers.

29. Ordnance Account Book.

30. *O.R.N.*, Vol. VIII, pp. 301, 420; Gragg, "Fort Fisher," pp. 59–69.

31. *O.R.N.*, Vol. XI, pp. 108–112, 252–261; Gragg, "Fort Fisher," pp. 69–75.

32. *O.R.A.*, Vol. XLII, pp. 1137, 1151–1152, 1160–1273; *O.R.N.*, XI, pp. 785–786; Gragg "Fort Fisher," pp. 76–88; William Lamb Diary, Swen Library, College of William and Mary, Williamsburg, Virginia; Pickett Papers, Entrances and Clearances of Bermuda; *Bermuda Gazette*, Vessel Entrances and Clearances.

33. *O.R.N.*, Vol. XI, pp. 207–245; Lamb Diary.

34. *O.R.N.*, Vol. XI, pp. 249–275; Fonvielle, "Fort Fisher," pp. 11–15; Gragg, "Fort Fisher," pp. 77–197.

35. *O.R.A.*, Vol. XLII, pp. 1318, 1326, 1330–1347; *O.R.N*, Vol. XI, p. 620; Arnold and Appleton Family Papers, Southern Historical Collection, University of North Carolina, Chapel Hill, North Carolina, Diary of Mary Ellen Arnold; Lamb Diary; Pickett Papers, Bermuda Entrances and Clearances; Bermuda Gazette, Vessel Entrances and Clearances; William Lamb, *Colonel Lamb's Story of Fort Fisher* (Wilmington: Wilmington Printing Company, 1966), p. 35.

36. Daniel Ammen, "Our Second Bombardment of Fort Fisher," *Military Order of the Loyal Legion of the United States, Commandery of the District of Columbia* (Washington: The Commandery, 1187), pp. 1–8.

37. *O.R.N.*, Vol. XI, pp. 785–786; *Civil War Naval Chronology*, Vol. VI, p. 211.

38. Wilkinson, *Narrative of a Blockade Runner*, pp. 228–248; Maffitt Papers.

39. Usina, *Blockade Running in Confederate Times*, pp. 38–39.

40. *O.R.N.*, Vol. XI, pp. 618, 620, 623, 624, 626–628.

41. Wilkinson, *Narrative of a Blockade Runner*, pp. 228–248.

42. Waddell Papers; Bermuda Consul, Reel 7, Jan. 23, 1865.

43. *O.R.N.*, Vol. XVI, pp. 36–37; "Blockade Running," p. 561; *Nassau Guardian*, Vessel Entrances and Clearances.

44. *Nassau Guardian*, Feb. 22, 1865; *O.R.N.*, Vol. XVI, p. 354; *Nassau Guardian*, Vessel Entrances and Clearances.

45. *Nassau Guardian*, Feb. 22, 1865; *O.R.N.*, Vol. XVI, p. 252; Charles Cowley, *Leaves from a Lawyer's Life Afloat* (Boston: Lee and Shepard, 1879), pp. 170–171.

46. *O.R.N.*, Vol. XVI, p. 252.

47. *Nassau Guardian*, Feb. 22, 1865; Nassau Consul, Reel 12, Feb. 24, 1864, Mar. 1, 1864.

48. Quartermaster Memorandum Book; *O.R.A.*, Ser. IV, Vol III, pp. 1039–1041.

49. *O.R.A.*, Ser. IV, Vol. III, pp. 986–991.

50. Wilkinson, *Narrative of a Blockade Runner*, p. 212; Vandiver, "The Food Supply of the Confederate Armies, 1865," *Tyler's Quarterly Historical and Genealogical Magazine* XXVI (October 1944), pp. 209–210; *O.R.A.*, Ser. IV, Vol. III, pp. 941, 955–958.

51. *O.R.A.*, Ser. IV, Vol. III, pp. 1076–1077; Vance Letters, Z. Vance to J. White, Feb. 28, 1865.

52. *O.R.A.*, Ser. IV, Vol. III, pp. 1071–1073; Liverpool Consul, Reel 31, May 11, 1865; *O.R.N.*, Vol. XVII, p. 820, Ser. II, Vol. II, pp. 804–806; Maffitt Papers, Mallory to Maffitt, Feb. 24, 1865; Havana Consul, Reel 46, Mar. 11, 1865.

53. Havana Consul, Reel 46, Sept. 9, 17, 1864, Oct. 8, 20, 1864; Correspondence of the Confederate Treasury Department, Reel 2, pp. 772–773, 799–801; Erlanger Loan, Cotton and Captured Property Records; Glover, "West Gulf Blockade," pp. 203–205.

54. Liverpool Consul, Reel 29, Nov. 4, 1864; Havana Consul, Reel 46, July 2, 1864, Feb. 10, 1865; *O.R.A.*, Ser. IV, Vol. III, pp. 625–626.

55. Havana Consul, Reel 46, Feb. 4, 1865; Correspondence of the Confederate Treasury Department, Reel 2, p. 812.

56. Glover, "West Gulf Blockade," pp. 188–190, 201–205; Taylor, *Running the Blockade*, pp. 157–158; Foreign Supply Office Letterbook for Marshal, Texas, 2 Vols. Confederate Museum, Richmond, Virginia; Wharncliffe Papers, Jan. 16, 1865; Havana Consul, Reel 46, Feb. 3, 24, 1865; *London Index*, Feb. 2, 1865.

57. *O.R.N.*, Vol. III, pp. 393–394, Vol. XXII, p. 124; Wendell E. Pierce, "The Blockade Runner *Acadia*," *Journal of the Confederate Historical Society* X (Winter 1973), pp. 147–168; Havana Consul, Reel 46, Feb. 3, 1865.

58. *O.R.N.*, Vol. XXII, pp. 27–32.

59. Ibid., pp. 32–37.

60. Havana Consul, Reel 46, Mar. 16, 1865, May 1, 16, 1865; Maffitt Papers; John F. Mackie, "Running the Blockade: Escape of the *Fox*," in *Under Both Flags*, ed. George M. Vickers (Chicago: C. F. Bagley and Company, 1896), pp. 329–332.

61. *O.R.N.*, Vol. XXII, pp. 142–170.

62. *O.R.N.*, Vol. III, pp. 415–426, 435, 440, 464–465, 524, 537, 540, 719–748; Havana Consul, Reel 46, May 11, 29, 1865.

63. Kerby, *Kirby Smith's Confederacy*, p. 378; Letterbooks for Marshall, Texas.

64. *O.R.N.*, Vol. XXII, pp. 198, 203, 205–207, 211, 216–217; Kerby, *Kirby Smith's Confederacy*, pp. 520–528; Garner, Galveston during the Civil War," pp. 217–218; Ogden, "Blockaded Seaport," pp. 173–174.

## Chapter Ten.  The Final Ledger

1. Charleston, Mobile, New Orleans, St. Marks and Galveston Cotton Bonds; Dudley Papers; Todd, *Confederate Finances*, p. 60; Charleston, Mobile, New Orleans, St. Marks, Galveston, Wilmington, and Savannah Entrances and Clearances; *Nassau Guardian*, Vessel Entrances and Clearances; *Bermuda Gazette*, Vessel Entrances and Clearances; Bermuda Manifests; Reports for the United States Consuls for Bermuda, Nassau and Havana; Fenner, "Confederate Finances Abroad," pp. 220, 223–224.

2. Liverpool Consul, Reel 31, Mar. 7, 10, May 9, 1865.

3. Wilkinson, *Narrative of a Blockade Runner*, pp. 249–250; Liverpool Consul, Reel 31, Dec. 14, 1864, Apr. 11, May 9, 19, 1865; Records Concerning Confederate Property in Europe, Treasury Department Records, Record Group 365, National Archives, Washington D.C.; Davis, *McRae*, pp. 77–81; Wren, Key West Admiralty Records; *The United States versus John Fraser and Company* (Charleston: H. P. Cooke and Company, n.d.), pp. 1–60; *The United States versus John Fraser and Company, et al.* (Charleston: Walker, Evans and Cogswell, 1873), pp. 1–23; U.S. Congress, House, *Fraser, Trenholm and Company*, Ex. Doc. No. 63, 39th Congress, 2d Sess., 1867.

4. Liverpool Consul, Reel 31, June 23, 1865; Glasgow Consul, Reel 7, Feb. 9, 1865; Taylor, *Running the Blockade*, pp. 163–164; Wharncliffe Manuscripts, A. Collie to Lord Wharncliffe, Feb. 28, Apr. 3, 7, Aug. 25, 1865, June 27, 1868, E. Spence to Lord Wharncliffe, Jan. 3, July 22, 1865, Feb. 10, 1866, Apr. 15, 1868, E. Stringer to Lord Wharncliffe, Apr. 9, 1868.

5. Records of Gazaway B. Lamar; Coddington, "Gazaway B. Lamar," pp. 33–36.

6. Wagner Papers, *Charleston Mercury*, Feb. 27, 1864, Jan. 20, 1865; Depositions of B. Mordecai, T. D. Jervey, W. C. Bee, R. Dowie, A. S. Johnston, Henry Cobia and G. W. Williams, Cotton and Captured Property Records; *Burckmyer Letters*, pp. 463–466; William C. Bee and Company Papers; Henry Buist Manuscript, Perkins Library, Duke University, Durham, North Carolina.

7. *O.R.A.*, Ser. IV, Vol. III, p. 1117; Clark, "The Raising, Organization and Equipment of North Carolina Troops," pp. 59–62; Boyd, "Fiscal and Economic Conditions of North

Carolina," pp. 200, 209; Bradlee, *Blockade Running during the Civil War*, pp. 137–139; Sprunt, "Running the Blockade," pp. 157–158.

8. Gorgas wrote after the war that the Confederacy produced just over 50,000 rifles and salvaged another 150,000 from the battlefields. At the start of the war the South had about 25,000 rifles taken from federal arsenals. From all reports there seems to have been very little private importation of arms, especially rifles. Gorgas, "Notes," pp. 90–94; Gorgas, "Ordnance," pp. 184–187; Connelly, "Vicksburg," p. 49; Ordnance Account Book; Correspondence of the Confederate Treasury Department, Reel II, pp. 11–17, 295–340, 397–409, 725–727; Memorandum Book.

# Bibliography

## Manuscripts

American Jewish Historical Society, Waltham, Massachusetts
  Cohen Family Papers
Atlanta Federal Archives and Records Center, East Point, Georgia
  Record Group 21:
    Key West Admiralty Records
Bahamas Archives, Nassau, Bahamas
  Letters received from the Colonial Office File, 1862–1863
Bermuda Archives, Hamilton, Bermuda
  Bermuda Custom Manifests
  *Talisman* Log
Boston Federal Archives and Records Center, Waltham, Massachusetts
  Record Group 21:
    Boston Admiralty Records
Center for Archival Collections, Bowling Green State University, Bowling Green, Ohio
  Eric Heyl Collection
College of William and Mary, Williamsburg, Virginia
  William Lamb Diary
Duke University Library, Durham, North Carolina
  Thomas Sterling Begbie Papers
  Catherine Buie Papers
  Henry Buist Papers
  Campbell Family Papers
  William W. Clark Papers
  John Clopton Papers
  Ann Thomas Coleman Papers
  Confederate States Archives Papers
  Francis Porteus Corbin Papers
  Kendall Cox and Company Papers
  Thomas Tingey Craven Papers
  Fuller Family Papers
  Hinsdale Family Papers
  Thomas William Hull Papers
  *Intended* Logbook

Edmund Jennings Lee II Papers
James M. Longacre Papers
Eliza J. McEwen Papers
Hugh McRae Papers
Munford-Ellis Family Papers
Naval Papers
A. J. Orme Papers
Samuel Finley Papers
Mary Jane Pursley Papers
S. C. Roberts Papers
William Dunlap Simpson Papers
Spanish Consulate, Charleston, S.C., Papers
Alexander Sprunt and Son, Inc. Papers
Charles Steedman Papers
Thomas Holdup Stevens Papers
Philip E. Walden Papers
Edward Mitchel Whaley Papers
East Carolina University Library, Greenville, North Carolina
Elizabeth Rudder Fearington Croom Collection
John G. Fennel Papers
James Clarence Galloway Collection
Sylvanus M. Hankins Papers
Hunter-Wills Family Papers
Richard Parson Paddington Papers
Sallie Lightfoot Tarleton Papers
Arthur Whitford Papers
Emory University Library, Atlanta, Georgia
Theodore Turner Fogle Papers
British Consulate, Savannah, Georgia, Papers
Virginia McBlair Papers
Charles Brown Thurston Papers
Florida State University Libraries
William A. Swan Papers
Fort Worth Federal Archives and Records Center, Fort Worth, Texas
Record Group 21:
New Orleans Admiralty Papers
Georgia Historical Society, Savannah, Georgia
Keith Reed Collection
Charles Steedman Papers
Paschal Nelson Strong Papers
Telfair Family Papers
Glasgow University Archives, Glasgow, Scotland

UCS1 Collection
Henry E. Huntington Library, San Marino, California
    Thomas Haines Dudley Papers
Johns Hopkins University Library, Baltimore, Maryland
    Sidney and Clifford Lanier Papers
Library of Congress, Washington, District of Columbia
    James Murry Mason Papers
    Eugene Mejan Correspondence
    Picket Papers
    George Alfred Trenholm Papers
    Edward Willis Papers
Mariners' Museum, Newport News, Virginia
    Edwin Eldredge Collection
Masachusetts Historical Society, Boston, Massachusetts
    Charles Francis Adams Diary
    Charles Francis Adams Letterbook
Merseyside Archives, Merseyside, England
    Charles K. Prioleau Papers
Museum of the Confederacy, Richmond, Virginia
    Ordnance Department, Account Letterbook of Captain John M. Payne
    Foreign Supply Office, Letterbook for Marshal, Texas
    Treasury Department, Press Copies of Letters Sent, Sept. 17–Nov. 28, 1864
Museum Department, City Museum, Mobile, Alabama
    George Tuthill Account Book
National Archives, Washington, District of Columbia
    Record Group 19:
        Ship Plans of Blockade Runners
    Record Group 36:
        Entrances and Clearances for New Orleans, Mobile, and Charleston
        Cargo Manifests for New Orleans, Mobile, and Charleston
    Record Group 41:
        Ships Registers and Enrollments
    Record Group 45:
        CSN Papers
        *Cornubia* Papers
    Record Group 56:
        Letters of the Confederate Secretary of the Treasury
        Cotton and Captured Property Records
    Record Group 84:
        Consular Despatches for Bermuda, Dublin, Liverpool, Nassau, Glasgow,
            Halifax, and Havana
    Record Group 109:

Vessel Papers
Memorandum Book Relating to Agents and Supplies
Miscellaneous Contract Book
Copies of Letters and Telegrams Sent and Received by Governor Zebulon B.
Vance
Letters Sent by the Confederate Secretary of War
Record Group 365:
Records Relating to the Erlanger Loan
Charleston Cotton Bonds
Inward and Outward Cargo Manifests for Charleston, S.C.
Records Concerning Federal Property in Europe
Confederate Collector's Correspondence
Record Group 366:
Records of Gazaway B. Lamar
Norfolk Public Library, Norfolk, Virginia
William Conway Whittle Papers
North Carolina State Archives, Raleigh, North Carolina
Charles A. Anderson Papers
John Julius Guthrie Papers
Edward Jones Hale Papers
Zebulon B. Vance Papers
Waddell Papers
Rosenburg Public Library, Galveston, Texas
George W. Grover Papers
Henry Sampson Papers
St. George Historical Society, St. George, Bermuda
Blockade Papers
Scott, Lithgow, Ltd., Glasgow, Scotland
John Scott and Sons Ship List and Builders Certificates
Sheffield City Libraries, Sheffield, England
Edward Stuart Wortley-Maskenzie (First Earl of Wharncliffe) Papers
South Carolina Historical Society, Charleston, South Carolina
William C. Bee and Company Papers
Fraser Family Papers
Grimball Family Papers
Hutson Lee Papers
Merchant Papers
Middleton Family Papers
Thomas Tobias Papers
Theodore D. Wagner Papers
South Caroliniana Library, University of South Carolina, Columbia, South
Carolina

Oskar Aickel Papers
Anonymous (Vincent) Papers
Oscar Charles Badger Papers
Percival Drayton Papers
Edward Harleston Edwards Papers
William R. Godfrey Papers
Ambrosio J. Gonzales Papers
John Berkely Grimball Papers
William A. Gyles Papers
Eugene P. Jervey Papers
James F. Izlar Diary
Elliott Keith Diary
John B. Lafitte Papers
Samuel Wells Leland Papers
Thomas Reeder Papers
George Alfred Trenholm Papers
Baxter Watson Papers
Southern Historical Collection, University of North Carolina, Chapel Hill, North
Carolina
Edward C. Anderson Papers
Arnold and Appleton Family Papers
Francis Thornton Chew Papers
Chisolm Family Papers
DeRossett Family Papers
*Florida* Log
Forrest Family Papers
Catherine E. Hanes Papers
John Newland Maffitt Papers
James Heward North Papers
*Oneida* Ship Diary
Richard Lucien Page Logs
James Ryder Randall Papers
Peter Evans Smith Papers
Henry Sumner Papers
Laura Cornelia Warlick Papers
Eugene Whitmore Papers
C. A. Withers Reminiscences
Suitland Federal Archives and Records Center, Suitland, Maryland
Record Group 21:
District of Columbia Admiralty Records
University of Texas Library, Austin, Texas
Thomas William House Papers

Jose San Roman Papers
University of West Virginia Library, Morgantown, West Virginia
  Isaac McNeel Papers
Western Reserve Historical Society, Cleveland, Ohio
  Braxton Bragg Papers
In the possession of Dr. Charles Peery, Charleston, South Carolina
  Charles Smith Peck Papers

## Newspapers

*Bahamas Herald*
*Bermuda Royal Gazette*
*Charleston Daily Courier*
*Charleston Mercury*
*DeBow's Review*
*Galveston Weekly News*
*Hunt's Merchant Magazine and Commercial Review*
*Liverpool Chronicle*
*London Index*
*London Times*
*Mobile Daily Advertiser and Register*
*Nassau Guardian*
*New Orleans Daily Picayune*
*Savannah Daily Republican*
*Wilmington Journal*

## Printed Primary Sources, Public Documents, and Reminiscences

### Books

*Acts of the General Assembly of the State of South Carolina Passed in December, 1861.* Columbia, South Carolina: Charles P. Pelham, 1862.

*Acts of the General Assembly of the State of South Carolina Passed in December, 1862 and February and April, 1863.* Columbia, South Carolina: Charles P. Pelham, 1863.

*Acts of the General Assembly of the State of South Carolina Passed in September and December, 1863.* Columbia, South Carolina: Charles P. Pelham, 1864.

*Acts of the General Assembly of the State of South Carolina Passed at the Sessions of 1864–1865.* Columbia, South Carolina: Julian A. Selby, 1866.

Anderson, Charles R., and Aubrey H. Starke, eds. *The Centennial Edition of the Works of Sidney Lanier.* 10 Vols. Baltimore: Johns Hopkins University Press, 1945.

Boyd, Belle. *Belle Boyd in Camp and Prison.* New York: Bielock and Company, 1865.

Boyer, Samuel P. *Naval Surgeon: The Diary of Dr. Samuel Pellman Boyer.* Edited by Elener and James Barnes. Bloomington: Indiana University Press, 1963.

*British and Foreign State Papers, 1864–1865.* Vol. LV. London: William Ridgeway, 1870.

Bulloch, James D. *The Secret Service of the Confederate States in Europe.* 2 Vols. New York: G. P. Putnam's Sons, 1884.

*Burckmyer Letters.* Columbia, South Carolina: The State Company, 1926.

*Cases Argued and Decided in the Supreme Court of the United States.* 450 Vols. Rochester: Lawyers Co-operative Publishing Company, 1901–.

Castlen, Harriet Gift. *Hope Bids Me Onward.* Savannah: Chatham Printing Company, 1945.

Clayton, William F. *A Narrative of the Confederate Navy.* Weldon, North Carolina: Harrell's Printing House, 1910.

Conrad, August. *Schatten Und Lichtblicke aus dem Amerikanischen Leben wahrend des Secessions-Krieges.* Hanover, Hanover: Th. Schulze's Buchhandlung, 1879.

Crowley, Charles. *Leaves from a Lawyer's Life Afloat.* Boston: Lee and Shepard, 1879.

Curtis, Walter Gilmer. *Reminiscences of Wilmington and Smithville—Southport, 1848–1900.* Southport, North Carolina: Herald Job Office, 1900.

Davis, Jefferson. *Rise and Fall of the Confederate Government.* New York: D. Appleton and Company, 1881.

Dawson, Francis W. *Reminiscences of Confederate Service.* Charleston and Courier Presses, 1882.

DeLeon, T. C. *Four Years in Rebel Capitals.* Mobile: Gossip Printing Company, 1890.

*Directory of Charleston, South Carolina, 1860.* Charleston: W. E. Ferslew, 1860.

Great Britain Foreign Office. *Correspondence Respecting the Seizure of the British Vessels Springbok and Peteroff by the United States Cruisers in 1863.* London: R. M. Stationary Office, 1900.

Great Britain Foreign Office. *Papers Relating to the Blockade of the Ports of the Confederate States.* London: Harrison, 1862.

Hague, Parthenia A. *A Blockaded Family: Life in Southern Alabama During the Civil War.* Boston: Houghton, Mifflin, 1885.

Hayes, John D., ed. *Samuel Francis Du Pont: A Selection from His Civil War Letters.* Ithaca: Cornell University Press, 1969.

Hobart-Hampden, Augustus C. *Never Caught.* London: John Camden Holton, 1867.

————. *Sketches of My Life.* New York: D. Appleton, 1887.

Hoole, Stanley W., ed. *Confederate Foreign Agent: The European Diary of Major Edward C. Anderson.* University, Alabama: Confederate Publishing Company, 1976.

Huse, Caleb. *The Supplies for the Confederate Army, How They Were Obtained in Europe and How Paid For. Personal Reminiscences and Unpublished History.* Boston: T. R. Marvin, 1904.

Johnston, Frontis W., ed. *The Papers of Zebulon Baird Vance.* Raleigh: Department of Archives and History, 1963.

Jones, John B. *A Rebel War Clerk's Diary.* New York: Sagamore Press, 1958.

Lamb, William. *Colonel Lamb's Story of Fort Fisher.* Wilmington: Wilmington Printing Company, 1966.

Lyon, David John, comp. *The Denny List.* 4 Vols. London: National Maritime Museum, 1975.

Mason, Virginia, ed. *The Public Life and Diplomatic Correspondence of James M. Mason, with Some Personal History.* Roanoke, Stone Printing Company, 1903.

Mitchel, C. Bradford, ed. *Merchant Steam Vessels of the United States 1790-1868.* Staten Island: Steamship Historical Society of America, 1975.

Morgan, James M. *Recollections of a Rebel Reefer.* New York: Houghton, Mifflin, 1917.

Palmer, Sir Roundell. *A Speech Delivered in the House of Commons on the North American Blockade, March 7, 1862.* London: J. Ridgeway, 1862.

Parry, Clive, ed. *The Consolidated Treaty Series.* 220 Vols. Dobbs Ferry: Oceana Publications, 1969.

Porter, A. Toomer. *Led On!* New York: G. P. Putnam and Sons, 1898.

Preble, George Henry. *Chase of the Rebel Steamer Oreto.* Cambridge, Massachusetts: n.p., 1862.

*Register of Officers of the Confederate Navy 1861-1865.* Washington: Government Printing Office, 1931.

*Report on the Harbor of Charleston, South Carolina.* Charleston: Walker, Evans, and Company, 1858.

Richardson, James D., ed. *Compilation of Messages and Papers of the Confederacy, including Diplomatic Correspondence, 1861-1865.* Nashville: U.S. Publishing Company, 1905.

Russell, William Howard. *My Diary North and South.* 2 vols. London: Bradbury and Evans, 1863.

Sands, Benjamin. *From Reefer to Rear Admiral.* New York: Frederick A. Stokes, 1899.

Semmes, Raphael. *Service Afloat.* Baltimore: Baltimore Publishing Company, 1887.

*Southern Business Directory.* Charleston: Walker and James, 1854.

Taylor, Thomas E. *Running the Blockade.* London: J. Murray, 1897.

United States Bureau of Census. *Census of the United States, Manufacturers in 1860.* Washington: Government Printing Office, 1865.

United States Circuit Court of Appeals. *The United States versus John Fraser and Company.* Charleston: Walker, Evans, and Cogswell, 1873.

_____. *The United States versus John Fraser and Company, et al.* Charleston: Walker, Evans, and Cogswell, 1873.

Usina, M. P. *Blockade Running in Confederate Times.* Savannah: George N. Nichols Press, 1895.

Vandiver, Frank, ed. *Confederate Blockade Running Through Bermuda, 1861–1865; Letter and Cargo Manifests.* Austin: University of Texas Press, 1947.

_____. *The Civil War Diary of General Josiah Gorgas.* University: University of Alabama Press, 1947.

Walker, Georgiana F. (Gholson). *Private Journal, 1862–1865, with Selections from the Post-War 1866–1876.* Tuscaloosa: Confederate Publishing Company, 1963.

*War of the Rebellion: A Compilation of the Official Records of the Union and Confederate Armies.* Washington: Government Printing Office, 1880–1901.

*War of the Rebellion: The Official Records of the Union and Confederate Navies.* Washington: Government Printing Office, 1896.

Watson, William. *The Adventures of a Blockade Runner; or, Trade in Time of War.* New York: Macmillan, 1892.

Wilkinson, John. *The Narrative of a Blockade Runner.* New York: Sheldon, 1877.

### Articles

Almy, John J. "Incidents of the Blockade." *Military Order of the Loyal Legion of the United States. The Commandery of the District of Columbia.* 4 vols. (Washington: The Commandery, 1892), I, 1–10.

Ammen, Daniel. "Our Second Bombardment of Fort Fisher." *Military Order of the Loyal Legion of the United States. The Commandery of the District of Columbia.* 4 vols. (Washington: The Commandery, 1887), I, 1–8.

Anderson, William H. "Blockade Life." *Military Order of the Loyal Legion of the United States. The Commandery of the State of Maine.* 3 Vols. (Portland, Maine: Thurston, 1898–1908), II, 1–10.

Beauregard, Pierre, G. T. "Torpedo Service in the Harbor and Water Defenses of Charleston." *Southern Historical Society Papers* V (April 1878), 145–161.

Brand, Robert. "Reminiscences of the Blockade off Charleston." *Military Order of the Loyal Legion of the United States. The Commandery of the State of Wisconsin.* 3 Vols. (Milwaukee: Burdick, Armitage, and Allen, 1891–1903), III, 14–32.

Chester, Colby M. "Chasing the Blockaders." *Military Order of the Loyal Legion of the United States. Commandery of the District of Columbia.* 4 Vols. (Washington: The Commandery, 1913), IV, 1–20.

Crenshaw, Edward. "The Diary of Edward Crenshaw. *Alabama Historical Quarterly* I (Fall 1930), 261–270, (Winter 1930), 438–452, II (Spring 1931), 52–71, (Summer 1931), 210–238.

Cushing, William Barker. "Outline Story of the War Experiences of William Barker Cushing as Told by Himself." *United States Naval Institute Proceedings* XXXVIII (September 1912), 941–991.

Dickinson, A. G. "Blockade Running from Wilmington." *Confederate Veteran* III (January–December 1895), 361.

————. "Running the Blockade." *Era* XIII (April 1904), 249–254.

Dundas, William O. "Blockade Running in the Civil War." *Bellman* XXVI (March 1919), 606–608.

————. "Running the Blockade in the Civil War." *United Daughters of the Confederacy Magazine* XV (November 1952), 5, 8–9, 12.

Evans, Paul, and Thomas P. Green, trans. and eds. "A Belgian Consul Reports on Conditions in the South in 1860 and 1862." *Journal of Southern History* III (November 1937), 478–491.

Gorgas, Josiah. "Ordnance of the Confederacy." *Army Ordnance* XVI (January–February 1936), 212–216, (March–April 1936), 283–288.

————. "Notes on the Ordnance Department of the Confederate Government." *Southern Historical Society Papers* XII (January–February 1884), 67–94.

Henry-Ruffin, Mrs. M. E. "Running the Blockade." in *Under Both Flags*, George M. Vickers, ed. (Boston: J. S. Round and Company, 1896), 556–567.

Jefferies, Clarence. "Running the Blockade on the Mississippi." *Confederate Veteran* XXII (January–December 1914), 22–23.

Jervey, Theodore D. "Charleston During the Civil War." *Annual Report of the American Historical Association for the Year 1913* I (1915), 167–177.

Johns, John. "Wilmington during the Blockade." *Harper's New Monthly Magazine* XXXIII (September 1866), 497–503.

Jones, Mary Caldwalder. "Chapters from Unwritten Biographies." *Bookman* LIX (April 1924), 158–163.

McEachern, Leora H., and Isabel M. Williams. "The Prevailing Epidemic—1862." *Lower Cape Fear Historical Society Bulletin* XI (November 1967), 1–20.

Mackie, John F. "Running the Blockade: Escape of the Fox." in *Under Both Flags*, George M. Vickers, ed. (Boston: J. S. Round and Company, 1896), 329–332.

Maffitt, John Newland. "Blockade Running." *United Service* VI (June 1882), 626–633, VII (July 1882), 14–22, new series, VII (February 1892), 147–173.

————. "Reminiscences of the Confederate Navy." *United Service* III (October 1880), 495–514.

Mahan, Alfred T. "Minor Trial of Blockade Duty." *Harper's Weekly* LI (October 1907), 1556.

Narrell, H. D. "Running the Blockade." *Confederate Veteran* XXI (January–December 1913), 591–592.

"Particulars of the Steamer *Arizona*." *Journal of the Franklin Institute* LXVII (January 1859), 208.

"Particulars of the Steamer *Austin*." *Journal of the Franklin Institute* LXIX (April 1860), 324.

"Particulars of the Steamer *Cecile*." *Journal of the Franklin Institute* LXIV (November 1857), 352.

"Particulars of the Steamer *Charles Morgan.*" *Journal of the Franklin Institute* LVII (February 1854), 131.

"Particulars of the Steamboat *Cuba.*" *Journal of the Franklin Institute* LIX (January 1885), 57.

"Particulars of the Steam Dredger *General Moultrie.*" *Journal of the Franklin Institute* LXII (December 1956), 407.

"Particulars of the Steamer *Florida.*" *Journal of the Franklin Institute* LXIX (January 1860), 136.

"Particulars of the Steamers *Galveston* and *Opelousas.*" *Journal of the Franklin Institute* LXIII (April 1857), 285.

"Particulars of the Steamer *Magnolia.*" *Journal of the Franklin Institute* LXV (January 1858), 60.

"Particulars of the Steamer *Nashville.*" *Journal of the Franklin Institute* LVII (March 1854), 200.

"Particulars of the Steamer *North Carolina.*" *Journal of the Franklin Institute* LXXII (July 1861), 202.

"Particulars of the Steamer *Orizaba No. 2.*" *Journal of the Franklin Institute* LXVI (August 1858), 121.

"Particulars of the Steamer *Tennessee.*" *Journal of the Franklin Institute* LVII (March 1854), 199.

"Particulars of the Steamer *William G. Hewes.*" *Journal of the Franklin Institute* LXXI (April 1861), 270.

"Particulars of the Steamer *William H. Webb.*" *Journal of the Franklin Institute* LXIII (January 1857), 48.

"Particulars of the Steamer *Yorktown.*" *Journal of the Franklin Institute* LXVIII (July 1859), 139.

Peck, W. F. G. "Four Years Under Fire at Charleston." *Harper's New Monthly Magazine* XXXI (August 1865), 358–366.

Plummer, E. C. "Running the Gauntlet." *New England Magazine* XIV (May 1896), 282–285.

Post, Charles A. "A Diary on the Blockade in 1863." *United States Naval Institute Proceedings* XLIV (October 1918), 2333–2350.

Romaine, Laurence B. "Blockade Runner Who Never Returned; The Story of James Dickson's Diary-Logbook—1861–1862." *Manuscripts* (April 1955), 166–172.

Sands, Francis P. B. "The Blockade and the Fall of Fort Fisher." *Military Order of the Loyal Legion of the United States. Commandery of the District of Columbia.* 4 Vols. (Washington: The Commandery, 1902), II, 1–30.

————. "My Messmates and Shipmates Who Are Now Gone." *Military Order of the Loyal Legion of the United States. Commandery of the District of Columbia.* 4 Vols. (Washington: The Commandery, 1908), IV, 1–22.

Semmes, Raphael. "The Sumter Runs the Mississippi Blockade." *Confederate Veteran* XXIV (January–December 1916), 502–503.

Sprunt, James. "Running the Blockade." *Southern Historical Society Papers* XXIV (January–December 1896), 157–165.

Staudenras, J. P., ed. "A War Correspondent's View of St. Augustine and Fernandina." *Florida Historical Quarterly* (July 1962), 60–65.

Vandiver, Frank E., ed. "The Capture of a Confederate Blockade Runner." *North Carolina Historical Review* (April 1944), 136–138.

West, Horatio L. "The Blockading Service." *Military Order of the Loyal Legion of the United States. The Commandery of the State of Illinois* 4 Vols. (Chicago: A. C. McClurg, 1891–1912), II, 211–252.

## Government Documents

United States. 36th Cong., 2d Sess. House Ex. Doc. No. 6 "Commerce and Navigation." Washington, 1860.

_____. 39th Cong. 2d Sess. House Ex. Doc. No. 63. "Fraser, Trenholm and Company." Washington, 1867.

_____. 36th Cong., 1st Sess. Senate Ex. Doc. No. 29. "In answer to a resolution of the Senate of the 21st instant, a report of the Secretary of the Navy, accompanied by copies of instructions given to the Officer of the United States Naval Forces on the coasts of Mexico to protect the persons and property of the citizens of the United States, and copies of the official reports of Captain Jarvis and Commander Turner of the capture of two Mexican war steamers, and the causes which led to said capture." Washington, 1860.

_____. 37th Cong., 2d Ses. House Report No. 36 "Permanent Fortifications and Sea Coast Defenses." Washington, 1862.

_____. 36th Cong., 2d Sess. House Ex. Doc. No. 14. "Report of the Superintendent of the Coast Survey Showing the Progress of the Survey During the Year 1860." Washington, 1861.

_____. 38th Cong., 2d Sess. House Ex. Doc. No. 11. "Report of the Superintendent of the Coast Survey Showing the Progress of the Survey During the Year 1863." Washington, 1863.

_____. 36th Cong., 2d Sess. House Ex. Doc. No. 6. "Report on the Commercial Relations of the United States with Foreign Nations for the Year Ending September 30, 1861." Washington, 1860.

_____. 50th Cong., 1st Sess. House Ex. Doc. No. 6. "Report on the Internal Commerce of the United States." Washington, 1887.

_____. 36th Cong., 1st Sess. House Ex. Doc. No. 33. "Statement Showing the Amount of Revenue Collected Annually in each Collection District from June 30, 1854 to June 30, 1859, together with the Amount Expended and the Persons Employed in each District." Washington, 1860.

_____. 38th Cong., 1st Sess. Senate Ex. Doc. No. 55. "Statistics of Foreign and Domestic Commerce of the United States." Washington, 1864.

---

## Secondary Sources

### Books

Albury, Paul. *The Story of the Bahamas*. London: Macmillan Caribbean, 1975.

Baughman, James P. *Charles Morgan and the Development of Southern Transportation*. Nashville: Vanderbilt University Press, 1968.

Barnath, Stuart L. *Squall Across the Atlantic*. Berkeley: University of California Press, 1970.

Black, Robert C. *The Railroads of the Confederacy*. Chapel Hill: University of North Carolina Press, 1952.

Blatchford, Samuel. *Reports of Cases Argued and Determined in the Courts of the United States for the Southern District of New York, 1861–1865*. Washington: Government Printing Office, 1866.

Bradless, Francis, B. C. *Blockade Running During the Civil War, and the Effect of Land and Water Transportation on the Confederacy*. Salem: Essex Institute, 1925.

Briggs, Herbert W. *The Doctrine of Continuous Voyage*. Baltimore: Johns Hopkins University Press, 1926.

Bright, Leslie S. *The Blockade Runner Modern Greece and Her Cargo*. Raleigh: Division of Archives and History, 1977.

Browne, Jefferson B. *Key West*. Gainesville: University of Florida Press, 1973.

Brutt, Frank. *Cross-Channel and Coastal Paddle Steamers*. London: Richard Tilling, 1934.

Burton, E. Milby. *The Siege of Charleston, 1861–1865*. Columbia: University of South Carolina Press, 1970.

Capers, Henry D. *The Life and Times of C. G. Memminger*. Richmond: Everett Waddey and Company, 1893.

Carse, Robert. *Blockade*. New York: Rinehart, 1958.

Carse, Lynn and Warren Spencer. *The United States and France: Civil War Diplomacy*. Philadelphia: University of Pennsylvania Press, 1970.

Chance, Franklin N., Paul C. Chance and David L. Topper. *Tangled Machinery and Charred Relics: The Historical and Archaeological Investigation of the C.S.S. Nashville*. Orangeburg: Sun Printing, 1985.

*Civil War Chronology*. Washington: Navy Department, 1971.

Cochrane, Hamilton. *Blockade Runners of the Confederacy*. Indianapolis: Bobbs-Merrill, 1958.

Connelly, Thomas L. *Army of the Heartland*. Baton Rouge: Louisiana State University Press, 1967.

Courtemanche, Regis A. *No Need of Glory: The British Navy in American Waters, 1860–1864*. Annapolis: Naval Institute Press, 1977.

Craton, Michael. *A History of the Bahamas*. London: Collins, 1962.

Cullum, George W. *Biographical Register of the Officers and Graduates of West Point*. 3 Vols. Boston: Houghton Mifflin and Company, 1891.

Daddysman, James W. *The Matamoras Trade*. Newark: University of Delaware Press, 1984.

Daniel, Larry J. and Riley W. Gunter. *Confederate Cannon Foundries*. Union City: Pioneer Press, 1977.

Davis, Carl L. *Arming the Union*. Port Washington, N.Y.: Kennikat Press, 1973.

Davis, Charles S. *Colin J. McRae, Confederate Financial Agent*. Tuscaloosa, Alabama, 1961.

Davis, George B., ed. *The Official Atlas of the Civil War*. New York: Arno Press, 1978.

Deak, Francis, and Philip C. Jessup, eds. *A Collection of Neutrality Laws, Regulations Treaties of Various Countries*. 2 Vols. Washington: Carnegie Endowment for International Peace, 1939.

Delaney, Caldwell. *Confederate Mobile*. Mobile: Haunted Book Shop, 1971.

Dew, Charles B. *Ironmaker to the Confederacy: Joseph R. Anderson and the Tredegar Iron Works*. New Haven: Yale University Press, 1966.

Dewey, Davis Rich. *Financial History of the United States*. New York: Longmans, Green, and Company, 1912.

Dufour, Charles L. *The Night the War Was Lost*. Garden City: Doubleday, 1960.

Durkin, Joseph T. *Stephen R. Mallory*. Chapel Hill: University of North Carolina Press, 1938.

Eaton, Clement. *A History of the Southern Confederacy*. London: Collier-Macmillan, 1954.

Edwards, William B. *Civil War Guns*. Harrisburg: Stackpole, 1962.

Ferris, Norman S. *Desperate Diplomacy*. Knoxville: University of Tennessee Press, 1976.

Fishbaugh, Charles Preston. *From Paddlewheels to Propellers*. Indianapolis: Indiana Historical Society, 1970.

Franke, Norman H. *Pharmaceutical Conditions and Drug Supply in the Confederacy*. Madison: American Institute of Pharmacy, 1955.

Fuller, Claude E. *The Rifled Musket*. New York; Bonanza Press, 1958.

Goff, Richard D. *Confederate Supply*. Durham: Duke University Press, 1969.

Guthrie, John. *A History of Marine Engineering*. London: Hutchinson, 1971.

Hammond, Bray. *Banks and Politics in America*. Princeton: Princeton University Press, 1957.

Hayward, Walter B. *Bermuda Past and Present*. New York: Dodd, Mead, and Company, 1911.

Heyl, Eric. *Early American Steamers*. 6 Vols. Buffalo: Eric Heyl, 1953–1969.

Holcombe, Robert. *Notes on the Classification of Confederate Ironclads*. Savannah: Corps of Engineers, 1980.

Hoole, William Stanley. *Four Years in the Confederate Navy*. Athens: University of Georgia Press, 1964.

Horner, David L. *The Blockade Runners: True Tales of Running the Yankee Blockade off the Confederate Coast.* New York: Dodd, Mead, and Company, 1968.

Hunter, Lewis C. *Steamboats on the Western Rivers.* New York: Octagon Books, 1969.

Jones, Virgil C. *The Civil War at Sea.* 3 Vols. New York: Holt, Rinehart, and Winston, 1960–1962.

Kerby, Robert Lee. *Kirby Smith's Confederacy: The Trans Mississippi South, 1863–1865.* New York: Columbia University Press, 1972.

King, Edward. *The Great South.* 2 Vols. New York: Burt Franklin, 1875.

Lawrence, Alexander A. *A Present for Mr. Lincoln.* Macon: Ardivan Press, 1961.

Lester, Richard I. *Confederate Finance and Purchasing in Great Britain.* Charlottesville: University of Virginia Press, 1975.

Lewis, Berkeley R. *Small Arms and Ammunition in the United States Service, 1776–1865.* Washington: Smithsonian Institution Press, 1968.

Lonn, Ella. *Salt as a Factor in the Confederacy.* University: University of Alabama Press, 1965.

Low, Alfred M. *Blockade and Contraband.* Washington: Columbian Printing, 1916.

Maffitt, Emma Martin. *The Life and Services of John Newland Maffitt.* New York: Neale Publishing Company, 1906.

Mahan, Alfred Thayer. *The Gulf and Inland Waters.* New York; Jack Brussel, n.d.

Marchand, John B. *Charleston Blockade.* Newport: Naval War College Press, 1976.

Merli, Frank J. *Great Britain and the Confederate Navy, 1861–1864.* Bloomington: Indiana University Press, 1970.

Mills, John M. *Canadian Coastal and Inland Steam Vessels, 1809–1930.* Providence: Steamship Society of America, 1979.

Mitchel, Wesley C. *Gold Prices and Wages under the Greenback Standard.* New York: Augustus M. Kelley, 1966.

Morrison, John H. *History of American Steam Navigation.* New York: Argosy-Antiquarian, 1967.

Nepveux, Ethel T. S. *George Alfred Trenholm: The Company That Went to War.* Charleston: Comprint, 1973.

Nichols, James L. *Confederate Quartermaster in the Trans-Mississippi.* Austin: University of Texas Press, 1964.

Niven, John. *Gideon Welles.* New York: Oxford University Press, 1973.

Orvin, Maxwell Clayton. *In South Carolina Waters, 1861–1865.* Charleston: Nelson's Southern Printing and Publishing Company, 1961.

Osterweis, Rollin G. *Romanticism and Nationalism in the Old South.* Baton Rouge: Louisiana State University Press, 1949.

Owsley, Frank L. *King Cotton Diplomacy: Foreign Relations of the Confederate States of America.* Chicago: University of Chicago Press, 1935.

Owsley, Frank L., Jr. *The CSS Florida: Her Building and Operations.* Philadelphia: University of Pennsylvania Press, 1965.

Oxley, J. M. *Baffling the Blockade.* London: Nelson, 1896.

Reed, Rowena. *Combined Operations in the Civil War.* Annapolis: Naval Institute Press, 1978.

Roberts, W. Adolphe. *Semmes of the Alabama.* Indianapolis: Bobbs-Merrill, 1938.

Robinson, Madeline. *An Introduction to the Papers of the New York Prize Court, 1861–1865.* New York: Columbia University Press, 1945.

Robinson, William Morrison. *The Confederate Privateers.* New Haven: Yale University Press, 1928.

Russel, Robert Royal. *Economic Aspects of Southern Sectionalism, 1840–1861.* Urbana: University of Illinois Press, 1924.

Savage, Carlton. *Policy of the United States Towards Maritime Commerce in War.* 2 Vols. New York: Kraus Reprint Company, 1969.

Scharf, J. Thomas. *History of the Confederate Navy.* 2 Vols. New York: Rogers and Sherwood, 1887.

Schwab, John C. *The Confederate States of America, 1861–1865; A Financial and Industrial History of the South during the Civil War.* New York: C. Scribner's Sons, 1901.

Shingleton, Royce Gorgon. *John Taylor Wood: Sea Ghost of the Confederacy.* Athens: University of Georgia Press, 1979.

Simons, Katherine Drayton. *Stories of Charleston Harbor.* Columbia: State Company, 1930.

Soley, James R. *The Blockade and the Cruisers.* New York: Scribner, 1883.

Sprunt, James. *Chronicles of the Cape Fear River.* Raleigh: Edwards and Broughton, 1916.

_____. *Derelicts: An Account of Ships Lost at Sea in General Commercial Traffic and a Brief History of Blockade Runners Stranded along the North Carolina Coast, 1861–1865.* Wilmington: n.p., 1919.

_____. *Tales of the Cape Fear Blockade: Being a Turn of the Century Account of Blockade Running.* Raleigh: Capital Printing, 1902.

_____. *Tales and Traditions of the Lower Cape Fear, 1661–1898.* Wilmington: LeGwin Brothers, 1898.

Stick, David. *Graveyard of the Atlantic: Shipwrecks of the North Carolina Coast.* Chapel Hill: University of North Carolina Press, 1958.

Still, William N. *Confederate Shipbuilding.* Athens: University of Georgia Press, 1969.

_____. *Iron Afloat.* Nashville: Vanderbilt University Press, 1971.

Thompson, Samuel B. *Confederate Purchasing Operations Abroad.* Chapel Hill: University of North Carolina Press, 1935.

Tyler, Ronnie C. *Santiago Vidaurri and the Southern Confederacy.* Austin: Texas State Historical Association, 1973.

Todd, Richard Cecil. *Confederate Finance.* Athens: University of Georgia Press, 1954.

Vandiver, Frank E. *Ploughshares into Swords: Josiah Gorgas and Confederate Ordnance.* Austin: University of Texas Press, 1952.

Walker, Jennie M. *The Life of Captain Fry.* Hartford: J. B. Burr, 1875.

Winks, Robin W. *Canada and the United States: The Civil War Years.* Baltimore: Johns Hopkins Press, 1960.

Wilkinson, Henry. *Bermuda From Sail to Steam.* London: Oxford University Press, 1973.

Winsor, Bell. *Texas in the Confederacy: Military Installations, Economy and People.* Hillsboro, Texas: Hill Junior College Press, 1978.

Winters, John D. *The Civil War in Louisiana.* Baton Rouge: Louisiana State University Press, 1963.

Zuill, W. E. S. *Bermuda Journey.* New York: Coward-McCann, 1946.

## Articles

Barr, Alwyn. "Texas Coast Defense, 1861–1865." *Southwestern Historical Quarterly* XLV (July 1961), 1–31.

"Blockade Running." *City of Charleston Yearbook, 1883.* 557–563.

Boyd, William K. "Fiscal and Economic Conditions in North Carolina during the Civil War." *North Carolina Booklet* XIV (April 1915), 195–219.

Clark, Walter. "The Raising, Organizing and Equipment of North Carolina Troops during the Civil War." *North Carolina Booklet* XIX (July–October 1919), 55–65.

Coddington, Edwin B. "Activities and Attitudes of a Confederate Businessman: Gazaway B. Lamar." *Journal of Southern History* IX (February 1943), 3–36.

_____. "The Civil War Blockade Reconsidered," in *Essays in History and International Relations in Honor of George Hubbard Blakeslee.* Dwight E. Lee and George E. McReynolds, eds. Worchester: Clark University Press, 1949, 284–305.

Connelly, Thomas L. "Vicksburg: Strategic Point or Propaganda Device?" *Military Affairs* XXXIV (April 1970), 49–53.

Diamond, William. "Imports of the Confederate Government from Europe and Mexico." *Journal of Southern History* VI (November 1940), 470–503.

Drysdale, Richard. "Blockade Running from Nassau." *History Today* XXVII (May 1977), 332–337.

Ellis, L. Tuffy. "Maritime Commerce on the Far Western Gulf, 1861–1865." *Southwestern Historical Quarterly* LXXVII (October 1973), 167–226.

Fredd, John P. "Civil War Blockade." *Recruiter's Bulletin* II (March 1916), 12.

Gentry, Edith Fenner. "A Confederate Success in Europe: The Erlanger Loan." *Journal of Southern History* XXVI (May 1970), 157–188.

Gleaves, Albert. "The Affair of the *Blanche.*" *United States Naval Institute Proceedings* XLVIII (October 1922), 1661–1676.

Graham, Gerald S. "The Ascendancy of the Sailing Ship, 1850–1885." *Economic History Review* IX (1956–1957), 74–88.

Green, Thomas W. "Major Caleb Huse C.S.A.—An Appreciation and Two Appendices." *Confederate Historical Society Journal* XII (Spring 1984), 17–29.

Hallock, C. "Bermuda in Blockade Times." *New England Magazine* VI (May 1892), 337–343.

Hamilton, F. E. "*Chicora*, A Blockade Runner Came to the Lakes." *Steamboat Bill of Facts* XII (September 1955), 49–52, 57.

Hanks, Carlos C. "Blockaders off the American Coast," *United States Naval Institute Proceedings* LXVII (February 1941), 172–175.

Hanna, Kathryn A. "Incidents of the Confederate Blockade." *Journal of Southern History* XI (May 1945), 214–229.

Hassler, Warren W. "How the Confederacy Controlled Blockade Running." *Civil War Times Illustrated* IV (October 1963), 43–49.

Hefferman, John B. "The Blockade of the Southern Confederacy." *Smithsonian Journal of History* II (Winter 1967–1968), 23–44.

Hendren, Paul. "The Confederate Blockade Runners." *United States Naval Institute Proceedings* LIX (April 1933), 505–512.

Heyl, Eric. "The Blockade Runner *Scotia*." *Steamboat Bill of Facts* XII (December 1955), 79–81.

———. "The Lady Was a Tramp." *Steamboat Bill of Facts* XX (Fall 1963), 73–77.

Hill, D. H. "The Confederate Ordnance Department." *Proceedings of the Twentieth and Twenty-first Annual Sessions of the State Literary and Historical Association of North Carolina.* Raleigh: 1922.

Holmes, Henry Schultz. "The Trenholm Family." *South Carolina Historical and Genealogical Magazine* XVI (October 1915), 151–163.

Hooper, W. R. "Blockade Running." *Harper's New Monthly Magazine* XLII (December 1870), 105–108.

Johnson, Ludwell H. "Blockade or Trade Monopoly: John A. Dix and the Union Occupation of Norfolk." *Virginia Magazine of History and Biography* XCIII (January 1985), 54–78.

———. "Commerce Between Northeastern Ports and the Confederacy." *Journal of American History* LIV (June 1967), 30–42.

———. "Trading with the Union: The Evolution of Confederate Policy." *Virginia Magazine of History and Biography* LXVIIII (July 1970), 308–325.

Johnson, Robert Erwin. "Investment by Sea: The Civil War Blockade." *American Neptune* XXXII (January 1972), 45–57.

Jones, Ivor Wayne. "America's Secret War in Welsh Waters." *Confederate Historical Society Journal* XII (Spring 1984), 2–13.

Jones, Virgil C. "Mr. Lincoln's Blockade." *Civil War Times Illustrated* X (December 1971), 10–24.

————. "Slipping through the Blockade." *Civil War Times Illustrated* II (October 1960), 4–6, 18–19.

"Klaxon, Stout Hearts." *Blackwood's Magazine* CCXXXVII (April 1935), 540–550.

Lawrie, William. "Letter in Correspondence Circular." *Confederate Historical Society Correspondence Circular* II (Summer 1985), 1.

Lebergott, Stanley. "Through the Blockade: The Profitability and Extent of Cotton Smuggling, 1861–1865." *Journal of Economic History* XLI (December 1981), 867–888.

McDiarmid, A. M. "American Civil War Precedents: Their Nature, Application, and Extension." *American Journal of International Law* XXXIV (April 1940), 220–237.

Mueller, Edward A. "East Coast Florida Steamboating, 1831–1861." *Florida Historical Quarterly* XL (January 1962), pp. 241–260.

Neblett, Thomas R. "Edward C. Anderson and the *Fingal*." *Georgia Historical Quarterly* LII (June 1968), 132–158.

O'Flaherty, Daniel C. "The Blockade that Failed." *American Heritage* VI (August 1955), 38–41, 104–105.

Owsley, Frank L. Jr. "The CSS *Florida*'s Tour de Force at Mobile Bay." *Alabama Review* XV (October 1962), 262–270.

Payne, Peter, and Frank J. Merli. "A Blockade Running Chapter, Spring 1862." *American Neptune* XXVI (April 1966), 134–137.

Peery, Charles V. "Blockade Running During the Civil War." *The American Society of Arms Collectors Bulletin* LIV (May 30–April 4, 1986), 32–40.

Pelzer, John, and Linda Pelzer. "Cotton, Cotton Everywhere." *Civil War Times Illustrated* XIX (January 1981), 10–17.

Peters, Thelma. "Running the Blockade in the Bahamas during the Civil War." *Tequesta* V (1945), 16–30.

Pierce, Wendell E. "The Blockade Runner *Acadia*." *Journal of the Confederate Historical Society* X (Winter 1973), 147–168.

Pratt, Fletcher. "Starvation Blockade." *American Mercury* XXXVI (November 1935), 334–342.

Price, Marcus W. "Blockade Running as a Business in South Carolina during the War between the States, 1861–1865." *American Neptune* IX (January 1949), 31–62.

————. "Four From Bristol." *American Neptune* XVII (October 1957), 249–261.

————. "Masters and Pilots Who Tested the Blockade of the Confederate Ports, 1861–1865." *American Neptune* (April 1961), 81–106.

————. "Ships that Tested the Blockade of the Carolina Ports, 1861–1865." *American Neptune* VIII (April 1948), 196–241.

————. "Ships that Tested the Blockade of the Georgian and East Florida Ports, 1861–1865." *American Neptune* XV (April 1955), 97–132.

_____. "Ships that Tested the Blockade of the Gulf Ports, 1861-1865." *American Neptune* XII (January-July 1952), 52-59, 154-161, 229-238.

Ramsdell, Charles W. "The Confederate Government and the Railroads." *American Historical Review* XXII (July 1917), 794-810.

Roberts, A. Sellew. "High Prices and the Blockade in the Confederacy." *South Atlantic Quarterly* XXIV (April 1925), 154-163.

"Running the Blockade." *Southern Historical Society Papers* XXIV (January-December 1896), 225-229.

Seward, Charles W. "William Barker Cushing." *United States Naval Institute Proceedings* XXXVIII (August-September 1912), 425-491, 913-939.

Sibley, Marilyn McAdams. "Charles Stillman: A Case Study of Entrepreneurship on the Rio Grande, 1861-1865." *Southwestern Historical Quarterly* LXXVII (October 1973), 227-240.

Simpson, W. A. C. "Britain and the Blockade." *Journal of the Confederate Historical Society* VI (Spring 1968), 6-26.

Skelton, Lynda Warley. "The Importing and Exporting Company of South Carolina." *South Carolina Historical Magazine* LXXV (Spring 1974), 24-32.

Still, William N. "The Common Sailor." *Civil War Times Illustrated* (February 1985), 24-39 (March 1985), 13-39.

_____. "A Naval Sieve: The Union Blockade in the Civil War." *Naval War College Review* XXXVI (May-June 1983), 38-45.

Stubbs, Jane. "Virginians Run the Sea Blockade." *Virginia Cavalcade* IX (Fall 1960), 17-22.

Taylor, Thomas E. "Blockade Buster—1863." *All Hands* No. 461 (July 1955), 59-63.

Vandiver, Frank E. "The Food Supply of the Confederate Armies, 1865." *Tyler's Quarterly Historical and Genealogical Magazine* XXVI (July 1944), 77-89.

_____. "A Sketch of Efforts Abroad to Equip the Confederate Army at Macon." *Georgia Historical Quarterly* XXVIII (March 1944), 34-40.

_____. "Texas and the Confederate Armies Meat Problem." *Southwestern Historical Quarterly* XLVII (January 1944), 225-233.

Wait, Horatio L. "The Blockade of the Confederacy." *Century Illustrated Magazine* XXXXIV (October 1898), 914-928.

Wardle, A. C. "British Built Blockade Runners." *Steamboat Bill of Facts* XI (December 1954), 77-80.

Williams, Jerry. "Wirral-Built Blockade Runners of the American Civil War." *Confederate Historical Society Journal* XIII (Summer 1985), 39-40.

Williams, Jerry, and John Vaughan. "American Civil War Land Marks in Great Britain, 19, Abercromby Square, Liverpool, Merseyside, England." *Confederate Historical Journal* XIII (Spring 1985), 9-12.

"Wilmington and the Blockade Runners." *Confederate Veteran* XXIX (January-December 1921), 258-259.

Wise, Stephen R. "Confederate Trade and Blockade Running during the American Civil War." *Conference on Historical Archaeology, Special Publication No. 4* (Boston 1985), 120–124.

Windham, William T. "The Problem of Supply in the Trans-Mississippi Confederacy." *Journal of Southern History* XXVII (May 1961), 149–168.

Wright, Michael F. "Vicksburg and the Trans-Mississippi Supply Line (1861–1863)." *Journal of Mississippi History* XLIII (August 1981), 210-225.

Wondrus, Harry and Tom Stretch. "Brief Notes on Arms Brought into the Confederacy by Blockade Runners." *Hobbies* LV (August 1950), 129–131.

**Theses and Dissertations and Other Unpublished Works**

Ashcraft, Allan C. "Texas: 1860–1866. The Lone Star State in the Civil War." Ph.D. dissertation, Columbia University, 1960.

Blume, Kenneth John. "The Mid-Atlantic Arena: The United States the Confederacy and the British West Indies, 1861–1865." Ph.D. dissertation, State University of New York, 1984.

Babin, Charles H. "The Economic Expansion of New Orleans Before the Civil War." Ph.D. dissertation, Tulane University, 1954.

Browning, Robert M. "The Blockade of Wilmington, 1861–1865." M.A. thesis, East Carolina University, 1980.

Cowling, Annie. "The Civil War Trade of the Lower Rio Grande Valley." M.A. thesis, University of Texas, 1926.

Davis, William Watson. "Civil War and Reconstruction in Florida." Ph.D. dissertation, Columbia University, 1913.

Edwards, Frank Tousley. "The United States Consular Service in the Bahamas During the American Civil War." Ph.D. dissertation, Catholic University, 1968.

Fenner, Judith Ann. "Confederate Finances Abroad." Ph.D. dissertation, Rice University, 1969.

Fonvielle, Chris. "The Fall of Fort Fisher." Unpublished manuscript in possession of the author.

Garner, Ruby. "Galveston during the Civil War." M.A. thesis, University of Texas, 1927.

Glover, Robert Warren. "The West Coast Blockade, 1861–1865: An Evaluation." Ph.D. dissertation, North Texas State University, 1974.

Graf, Leroy P. "Economic History of the Lower Rio Grande Valley, 1820–1865." Ph.D. dissertation, Harvard University, 1942.

Gragg, Rod. "Fort Fisher: The Confederate Goliath, 1861–1864." M.A. thesis, University of South Carolina, 1979.

Greb, Gregory Allen. "Charleston, South Carolina, Merchants, 1815–1860: Urban Leadership in the Antebellum South." Ph.D. dissertation, University of California, San Diego, 1975.

Griffin, James D. "Savannah Georgia during the Civil War." Ph.D. dissertation, University of Georgia, 1963.

Haberlein, Charles R. "Former Blockade Runners in the United States Navy." B.A. Paper, Kalamazoo College, 1965.

Hoovestol, Paeder Joel. "Galveston during the Civil War." M.A. thesis, University of Houston, 1950.

Jackson, Vivian Gladys. "A History of Sabine Pass," M.A. thesis, University of Texas, 1930.

Johns, John Edwin. "Florida in the Confederacy." Ph.D. dissertation, University of North Carolina, Chapel Hill, 1959.

McLain, Minor. "Prison Conditions in Fort Warren, Boston, during the Civil War." Ph.D. dissertation, Boston University, 1955.

Marifield, Edward F. "The Seaboard War: A History of the North Atlantic Blockading Squadron 1861–1865." Ph.D. dissertation, Case Western University, 1975.

Melton, Maurice K. "Major Military Industries of the Confederate Government." Ph.D. dissertation, Emory University, 1978.

Ogden, Brother August Raymond. "A Blockaded Seaport, Galveston, Texas, C.S.A." M.A. thesis, St. Mary's University, 1939.

Racine, Philip. "Thurston Correspondence." Unpublished Honors Paper, Bowdoin College, 1964.

Sheridan, Robert Neal. "The Confederate Naval Effort at New Orleans." M.A. thesis, University of South Carolina, 1954.

Todd, Herbert II. "The Building of a Confederate States Navy in Europe." Ph.D. dissertation, Vanderbilt University, 1940.

Tyler, Ronnie Curtis. "The Age of Cotton: Santiago Vidaurri and the Confederacy, 1861–1864." Ph.D. dissertation, Texas Christian University, 1968.

Wardle, Arthur C. "Blockade Runners Built on Merseyside and Registered at the Port of Liverpool During the American Civil War, 1861–1865." Unpublished manuscript, Liverpool Public Library, 1941.

Wise, Stephen R. "The Campaign for Morris Island." M.A. thesis, Bowling Green State University, 1978.

Wood, Richard E. "Port Town at War: Wilmington, North Carolina, 1860–1865." Ph.D. dissertation, Florida State University, 1976.

# Index